Tell us what you think about Shojo Beat Manga!

Our survey is now available online. Go to:

shojobeat.com/mangasurvey

Help us make our product offerings better!

La Corda d'Oro™

by Yuki Kure

Ordinary student Kahoko couldn't be less qualified to participate in her school's music competition. But when she spots a magical fairy who grants her amazing musical talent, Kahoko finds herself in the company of some very musical—not to mention hot—guys!

Only $8.99

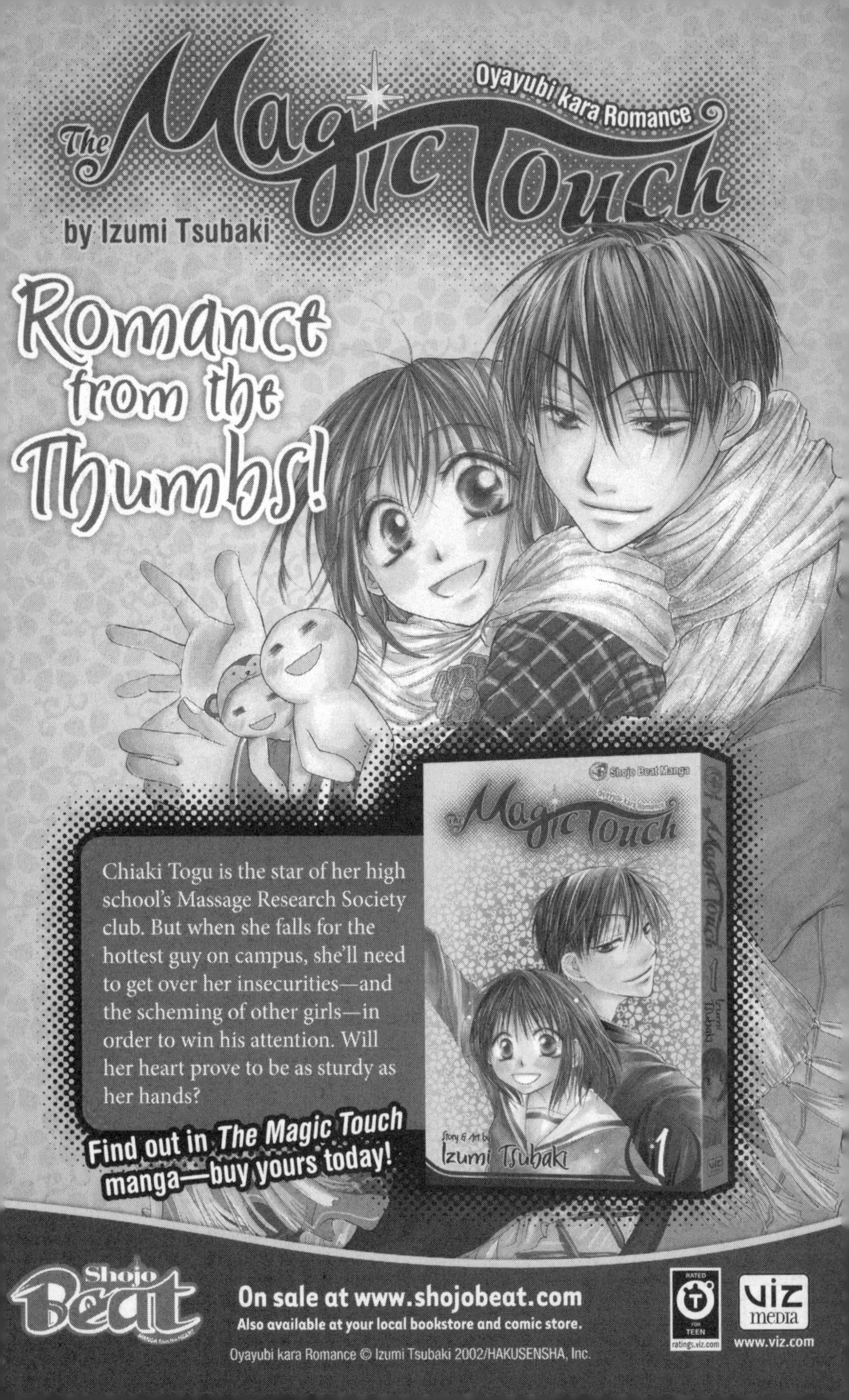
Oyayubi kara Romance
The Magic Touch
by Izumi Tsubaki
Romance from the Thumbs!
Shojo Beat Manga
Oyayubi kara Romance
The Magic Touch
Story & Art by
Izumi Tsubaki
1
Chiaki Togu is the star of her high school's Massage Research Society club. But when she falls for the hottest guy on campus, she'll need to get over her insecurities—and the scheming of other girls—in order to win his attention. Will her heart prove to be as sturdy as her hands?
Find out in The Magic Touch manga—buy yours today!
Shojo Beat
On sale at www.shojobeat.com
Also available at your local bookstore and comic store.
RATED T FOR TEEN
ratings.viz.com
VIZ media
www.viz.com
Oyayubi kara Romance © Izumi Tsubaki 2002/HAKUSENSHA, Inc.

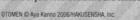

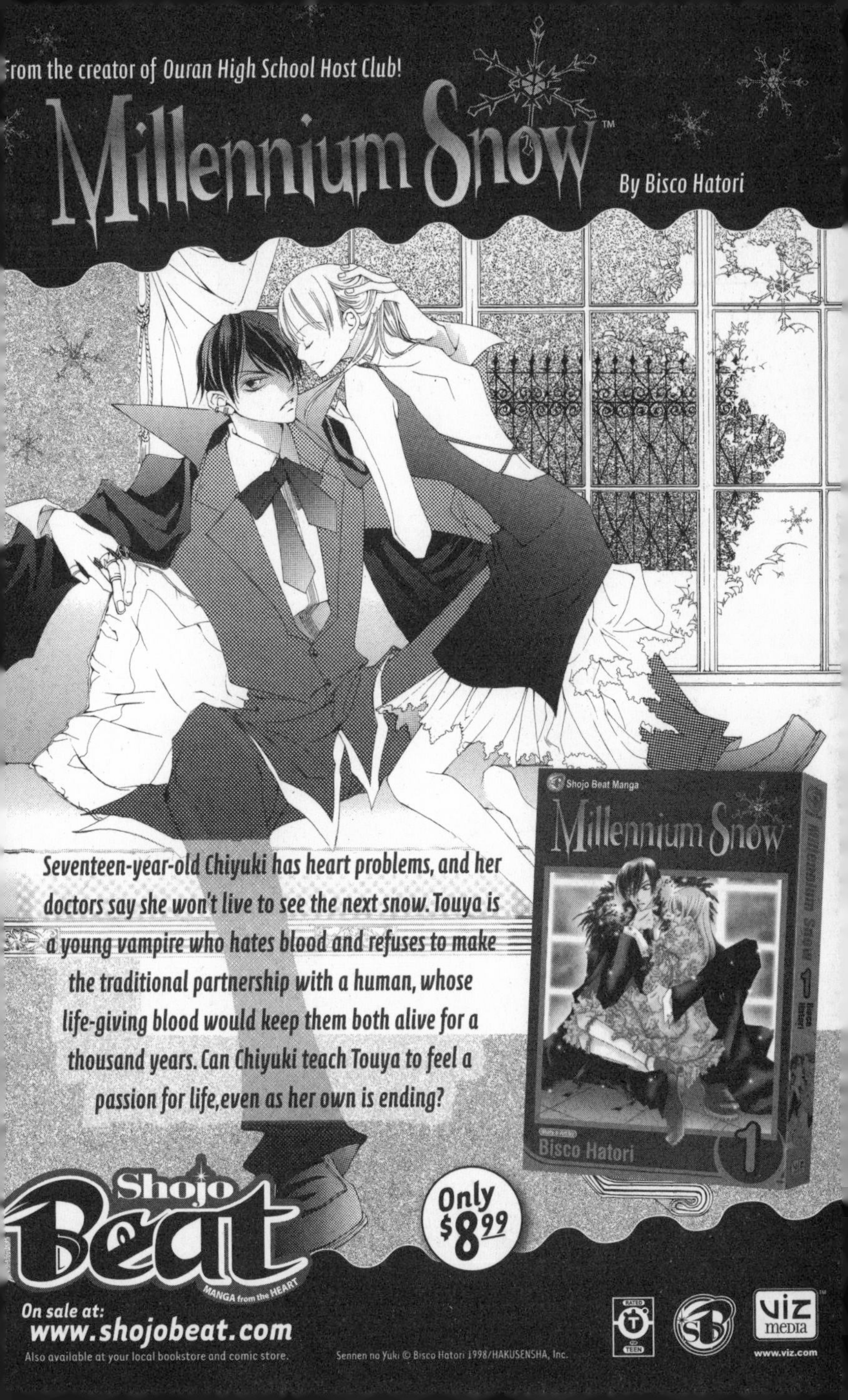
From the creator of Ouran High School Host Club!
Millennium Snow™
By Bisco Hatori
Seventeen-year-old Chiyuki has heart problems, and her doctors say she won't live to see the next snow. Touya is a young vampire who hates blood and refuses to make the traditional partnership with a human, whose life-giving blood would keep them both alive for a thousand years. Can Chiyuki teach Touya to feel a passion for life,even as her own is ending?
Shojo Beat Manga
Millennium Snow
1
Bisco Hatori
Only $8.99
Shojo Beat
MANGA from the HEART
On sale at:
www.shojobeat.com
Also available at your local bookstore and comic store.
Sennen no Yuki © Bisco Hatori 1998/HAKUSENSHA, Inc.
RATED T TEEN
VIZ media
www.viz.com

OURAN HIGH SCHOOL HOST CLUB
Vol. 12
The Shojo Beat Manga Edition

STORY AND ART BY BISCO HATORI

Translation/Masumi Matsumoto
Touch-up Art & Lettering/Gia Cam Luc
Graphic Design/Amy Martin
Editor/Nancy Thistlethwaite

Editor in Chief, Books/Alvin Lu
Editor in Chief, Magazines/Marc Weidenbaum
VP, Publishing Licensing/Rika Inouye
VP, Sales & Product Marketing/Gonzalo Ferreyra
VP, Creative/Linda Espinosa
Publisher/Hyoe Narita

Printed in Canada

Published by VIZ Media, LLC
P.O. Box 77010
San Francisco, CA 94107

Shojo Beat Manga Edition
10 9 8 7 6 5 4 3 2 1
First printing, June 2009

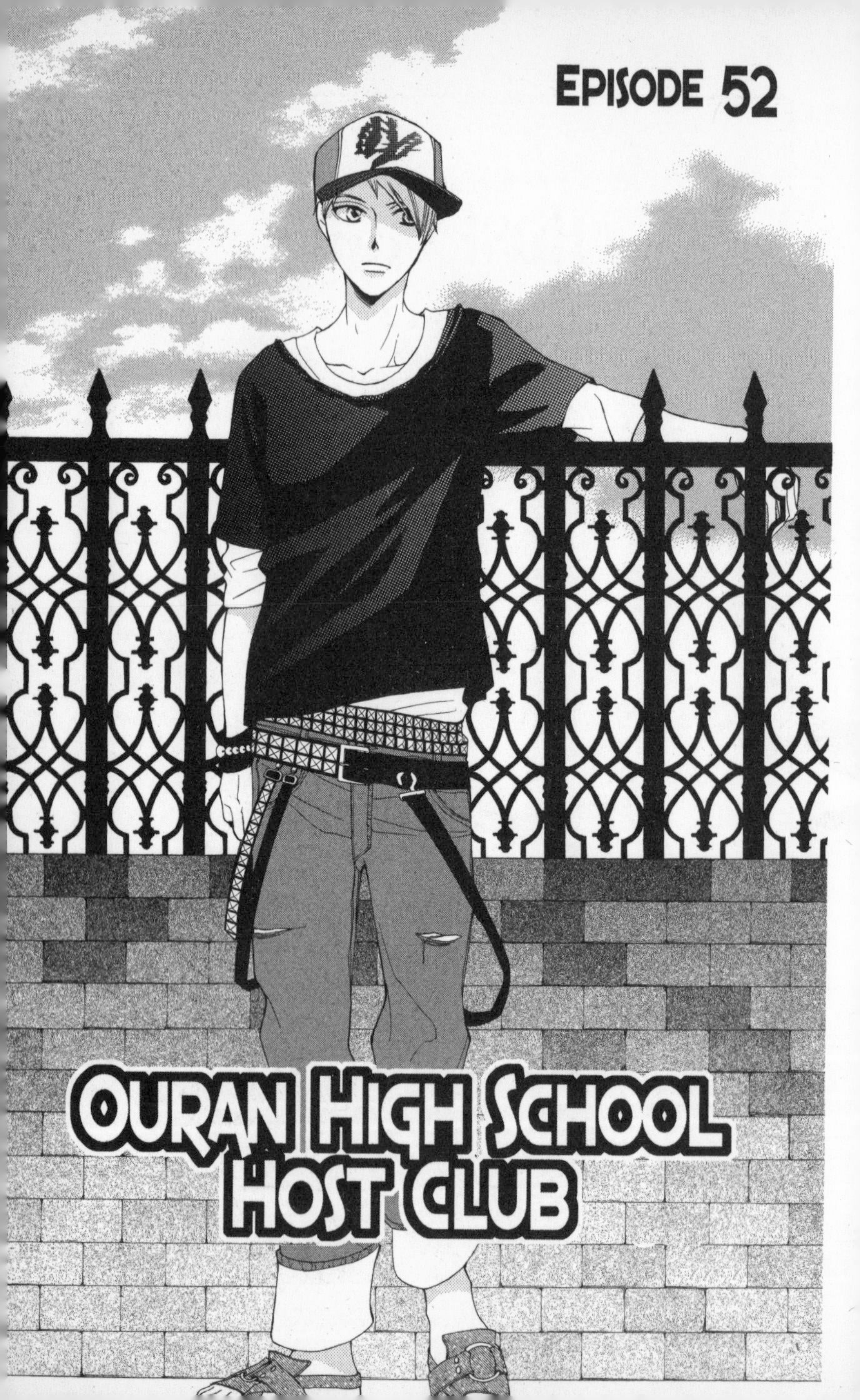
EPISODE 52
OURAN HIGH SCHOOL
HOST CLUB

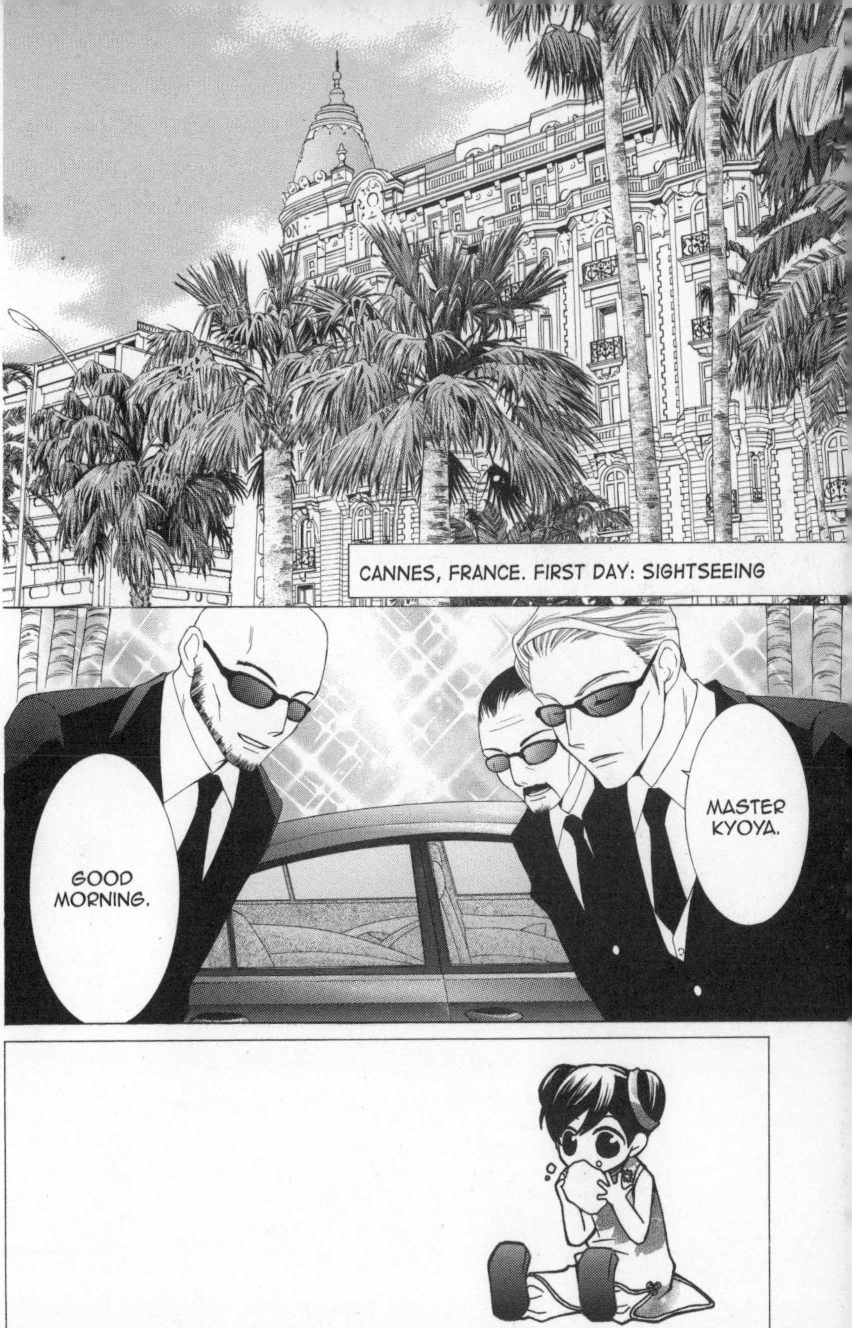
CANNES, FRANCE. FIRST DAY: SIGHTSEEING
MASTER KYOYA.
GOOD MORNING.

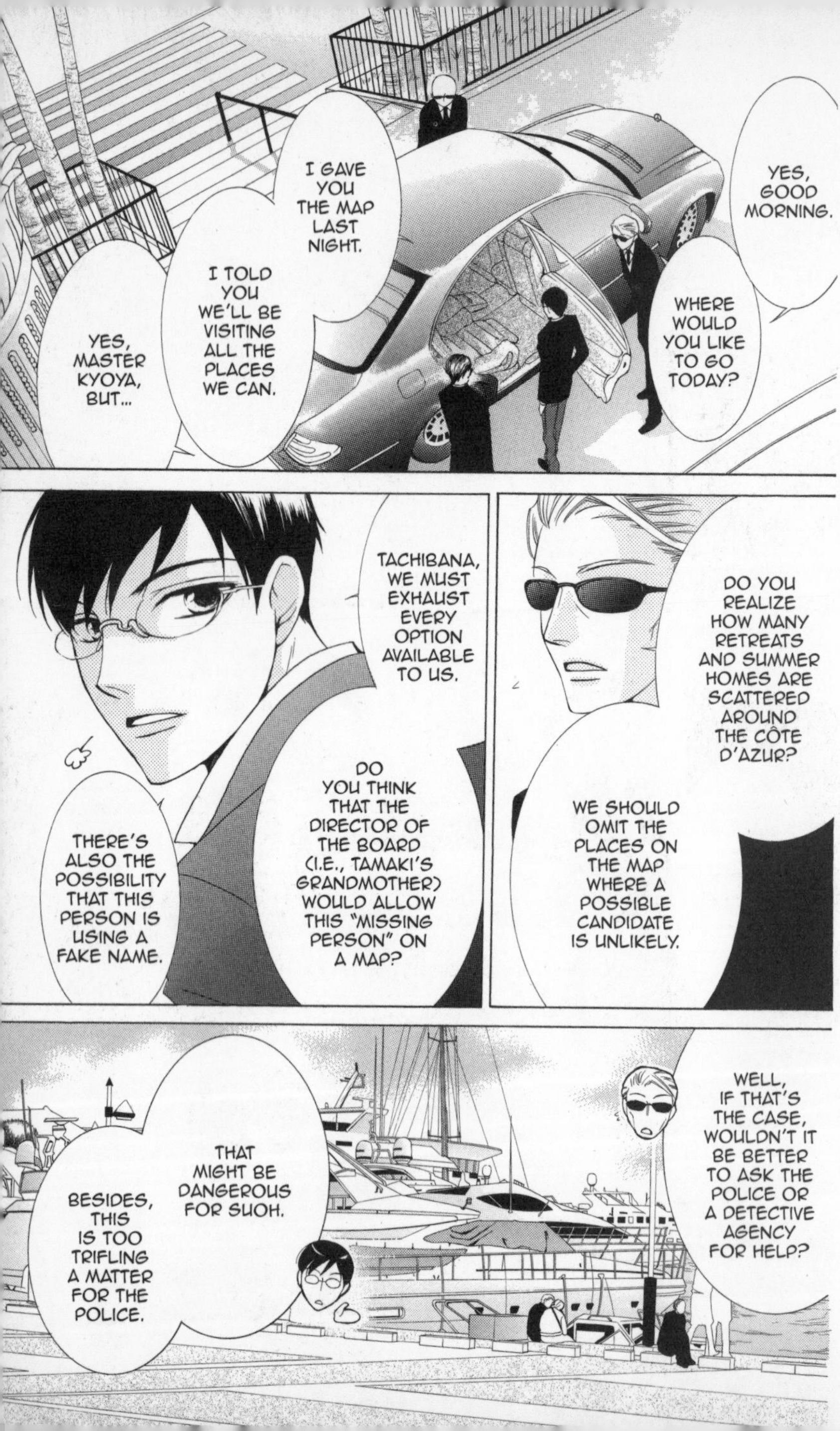
YES, GOOD MORNING.
WHERE WOULD YOU LIKE TO GO TODAY?
I GAVE YOU THE MAP LAST NIGHT.
I TOLD YOU WE'LL BE VISITING ALL THE PLACES WE CAN.
YES, MASTER KYOYA, BUT...
DO YOU REALIZE HOW MANY RETREATS AND SUMMER HOMES ARE SCATTERED AROUND THE CÔTE D'AZUR?
WE SHOULD OMIT THE PLACES ON THE MAP WHERE A POSSIBLE CANDIDATE IS UNLIKELY.
TACHIBANA, WE MUST EXHAUST EVERY OPTION AVAILABLE TO US.
DO YOU THINK THAT THE DIRECTOR OF THE BOARD (I.E., TAMAKI'S GRANDMOTHER) WOULD ALLOW THIS "MISSING PERSON" ON A MAP?
THERE'S ALSO THE POSSIBILITY THAT THIS PERSON IS USING A FAKE NAME.
WELL, IF THAT'S THE CASE, WOULDN'T IT BE BETTER TO ASK THE POLICE OR A DETECTIVE AGENCY FOR HELP?
THAT MIGHT BE DANGEROUS FOR SUOH.
BESIDES, THIS IS TOO TRIFLING A MATTER FOR THE POLICE.

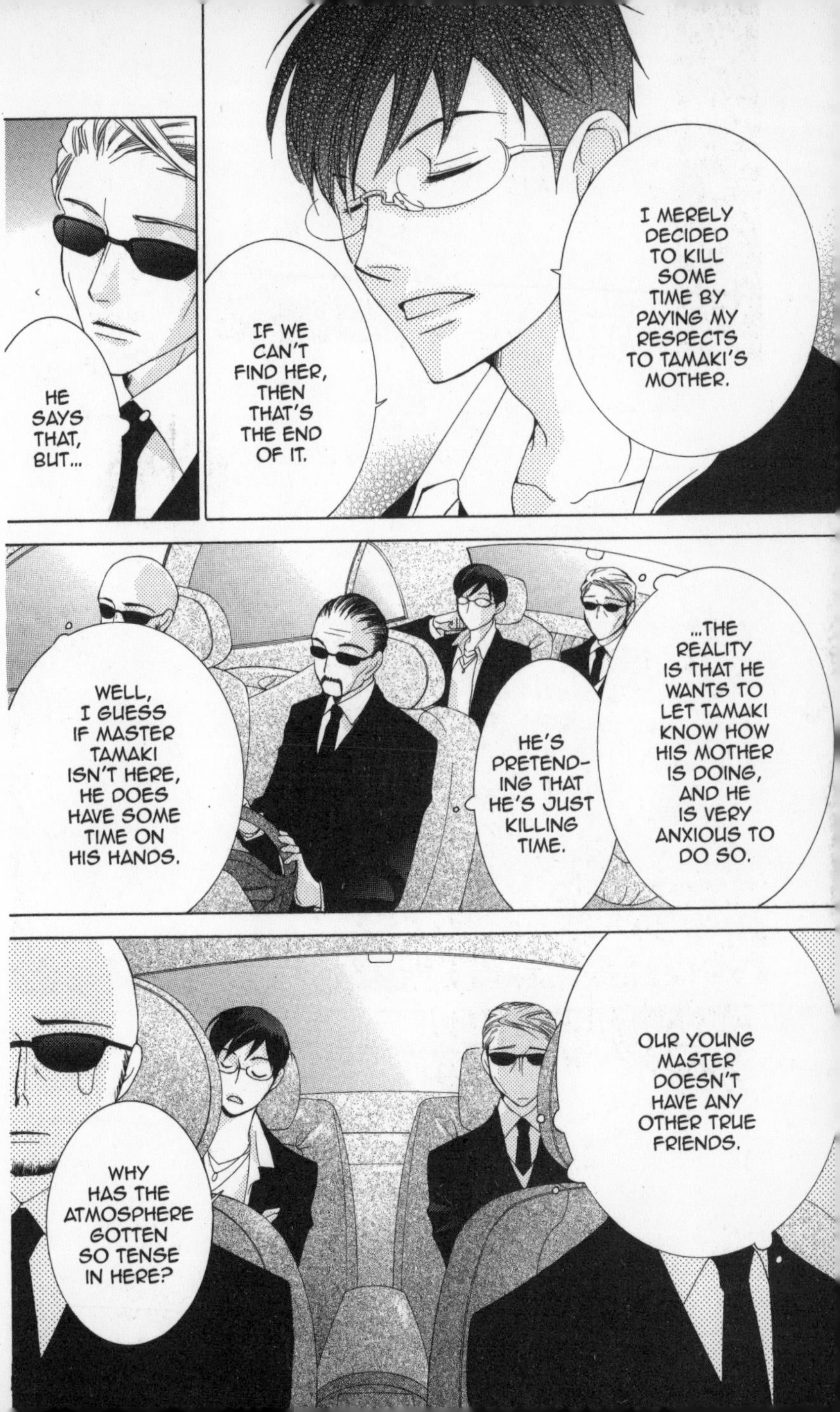
I MERELY DECIDED TO KILL SOME TIME BY PAYING MY RESPECTS TO TAMAKI'S MOTHER.
IF WE CAN'T FIND HER, THEN THAT'S THE END OF IT.
HE SAYS THAT, BUT...
HE'S PRETENDING THAT HE'S JUST KILLING TIME.
...THE REALITY IS THAT HE WANTS TO LET TAMAKI KNOW HOW HIS MOTHER IS DOING, AND HE IS VERY ANXIOUS TO DO SO.
WELL, I GUESS IF MASTER TAMAKI ISN'T HERE, HE DOES HAVE SOME TIME ON HIS HANDS.
OUR YOUNG MASTER DOESN'T HAVE ANY OTHER TRUE FRIENDS.
WHY HAS THE ATMOSPHERE GOTTEN SO TENSE IN HERE?

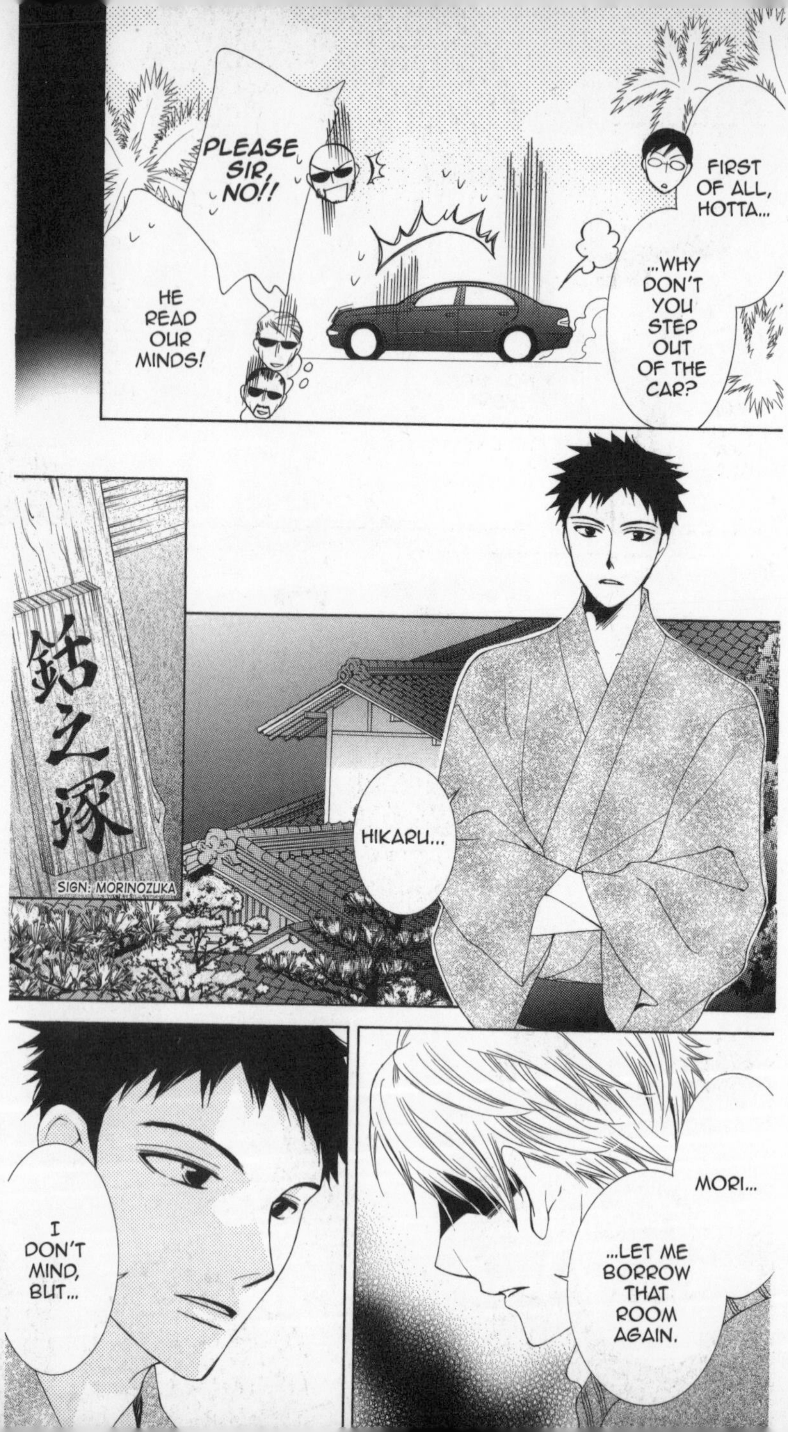
FIRST OF ALL, HOTTA...
...WHY DON'T YOU STEP OUT OF THE CAR?
PLEASE SIR, NO!!
HE READ OUR MINDS!
HIKARU...
銛之塚
SIGN: MORINOZUKA
MORI...
...LET ME BORROW THAT ROOM AGAIN.
I DON'T MIND, BUT...

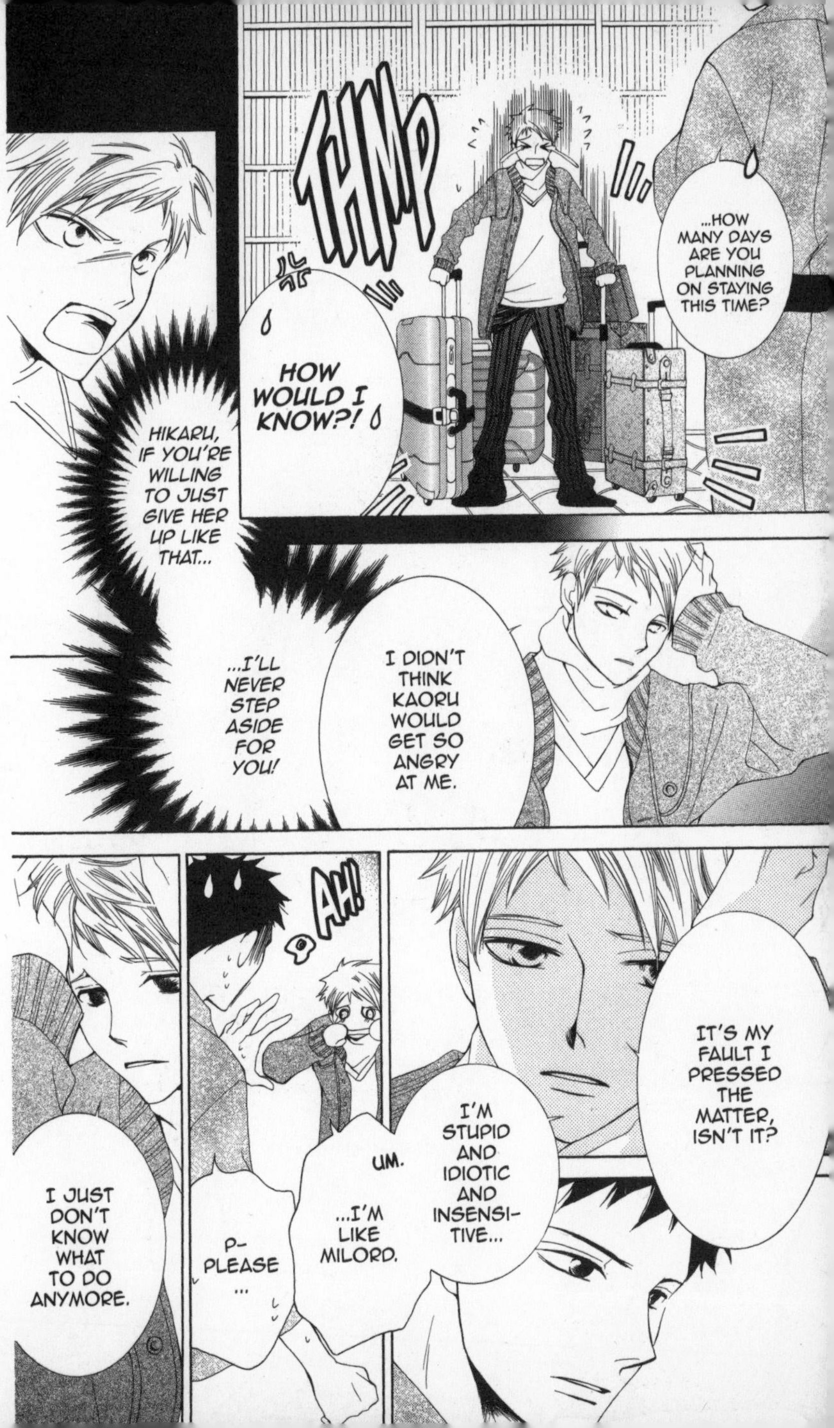
...HOW MANY DAYS ARE YOU PLANNING ON STAYING THIS TIME?
THMP
HOW WOULD I KNOW?!
I DIDN'T THINK KAORU WOULD GET SO ANGRY AT ME.
HIKARU, IF YOU'RE WILLING TO JUST GIVE HER UP LIKE THAT...
...I'LL NEVER STEP ASIDE FOR YOU!
IT'S MY FAULT I PRESSED THE MATTER, ISN'T IT?
I'M STUPID AND IDIOTIC AND INSENSI-TIVE...
...I'M LIKE MILORD.
AH!
UM.
P-PLEASE ...
I JUST DON'T KNOW WHAT TO DO ANYMORE.

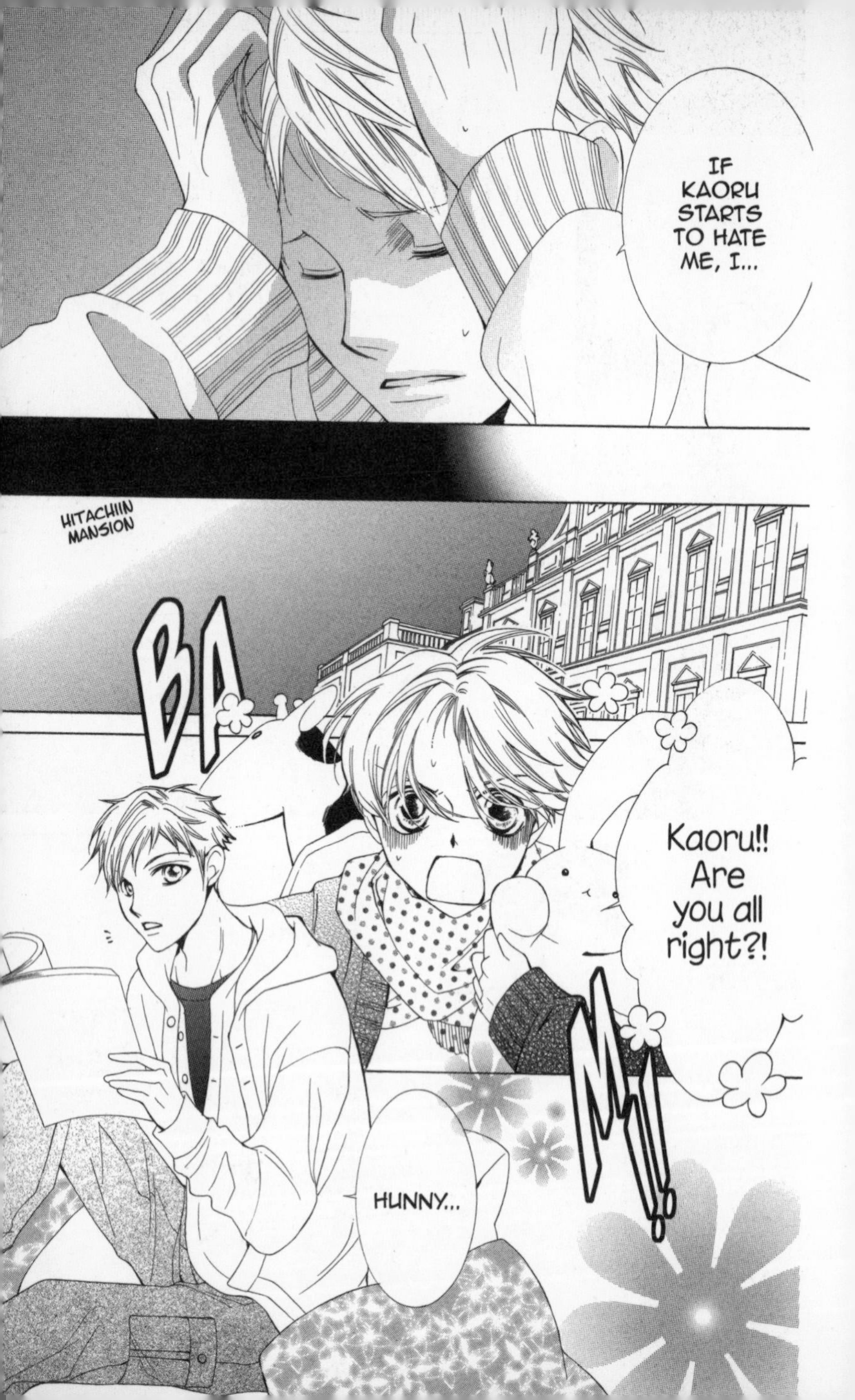
IF KAORU STARTS TO HATE ME, I...
HITACHIIN MANSION
BA
Kaoru!! Are you all right?!
M
HUNNY...

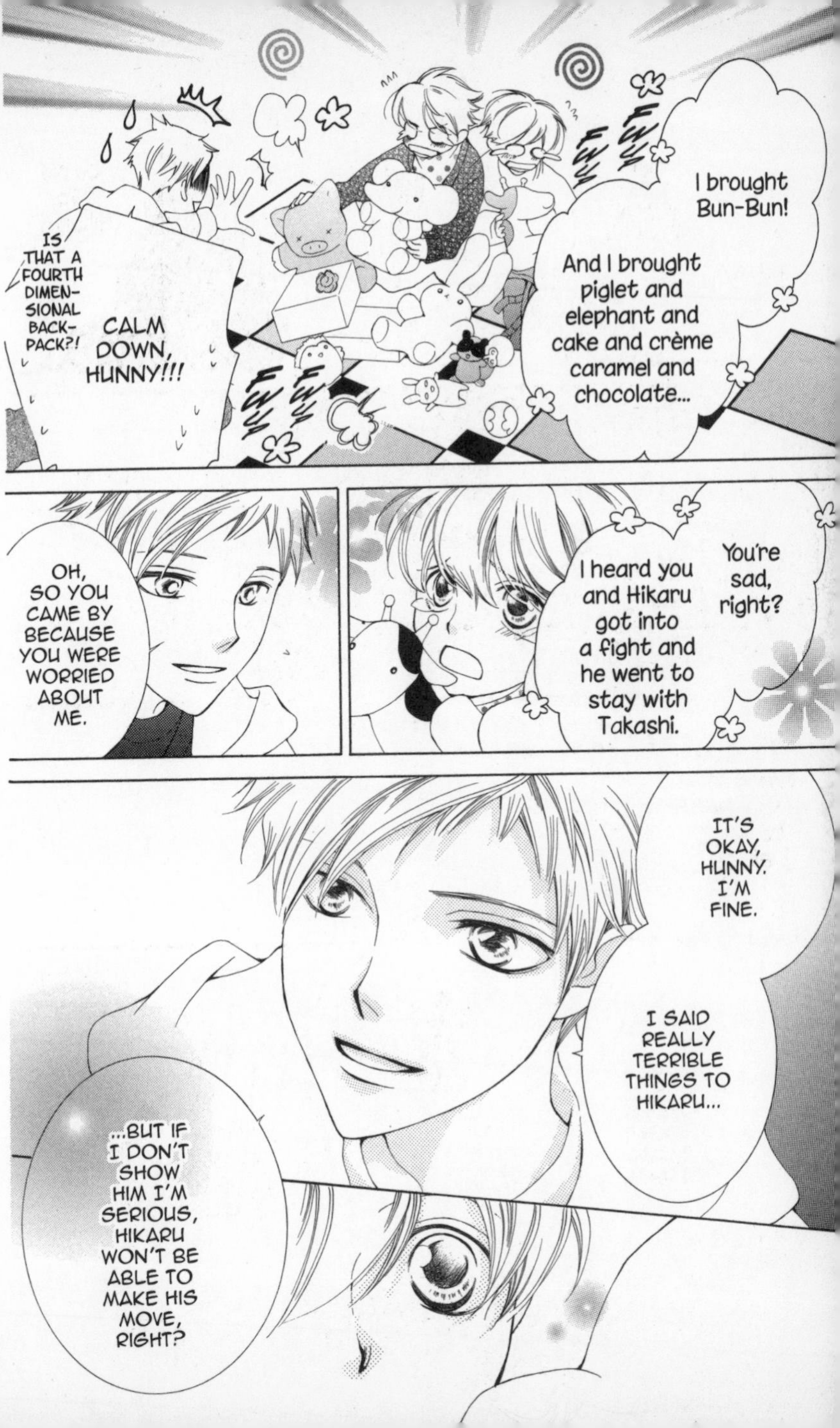
I brought Bun-Bun!
And I brought piglet and elephant and cake and crème caramel and chocolate...
CALM DOWN, HUNNY!!!
IS THAT A FOURTH DIMENSIONAL BACKPACK?!
You're sad, right?
I heard you and Hikaru got into a fight and he went to stay with Takashi.
OH, SO YOU CAME BY BECAUSE YOU WERE WORRIED ABOUT ME.
IT'S OKAY, HUNNY. I'M FINE.
I SAID REALLY TERRIBLE THINGS TO HIKARU...
...BUT IF I DON'T SHOW HIM I'M SERIOUS, HIKARU WON'T BE ABLE TO MAKE HIS MOVE, RIGHT?

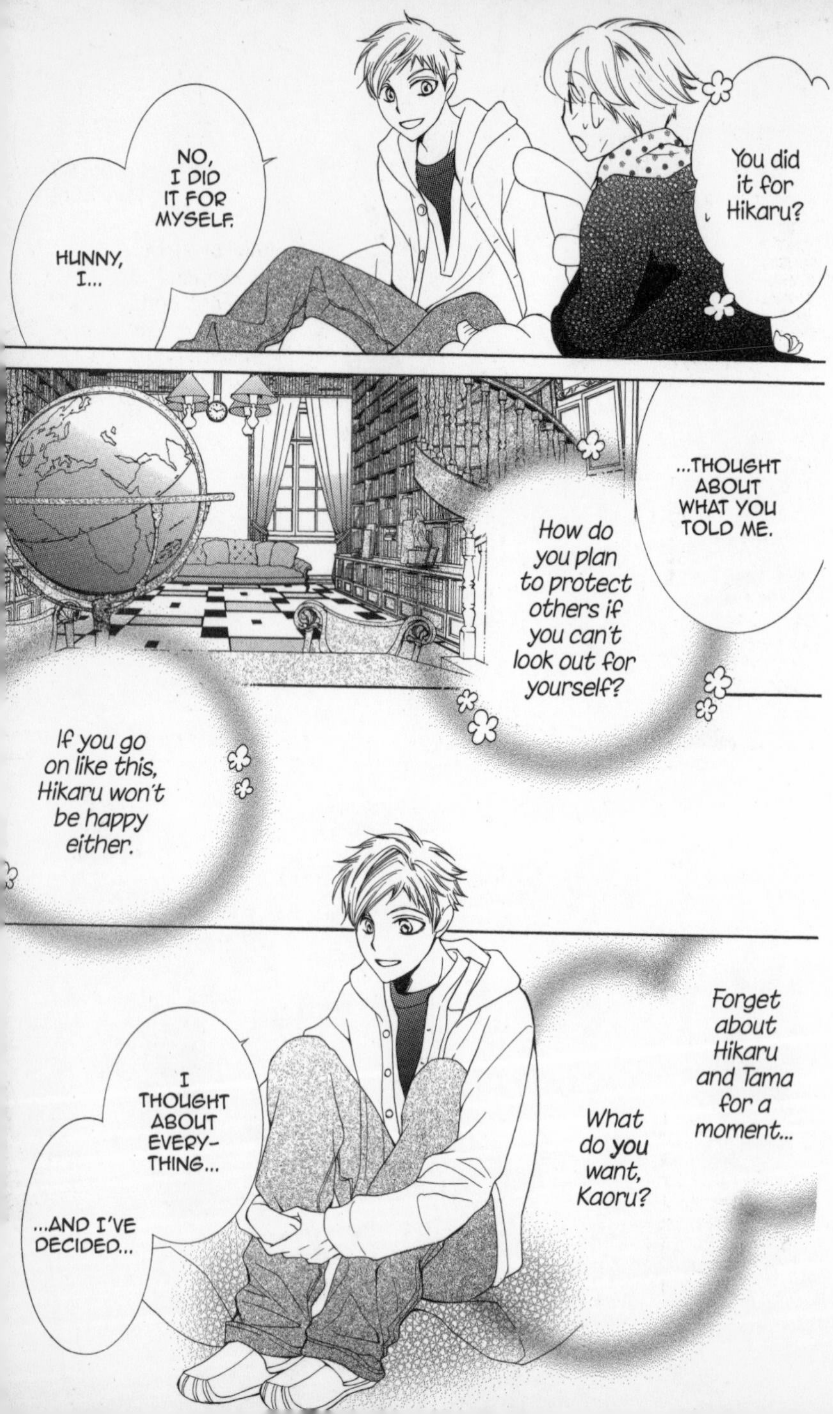
You did it for Hikaru?
NO, I DID IT FOR MYSELF.
HUNNY, I...
...THOUGHT ABOUT WHAT YOU TOLD ME.
How do you plan to protect others if you can't look out for yourself?
If you go on like this, Hikaru won't be happy either.
Forget about Hikaru and Tama for a moment...
What do you want, Kaoru?
I THOUGHT ABOUT EVERYTHING...
...AND I'VE DECIDED...

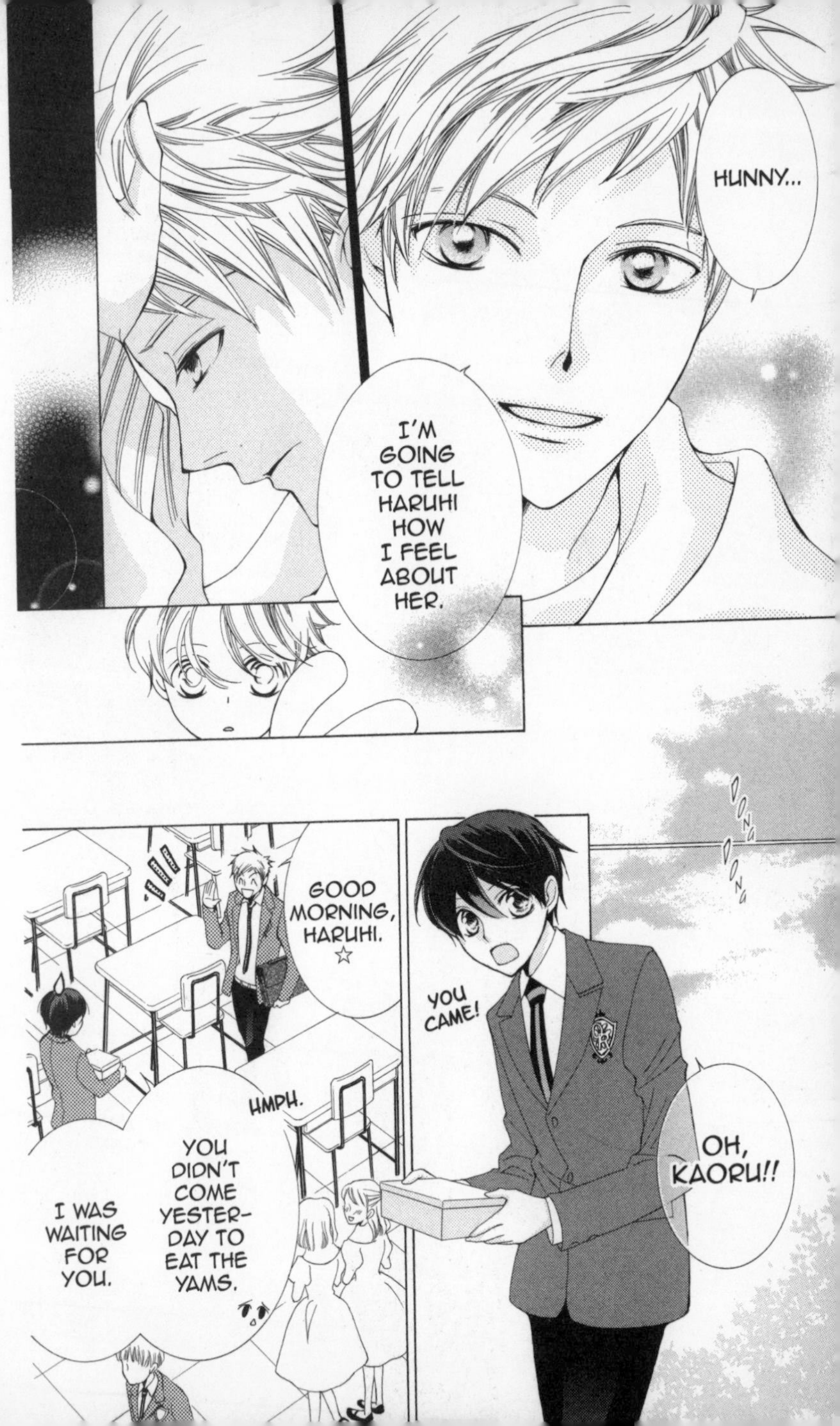
HUNNY...
I'M GOING TO TELL HARUHI HOW I FEEL ABOUT HER.
DONG
DONG
OH, KAORU!!
YOU CAME!
GOOD MORNING, HARUHI. ☆
HMPH.
YOU DIDN'T COME YESTER-DAY TO EAT THE YAMS.
I WAS WAITING FOR YOU.

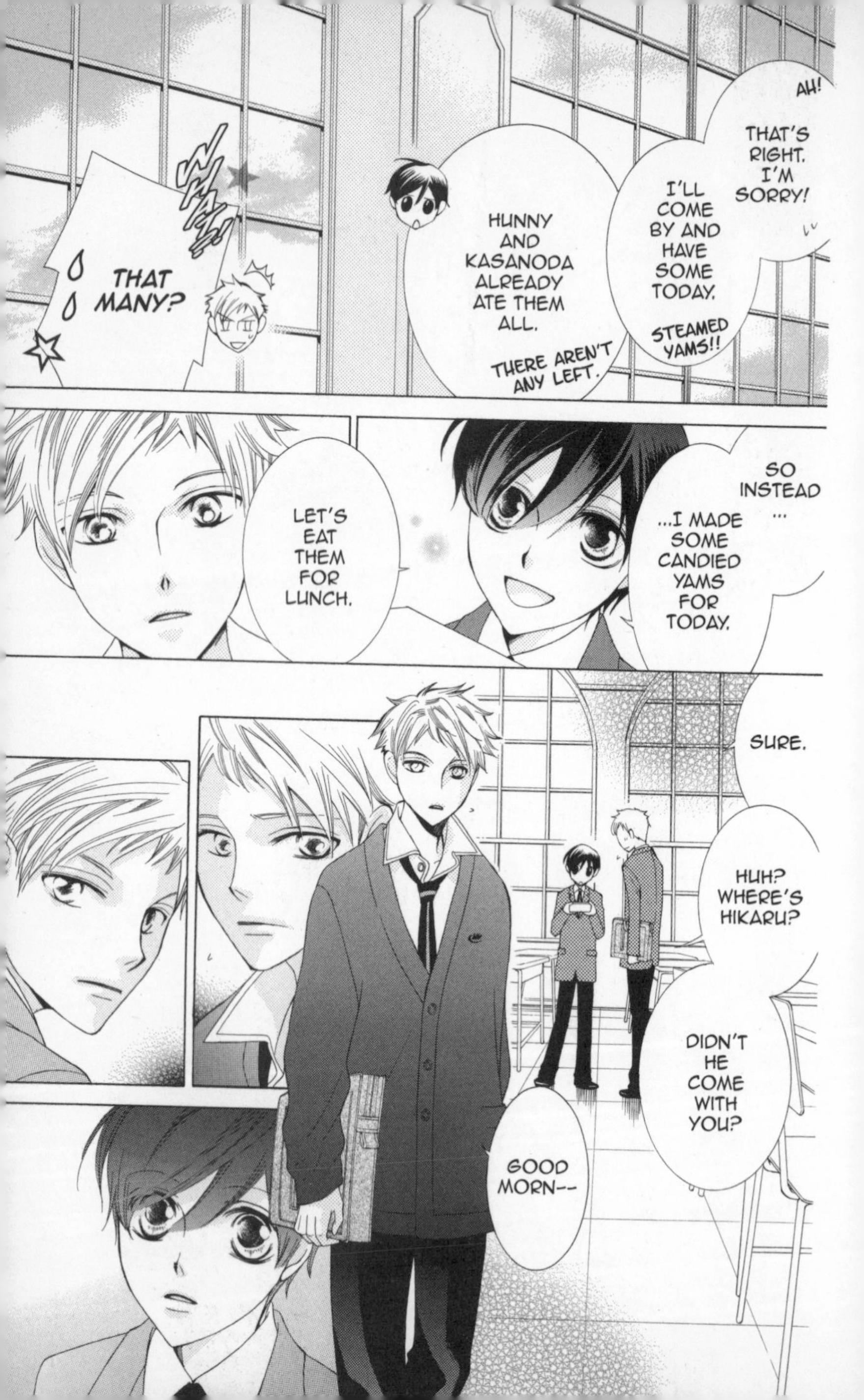
AH!
THAT'S RIGHT. I'M SORRY!
I'LL COME BY AND HAVE SOME TODAY.
STEAMED YAMS!!
HUNNY AND KASANODA ALREADY ATE THEM ALL.
THERE AREN'T ANY LEFT.
THAT MANY?
SO INSTEAD ...
...I MADE SOME CANDIED YAMS FOR TODAY.
LET'S EAT THEM FOR LUNCH.
SURE.
HUH? WHERE'S HIKARU?
DIDN'T HE COME WITH YOU?
GOOD MORN--

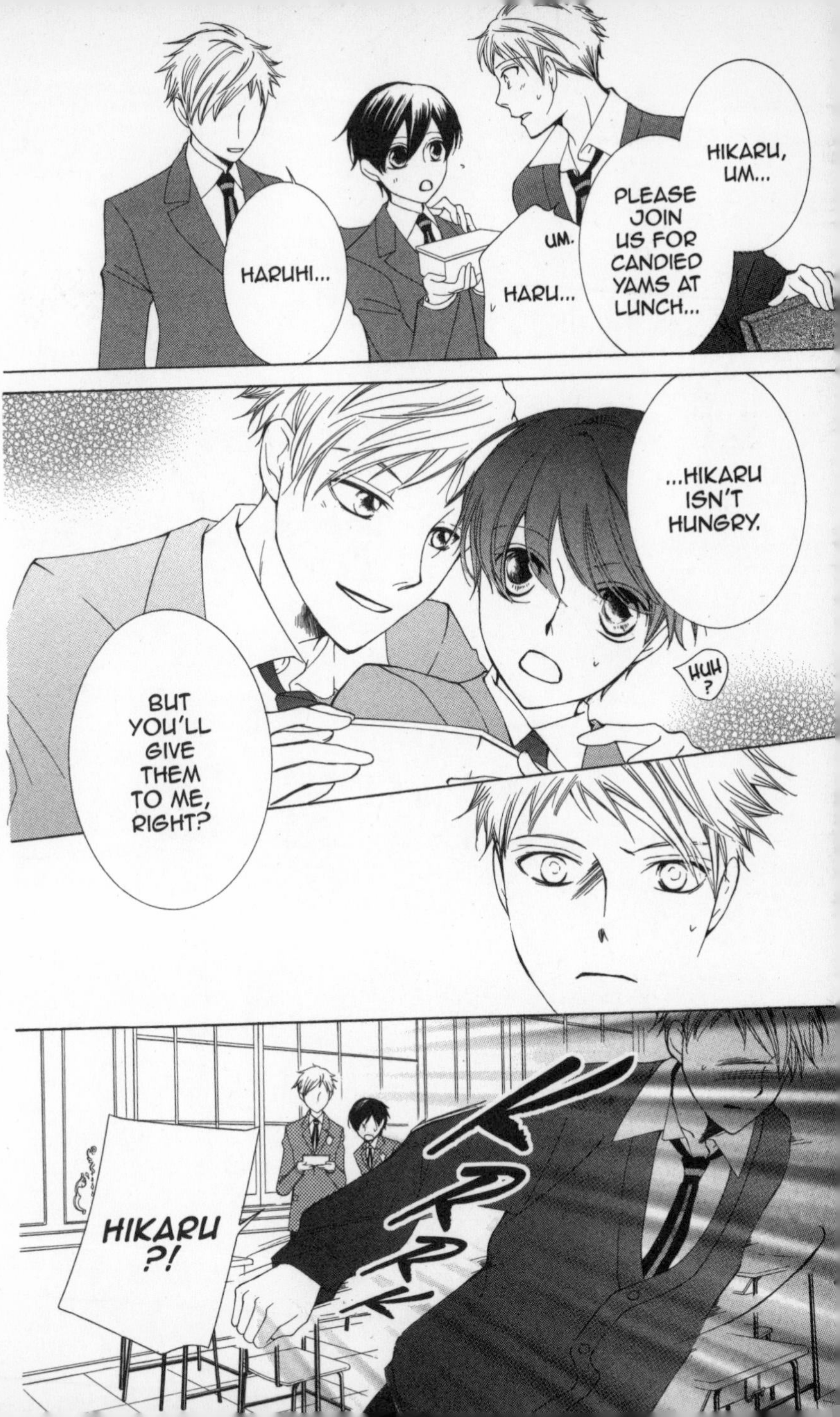
HIKARU, UM...
PLEASE JOIN US FOR CANDIED YAMS AT LUNCH...
UM.
HARU...
HARUHI...
...HIKARU ISN'T HUNGRY.
HUH?
BUT YOU'LL GIVE THEM TO ME, RIGHT?
HIKARU ?!

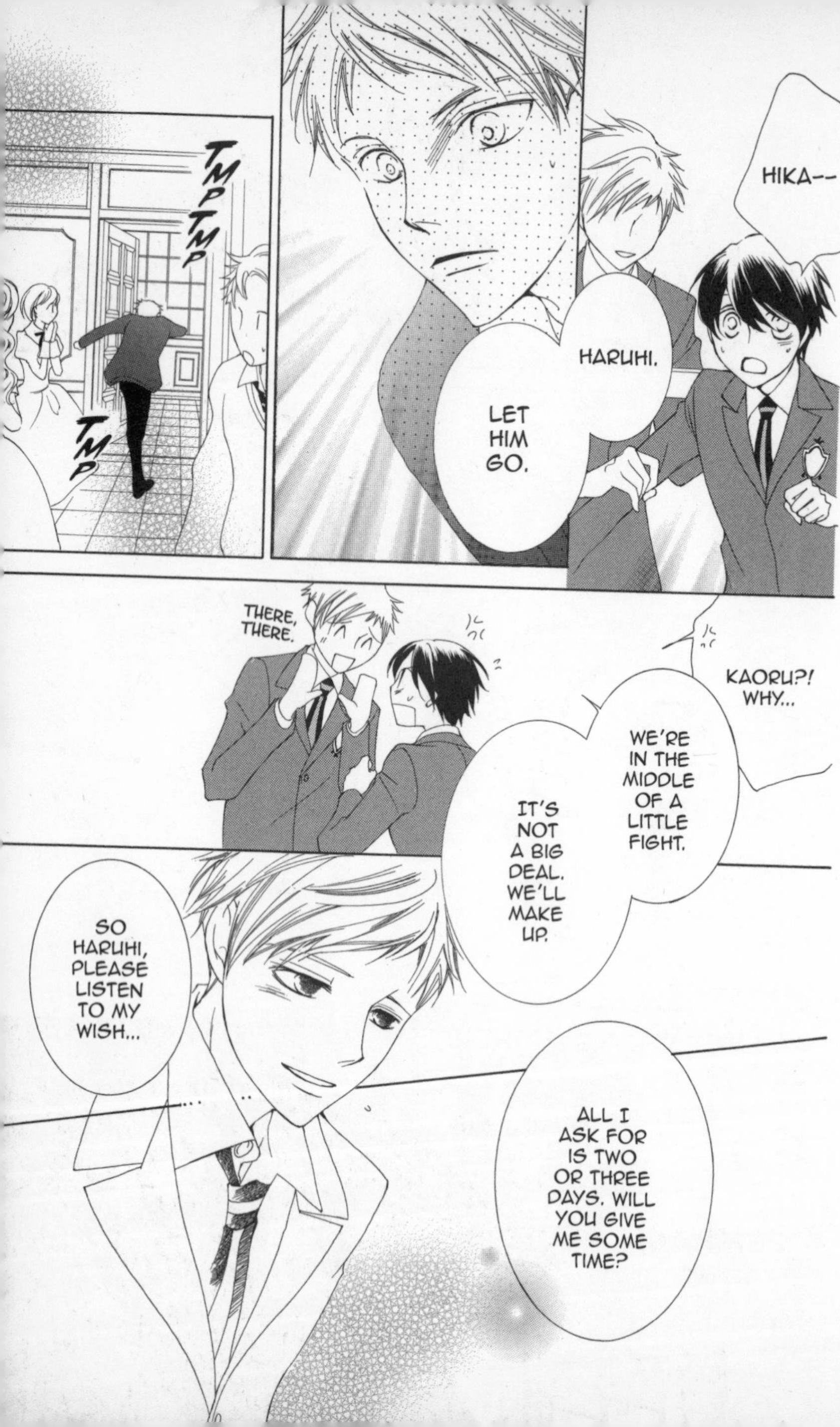
HIKA--
HARUHI.
LET HIM GO.
TMPTMP
TMP
KAORU?! WHY...
WE'RE IN THE MIDDLE OF A LITTLE FIGHT.
IT'S NOT A BIG DEAL. WE'LL MAKE UP.
THERE, THERE.
SO HARUHI, PLEASE LISTEN TO MY WISH...
... ...
ALL I ASK FOR IS TWO OR THREE DAYS. WILL YOU GIVE ME SOME TIME?

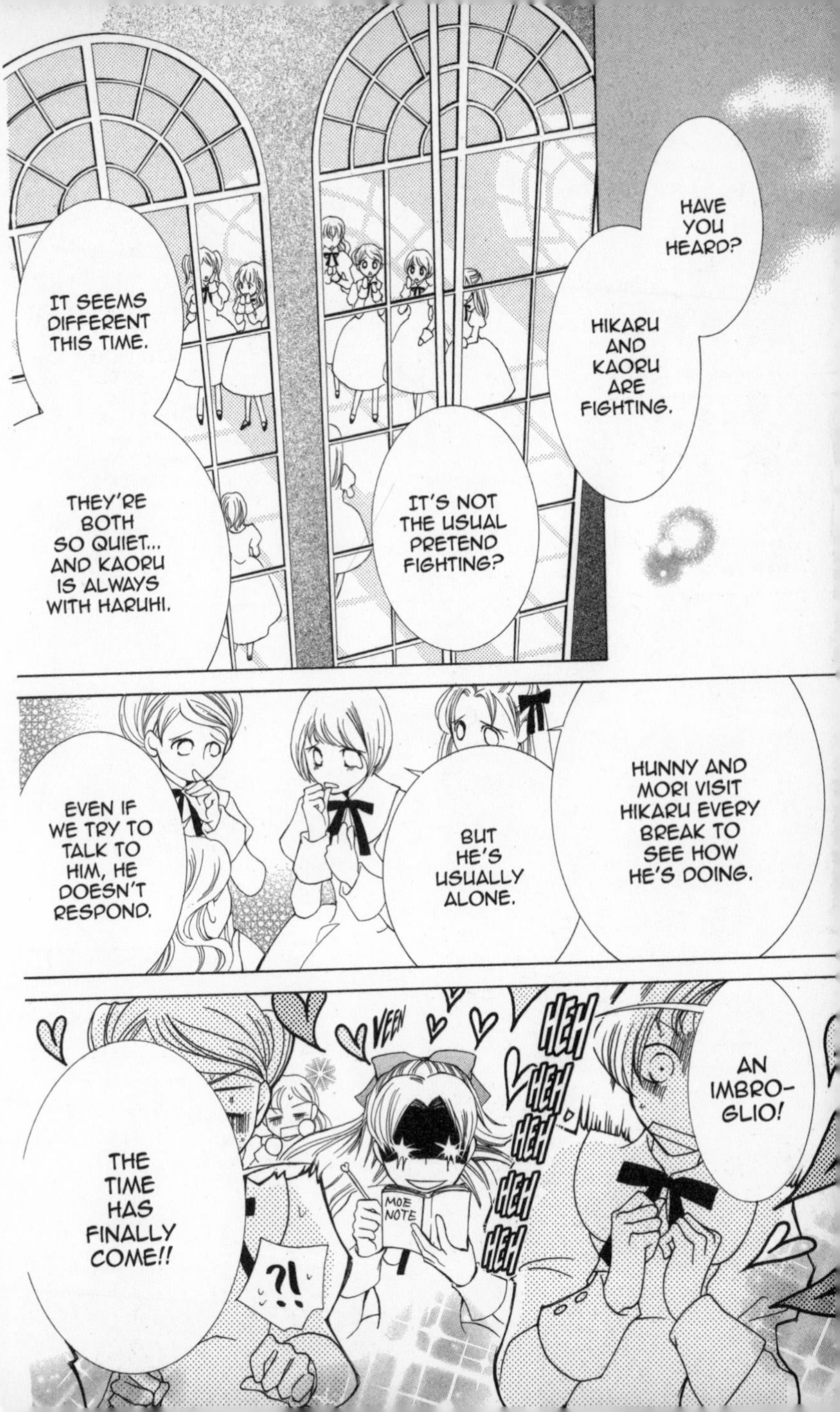
HAVE YOU HEARD?
HIKARU AND KAORU ARE FIGHTING.
IT'S NOT THE USUAL PRETEND FIGHTING?
IT SEEMS DIFFERENT THIS TIME.
THEY'RE BOTH SO QUIET... AND KAORU IS ALWAYS WITH HARUHI.
HUNNY AND MORI VISIT HIKARU EVERY BREAK TO SEE HOW HE'S DOING.
BUT HE'S USUALLY ALONE.
EVEN IF WE TRY TO TALK TO HIM, HE DOESN'T RESPOND.
AN IMBROGLIO!
HEH HEH HEH HEH HEH
VEEN
MOE NOTE
THE TIME HAS FINALLY COME!!
?!

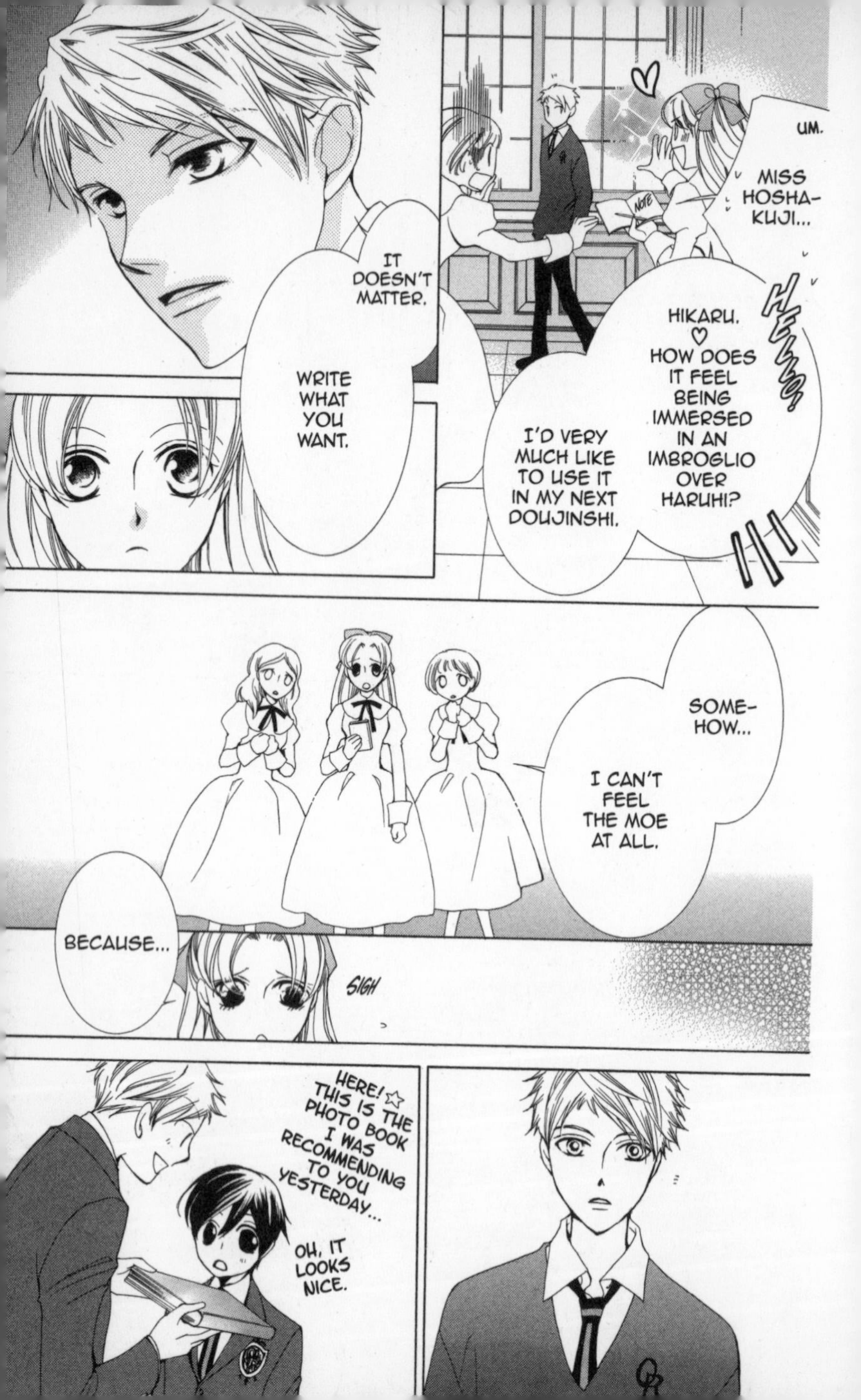
UM.
MISS HOSHA-KUJI...
HIKARU. ♡ HOW DOES IT FEEL BEING IMMERSED IN AN IMBROGLIO OVER HARUHI?
I'D VERY MUCH LIKE TO USE IT IN MY NEXT DOUJINSHI.
IT DOESN'T MATTER.
WRITE WHAT YOU WANT.
SOME-HOW...
I CAN'T FEEL THE MOE AT ALL.
BECAUSE...
SIGH
HERE! ☆ THIS IS THE PHOTO BOOK I WAS RECOMMENDING TO YOU YESTERDAY...
OH, IT LOOKS NICE.

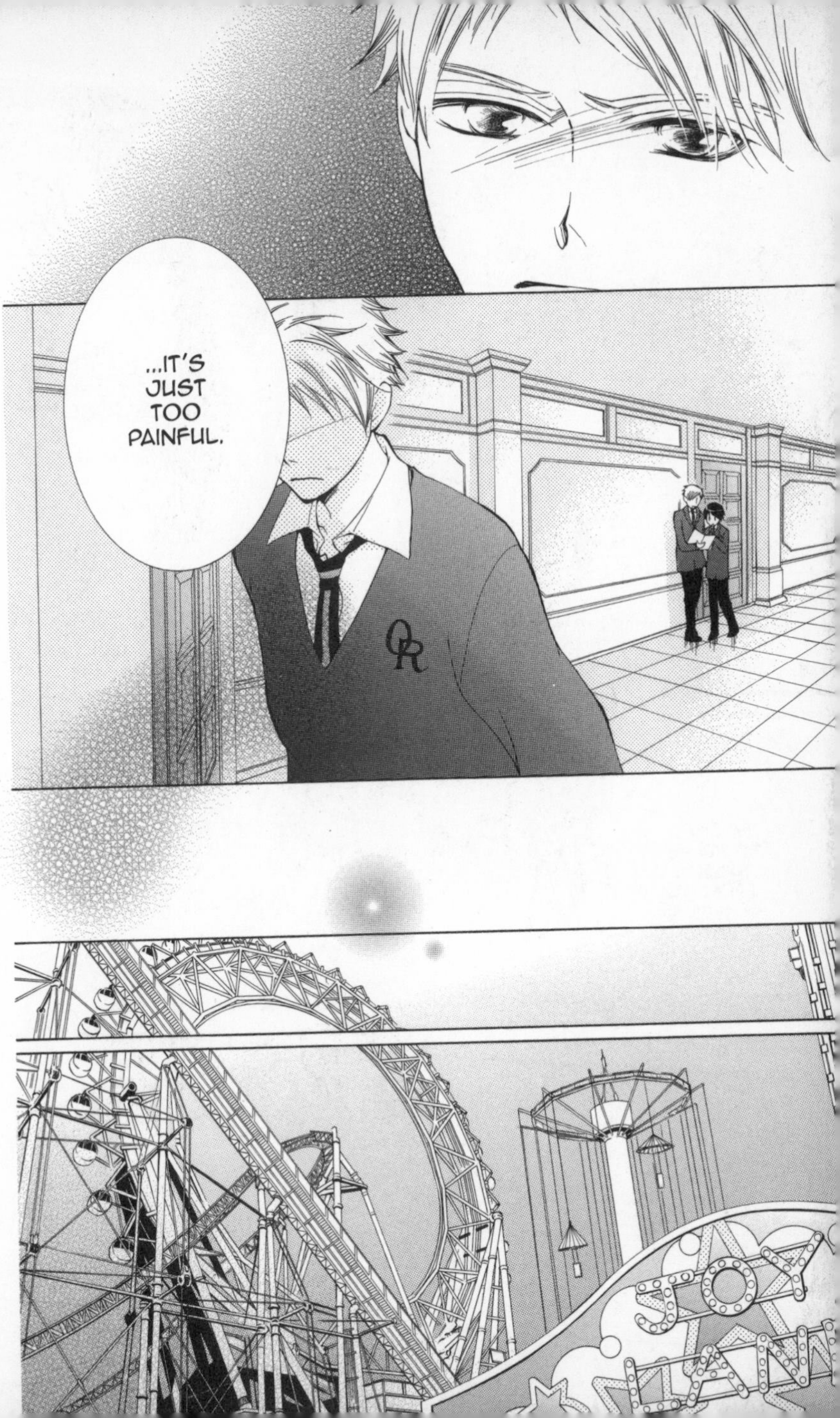
...IT'S JUST TOO PAINFUL.
JOY

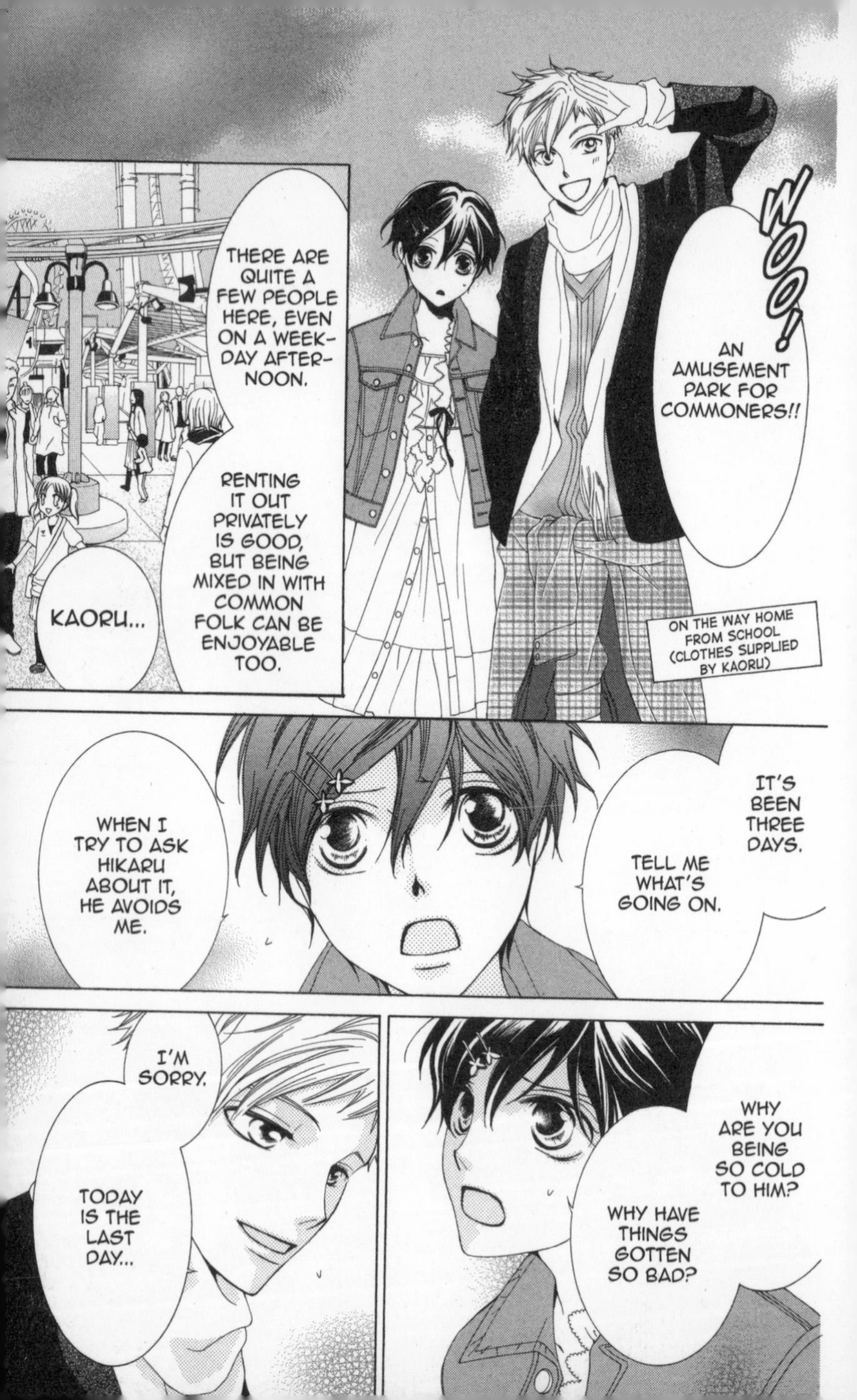
WOOO!
AN AMUSEMENT PARK FOR COMMONERS!!
ON THE WAY HOME FROM SCHOOL (CLOTHES SUPPLIED BY KAORU)
THERE ARE QUITE A FEW PEOPLE HERE, EVEN ON A WEEK-DAY AFTER-NOON.
RENTING IT OUT PRIVATELY IS GOOD, BUT BEING MIXED IN WITH COMMON FOLK CAN BE ENJOYABLE TOO.
KAORU...
IT'S BEEN THREE DAYS.
TELL ME WHAT'S GOING ON.
WHEN I TRY TO ASK HIKARU ABOUT IT, HE AVOIDS ME.
WHY ARE YOU BEING SO COLD TO HIM?
WHY HAVE THINGS GOTTEN SO BAD?
I'M SORRY.
TODAY IS THE LAST DAY...

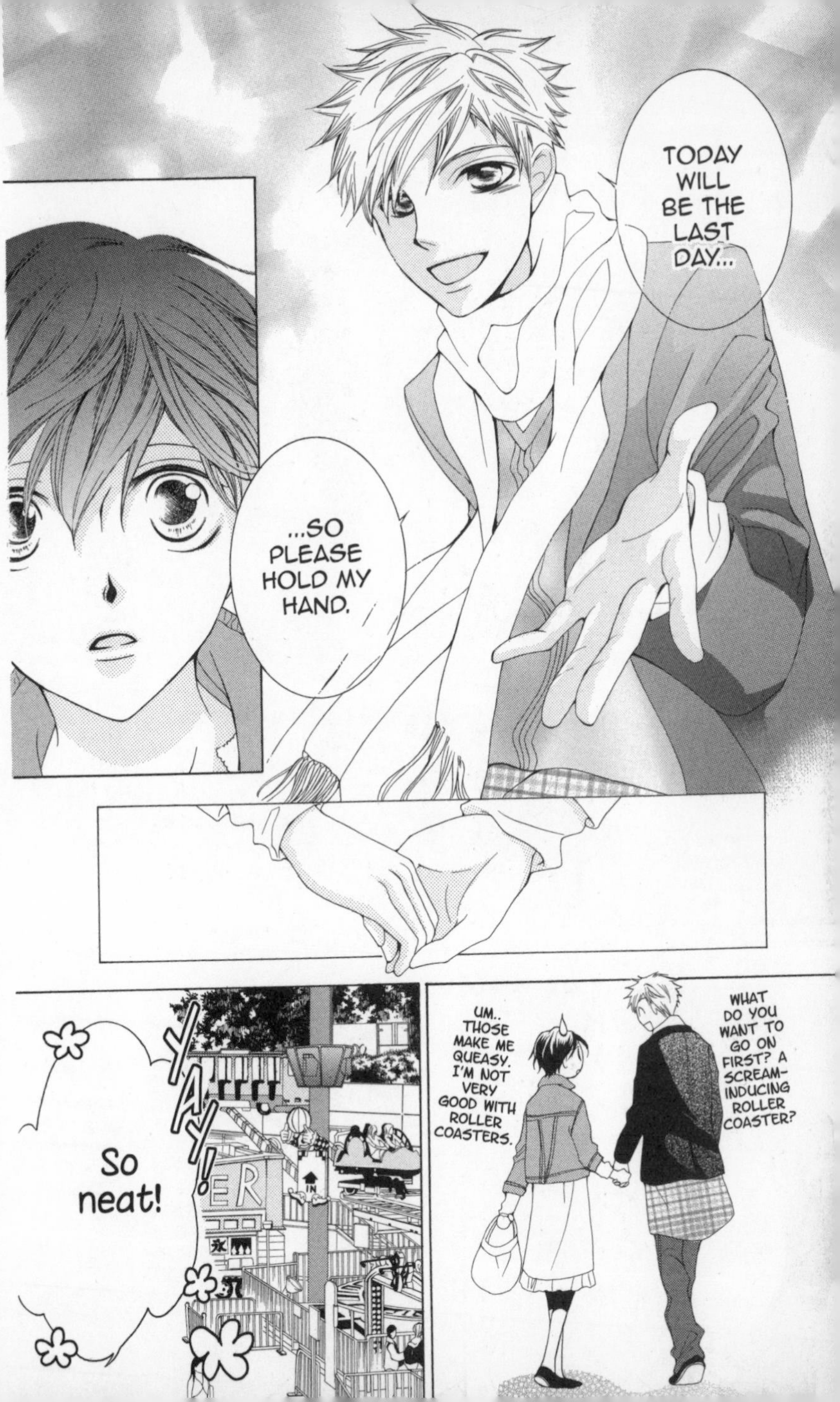
TODAY WILL BE THE LAST DAY...
...SO PLEASE HOLD MY HAND.
WHAT DO YOU WANT TO GO ON FIRST? A SCREAM-INDUCING ROLLER COASTER?
UM.. THOSE MAKE ME QUEASY. I'M NOT VERY GOOD WITH ROLLER COASTERS.
YAY!
So neat!

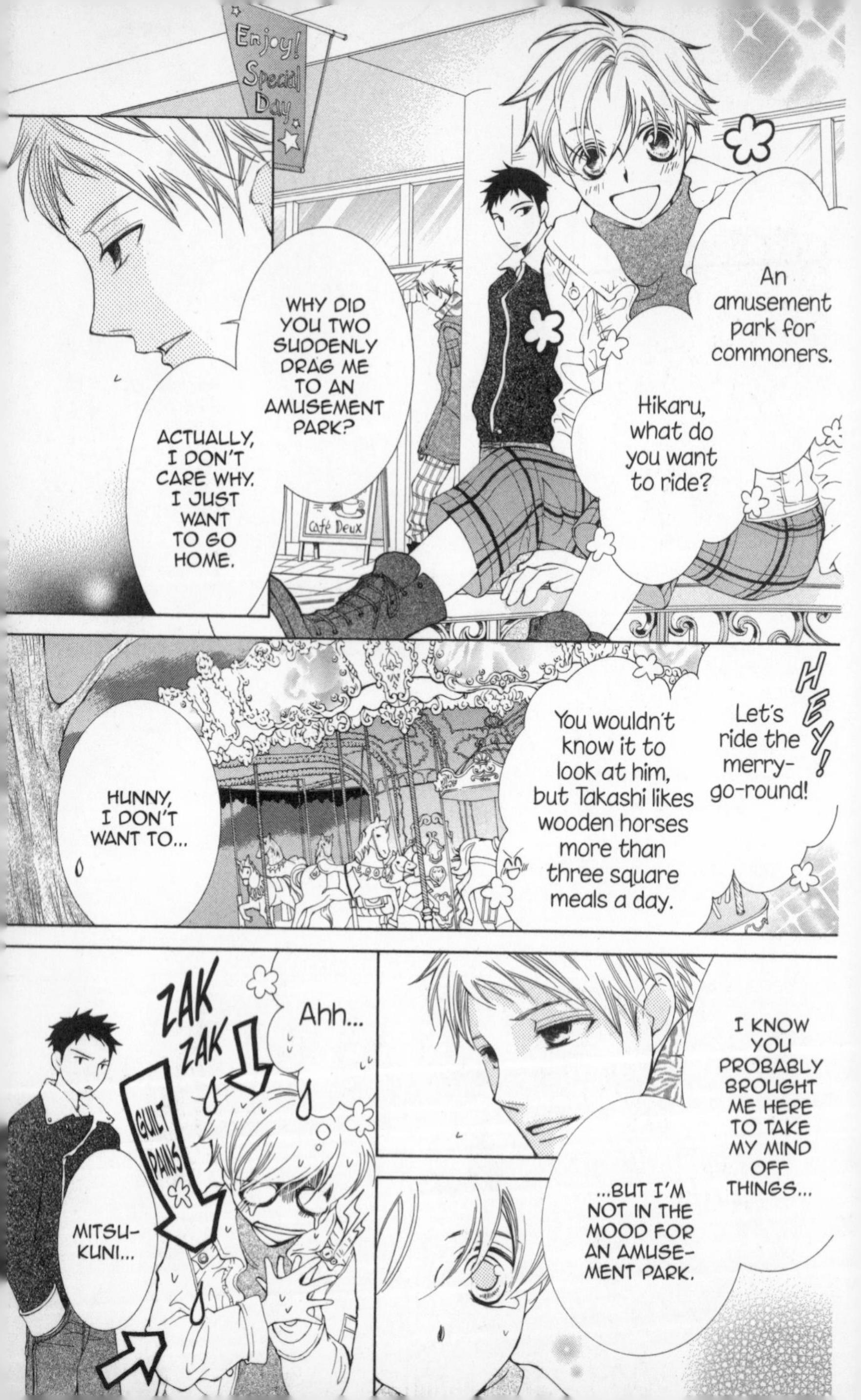
Enjoy! Special Day
An amusement park for commoners.
Hikaru, what do you want to ride?
Café Deux
WHY DID YOU TWO SUDDENLY DRAG ME TO AN AMUSEMENT PARK?
ACTUALLY, I DON'T CARE WHY. I JUST WANT TO GO HOME.
HEY!
Let's ride the merry-go-round!
You wouldn't know it to look at him, but Takashi likes wooden horses more than three square meals a day.
HUNNY, I DON'T WANT TO...
I KNOW YOU PROBABLY BROUGHT ME HERE TO TAKE MY MIND OFF THINGS...
...BUT I'M NOT IN THE MOOD FOR AN AMUSEMENT PARK.
Ahh...
ZAK ZAK
GUILT PAINS
MITSU-KUNI...

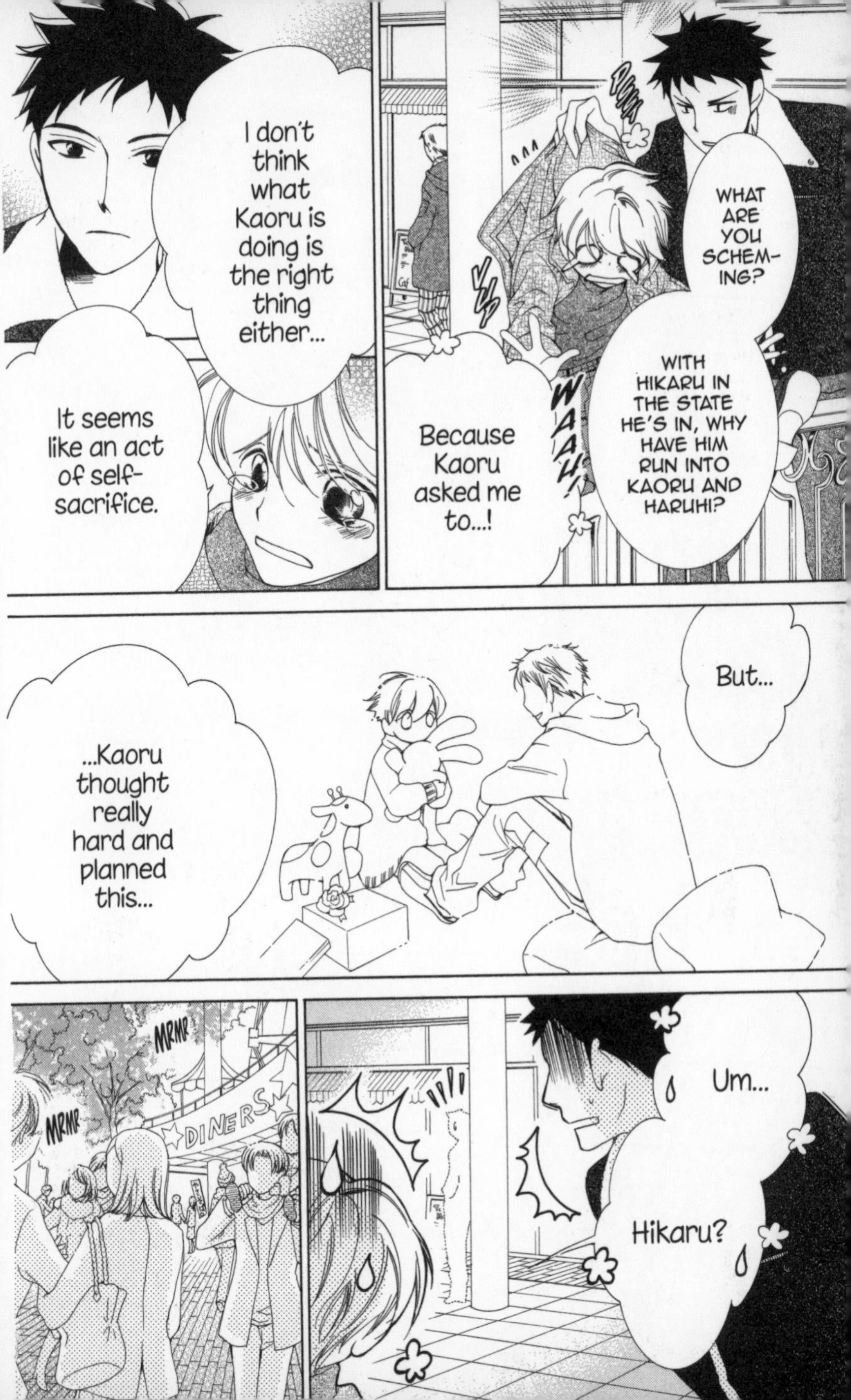
WHAT ARE YOU SCHEM-ING?
WITH HIKARU IN THE STATE HE'S IN, WHY HAVE HIM RUN INTO KAORU AND HARUHI?
WAAAH!
Because Kaoru asked me to...!
I don't think what Kaoru is doing is the right thing either...
It seems like an act of self-sacrifice.
But...
...Kaoru thought really hard and planned this...
Um...
Hikaru?
MRMR
DINERS
MRMR

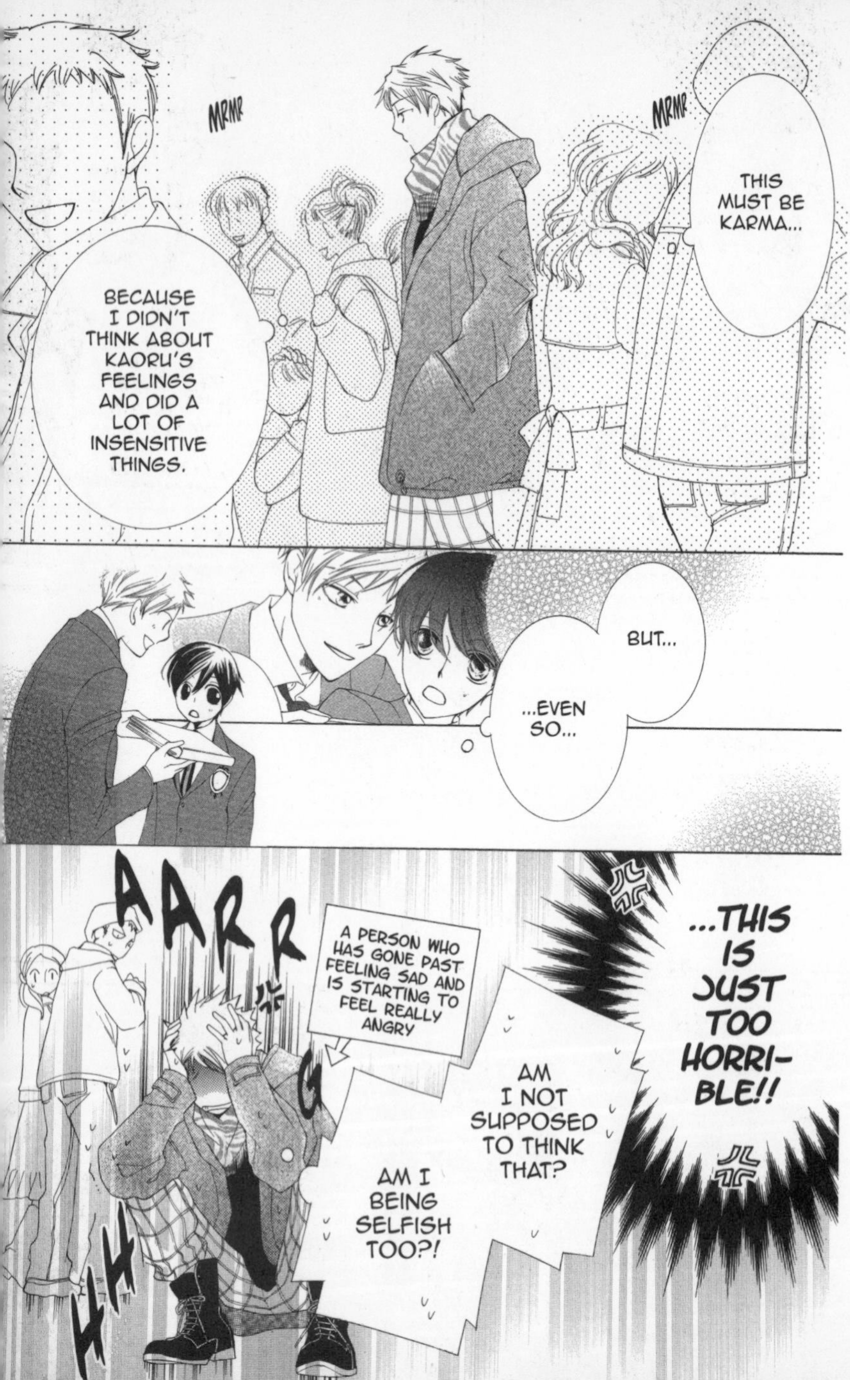
MRMR
THIS MUST BE KARMA...
MRMR
BECAUSE I DIDN'T THINK ABOUT KAORU'S FEELINGS AND DID A LOT OF INSENSITIVE THINGS.
BUT...
...EVEN SO...
...THIS IS JUST TOO HORRIBLE!!
AM I NOT SUPPOSED TO THINK THAT?
AM I BEING SELFISH TOO?!
A PERSON WHO HAS GONE PAST FEELING SAD AND IS STARTING TO FEEL REALLY ANGRY
AARRGHH

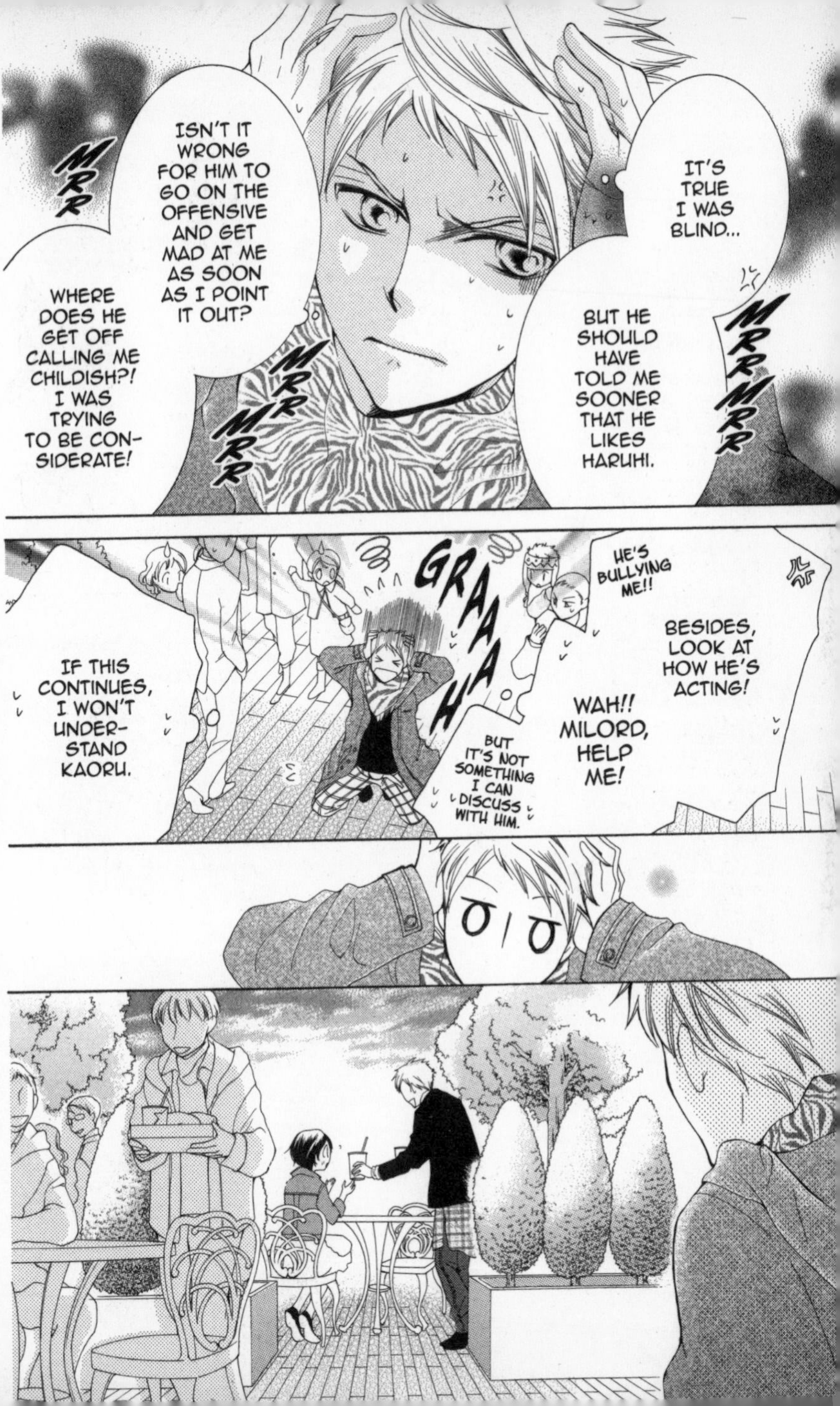
IT'S TRUE I WAS BLIND...
BUT HE SHOULD HAVE TOLD ME SOONER THAT HE LIKES HARUHI.
MRRMRR
MRR MRR
ISN'T IT WRONG FOR HIM TO GO ON THE OFFENSIVE AND GET MAD AT ME AS SOON AS I POINT IT OUT?
WHERE DOES HE GET OFF CALLING ME CHILDISH?! I WAS TRYING TO BE CON-SIDERATE!
MRR
BESIDES, LOOK AT HOW HE'S ACTING!
HE'S BULLYING ME!!
WAH!! MILORD, HELP ME!
BUT IT'S NOT SOMETHING I CAN DISCUSS WITH HIM.
GRAAAAH
IF THIS CONTINUES, I WON'T UNDER-STAND KAORU.

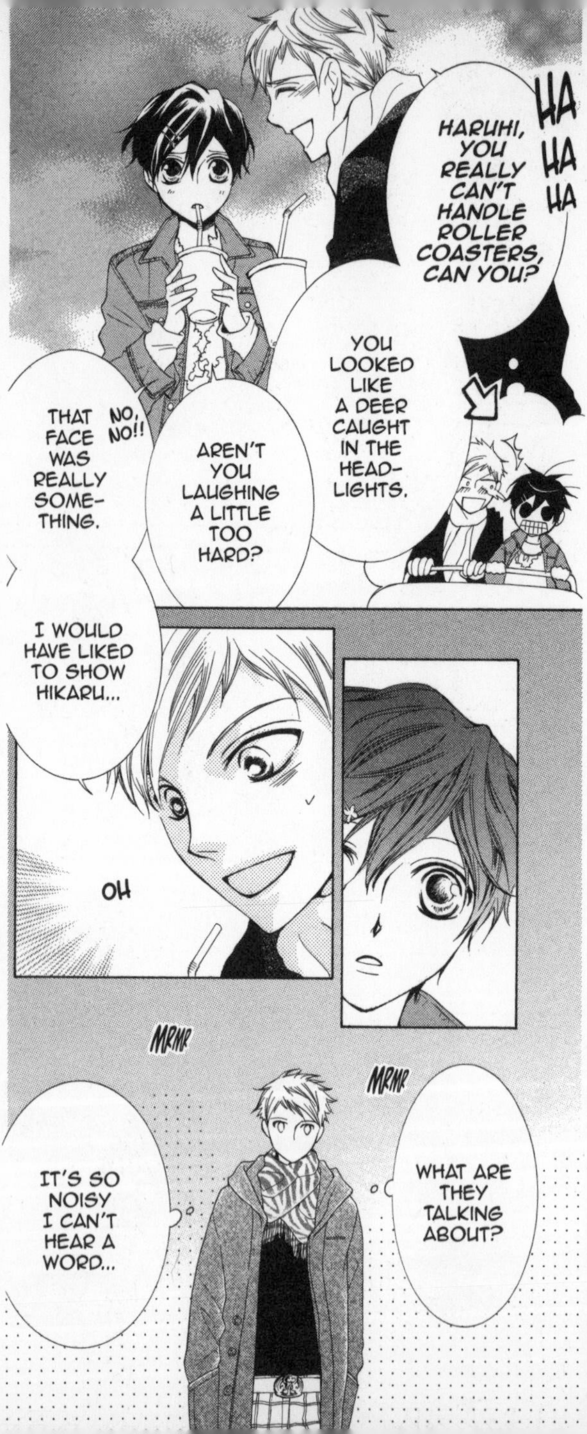
HA HA HA
HARUHI, YOU REALLY CAN'T HANDLE ROLLER COASTERS, CAN YOU?
YOU LOOKED LIKE A DEER CAUGHT IN THE HEAD-LIGHTS.
THAT FACE WAS REALLY SOME-THING.
NO, NO!!
AREN'T YOU LAUGHING A LITTLE TOO HARD?
I WOULD HAVE LIKED TO SHOW HIKARU...
OH
MRMP
MRMP
WHAT ARE THEY TALKING ABOUT?
IT'S SO NOISY I CAN'T HEAR A WORD...

1

✿HELLO!!
HAVE YOU ALL BEEN WELL?

THIS IS HATORI.✿

THIS IS HOST CLUB VOLUME 12. EACH OF THESE STORIES IS ONE WHERE I WAS FEELING, "OH, I'VE FINALLY COME TO THE POINT WHERE I CAN WRITE ABOUT THIS." I WAS REMINISCING AND THINKING ABOUT IT, BUT ALSO WRITING THE STORY WITH THE UTMOST NERVOUSNESS. I'D BE HAPPY IF YOU COULD ENJOY IT.

✿BY THE WAY, THE OTHER DAY, I COULDN'T FIND MY REMOTE CONTROL FOR ABOUT FOUR DAYS, AND I COULDN'T FIND IT EVEN AFTER SEARCHING EVERY-WHERE IN MY HOUSE. I HAD GIVEN UP WHEN I DISCOVERED IT WAS PLACED IN FRONT OF MY TV, CASUALLY STUCK IN A MAGAZINE.

THINGS LIKE THIS HAPPEN OFTEN, DON'T THEY?!

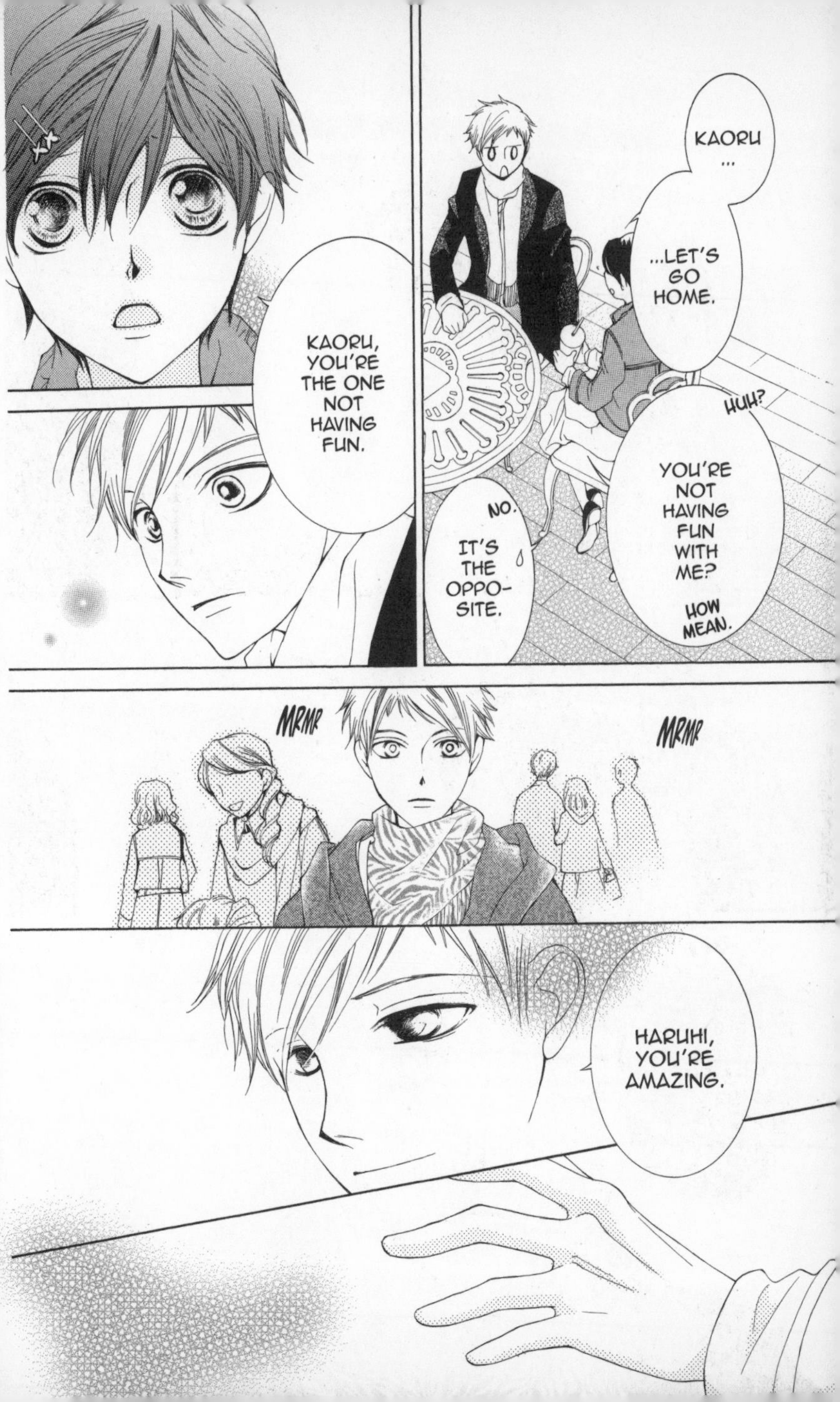
KAORU ...
...LET'S GO HOME.
HUH?
YOU'RE NOT HAVING FUN WITH ME?
HOW MEAN.
NO.
IT'S THE OPPOSITE.
KAORU, YOU'RE THE ONE NOT HAVING FUN.
MRMR
MRMR
HARUHI, YOU'RE AMAZING.

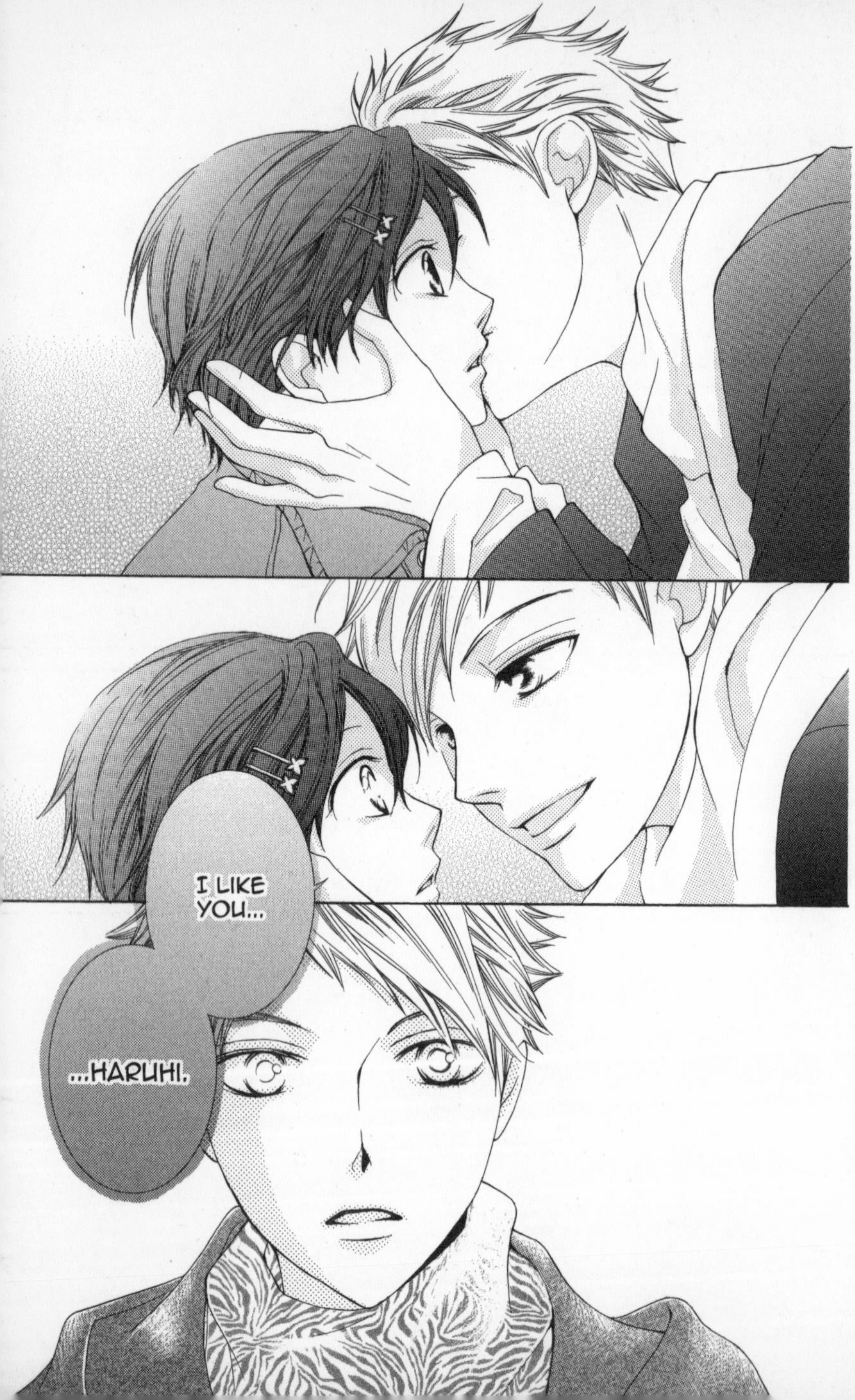
I LIKE YOU...
...HARUHI.

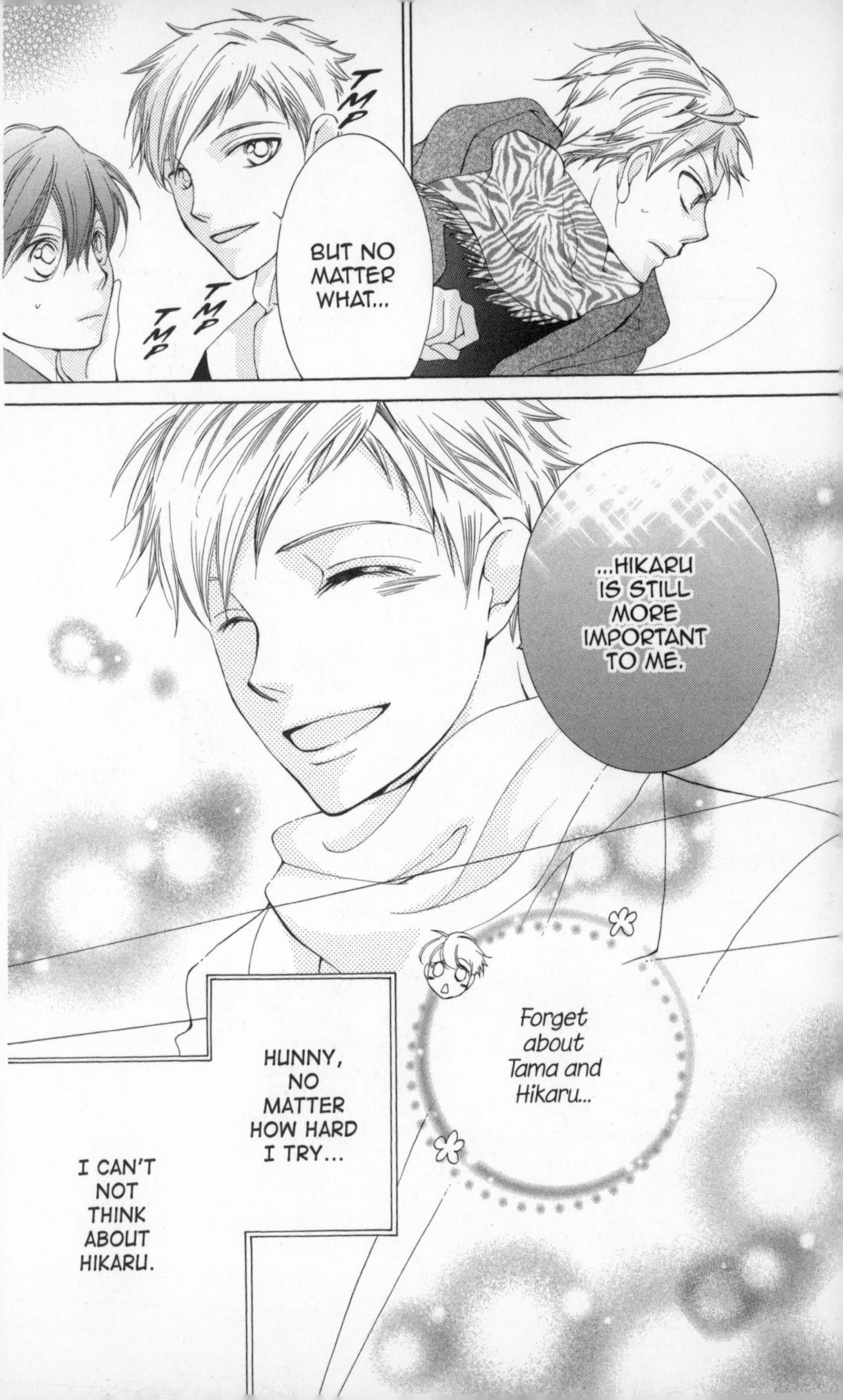
TMP
BUT NO MATTER WHAT...
TMP
TMP
...HIKARU IS STILL MORE IMPORTANT TO ME.
Forget about Tama and Hikaru...
HUNNY, NO MATTER HOW HARD I TRY...
I CAN'T NOT THINK ABOUT HIKARU.

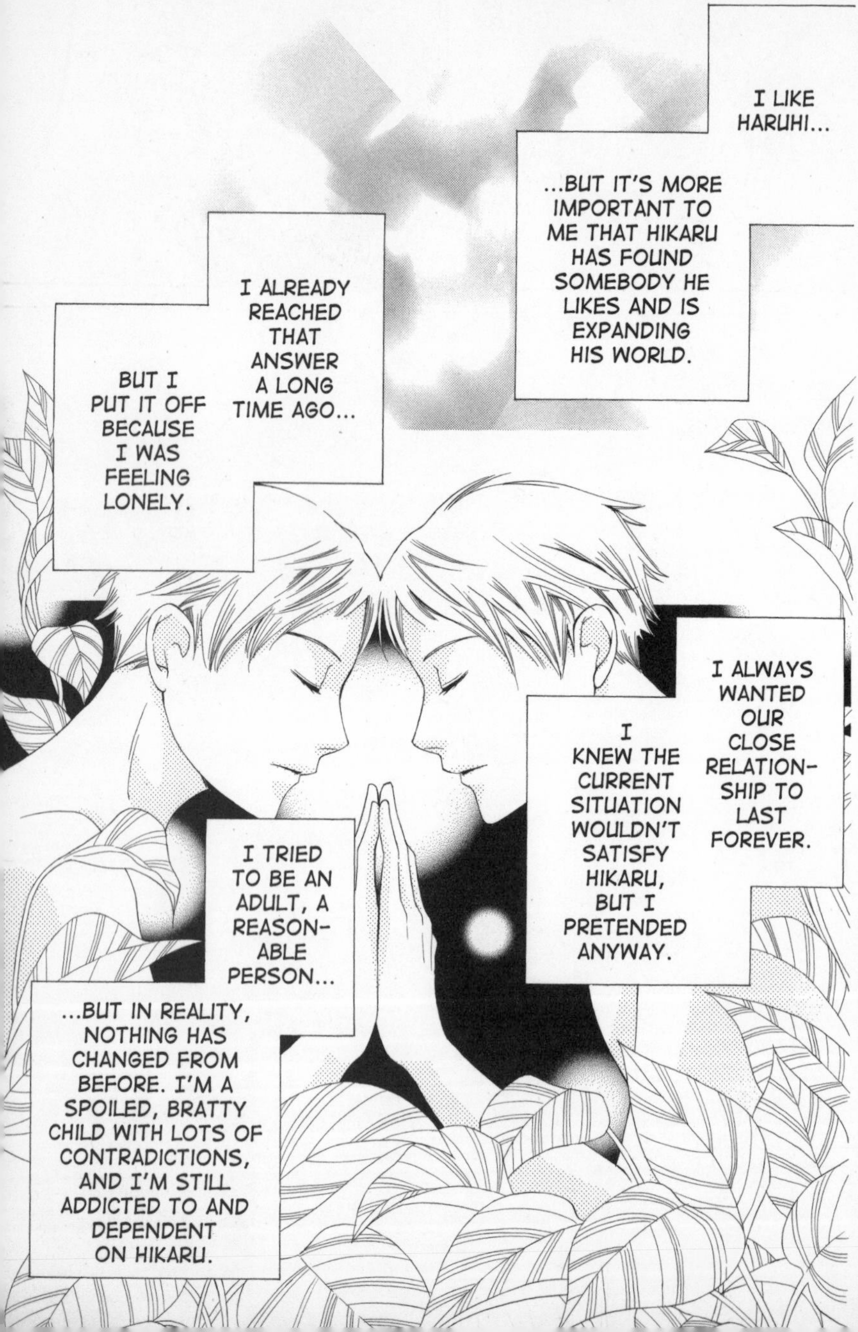
I LIKE HARUHI...
...BUT IT'S MORE IMPORTANT TO ME THAT HIKARU HAS FOUND SOMEBODY HE LIKES AND IS EXPANDING HIS WORLD.
I ALREADY REACHED THAT ANSWER A LONG TIME AGO...
BUT I PUT IT OFF BECAUSE I WAS FEELING LONELY.
I ALWAYS WANTED OUR CLOSE RELATION-SHIP TO LAST FOREVER.
I KNEW THE CURRENT SITUATION WOULDN'T SATISFY HIKARU, BUT I PRETENDED ANYWAY.
I TRIED TO BE AN ADULT, A REASON-ABLE PERSON...
...BUT IN REALITY, NOTHING HAS CHANGED FROM BEFORE. I'M A SPOILED, BRATTY CHILD WITH LOTS OF CONTRADICTIONS, AND I'M STILL ADDICTED TO AND DEPENDENT ON HIKARU.

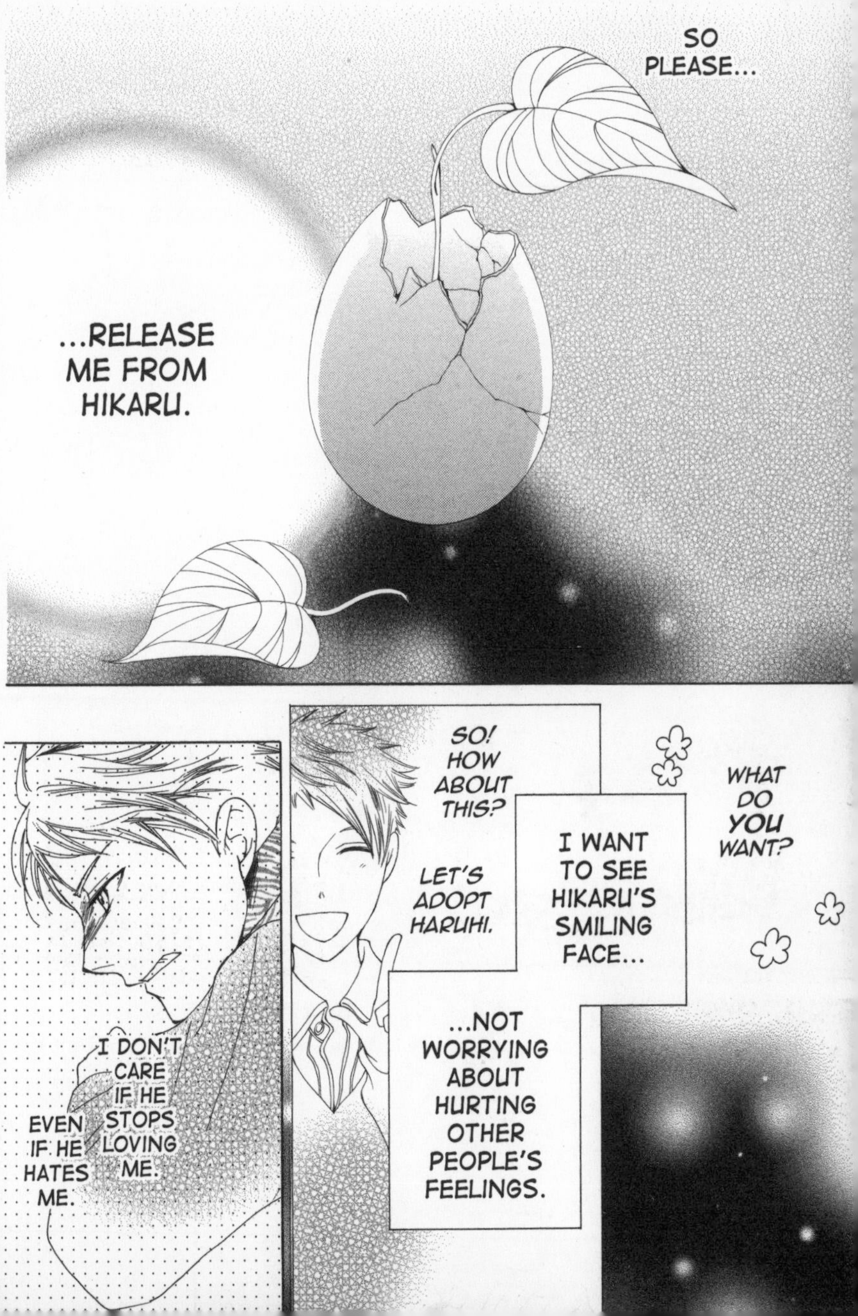
SO PLEASE...
...RELEASE ME FROM HIKARU.
WHAT DO YOU WANT?
I WANT TO SEE HIKARU'S SMILING FACE...
SO! HOW ABOUT THIS?
LET'S ADOPT HARUHI.
...NOT WORRYING ABOUT HURTING OTHER PEOPLE'S FEELINGS.
I DON'T CARE IF HE STOPS LOVING ME.
EVEN IF HE HATES ME.

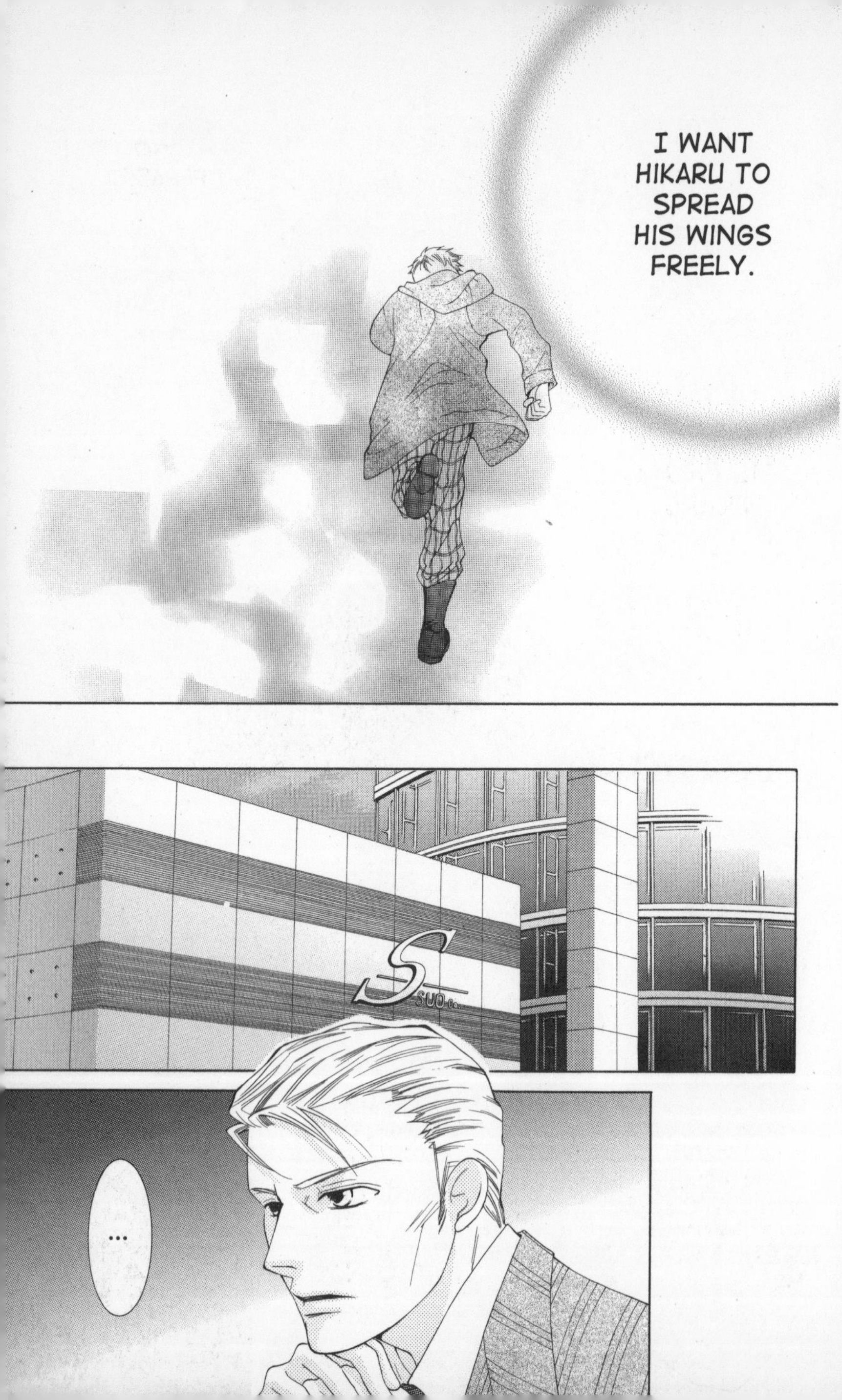
I WANT HIKARU TO SPREAD HIS WINGS FREELY.
SUO Co.
...

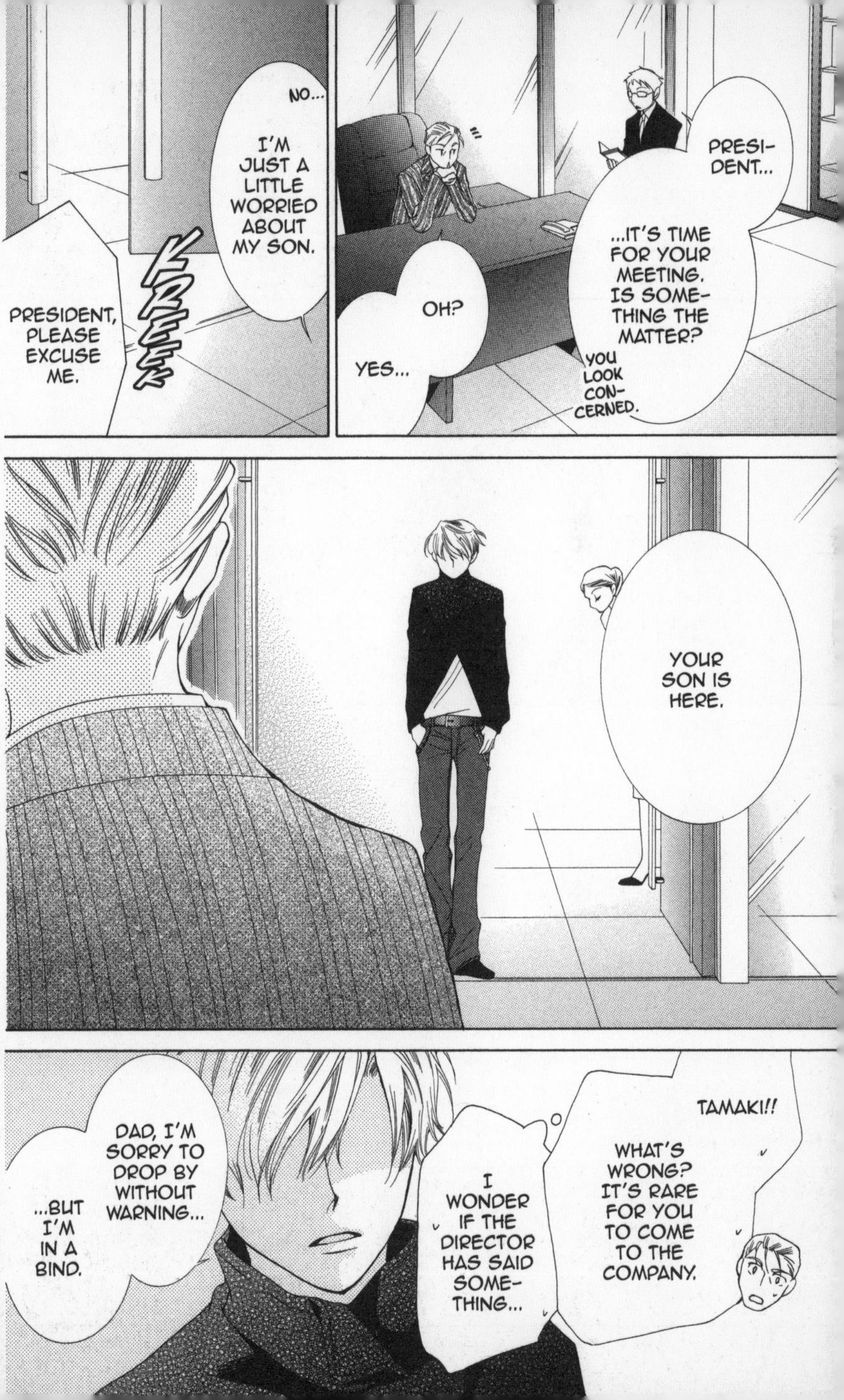
PRESI-DENT...
...IT'S TIME FOR YOUR MEETING. IS SOME-THING THE MATTER?
YOU LOOK CON-CERNED.
OH?
YES...
NO...
I'M JUST A LITTLE WORRIED ABOUT MY SON.
PRESIDENT, PLEASE EXCUSE ME.
YOUR SON IS HERE.
TAMAKI!!
WHAT'S WRONG? IT'S RARE FOR YOU TO COME TO THE COMPANY.
I WONDER IF THE DIRECTOR HAS SAID SOME-THING...
DAD, I'M SORRY TO DROP BY WITHOUT WARNING...
...BUT I'M IN A BIND.

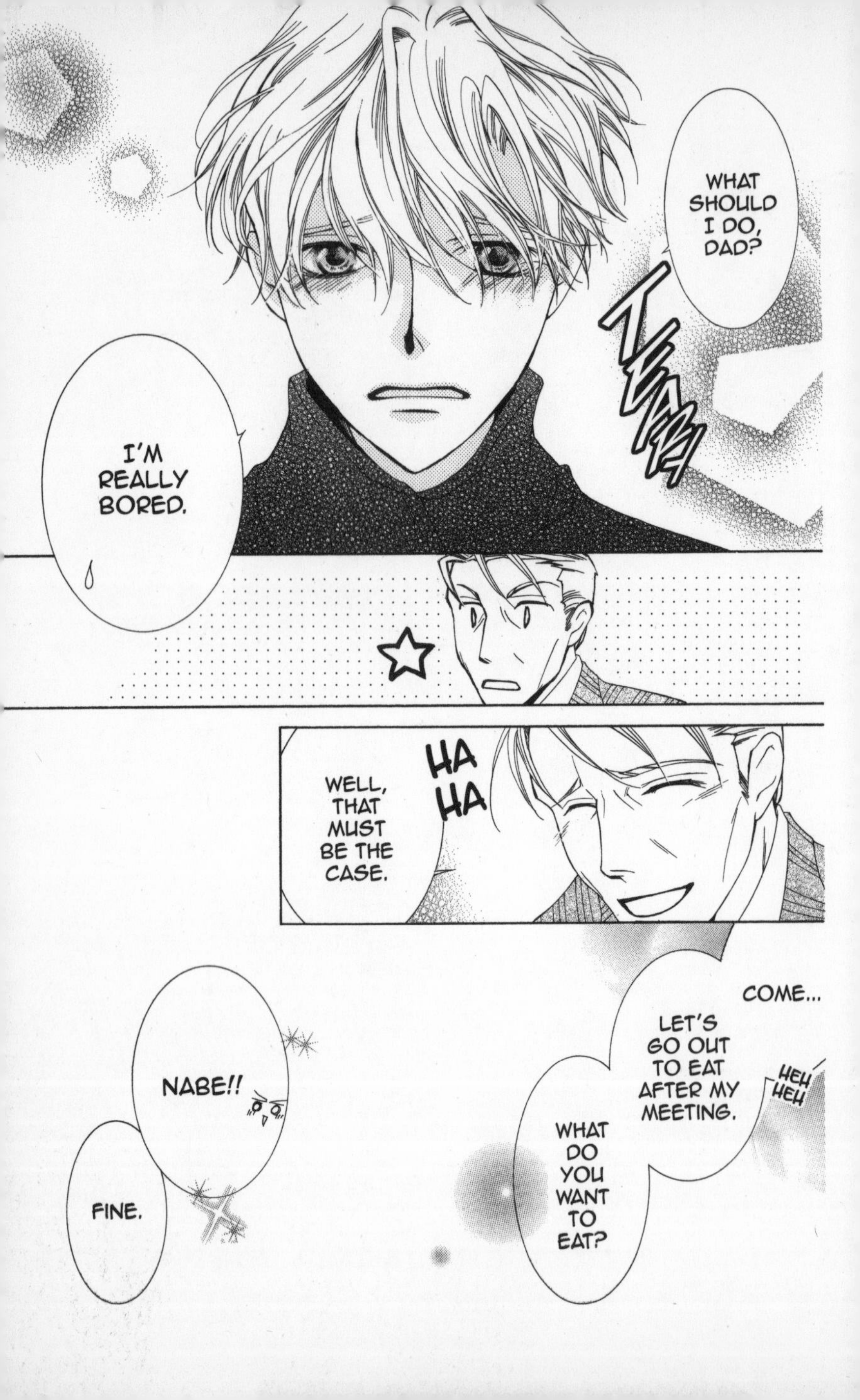
WHAT SHOULD I DO, DAD?
I'M REALLY BORED.
HA HA
WELL, THAT MUST BE THE CASE.
COME...
LET'S GO OUT TO EAT AFTER MY MEETING.
HEH HEH
WHAT DO YOU WANT TO EAT?
NABE!!
FINE.

YAMASHII: "THANK YOU FOR YOUR WORK" SPECIAL

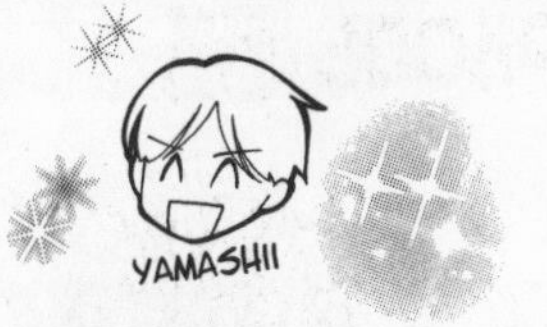
YAMASHII

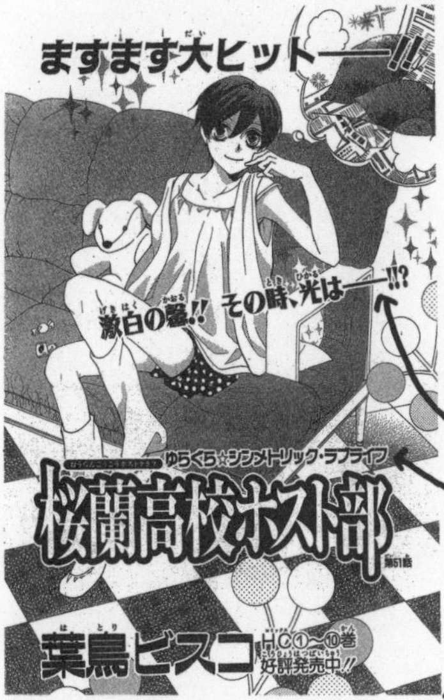
ますます大ヒット——!!
激白の馨!! その時、光は——!!?
ゆらくら☆シンメトリック・ラブライフ
桜蘭高校ホスト部
第51話
葉鳥ビスコ
H.C①～⑩巻
好評発売中!!

HERE'S THE "GEMLIKE TAGLINE" SPECIAL FEATURE! IT'S BEEN FIVE AND A HALF YEARS (!!) SINCE *HOST CLUB* STARTED. WE'RE SHOWING ALL THE TAGLINES MY EDITOR YAMASHII THOUGHT UP--ALL AT ONCE.

TAKE YOUR JAPANESE MAGAZINES AND COMPARE IT TO THE FINAL VERSION.

THIS LEAD COPY IS PRODUCED BY YAMASHII TOO, OF COURSE.
HERE ARE THE TAGLINES.

※ IN SOME PLACES IF THE TAGLINE IS MISSING, THIS IS BECAUSE THERE WAS NONE, OR BECAUSE HATORI DOESN'T HAVE IT HANDY. I'M SORRY!!

03 COLORFUL☆HEART-RACING LOVE-LIFE
04 SPRINGTIME✿SPARKLING LOVE-LIFE
05 SPRINGTIME★EPIPHANY LOVE-LIFE
06 COLORFUL SHINING ORIENTAL LOVE★LIFE (LONG!!)
07 COLORFUL☆SHINING☆ LOVE LIFE
08 SUMMERTIME RUSTLING LOVE-LIFE
09 SUMMERTIME UPSETTING LOVE-LIFE
10 LOSING BALANCE☆ WHISPERING LOVE LIFE
11 RUSTLING HAPPY♪ LOVE-LIFE
12 RUSTLING HEART-RACING★ LOVE-LIFE
13 LOSING BALANCE☆SECRET LOVE LIFE
14 HEART-RACING☆MELTING LOVE♫ LIFE
15 SURPRISING☆EXCITING♪ LOVE LIFE
16 SPARKLING☆FLOWERING LOVE-LIFE♪
17 SWEET★GLISTENING♫ LOVE-LIFE
18 REFRESHING☆EFFERVESCENT ♡LOVE LIFE
19 REFRESHING SUNNY LOVE-LIFE
20 MYSTERIOUS★HEART-RACING LOVE LIFE

NOW THAT I LOOK BACK AT IT, SOME OF THEM ARE SPELLED "LOVE LIFE" AND SOME ARE "LOVE-LIFE." YAMASHII, I WONDER WHY.

← THE REST IS ON THE NEXT FILLER PAGE.

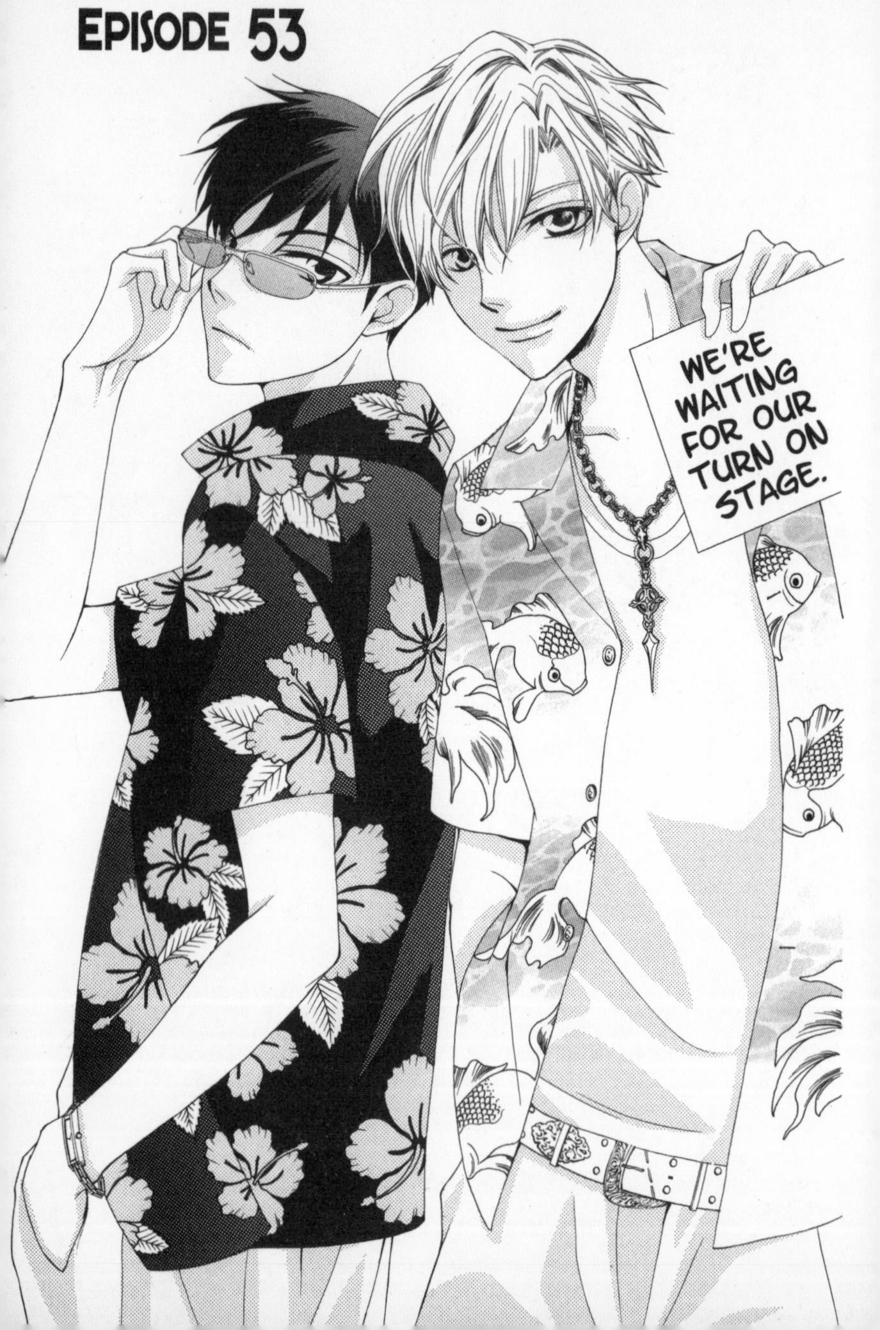
EPISODE 53
WE'RE WAITING FOR OUR TURN ON STAGE.

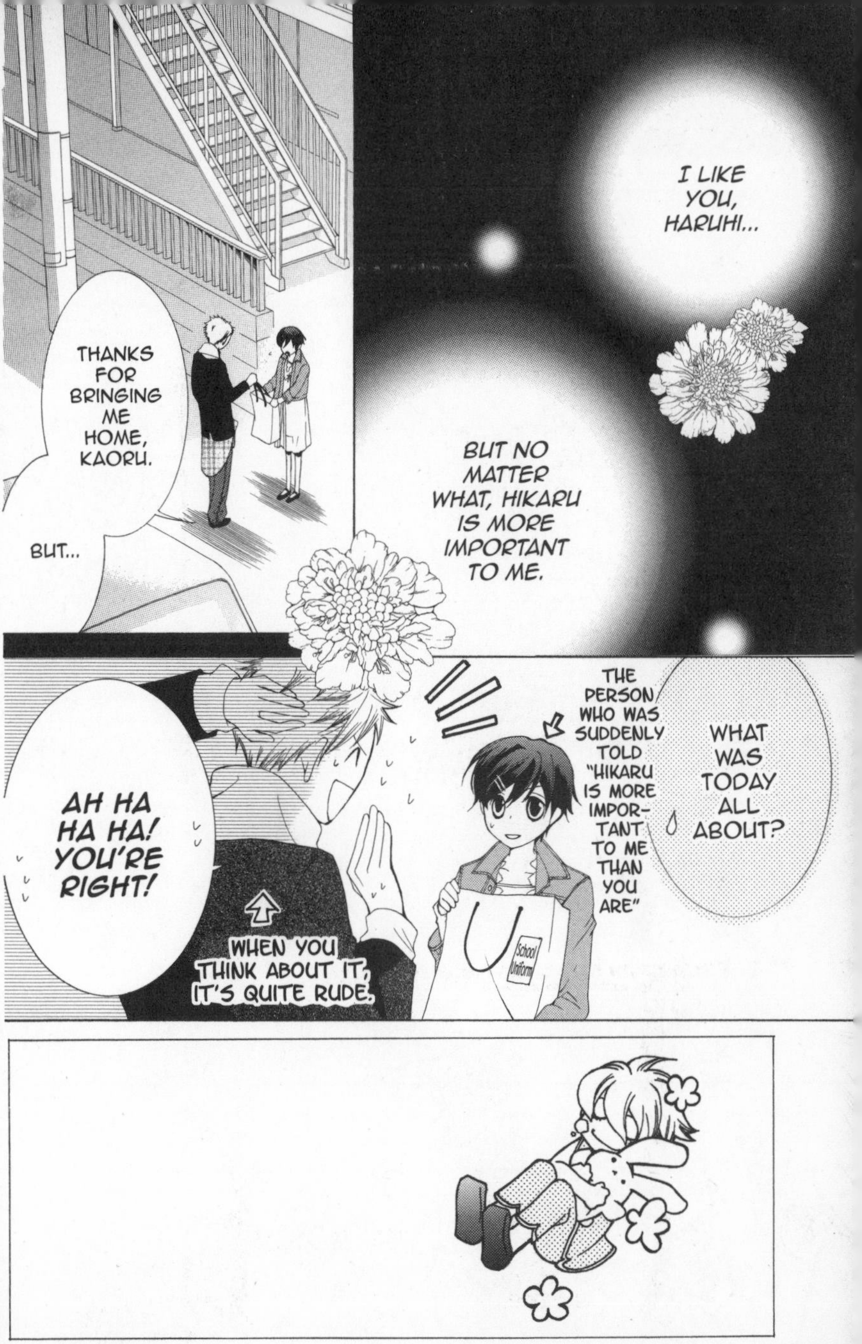
I LIKE YOU, HARUHI...
BUT NO MATTER WHAT, HIKARU IS MORE IMPORTANT TO ME.
THANKS FOR BRINGING ME HOME, KAORU.
BUT...
WHAT WAS TODAY ALL ABOUT?
THE PERSON WHO WAS SUDDENLY TOLD "HIKARU IS MORE IMPOR-TANT TO ME THAN YOU ARE"
School Uniform
AH HA HA HA! YOU'RE RIGHT!
WHEN YOU THINK ABOUT IT, IT'S QUITE RUDE.

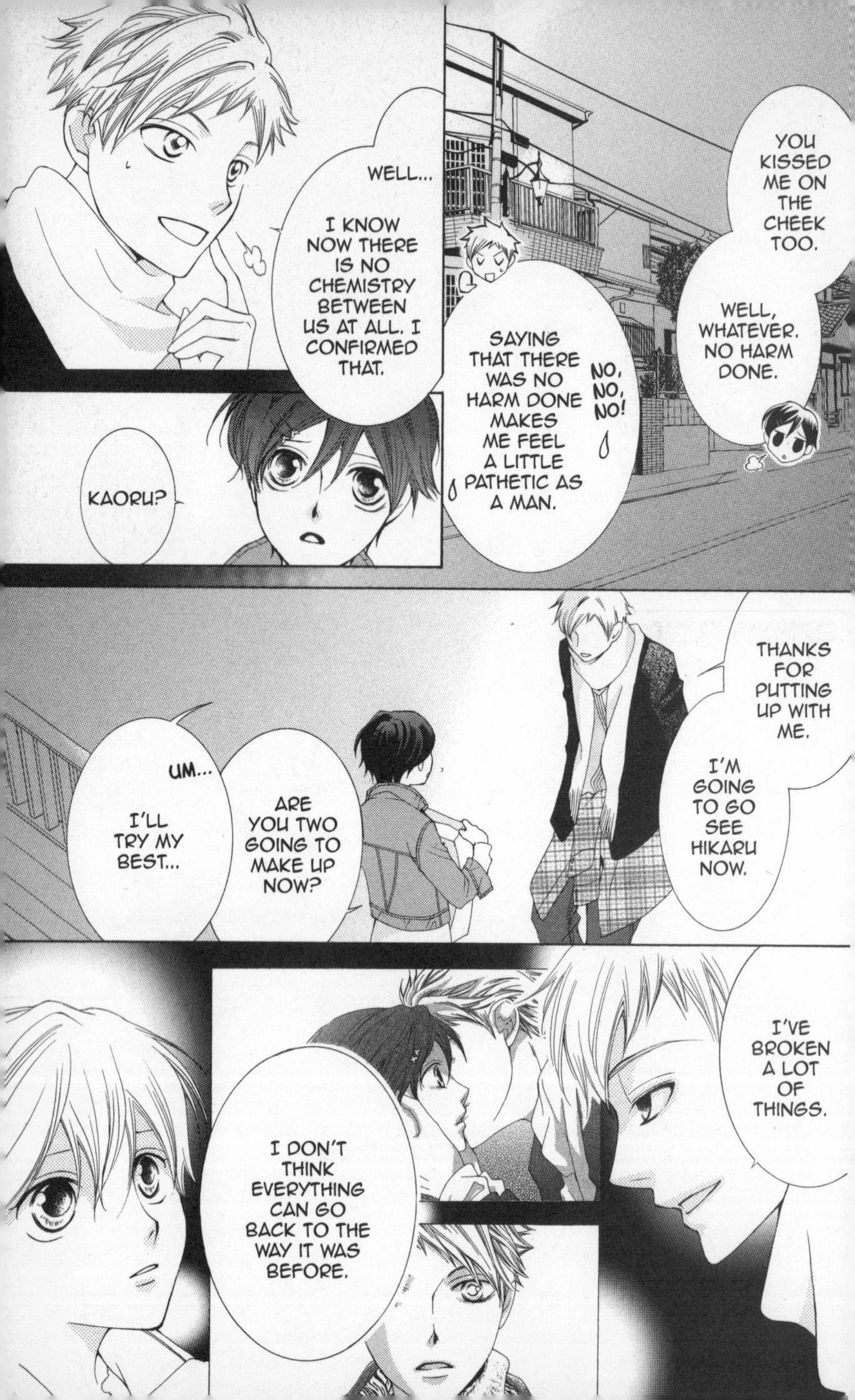
YOU KISSED ME ON THE CHEEK TOO.
WELL, WHATEVER. NO HARM DONE.
SAYING THAT THERE WAS NO HARM DONE MAKES ME FEEL A LITTLE PATHETIC AS A MAN.
NO, NO, NO!
WELL...
I KNOW NOW THERE IS NO CHEMISTRY BETWEEN US AT ALL. I CONFIRMED THAT.
KAORU?
THANKS FOR PUTTING UP WITH ME.
I'M GOING TO GO SEE HIKARU NOW.
ARE YOU TWO GOING TO MAKE UP NOW?
UM...
I'LL TRY MY BEST...
I'VE BROKEN A LOT OF THINGS.
I DON'T THINK EVERYTHING CAN GO BACK TO THE WAY IT WAS BEFORE.

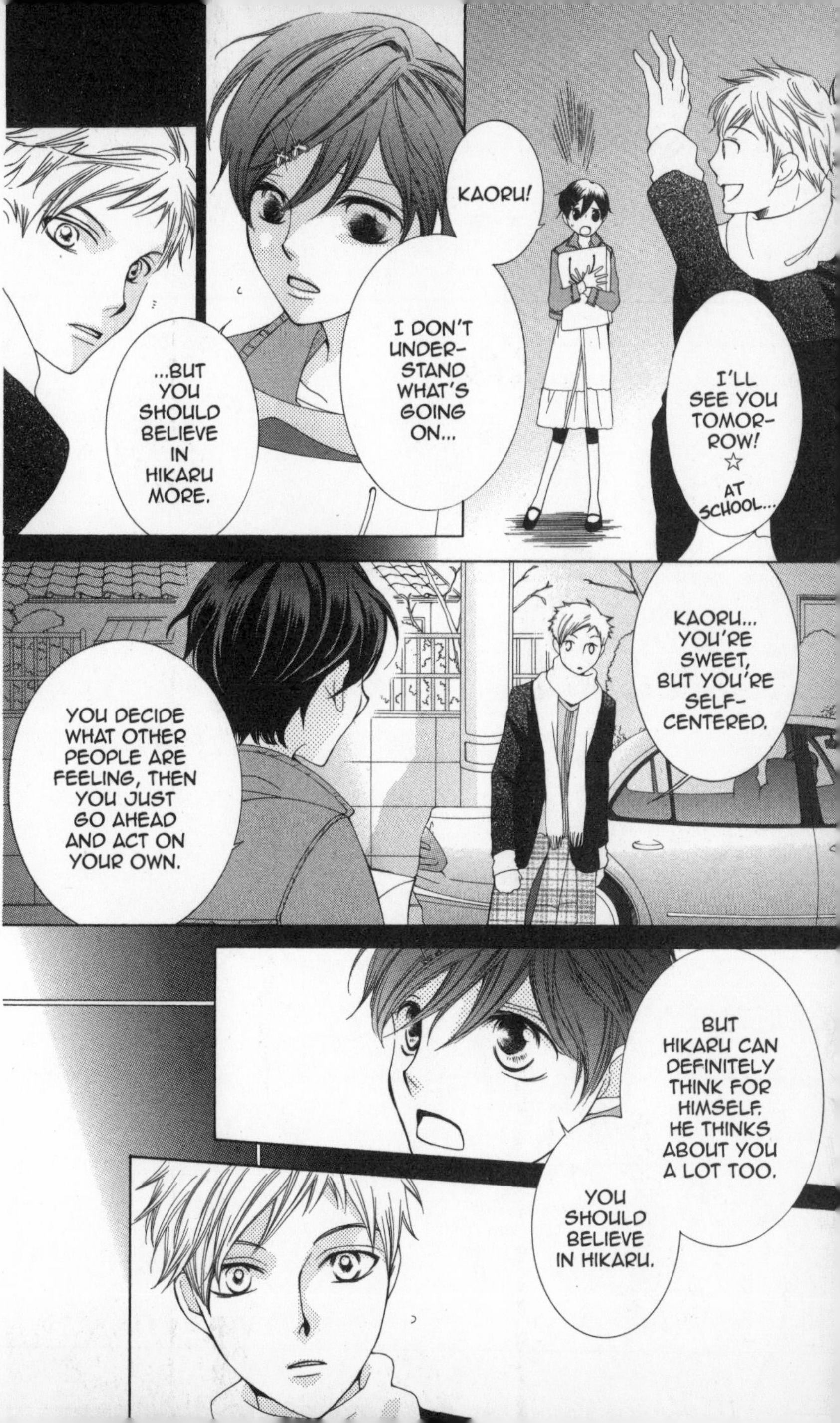
KAORU!
I'LL SEE YOU TOMORROW! ☆ AT SCHOOL...
I DON'T UNDERSTAND WHAT'S GOING ON...
...BUT YOU SHOULD BELIEVE IN HIKARU MORE.
KAORU... YOU'RE SWEET, BUT YOU'RE SELF-CENTERED.
YOU DECIDE WHAT OTHER PEOPLE ARE FEELING, THEN YOU JUST GO AHEAD AND ACT ON YOUR OWN.
BUT HIKARU CAN DEFINITELY THINK FOR HIMSELF. HE THINKS ABOUT YOU A LOT TOO.
YOU SHOULD BELIEVE IN HIKARU.

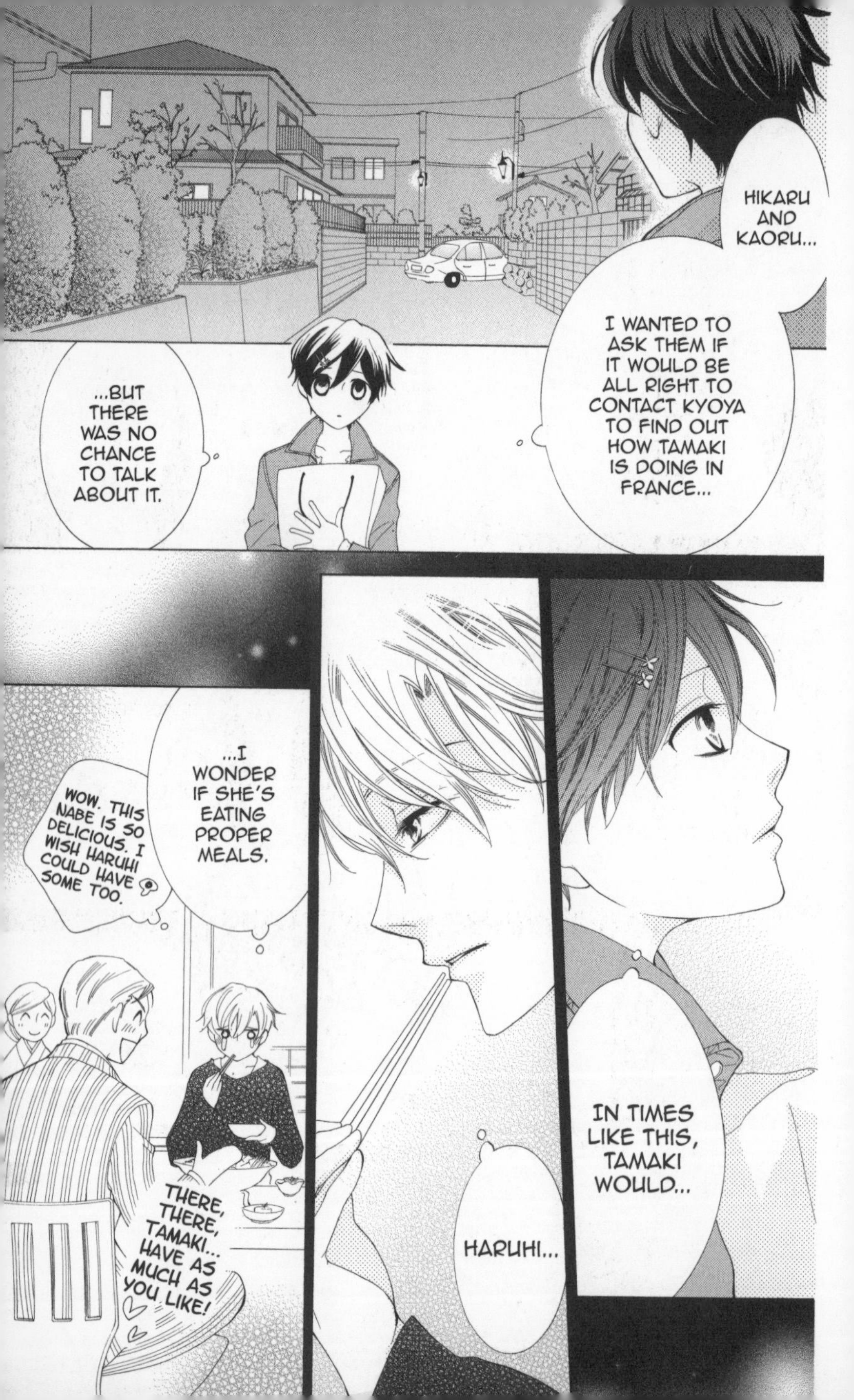
HIKARU AND KAORU...
I WANTED TO ASK THEM IF IT WOULD BE ALL RIGHT TO CONTACT KYOYA TO FIND OUT HOW TAMAKI IS DOING IN FRANCE...
...BUT THERE WAS NO CHANCE TO TALK ABOUT IT.
IN TIMES LIKE THIS, TAMAKI WOULD...
HARUHI...
...I WONDER IF SHE'S EATING PROPER MEALS.
WOW. THIS NABE IS SO DELICIOUS. I WISH HARUHI COULD HAVE SOME TOO.
THERE, THERE, TAMAKI... HAVE AS MUCH AS YOU LIKE!

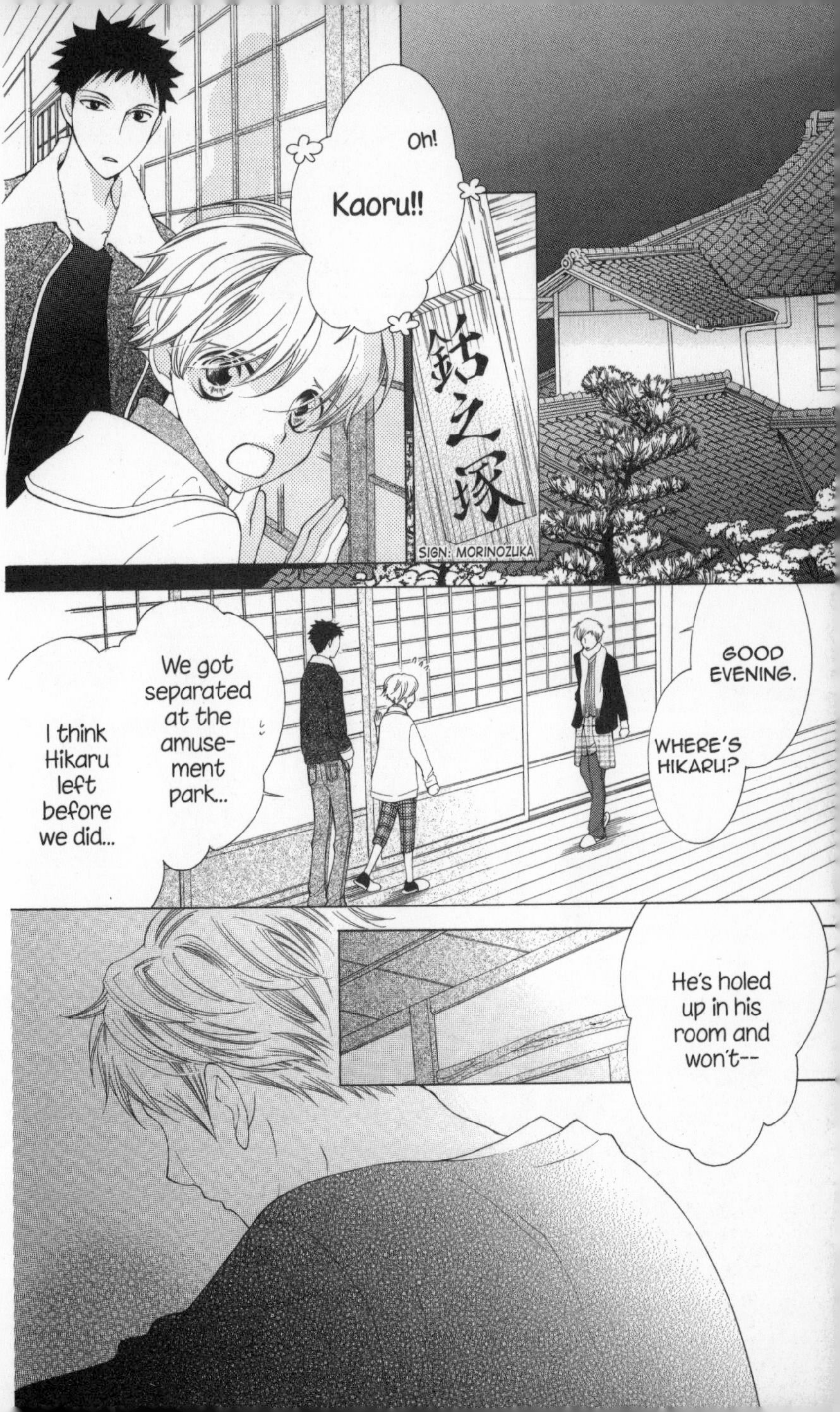
Oh!
Kaoru!!
鋲之塚
SIGN: MORINOZUKA
GOOD EVENING.
WHERE'S HIKARU?
We got separated at the amusement park...
I think Hikaru left before we did...
He's holed up in his room and won't--

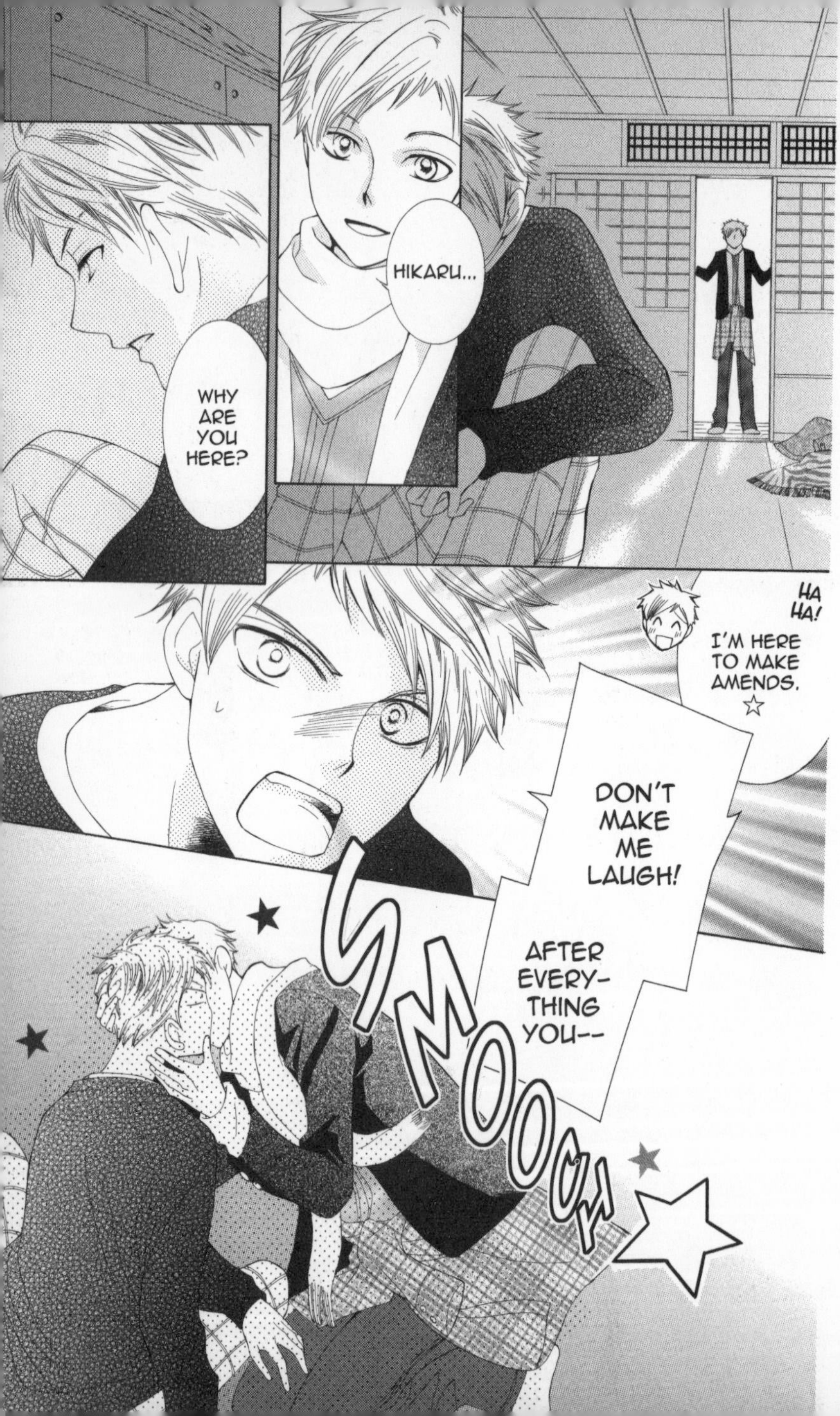
HIKARU...
WHY ARE YOU HERE?
HA HA! I'M HERE TO MAKE AMENDS. ☆
DON'T MAKE ME LAUGH!
AFTER EVERY-THING YOU--
SMOOCH

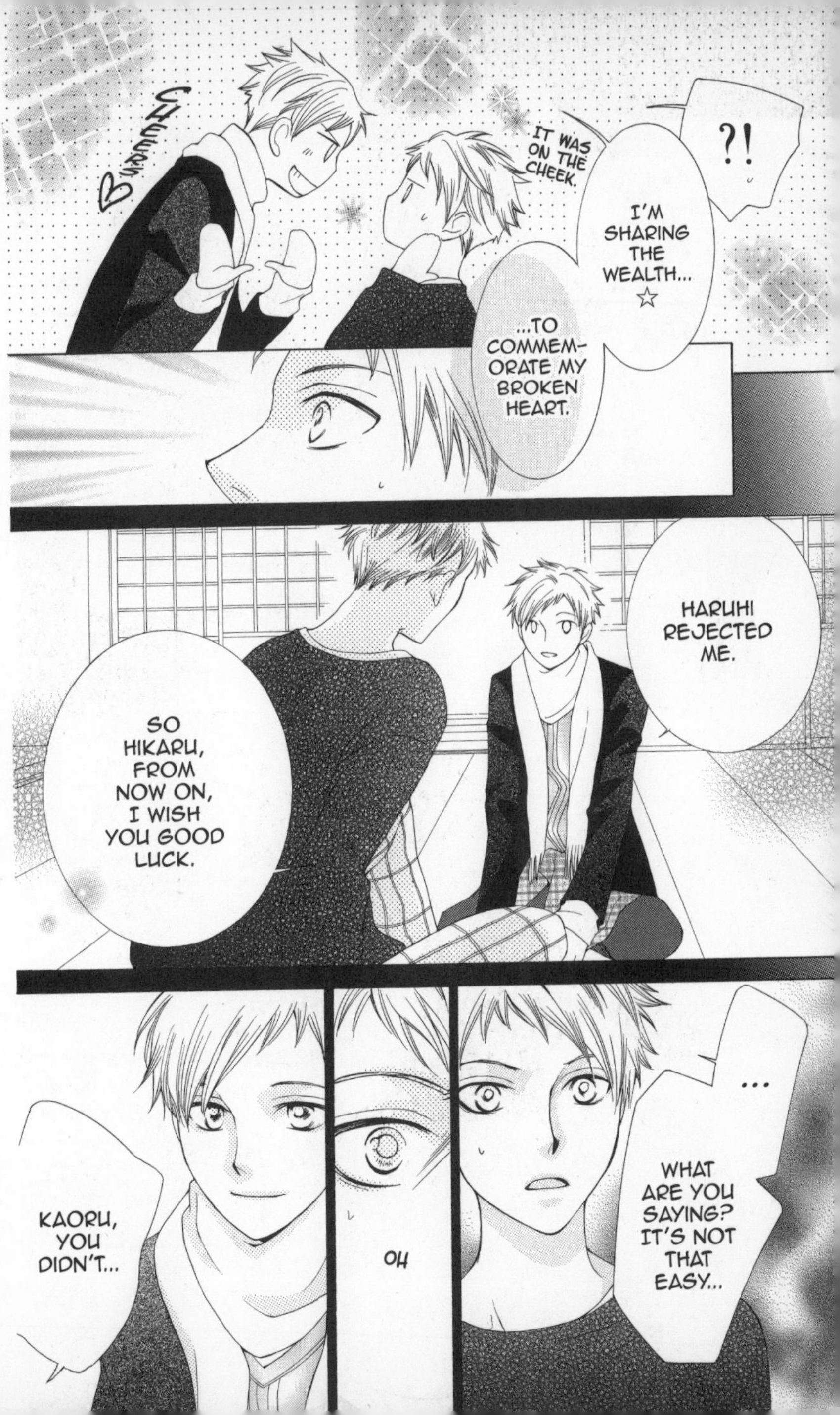
?!
I'M SHARING THE WEALTH... ☆
IT WAS ON THE CHEEK.
CHEERS♡
...TO COMMEMORATE MY BROKEN HEART.
HARUHI REJECTED ME.
SO HIKARU, FROM NOW ON, I WISH YOU GOOD LUCK.
...
WHAT ARE YOU SAYING? IT'S NOT THAT EASY...
OH
KAORU, YOU DIDN'T...

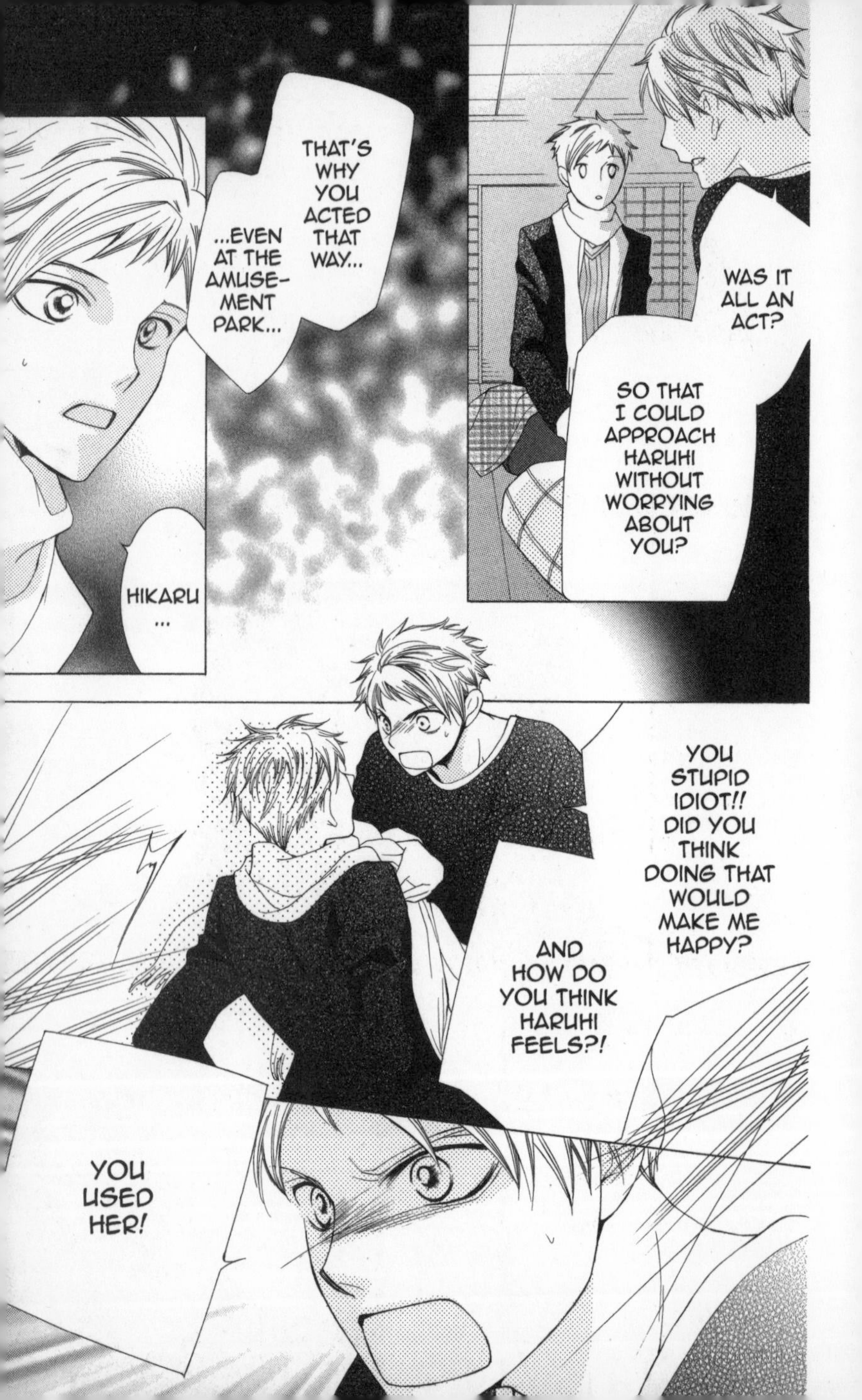
WAS IT ALL AN ACT?
SO THAT I COULD APPROACH HARUHI WITHOUT WORRYING ABOUT YOU?
THAT'S WHY YOU ACTED THAT WAY...
...EVEN AT THE AMUSEMENT PARK...
HIKARU...
YOU STUPID IDIOT!! DID YOU THINK DOING THAT WOULD MAKE ME HAPPY?
AND HOW DO YOU THINK HARUHI FEELS?!
YOU USED HER!

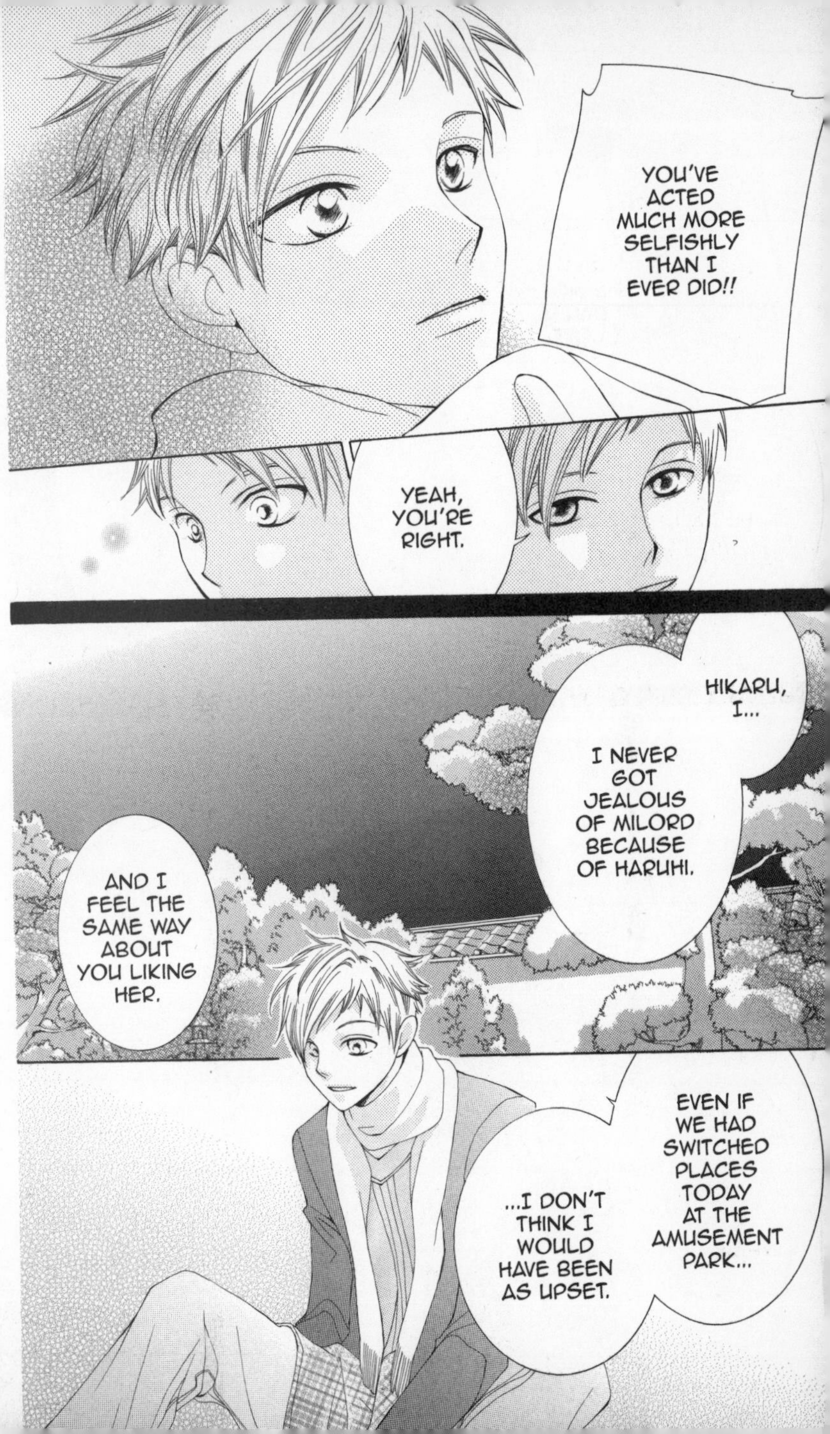
YOU'VE ACTED MUCH MORE SELFISHLY THAN I EVER DID!!
YEAH, YOU'RE RIGHT.
HIKARU, I...
I NEVER GOT JEALOUS OF MILORD BECAUSE OF HARUHI.
AND I FEEL THE SAME WAY ABOUT YOU LIKING HER.
EVEN IF WE HAD SWITCHED PLACES TODAY AT THE AMUSEMENT PARK...
...I DON'T THINK I WOULD HAVE BEEN AS UPSET.

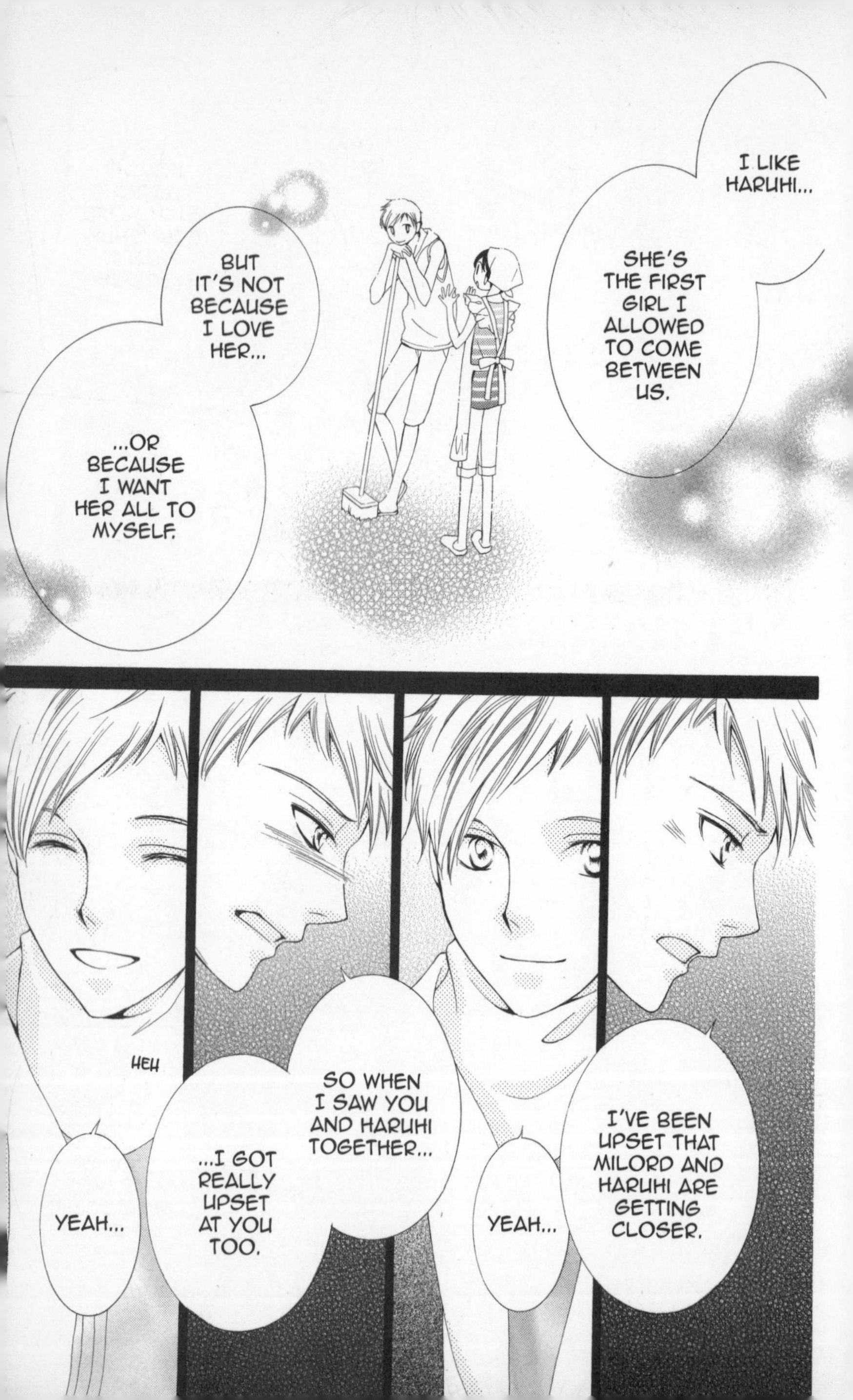
I LIKE HARUHI...
SHE'S THE FIRST GIRL I ALLOWED TO COME BETWEEN US.
BUT IT'S NOT BECAUSE I LOVE HER...
...OR BECAUSE I WANT HER ALL TO MYSELF.
I'VE BEEN UPSET THAT MILORD AND HARUHI ARE GETTING CLOSER.
YEAH...
SO WHEN I SAW YOU AND HARUHI TOGETHER...
...I GOT REALLY UPSET AT YOU TOO.
HEH
YEAH...

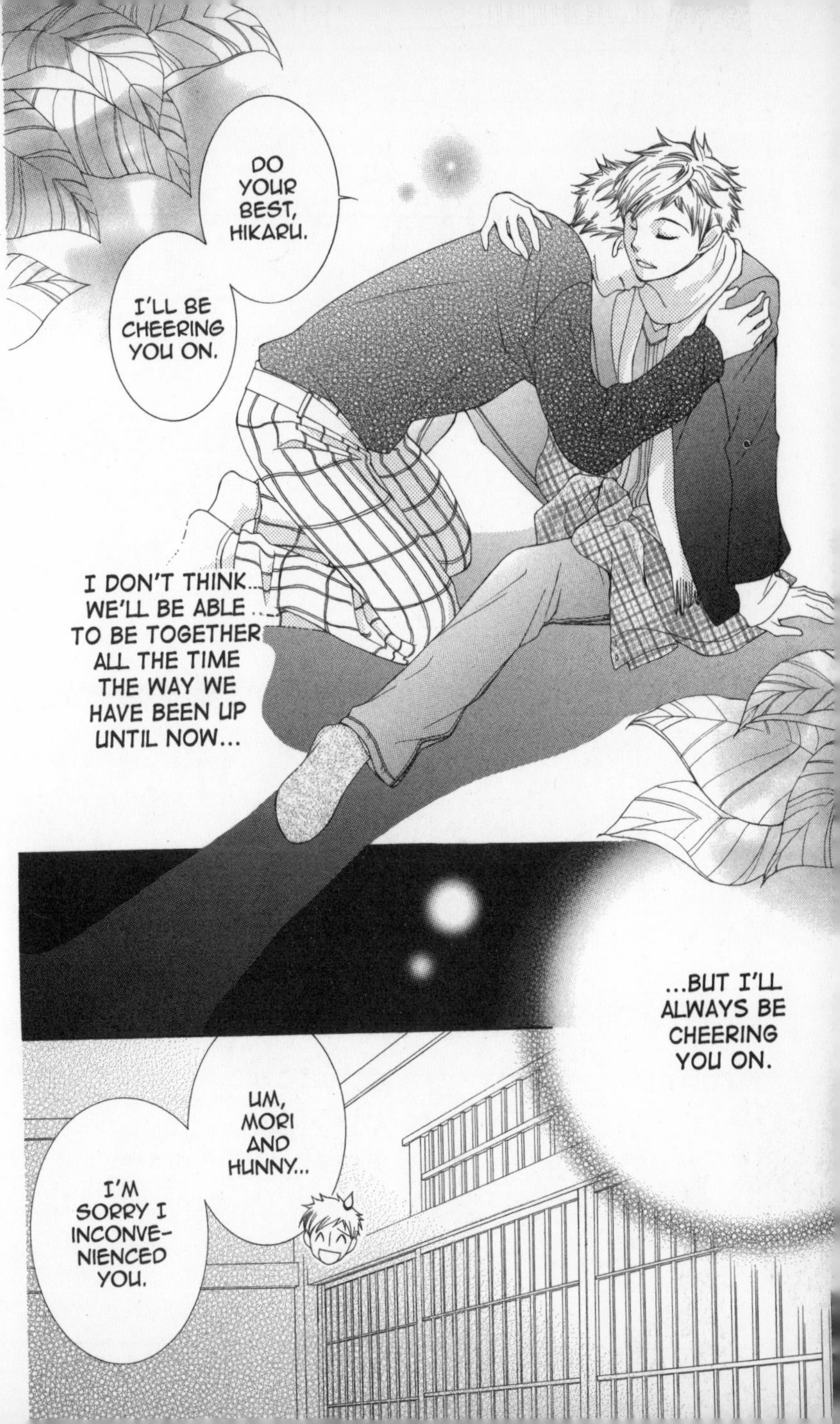
DO YOUR BEST, HIKARU.
I'LL BE CHEERING YOU ON.
I DON'T THINK... WE'LL BE ABLE... TO BE TOGETHER ALL THE TIME THE WAY WE HAVE BEEN UP UNTIL NOW...
...BUT I'LL ALWAYS BE CHEERING YOU ON.
UM, MORI AND HUNNY...
I'M SORRY I INCONVENIENCED YOU.

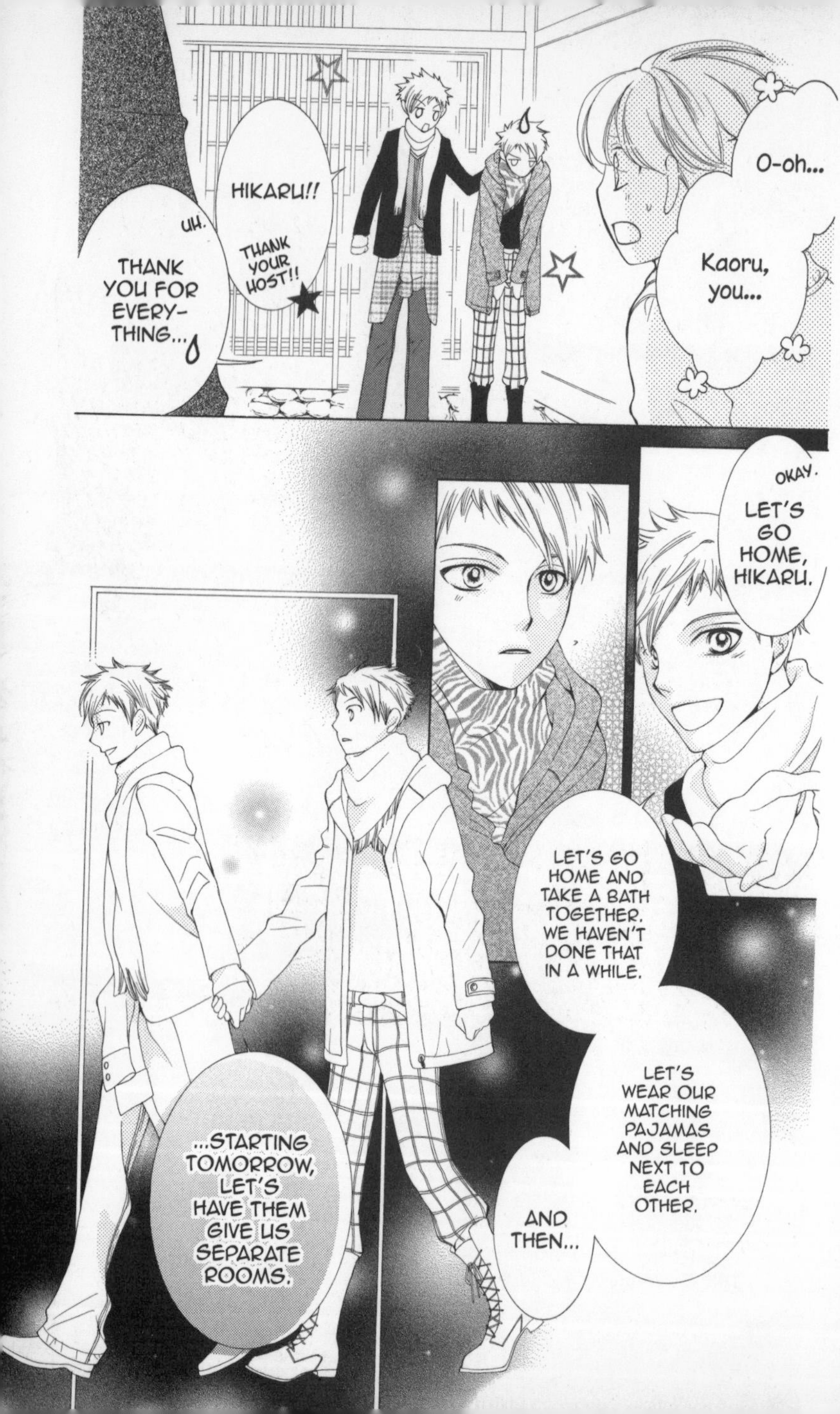
O-oh...
Kaoru, you...
HIKARU!!
THANK YOUR HOST!!
UH.
THANK YOU FOR EVERY-THING...
OKAY.
LET'S GO HOME, HIKARU.
LET'S GO HOME AND TAKE A BATH TOGETHER. WE HAVEN'T DONE THAT IN A WHILE.
LET'S WEAR OUR MATCHING PAJAMAS AND SLEEP NEXT TO EACH OTHER.
AND THEN...
...STARTING TOMORROW, LET'S HAVE THEM GIVE US SEPARATE ROOMS.

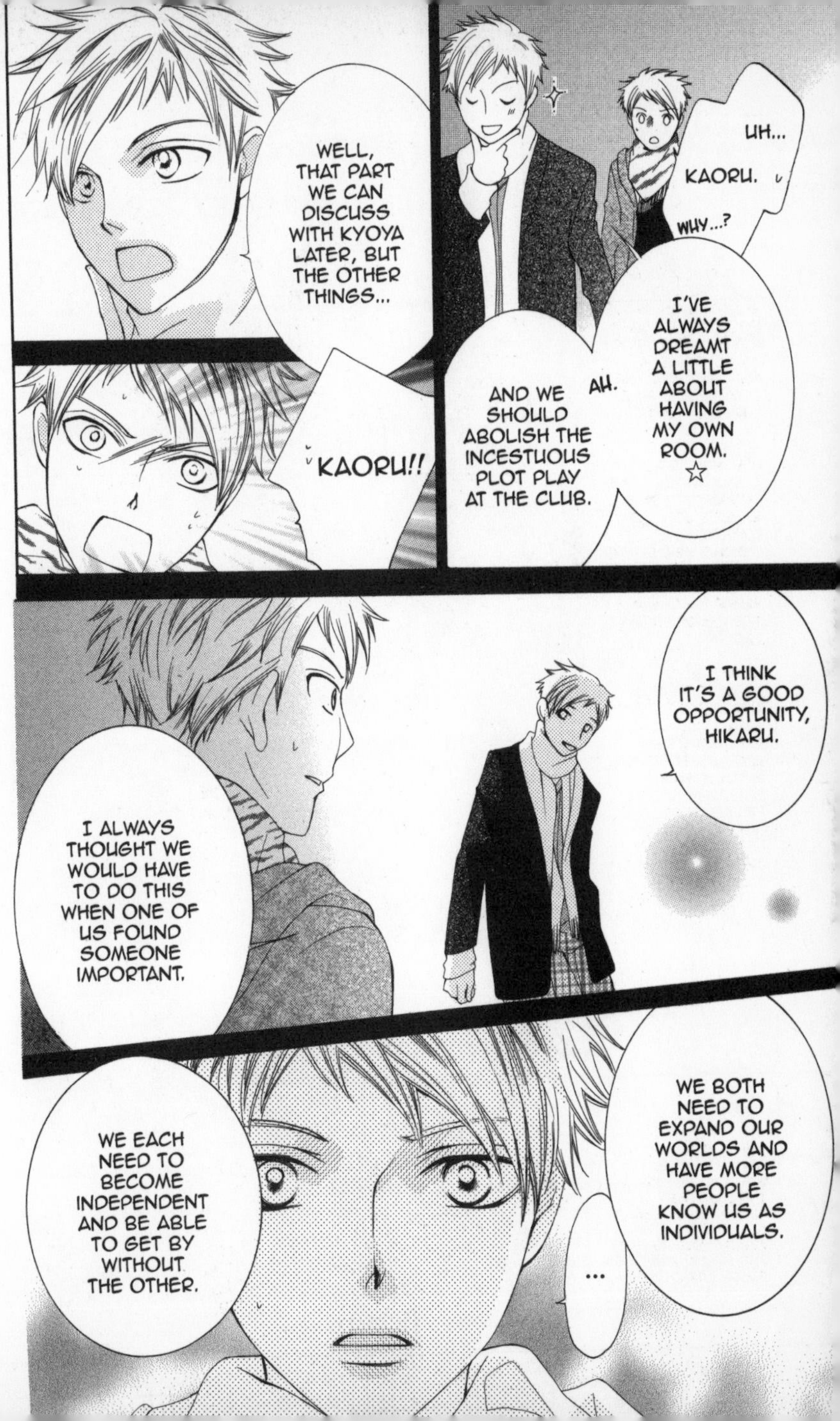
UH...
KAORU.
WHY...?
I'VE ALWAYS DREAMT A LITTLE ABOUT HAVING MY OWN ROOM. ☆
AH.
AND WE SHOULD ABOLISH THE INCESTUOUS PLOT PLAY AT THE CLUB.
WELL, THAT PART WE CAN DISCUSS WITH KYOYA LATER, BUT THE OTHER THINGS...
KAORU!!
I THINK IT'S A GOOD OPPORTUNITY, HIKARU.
I ALWAYS THOUGHT WE WOULD HAVE TO DO THIS WHEN ONE OF US FOUND SOMEONE IMPORTANT.
WE BOTH NEED TO EXPAND OUR WORLDS AND HAVE MORE PEOPLE KNOW US AS INDIVIDUALS.
...
WE EACH NEED TO BECOME INDEPENDENT AND BE ABLE TO GET BY WITHOUT THE OTHER.

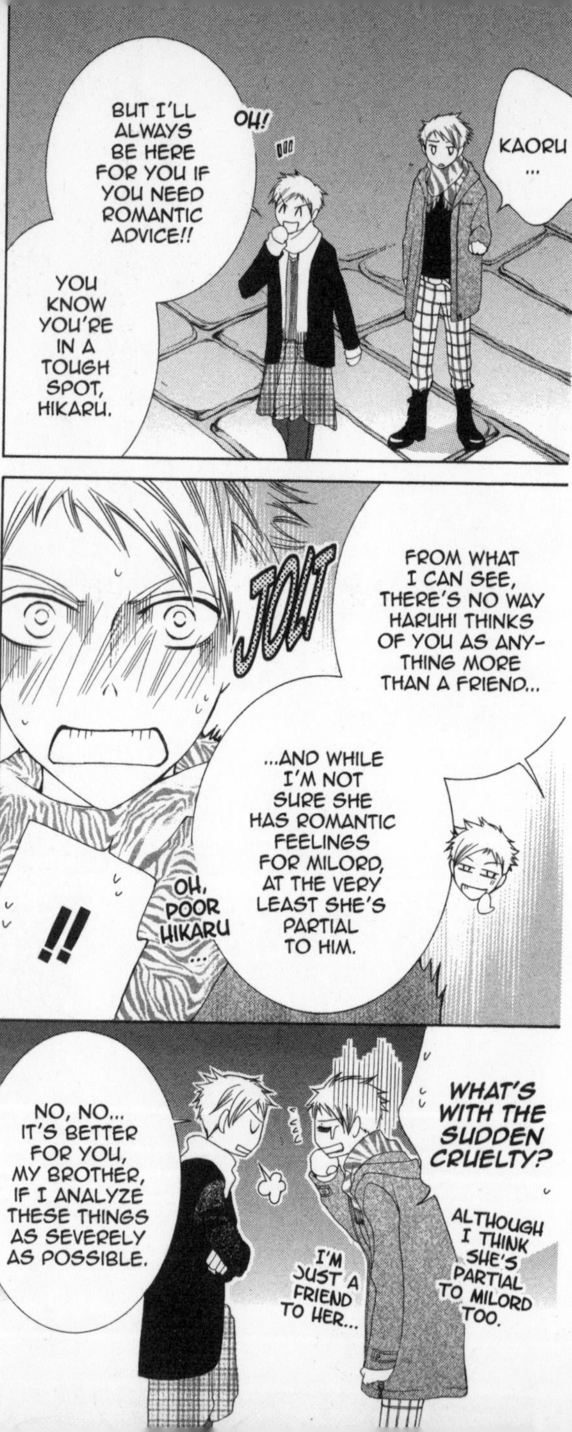
KAORU ...
OH!
BUT I'LL ALWAYS BE HERE FOR YOU IF YOU NEED ROMANTIC ADVICE!!
YOU KNOW YOU'RE IN A TOUGH SPOT, HIKARU.
FROM WHAT I CAN SEE, THERE'S NO WAY HARUHI THINKS OF YOU AS ANYTHING MORE THAN A FRIEND...
JOLT
...AND WHILE I'M NOT SURE SHE HAS ROMANTIC FEELINGS FOR MILORD, AT THE VERY LEAST SHE'S PARTIAL TO HIM.
OH, POOR HIKARU ...
!!
WHAT'S WITH THE SUDDEN CRUELTY?
ALTHOUGH I THINK SHE'S PARTIAL TO MILORD TOO.
I'M JUST A FRIEND TO HER...
NO, NO... IT'S BETTER FOR YOU, MY BROTHER, IF I ANALYZE THESE THINGS AS SEVERELY AS POSSIBLE.

2

✿ THEN I THOUGHT THAT THE DVD REMOTE WAS BROKEN, SO I CALLED THE ELECTRONICS STORE AND ORDERED A NEW ONE. BUT THE REMOTE WAS FINE THE NEXT DAY.

MAYBE IT'S REVENGE FOR USING KYOYA AND GETTING LAUGHS WITH THE REMOTE CONTROL MATERIAL. WELL, I DIDN'T REALLY THINK THAT, BUT THIS YEAR, I'M PLANNING ON BEING CAREFUL WITH THE REMOTE CONTROL.

✿ HATORI IS A USELESS PERSON AND LOSES THINGS A LOT. THE MOST PROBLEMATIC IS LOSING MECHANICAL PENCILS. WHEN I GET UP TO GET TEA OR GO TO THE BATHROOM, MORE OFTEN THAN NOT THE PENCIL IS NOT THERE WHEN I RETURN.

I ALSO FREQUENTLY LOSE RULERS AND ERASERS, AND THEN I SPEND TIME LOOKING FOR THEM. SO I ALWAYS KEEP ABOUT THREE RULERS AND MECHANICAL PENCILS HANDY.

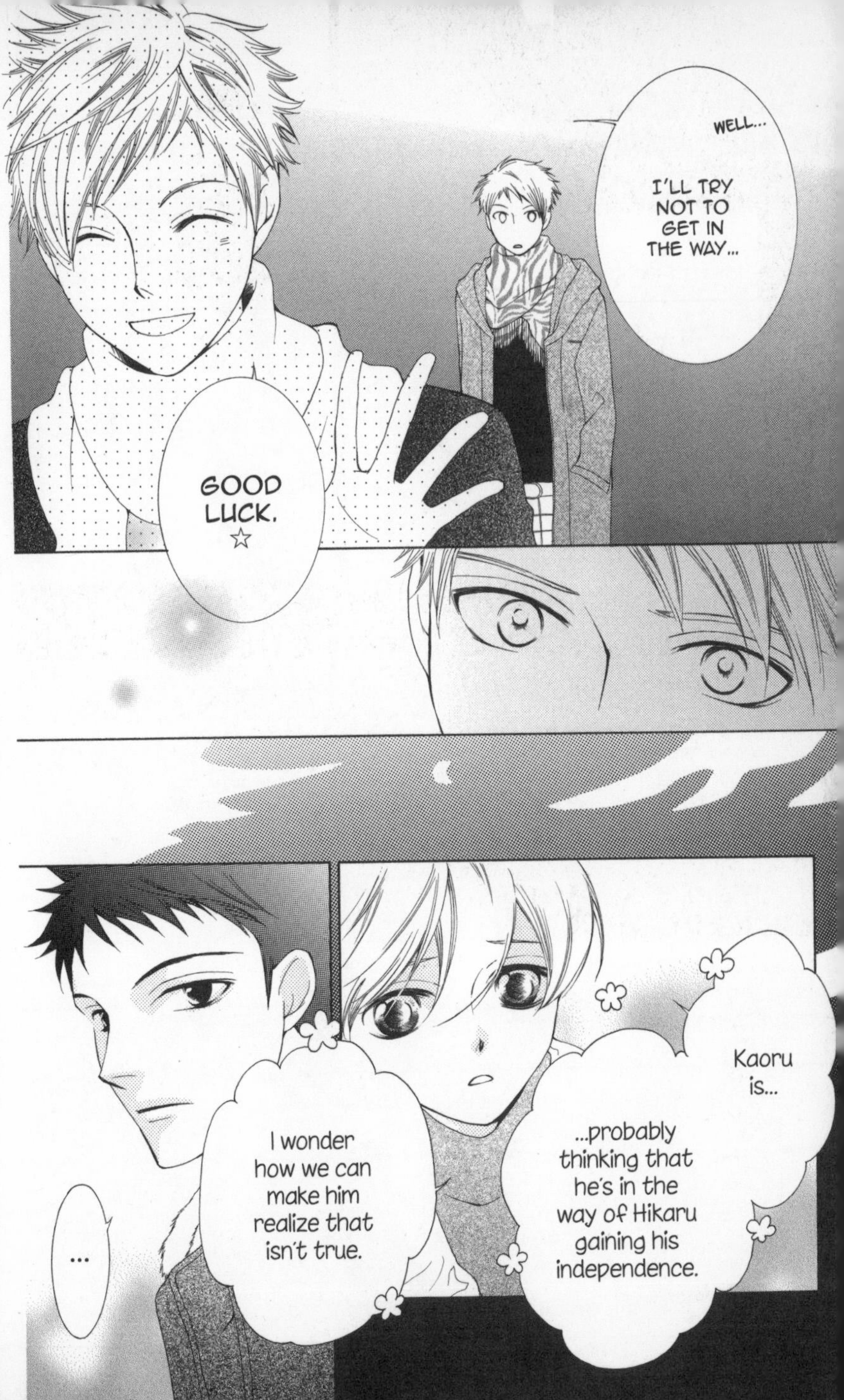
WELL...
I'LL TRY NOT TO GET IN THE WAY...
GOOD LUCK. ☆
Kaoru is...
...probably thinking that he's in the way of Hikaru gaining his independence.
I wonder how we can make him realize that isn't true.
...

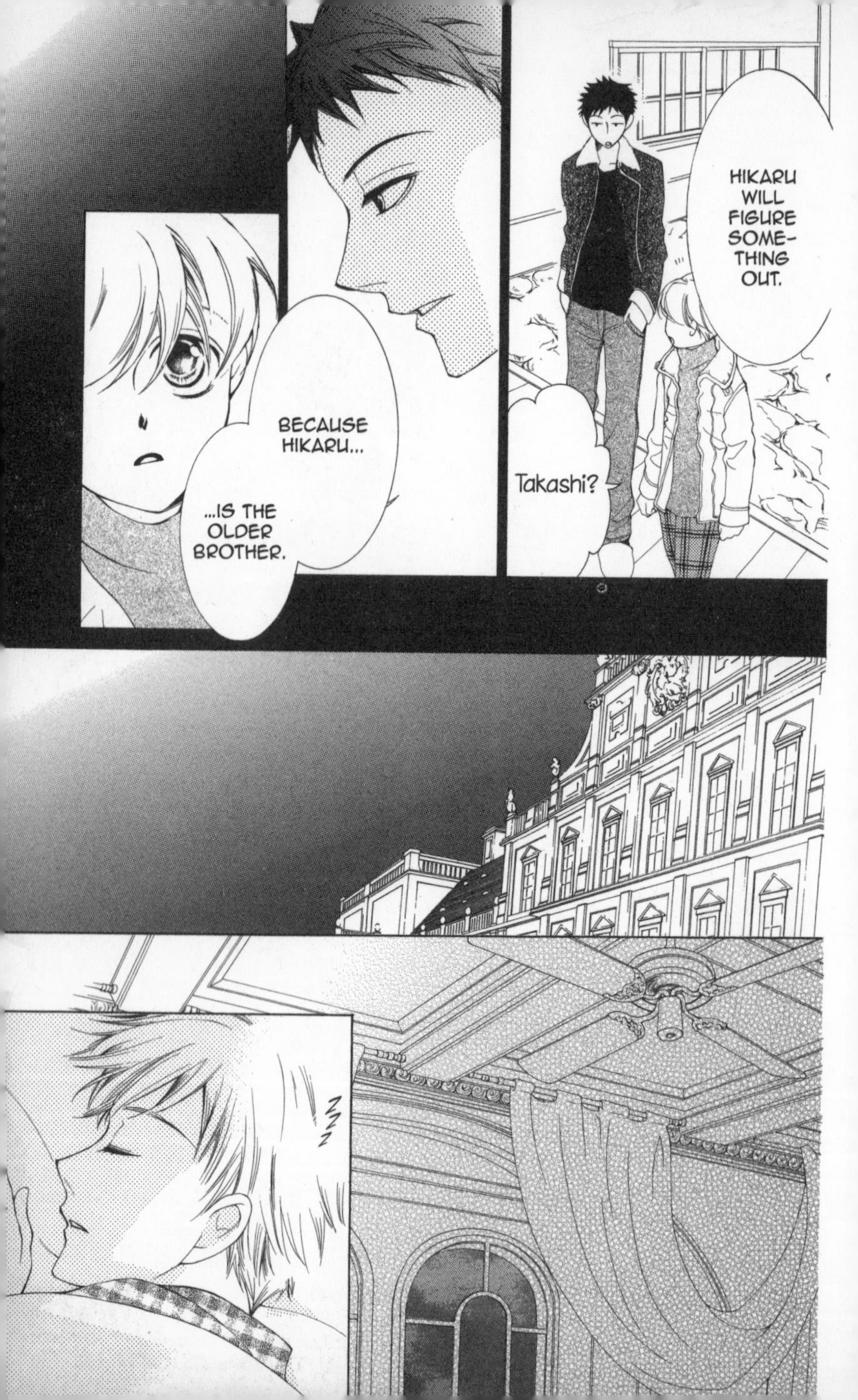
HIKARU WILL FIGURE SOME-THING OUT.
Takashi?
BECAUSE HIKARU...
...IS THE OLDER BROTHER.
ZZZ

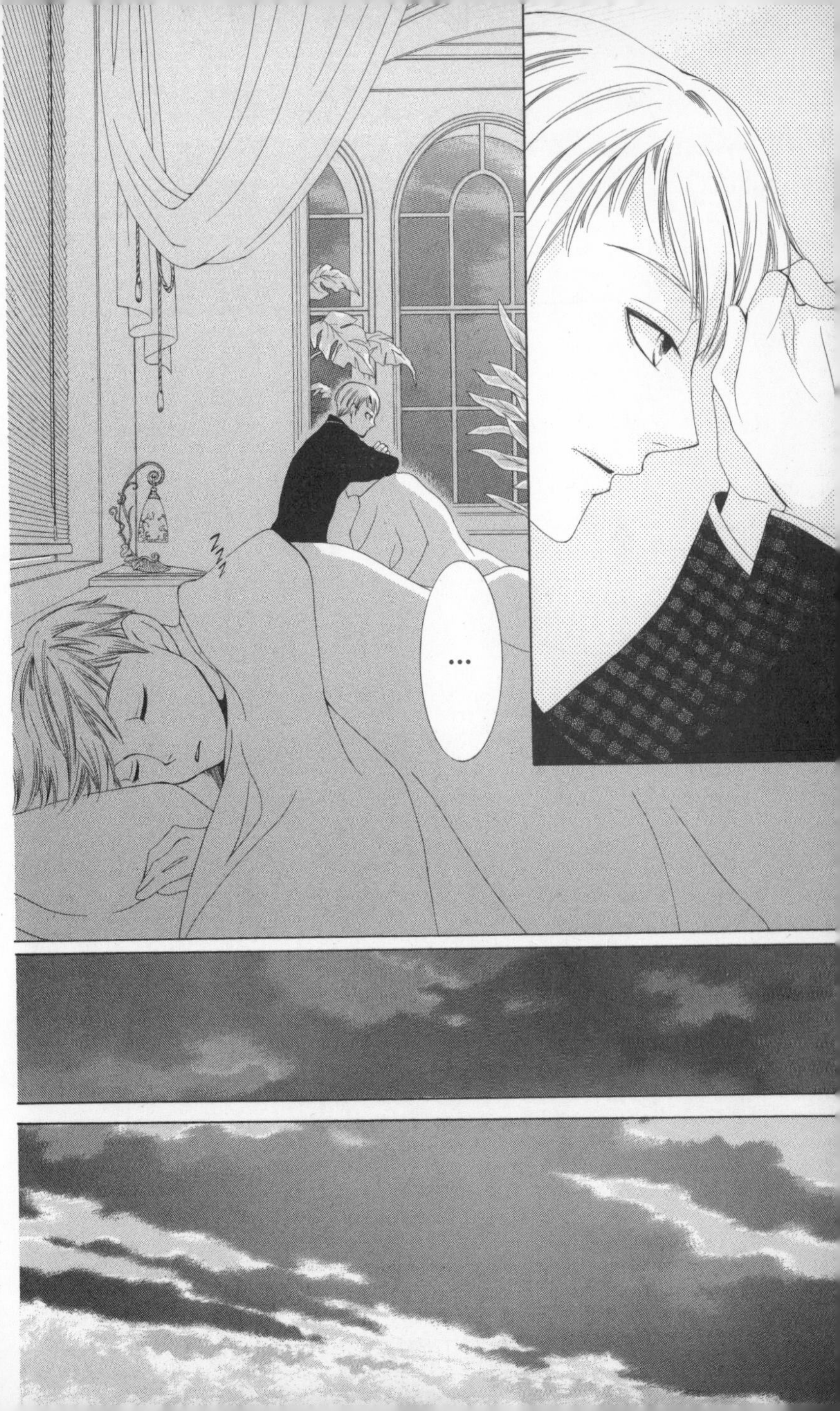
...
ZZZ

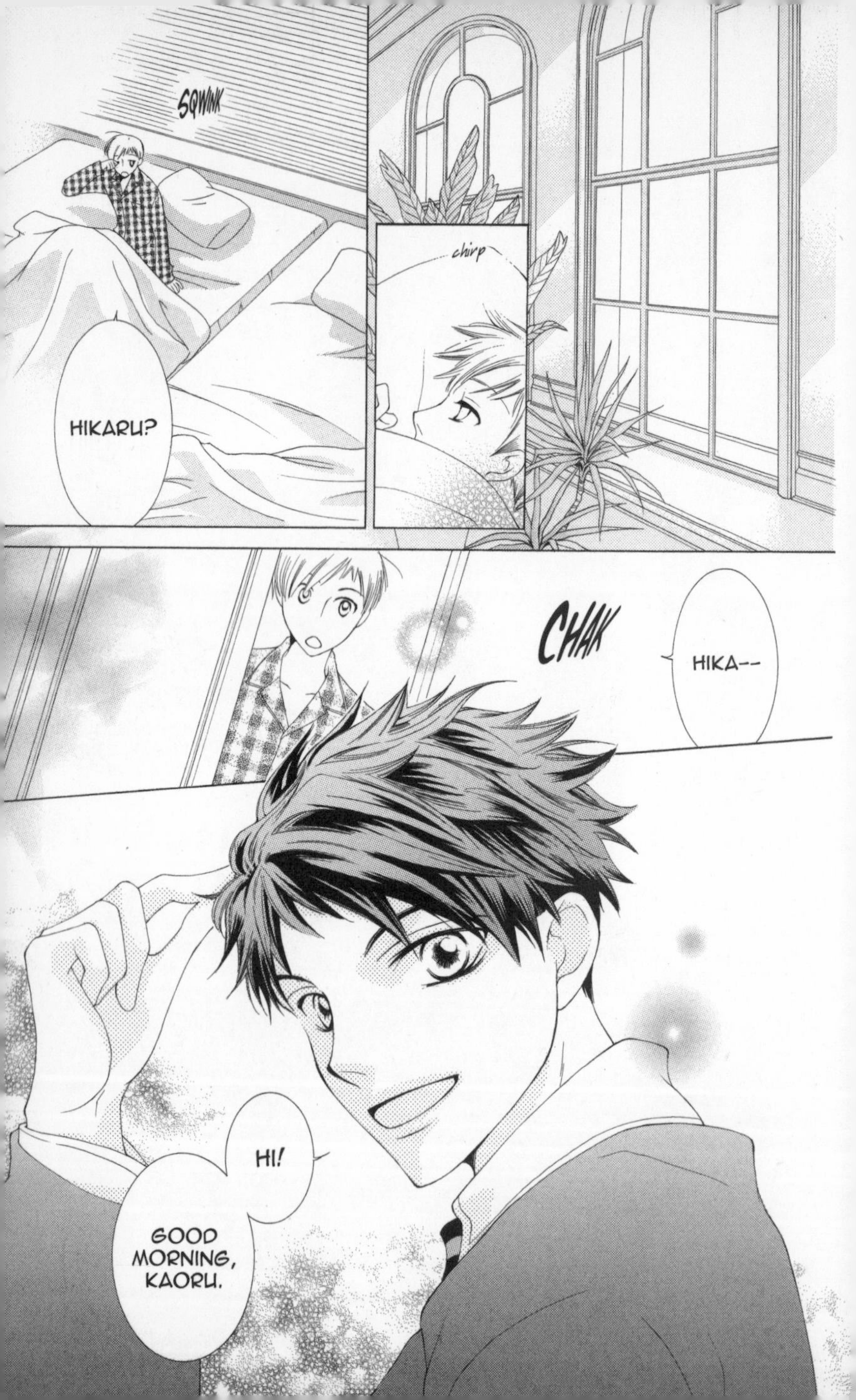
chirp
SQWINK
HIKARU?
CHAK
HIKA--
HI!
GOOD MORNING, KAORU.

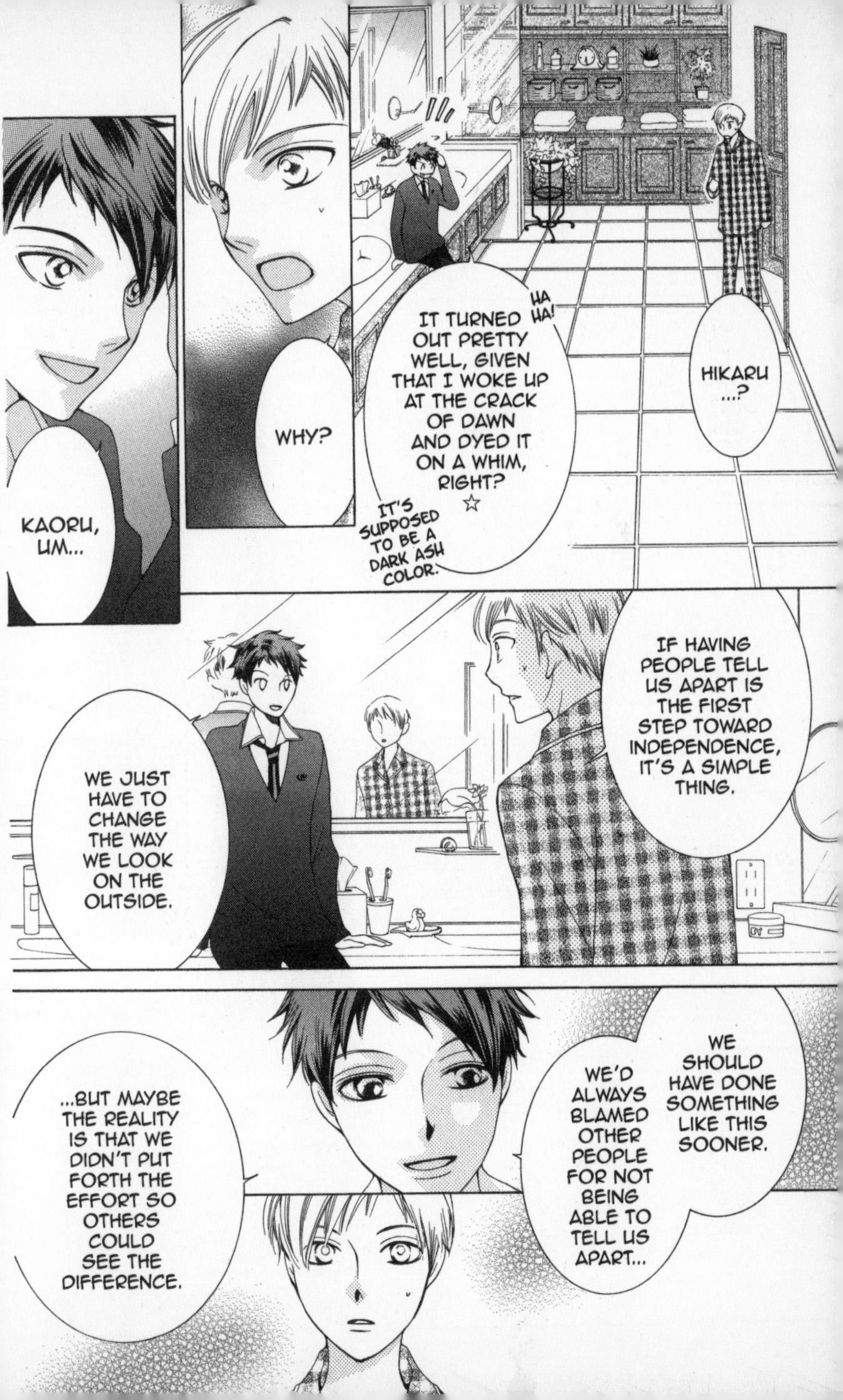
HIKARU ...?
IT TURNED OUT PRETTY WELL, GIVEN THAT I WOKE UP AT THE CRACK OF DAWN AND DYED IT ON A WHIM, RIGHT? ☆
HA HA!
IT'S SUPPOSED TO BE A DARK ASH COLOR.
WHY?
KAORU, UM...
IF HAVING PEOPLE TELL US APART IS THE FIRST STEP TOWARD INDEPENDENCE, IT'S A SIMPLE THING.
WE JUST HAVE TO CHANGE THE WAY WE LOOK ON THE OUTSIDE.
WE SHOULD HAVE DONE SOMETHING LIKE THIS SOONER.
WE'D ALWAYS BLAMED OTHER PEOPLE FOR NOT BEING ABLE TO TELL US APART...
...BUT MAYBE THE REALITY IS THAT WE DIDN'T PUT FORTH THE EFFORT SO OTHERS COULD SEE THE DIFFERENCE.

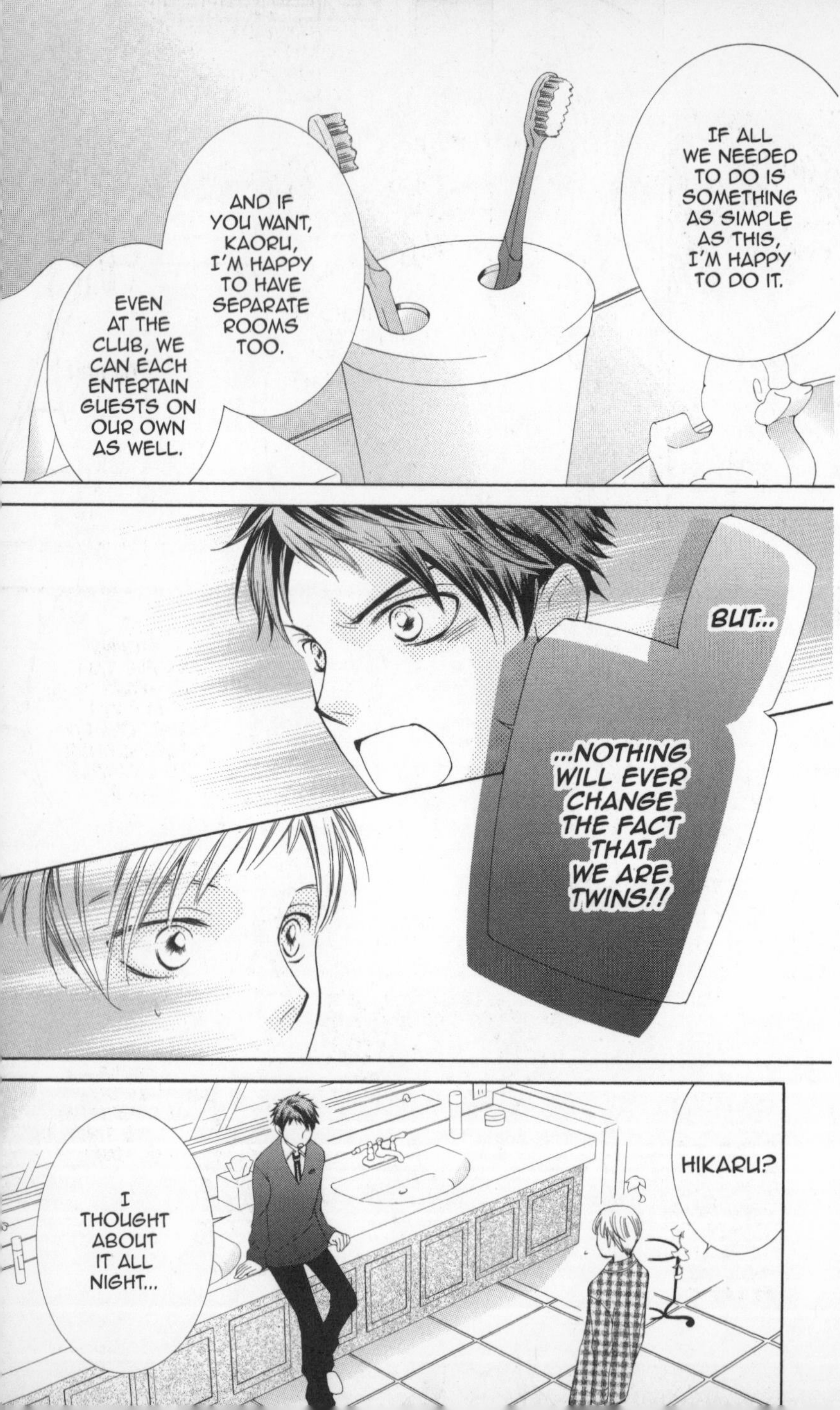
IF ALL WE NEEDED TO DO IS SOMETHING AS SIMPLE AS THIS, I'M HAPPY TO DO IT.
AND IF YOU WANT, KAORU, I'M HAPPY TO HAVE SEPARATE ROOMS TOO.
EVEN AT THE CLUB, WE CAN EACH ENTERTAIN GUESTS ON OUR OWN AS WELL.
BUT...
...NOTHING WILL EVER CHANGE THE FACT THAT WE ARE TWINS!!
HIKARU?
I THOUGHT ABOUT IT ALL NIGHT...

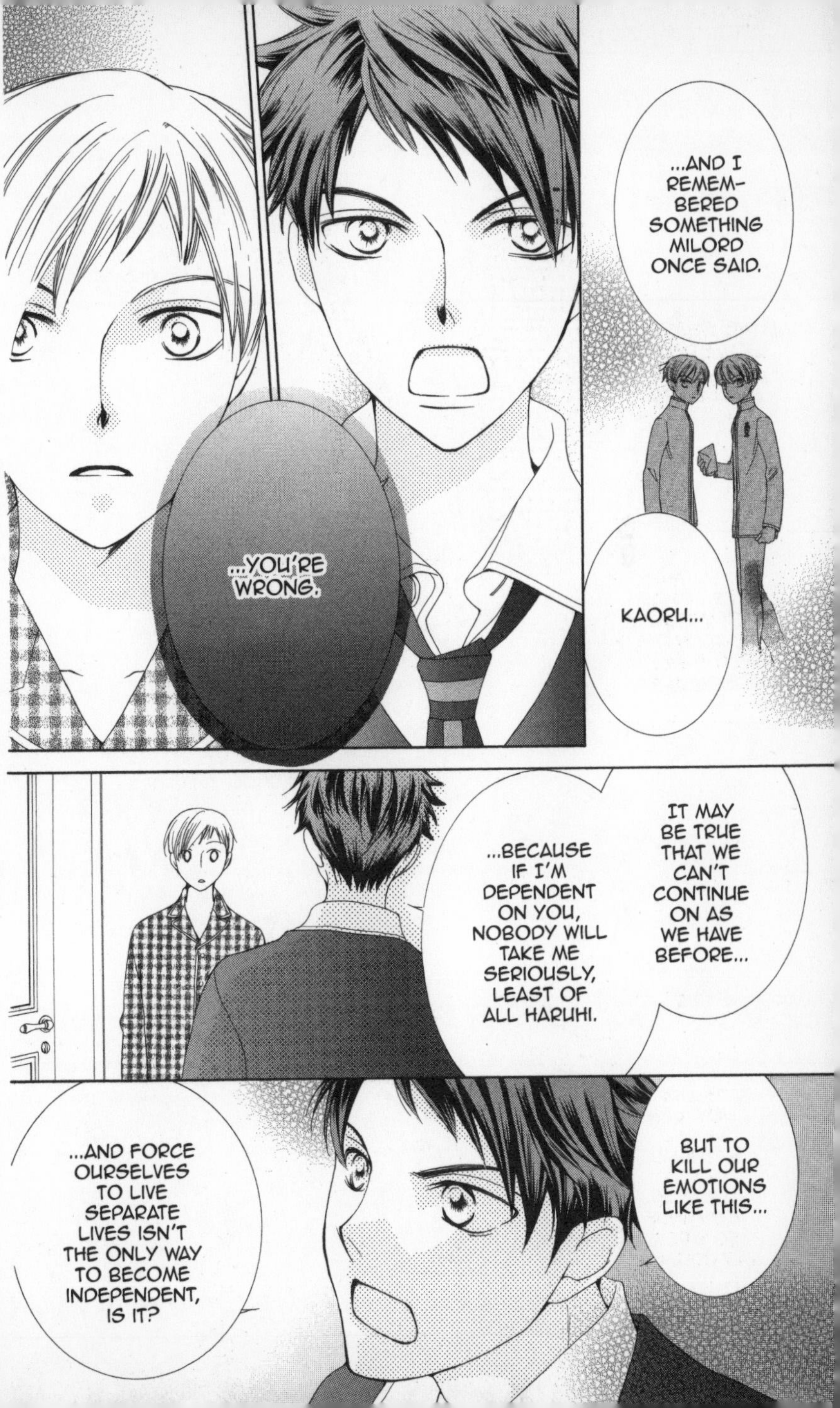
...AND I REMEMBERED SOMETHING MILORD ONCE SAID.
KAORU...
...YOU'RE WRONG.
IT MAY BE TRUE THAT WE CAN'T CONTINUE ON AS WE HAVE BEFORE...
...BECAUSE IF I'M DEPENDENT ON YOU, NOBODY WILL TAKE ME SERIOUSLY, LEAST OF ALL HARUHI.
BUT TO KILL OUR EMOTIONS LIKE THIS...
...AND FORCE OURSELVES TO LIVE SEPARATE LIVES ISN'T THE ONLY WAY TO BECOME INDEPENDENT, IS IT?

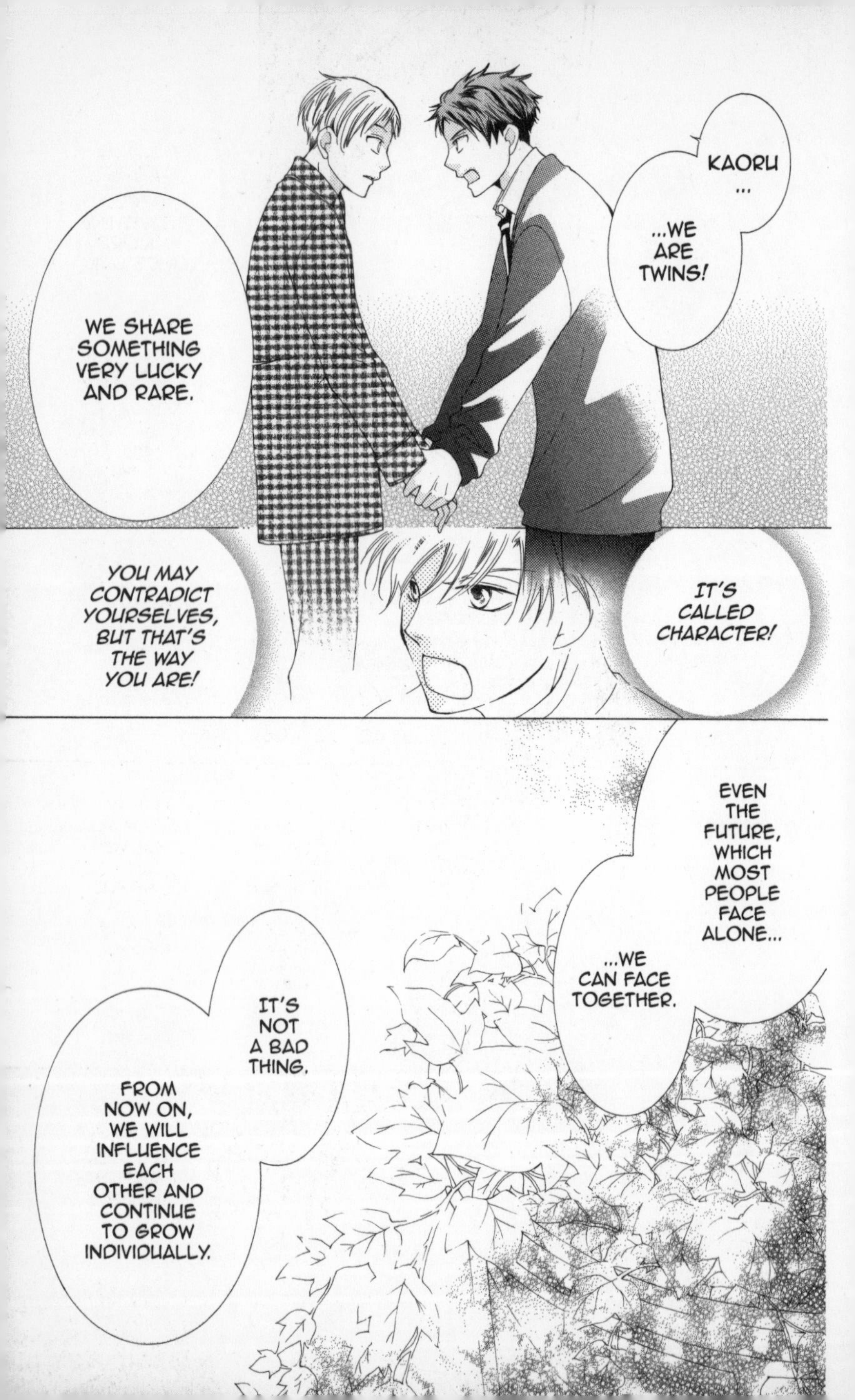
KAORU ... ...WE ARE TWINS!
WE SHARE SOMETHING VERY LUCKY AND RARE.
IT'S CALLED CHARACTER!
YOU MAY CONTRADICT YOURSELVES, BUT THAT'S THE WAY YOU ARE!
EVEN THE FUTURE, WHICH MOST PEOPLE FACE ALONE...
...WE CAN FACE TOGETHER.
IT'S NOT A BAD THING.
FROM NOW ON, WE WILL INFLUENCE EACH OTHER AND CONTINUE TO GROW INDIVIDUALLY.

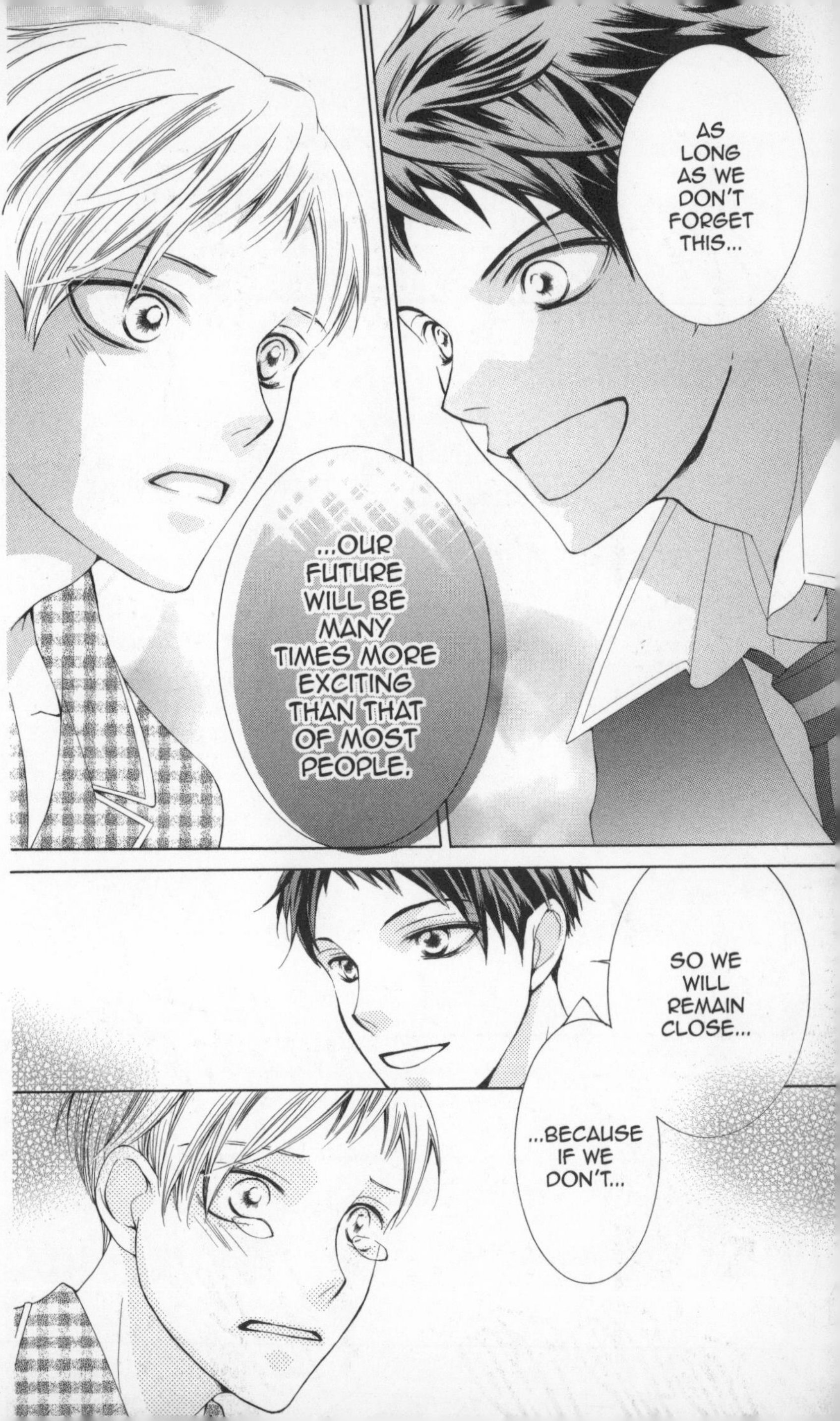
AS LONG AS WE DON'T FORGET THIS...
...OUR FUTURE WILL BE MANY TIMES MORE EXCITING THAN THAT OF MOST PEOPLE.
SO WE WILL REMAIN CLOSE...
...BECAUSE IF WE DON'T...

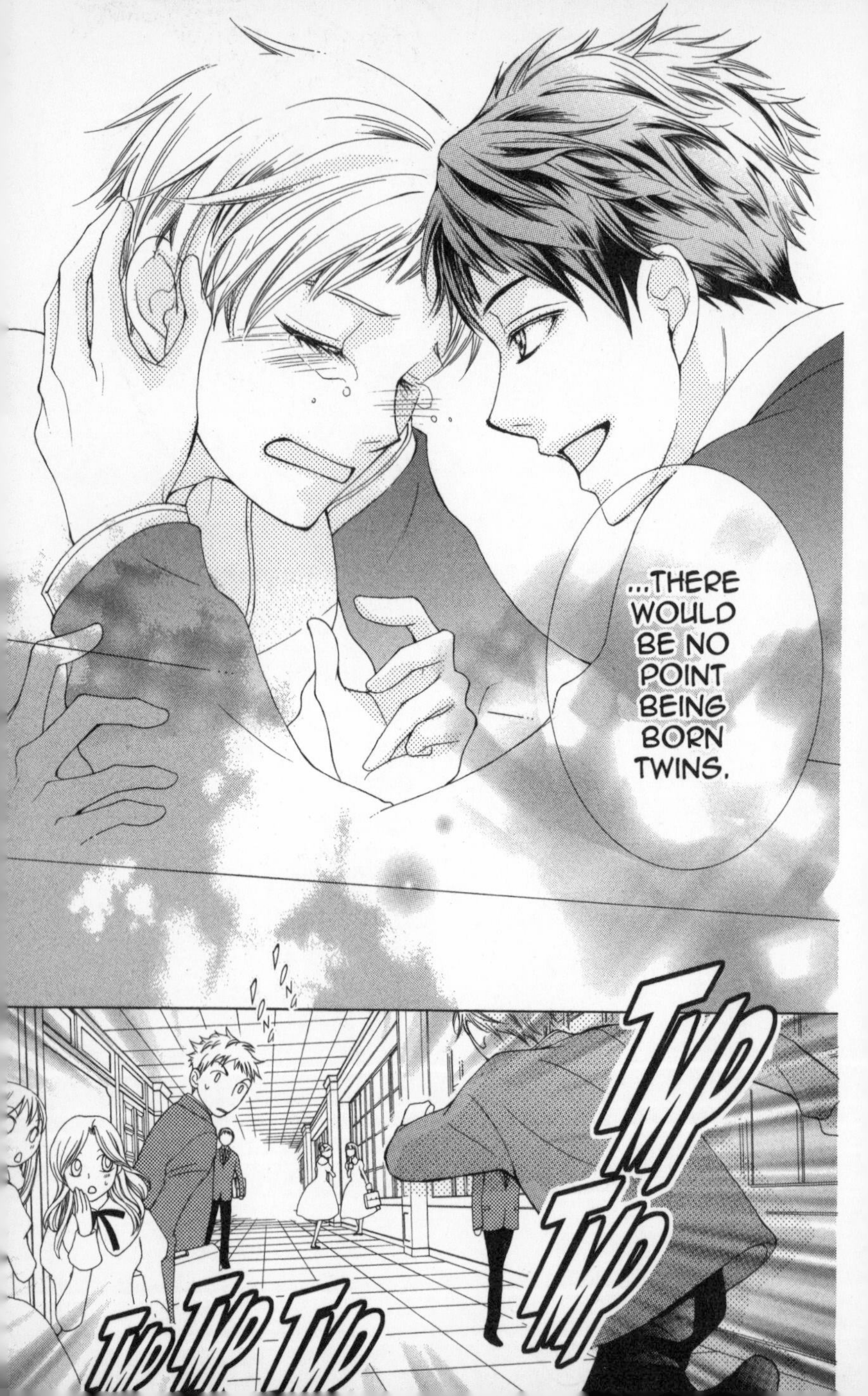
...THERE WOULD BE NO POINT BEING BORN TWINS.
DONG DONG
TMP TMP
TMP TMP TMP

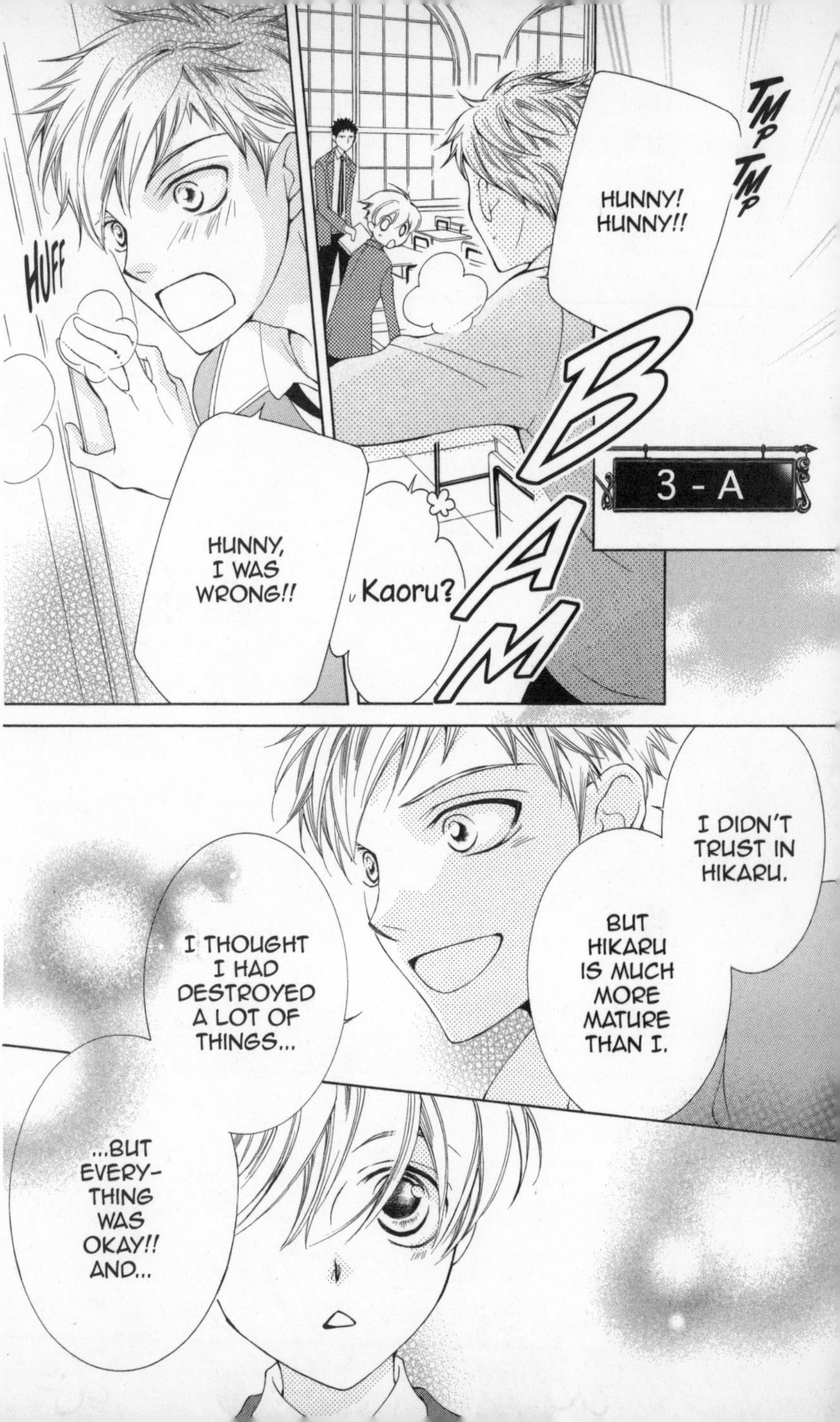
TMP TMP
HUNNY! HUNNY!!
3 - A
BAM
HUFF
Kaoru?
HUNNY, I WAS WRONG!!
I DIDN'T TRUST IN HIKARU.
BUT HIKARU IS MUCH MORE MATURE THAN I.
I THOUGHT I HAD DESTROYED A LOT OF THINGS...
...BUT EVERY-THING WAS OKAY!! AND...

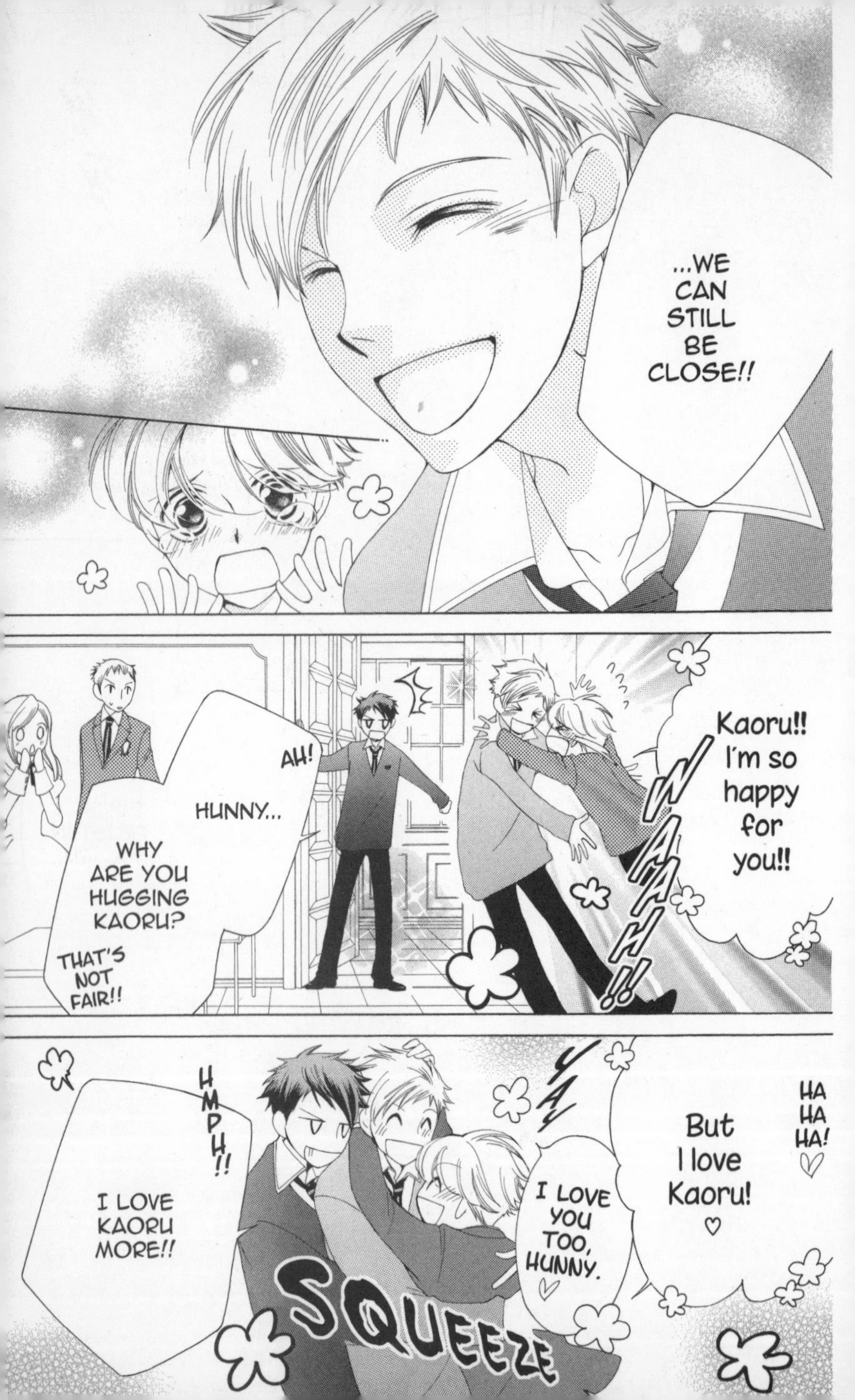
...WE CAN STILL BE CLOSE!!
...
Kaoru!! I'm so happy for you!!
WAAHH!!
AH!
HUNNY...
WHY ARE YOU HUGGING KAORU?
THAT'S NOT FAIR!!
HA HA HA! ♡
But I love Kaoru! ♡
YAY
I LOVE YOU TOO, HUNNY. ♡
HMPH!!
I LOVE KAORU MORE!!
SQUEEZE

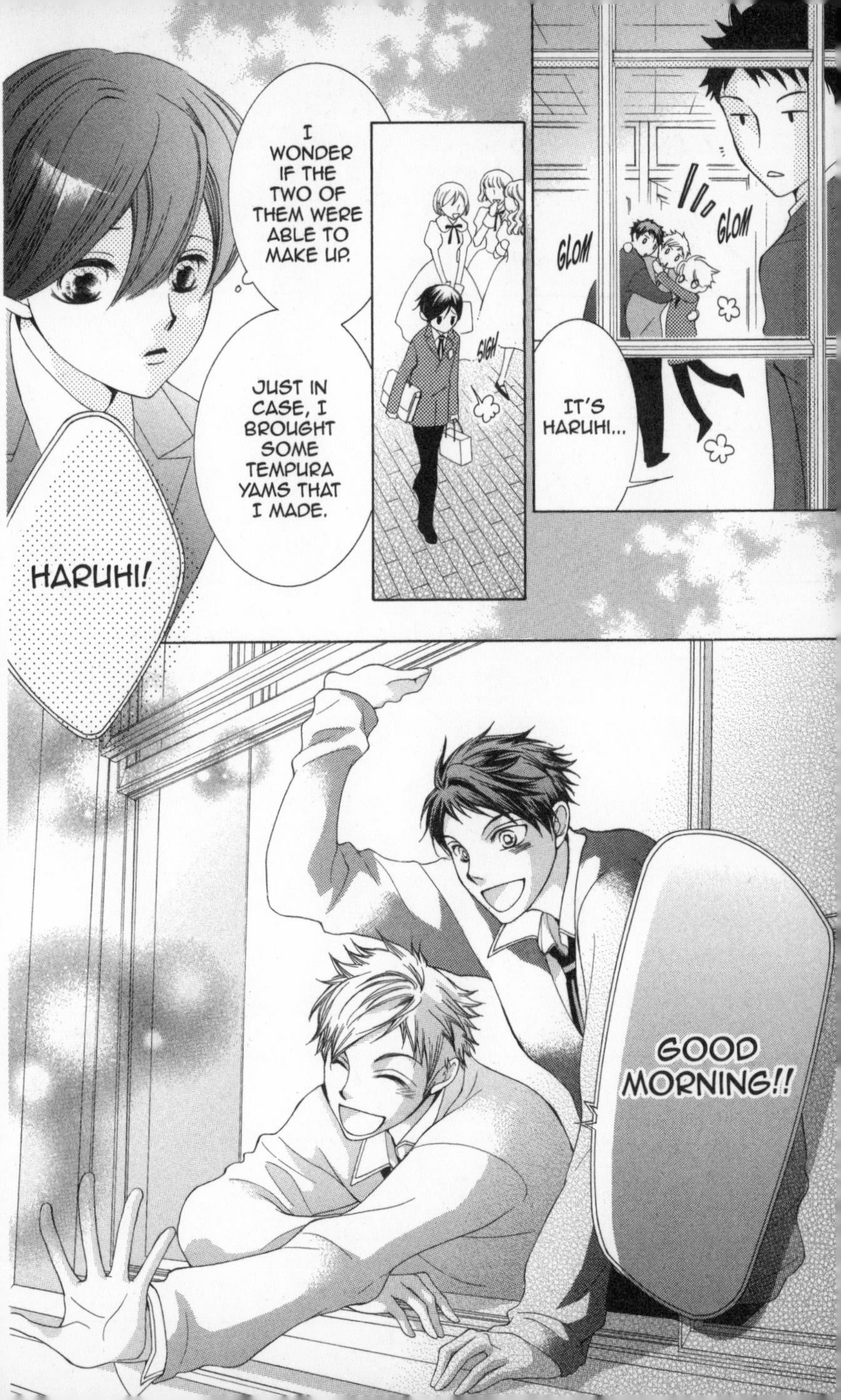
GLOM
GLOM
IT'S HARUHI...
I WONDER IF THE TWO OF THEM WERE ABLE TO MAKE UP.
JUST IN CASE, I BROUGHT SOME TEMPURA YAMS THAT I MADE.
SIGH
HARUHI!
GOOD MORNING!!

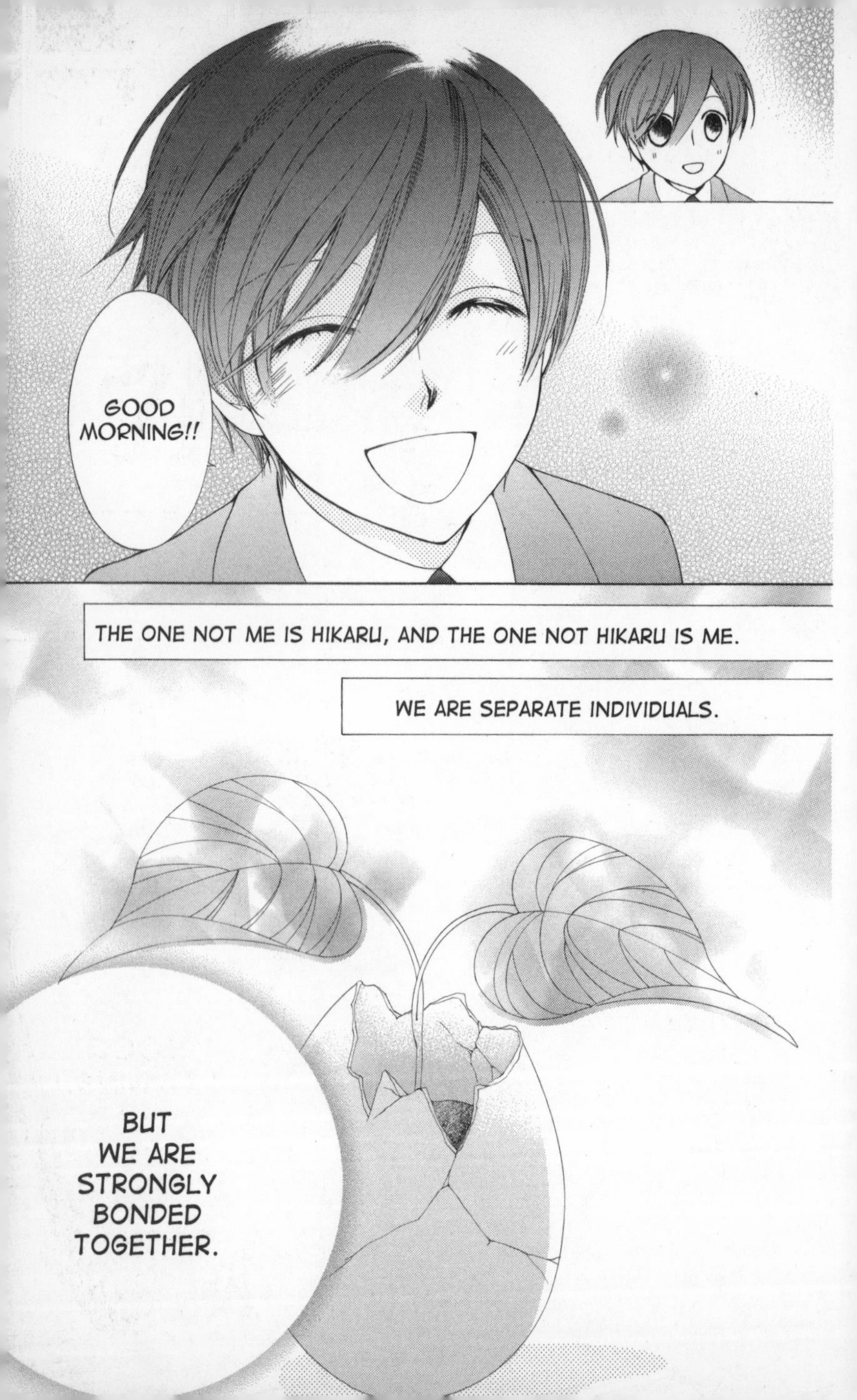
GOOD MORNING!!
THE ONE NOT ME IS HIKARU, AND THE ONE NOT HIKARU IS ME.
WE ARE SEPARATE INDIVIDUALS.
BUT WE ARE STRONGLY BONDED TOGETHER.

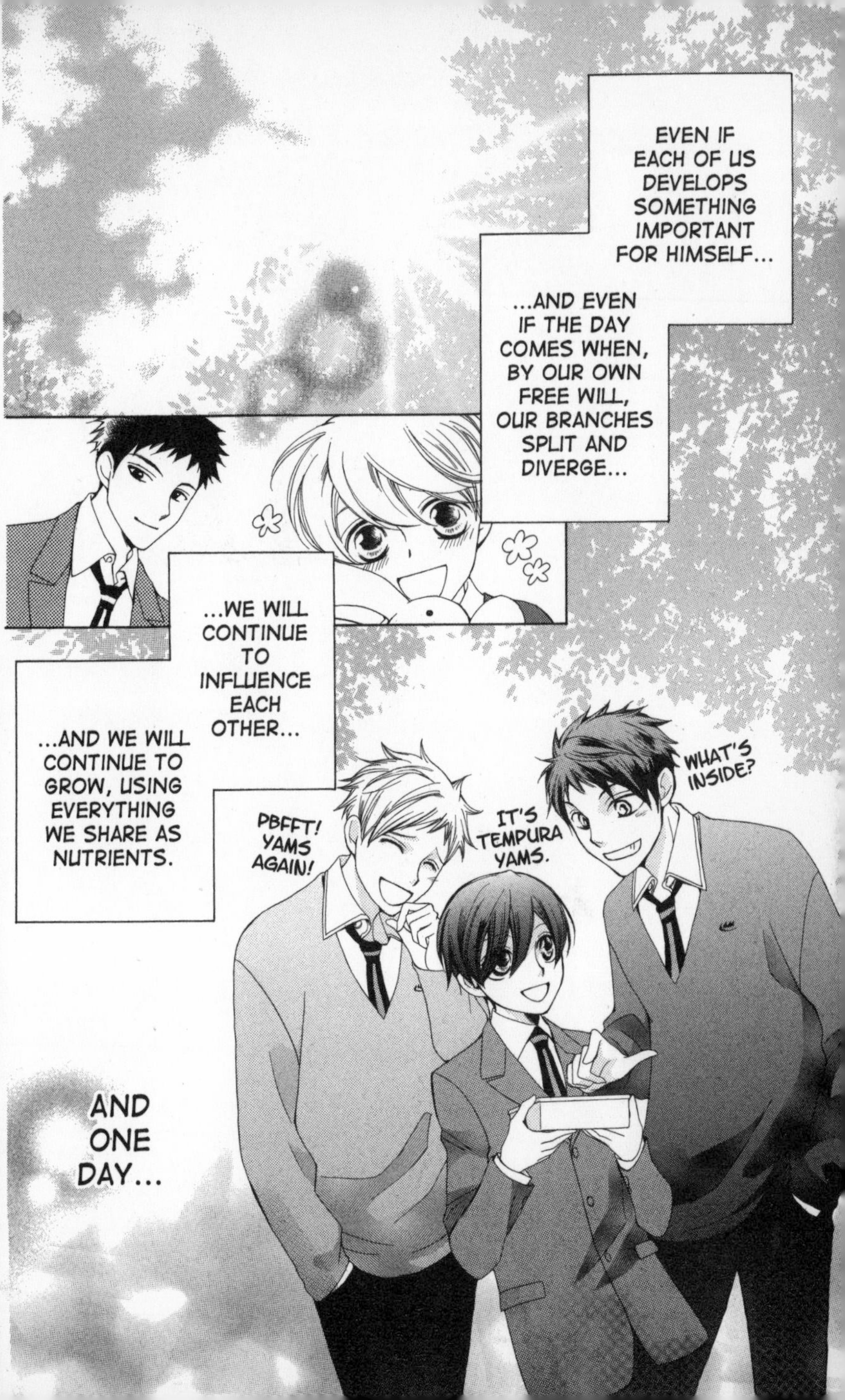
EVEN IF EACH OF US DEVELOPS SOMETHING IMPORTANT FOR HIMSELF...
...AND EVEN IF THE DAY COMES WHEN, BY OUR OWN FREE WILL, OUR BRANCHES SPLIT AND DIVERGE...
...WE WILL CONTINUE TO INFLUENCE EACH OTHER...
...AND WE WILL CONTINUE TO GROW, USING EVERYTHING WE SHARE AS NUTRIENTS.
WHAT'S INSIDE?
IT'S TEMPURA YAMS.
PBFFT! YAMS AGAIN!
AND ONE DAY...

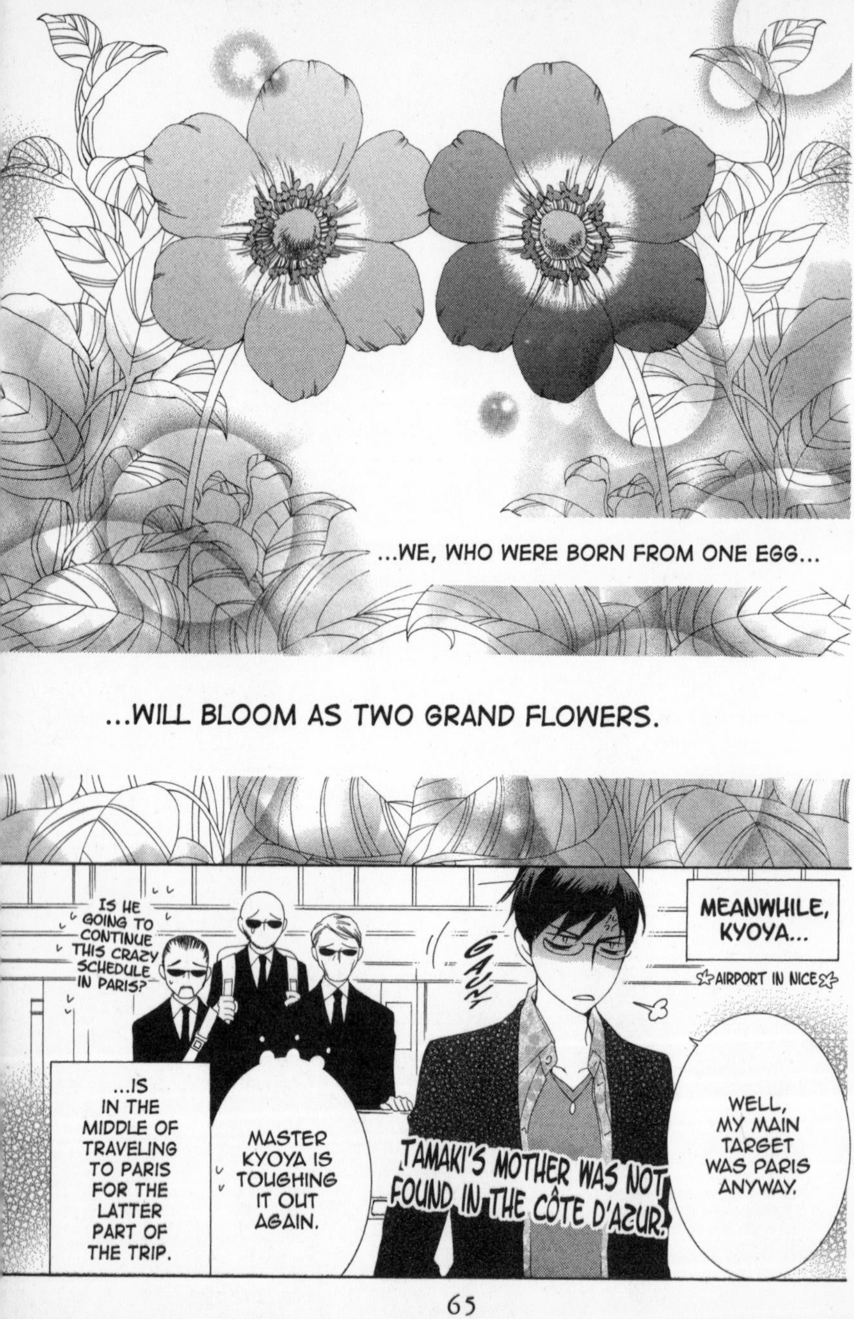
...WE, WHO WERE BORN FROM ONE EGG...
...WILL BLOOM AS TWO GRAND FLOWERS.
MEANWHILE, KYOYA...
AIRPORT IN NICE
GAUN
WELL, MY MAIN TARGET WAS PARIS ANYWAY.
TAMAKI'S MOTHER WAS NOT FOUND IN THE CÔTE D'AZUR.
IS HE GOING TO CONTINUE THIS CRAZY SCHEDULE IN PARIS?
MASTER KYOYA IS TOUGHING IT OUT AGAIN.
...IS IN THE MIDDLE OF TRAVELING TO PARIS FOR THE LATTER PART OF THE TRIP.

YAMASHII: "THANK YOU FOR YOUR WORK" SPECIAL "GEMLIKE TAGLINE" SPECIAL FEATURE PART ②

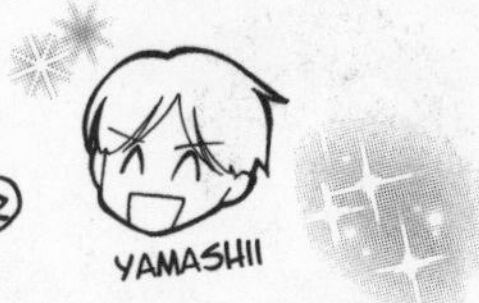
YAMASHII

21: RACING HEART THRILLING LOVE LIFE

23: RACING HEART★MYSTERY-SOLVING ⓘ LOVE-LIFE♫

25: EFFERVESCENT♡FLYING LOVE-LIFE

27: DELICIOUS♡MUNCHING☺LOVE-LIFE

29: RULES → TRYING HARD ★ LOVE-LIFE

31: FLUTTERING♪SPARKLING LOVE-LIFE

22: WHISPERING MYSTERIOUS LOVE★LIFE

24: SWAYING☆DIZZYING LOVE-LIFE♫

26: KLIP KLOP KLIP KLOP LOVE-LIFE ← HOW RAUCOUS (HA!)

28: ELEGANT ◆ STRONG ♠ LOVE-LIFE

30: IRRITATED✸AGGRESSIVE♠LOVE-LIFE

32: PASSIONATE★BULL'S EYE LOVE-LIFE

33: WAVERING WARM LOVE-LIFE ← I WONDER IF THIS WARMTH REFERS TO THE KOTATSU.

34: EYE POWER ⚒ PUNCHING ✸ LOVE-LIFE

36: FLYING AWAY☆BLOWN AWAY LOVE-LIFE

38: SPARKLING♡GLIMMERING LOVE-LIFE

42: SUMMER VACATION♡EXCITING★ LOVE-LIFE

44: SUMMER VACATION ★ HEART-RACING ♡LOVE-LIFE

46: DIZZY♡WOOZY LOVE-LIFE

48: HUSTLE MUSCLE★LOVE-LIFE

50: CHILLING♡ EXCITING LOVE-LIFE

53: SWAYING ★ SYMMETRIC LOVE-LIFE

35: BRIGHT RED♫ HAIR♫ LOVE-LIFE ← WHAT IS THIS ABOUT? (HA!)

37: TWO PEOPLE AS ONE LOVE-LIFE

40: HEART-RACING♡WHISPERING LOVE-LIFE

43: SUMMER VACATION★HEART-RACING♡ LOVE-LIFE

45: SUMMER VACATION★CLIMAX♡LOVE-LIFE

47: GUTS!★FIGHT!☆LOVE-LIFE

49: STURDY GUTS★LOVE-LIFE

52: SWAGGERING★SYMMETRIC LOVE-LIFE

56: THE TRUTH★DISCOVERED♫LOVE-LIFE

AM I THE ONLY ONE THAT FEELS LIKE YAMASHII IS BEGINNING TO BREAK DOWN AROUND NUMBER 26?

THE TAGLINE FOR 57 IS ANOTHER EXTREMELY NICE ONE,
BUT IT'S IN THE NEXT VOLUME, SO I'M DISAPPOINTED I CAN'T LIST IT HERE.

YAMASHII, THANK YOU SO MUCH FOR YOUR EFFORTS. EVEN WHEN YOU GO TO ANOTHER PLANET (A DIFFERENT PUBLICATION), I HOPE YOU CONTINUE TO CREATE WONDERFUL TAGLINES AND LEADS!!

AND THE NEW EDITOR...WE'LL HAVE TO SEE IF HE CONTINUES ON WITH THIS STYLE OF WRITING, OR IF HE ADOPTS A NEW SYSTEM. I HOPE YOU STAY TUNED AND LOOK FORWARD TO IT.

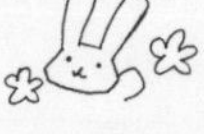

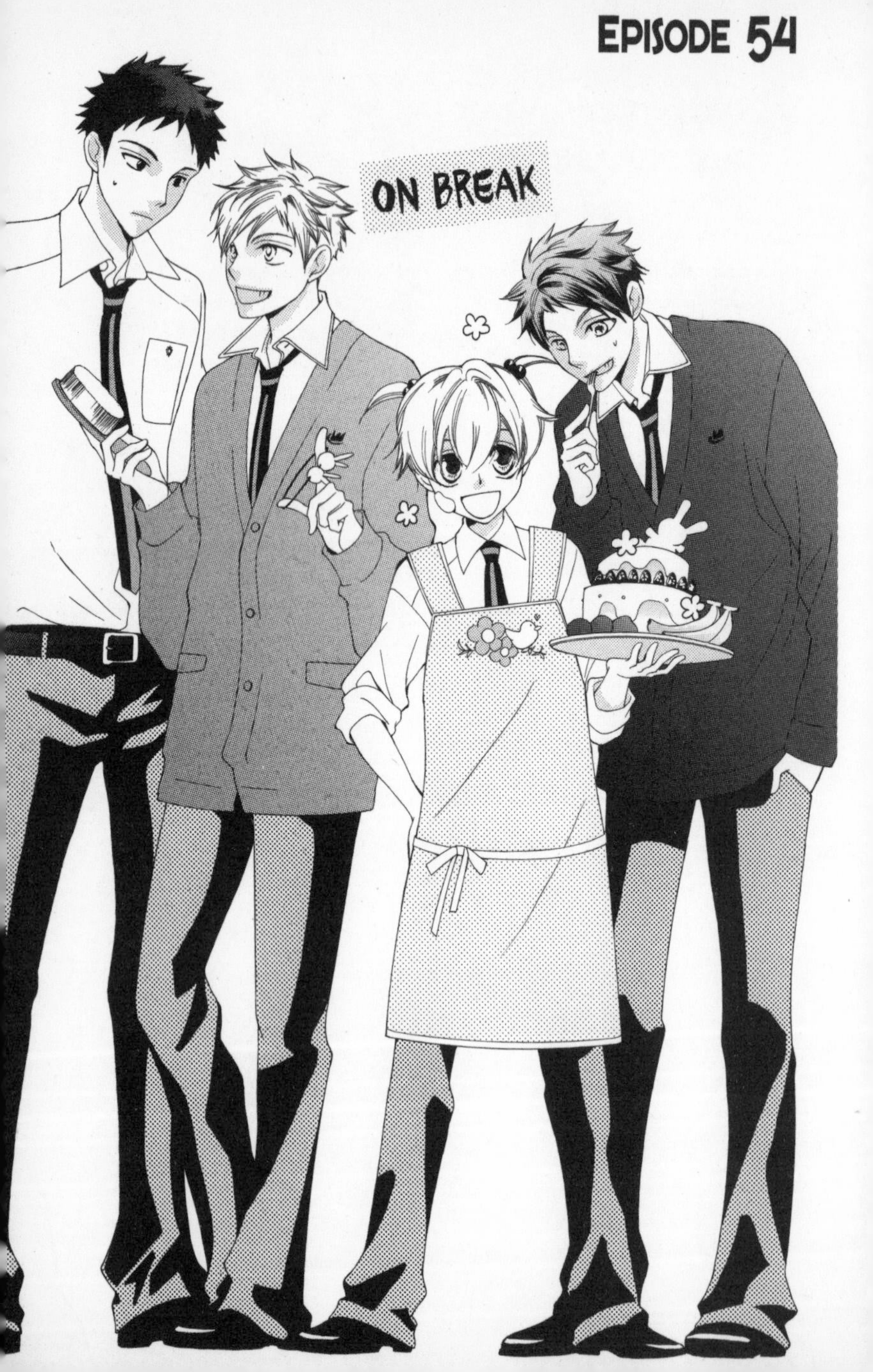
EPISODE 54
ON BREAK

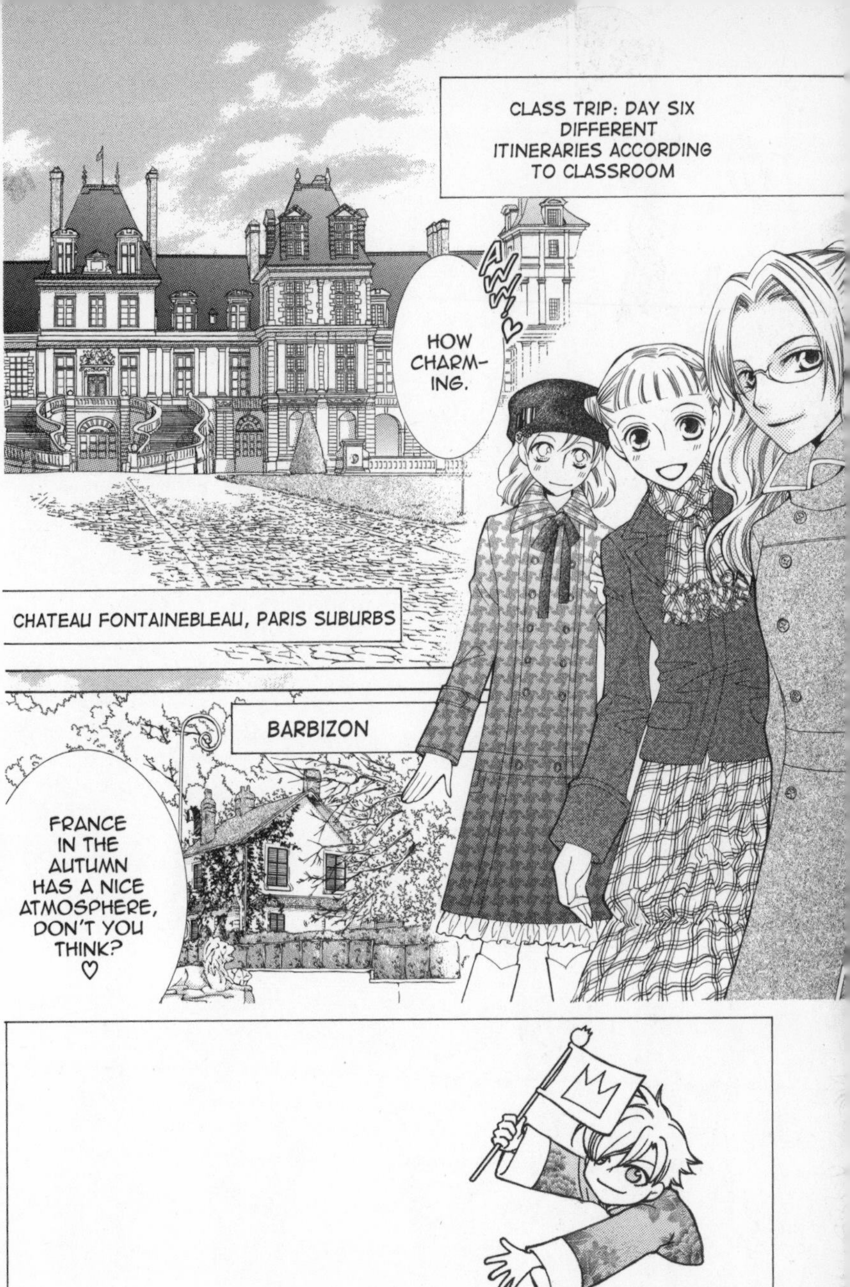
CLASS TRIP: DAY SIX
DIFFERENT ITINERARIES ACCORDING TO CLASSROOM
AWW! ♡
HOW CHARM-ING.
CHATEAU FONTAINEBLEAU, PARIS SUBURBS
BARBIZON
FRANCE IN THE AUTUMN HAS A NICE ATMOSPHERE, DON'T YOU THINK? ♡

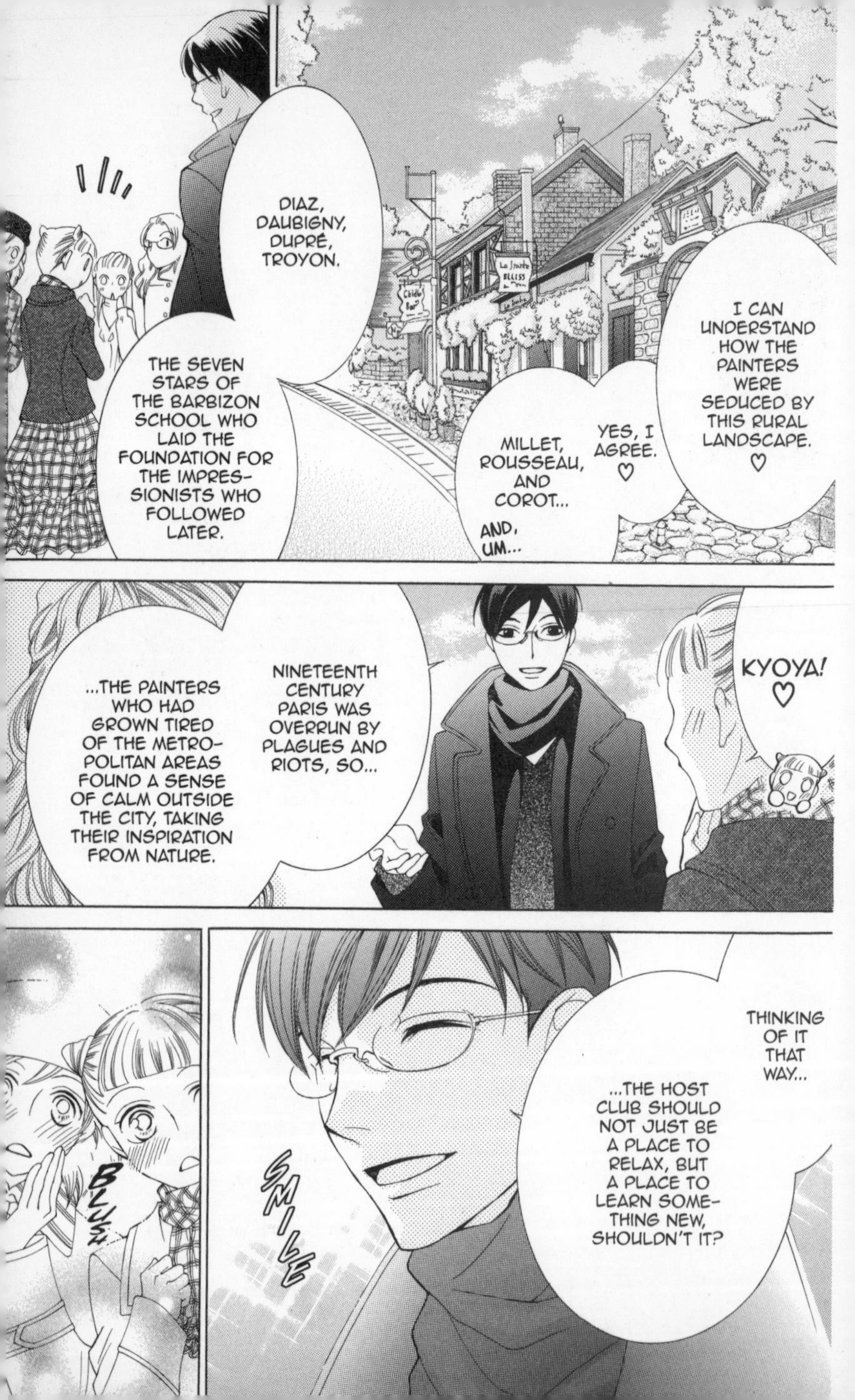
I CAN UNDERSTAND HOW THE PAINTERS WERE SEDUCED BY THIS RURAL LANDSCAPE. ♡
YES, I AGREE. ♡
MILLET, ROUSSEAU, AND COROT...
AND, UM...
DIAZ, DAUBIGNY, DUPRÉ, TROYON.
THE SEVEN STARS OF THE BARBIZON SCHOOL WHO LAID THE FOUNDATION FOR THE IMPRES-SIONISTS WHO FOLLOWED LATER.
KYOYA! ♡
NINETEENTH CENTURY PARIS WAS OVERRUN BY PLAGUES AND RIOTS, SO...
...THE PAINTERS WHO HAD GROWN TIRED OF THE METRO-POLITAN AREAS FOUND A SENSE OF CALM OUTSIDE THE CITY, TAKING THEIR INSPIRATION FROM NATURE.
THINKING OF IT THAT WAY...
...THE HOST CLUB SHOULD NOT JUST BE A PLACE TO RELAX, BUT A PLACE TO LEARN SOME-THING NEW, SHOULDN'T IT?
SMILE
BLUSH

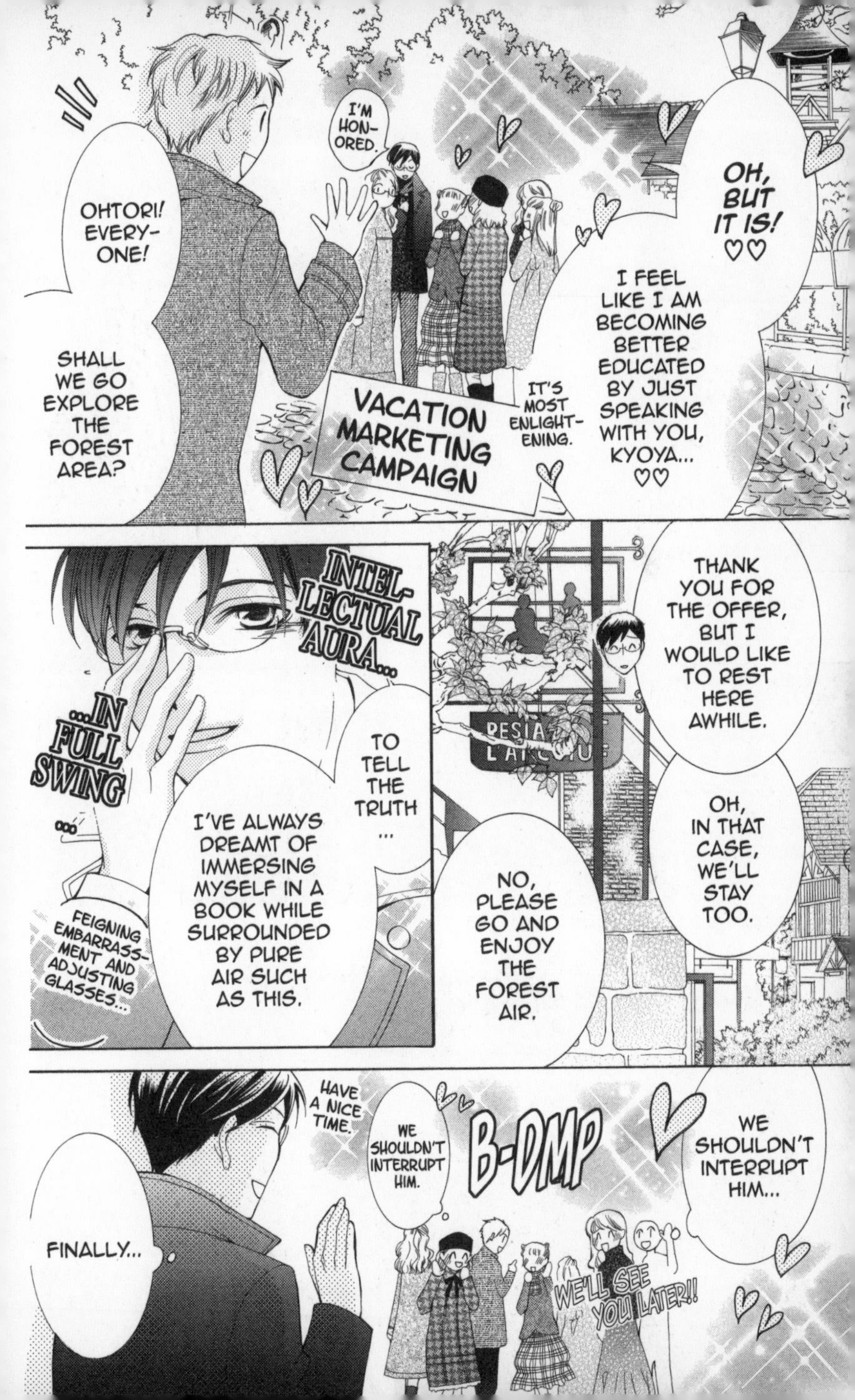
OH, BUT IT IS! ♡♡
I FEEL LIKE I AM BECOMING BETTER EDUCATED BY JUST SPEAKING WITH YOU, KYOYA... ♡♡
I'M HON-ORED.
IT'S MOST ENLIGHT-ENING.
VACATION MARKETING CAMPAIGN
OHTORI! EVERY-ONE!
SHALL WE GO EXPLORE THE FOREST AREA?
THANK YOU FOR THE OFFER, BUT I WOULD LIKE TO REST HERE AWHILE.
OH, IN THAT CASE, WE'LL STAY TOO.
NO, PLEASE GO AND ENJOY THE FOREST AIR.
INTEL-LECTUAL AURA...
TO TELL THE TRUTH...
I'VE ALWAYS DREAMT OF IMMERSING MYSELF IN A BOOK WHILE SURROUNDED BY PURE AIR SUCH AS THIS.
...IN FULL SWING
...
FEIGNING EMBARRASS-MENT AND ADJUSTING GLASSES...
WE SHOULDN'T INTERRUPT HIM...
B-DMP
WE SHOULDN'T INTERRUPT HIM.
HAVE A NICE TIME.
WE'LL SEE YOU LATER!!
FINALLY...

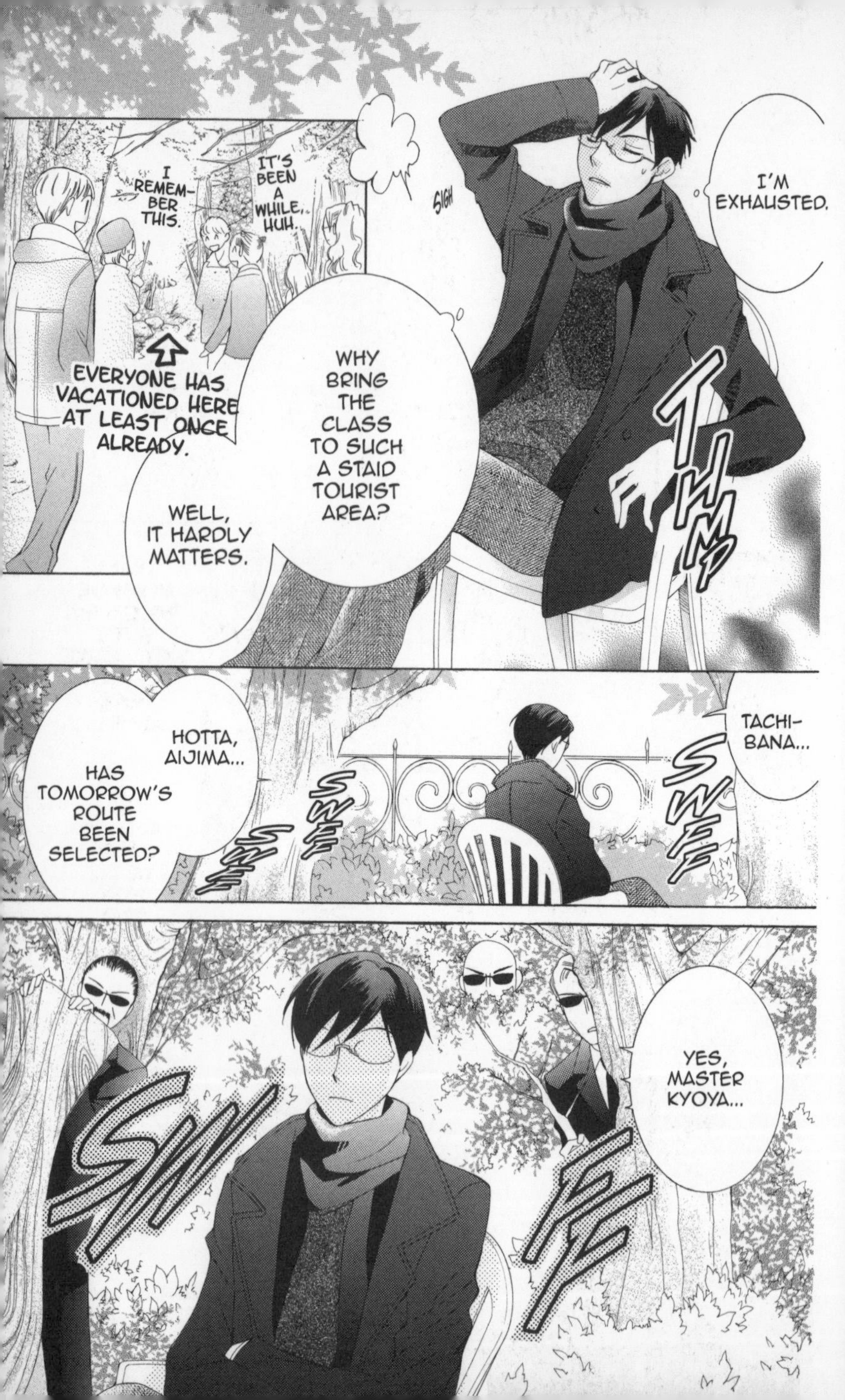
I'M EXHAUSTED.
SIGH
THUMP
WHY BRING THE CLASS TO SUCH A STAID TOURIST AREA?
IT'S BEEN A WHILE, HUH.
I REMEMBER THIS.
EVERYONE HAS VACATIONED HERE AT LEAST ONCE ALREADY.
WELL, IT HARDLY MATTERS.
TACHI-BANA...
SWFF
HOTTA, AIJIMA...
HAS TOMORROW'S ROUTE BEEN SELECTED?
SWFF
SWFF
YES, MASTER KYOYA...
SH
FF

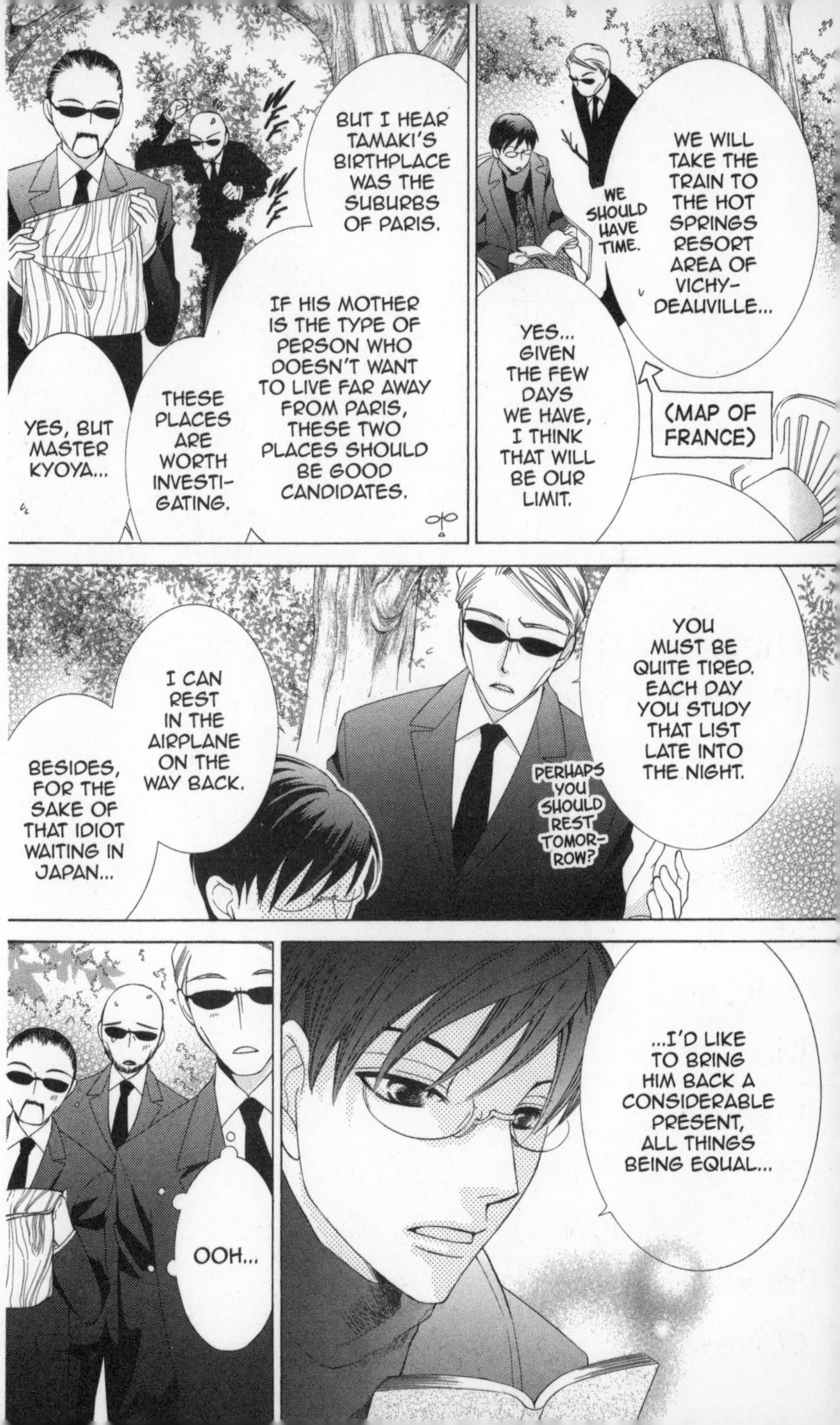
WE WILL TAKE THE TRAIN TO THE HOT SPRINGS RESORT AREA OF VICHY-DEAUVILLE...
WE SHOULD HAVE TIME.
(MAP OF FRANCE)
YES... GIVEN THE FEW DAYS WE HAVE, I THINK THAT WILL BE OUR LIMIT.
BUT I HEAR TAMAKI'S BIRTHPLACE WAS THE SUBURBS OF PARIS.
WFF WFF
IF HIS MOTHER IS THE TYPE OF PERSON WHO DOESN'T WANT TO LIVE FAR AWAY FROM PARIS, THESE TWO PLACES SHOULD BE GOOD CANDIDATES.
THESE PLACES ARE WORTH INVESTI-GATING.
YES, BUT MASTER KYOYA...
YOU MUST BE QUITE TIRED. EACH DAY YOU STUDY THAT LIST LATE INTO THE NIGHT.
PERHAPS YOU SHOULD REST TOMOR-ROW?
I CAN REST IN THE AIRPLANE ON THE WAY BACK.
BESIDES, FOR THE SAKE OF THAT IDIOT WAITING IN JAPAN...
...I'D LIKE TO BRING HIM BACK A CONSIDERABLE PRESENT, ALL THINGS BEING EQUAL...
OOH...

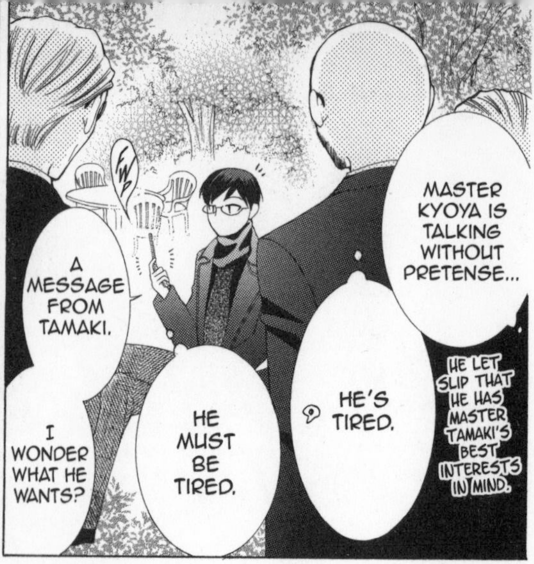
MASTER KYOYA IS TALKING WITHOUT PRETENSE...
HE LET SLIP THAT HE HAS MASTER TAMAKI'S BEST INTERESTS IN MIND.
HE'S TIRED.
A MESSAGE FROM TAMAKI.
HE MUST BE TIRED.
I WONDER WHAT HE WANTS?

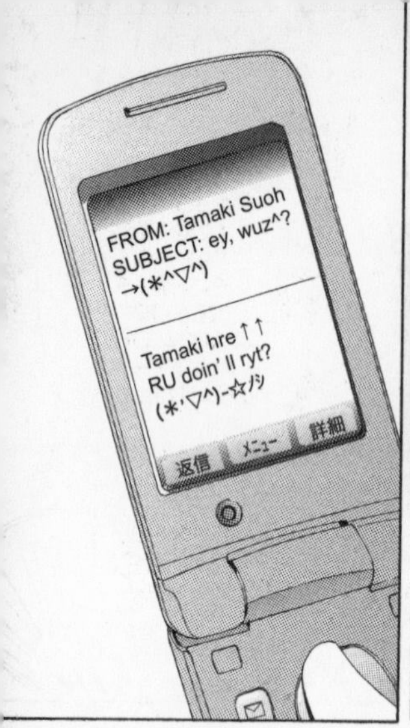
FROM: Tamaki Suoh
SUBJECT: ey, wuz^?
→(*^▽^)
Tamaki hre ↑↑
RU doin' ll ryt?
(*'▽^)-☆ノシ
返信
メニュー
詳細

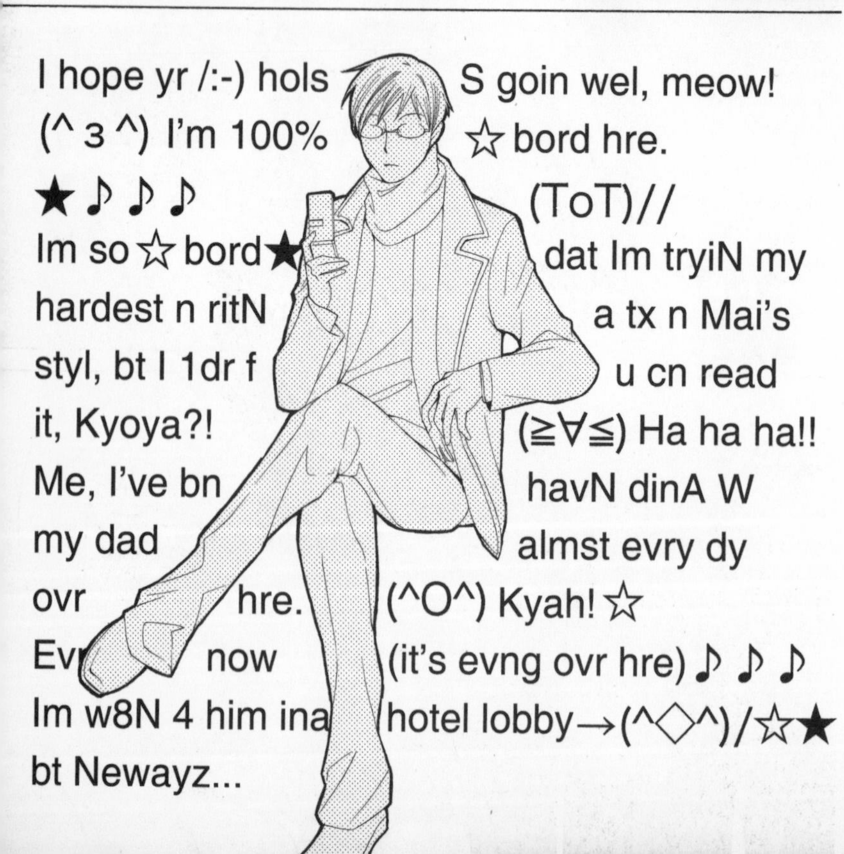
I hope yr /:-) hols S goin wel, meow!
(^ з ^) I'm 100% ☆ bord hre.
★♪♪♪ (ToT)//
Im so ☆ bord★ dat Im tryiN my
hardest n ritN a tx n Mai's
styl, bt I 1dr f u cn read
it, Kyoya?! (≧∀≦) Ha ha ha!!
Me, I've bn havN dinA W
my dad almst evry dy
ovr hre. (^O^) Kyah! ☆
Evr now (it's evng ovr hre) ♪♪♪
Im w8N 4 him ina hotel lobby→(^◇^)/☆★
bt Newayz...

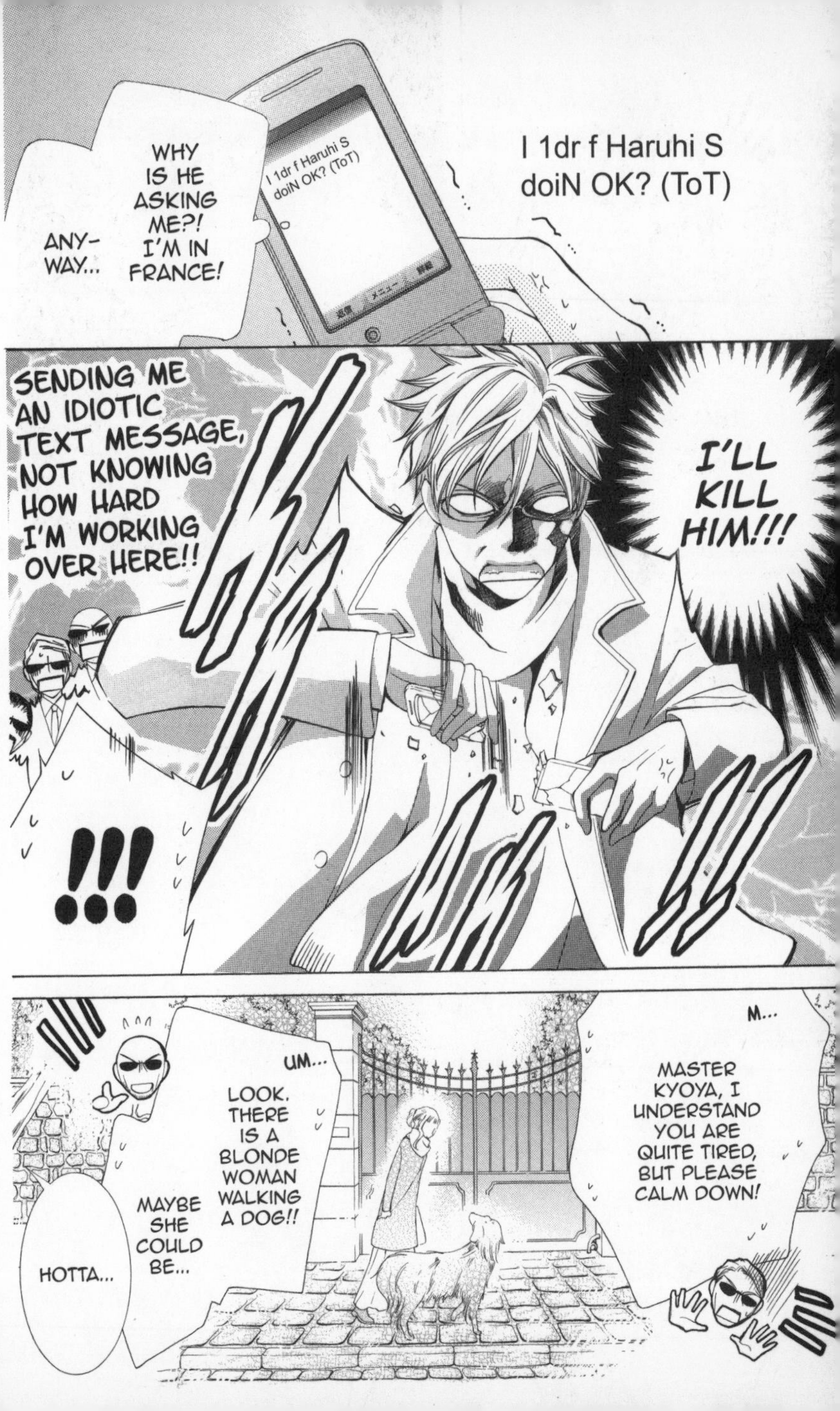
I 1dr f Haruhi S doiN OK? (ToT)
I 1dr f Haruhi S doiN OK? (ToT)
WHY IS HE ASKING ME?! I'M IN FRANCE!
ANY-WAY...
I'LL KILL HIM!!!
SENDING ME AN IDIOTIC TEXT MESSAGE, NOT KNOWING HOW HARD I'M WORKING OVER HERE!!
!!!
M...
MASTER KYOYA, I UNDERSTAND YOU ARE QUITE TIRED, BUT PLEASE CALM DOWN!
UM...
LOOK. THERE IS A BLONDE WOMAN WALKING A DOG!!
MAYBE SHE COULD BE...
HOTTA...

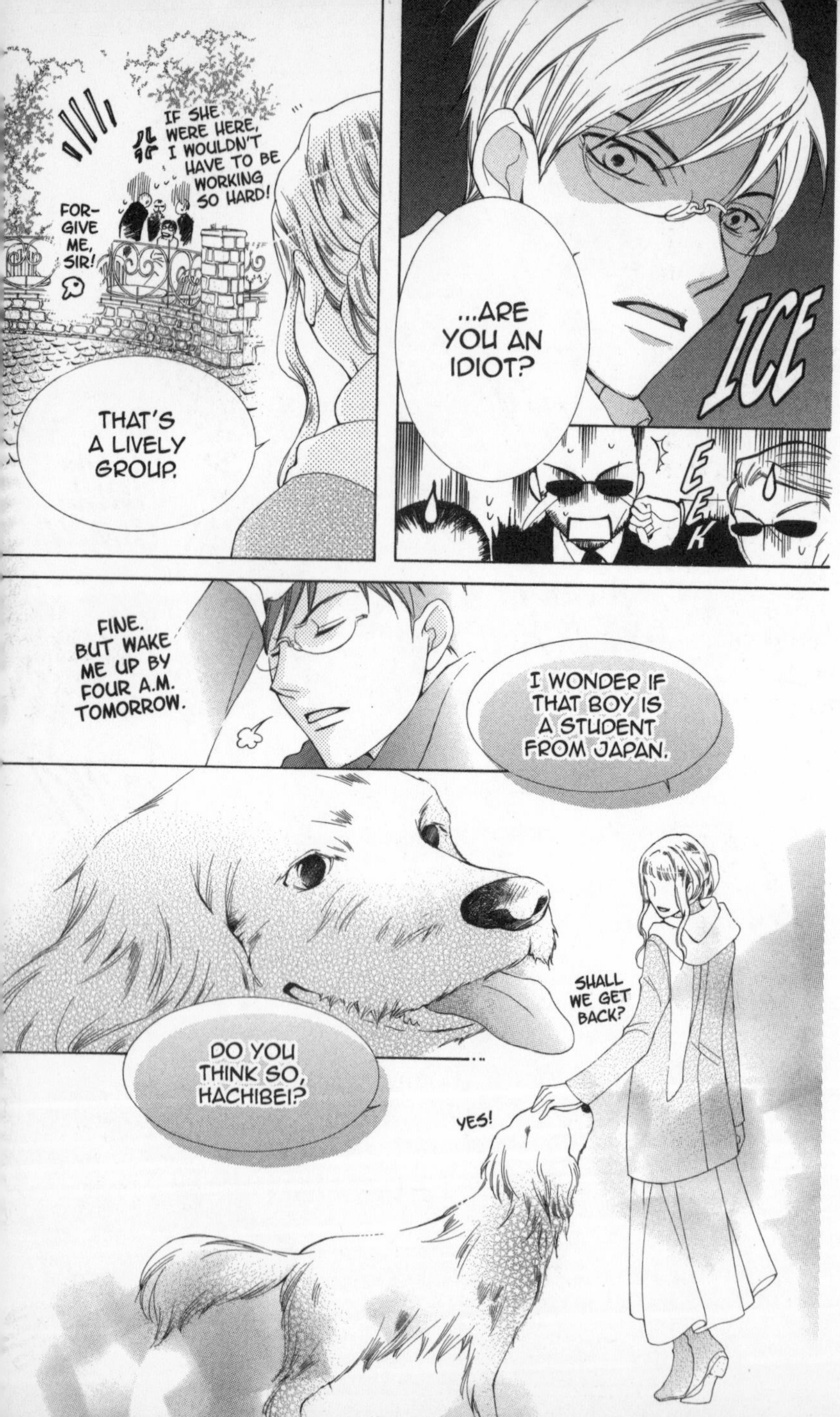
...ARE YOU AN IDIOT?
ICE
EEK
IF SHE WERE HERE, I WOULDN'T HAVE TO BE WORKING SO HARD!
FOR-GIVE ME, SIR!
THAT'S A LIVELY GROUP.
FINE. BUT WAKE ME UP BY FOUR A.M. TOMORROW.
I WONDER IF THAT BOY IS A STUDENT FROM JAPAN.
SHALL WE GET BACK?
DO YOU THINK SO, HACHIBEI?
YES!

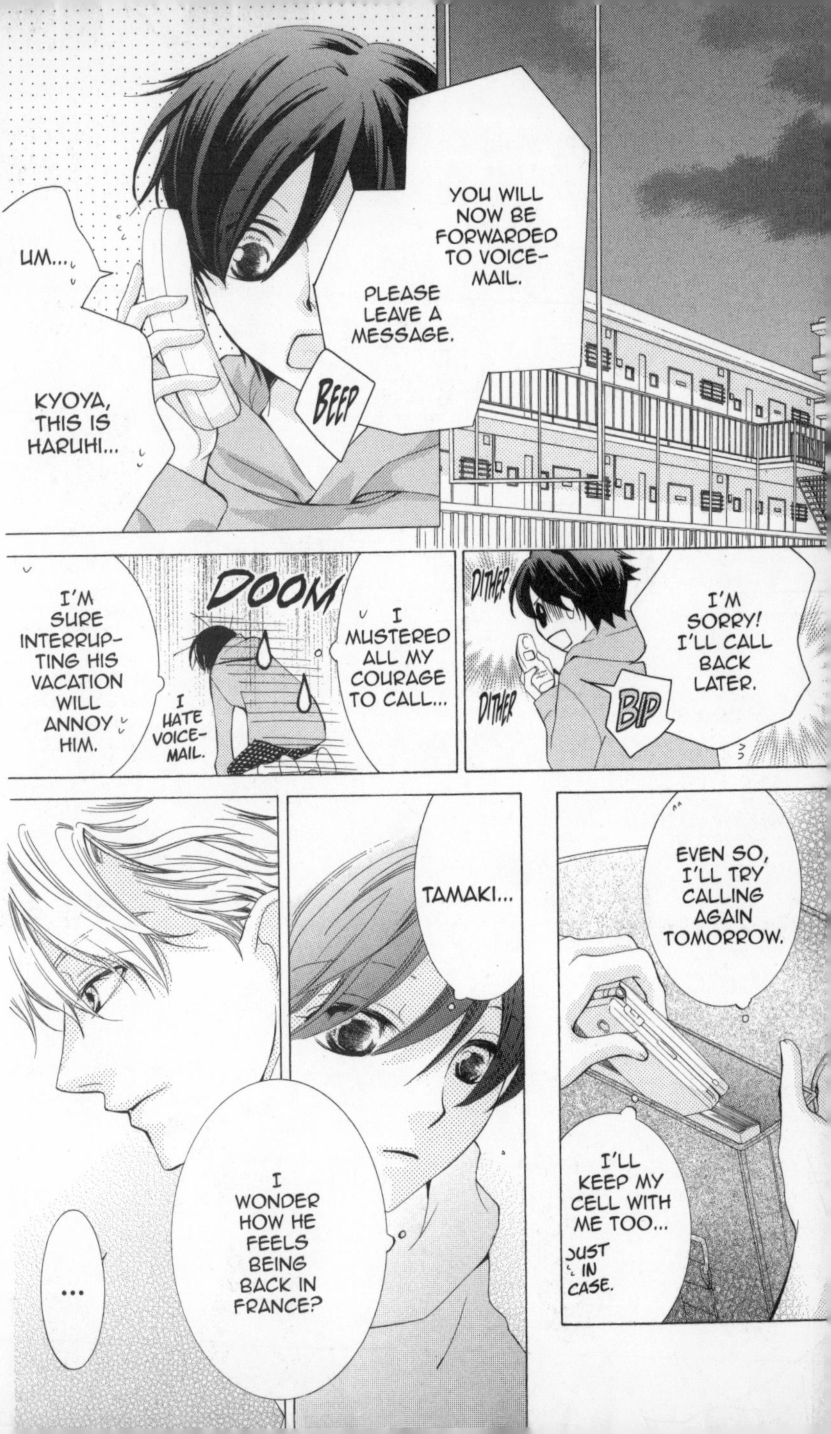
YOU WILL NOW BE FORWARDED TO VOICE-MAIL.
PLEASE LEAVE A MESSAGE.
BEEP
UM...
KYOYA, THIS IS HARUHI...
DITHER
DITHER
I'M SORRY! I'LL CALL BACK LATER.
BIP
I MUSTERED ALL MY COURAGE TO CALL...
DOOM
I HATE VOICE-MAIL.
I'M SURE INTERRUPTING HIS VACATION WILL ANNOY HIM.
EVEN SO, I'LL TRY CALLING AGAIN TOMORROW.
I'LL KEEP MY CELL WITH ME TOO...
JUST IN CASE.
TAMAKI...
I WONDER HOW HE FEELS BEING BACK IN FRANCE?
...

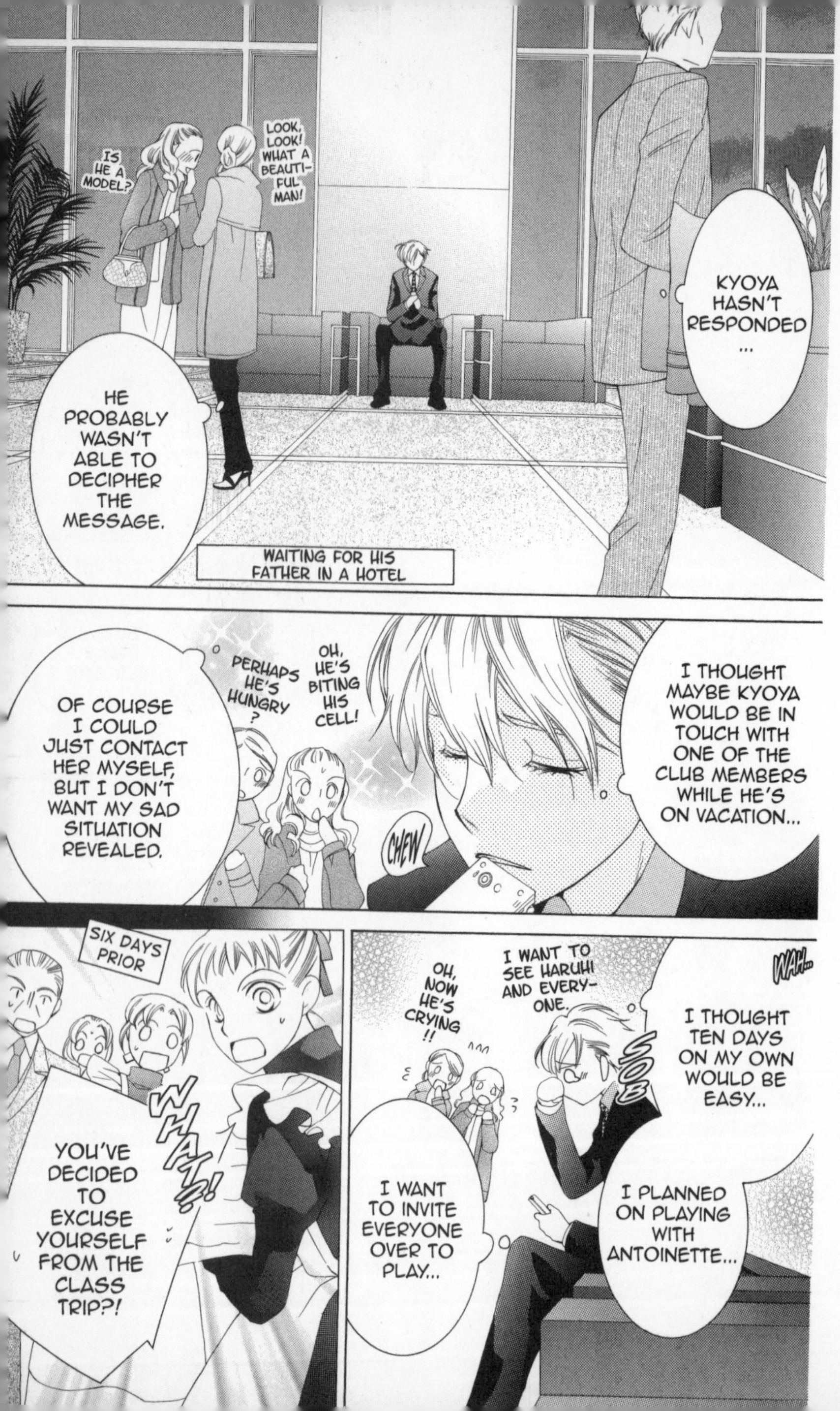
KYOYA HASN'T RESPONDED ...
LOOK, LOOK! WHAT A BEAUTIFUL MAN!
IS HE A MODEL?
HE PROBABLY WASN'T ABLE TO DECIPHER THE MESSAGE.
WAITING FOR HIS FATHER IN A HOTEL
I THOUGHT MAYBE KYOYA WOULD BE IN TOUCH WITH ONE OF THE CLUB MEMBERS WHILE HE'S ON VACATION...
CHEW
OH, HE'S BITING HIS CELL!
PERHAPS HE'S HUNGRY?
OF COURSE I COULD JUST CONTACT HER MYSELF, BUT I DON'T WANT MY SAD SITUATION REVEALED.
WAH...
I THOUGHT TEN DAYS ON MY OWN WOULD BE EASY...
SOB
I WANT TO SEE HARUHI AND EVERYONE.
OH, NOW HE'S CRYING!!
I PLANNED ON PLAYING WITH ANTOINETTE...
I WANT TO INVITE EVERYONE OVER TO PLAY...
SIX DAYS PRIOR
WHAT?!
YOU'VE DECIDED TO EXCUSE YOURSELF FROM THE CLASS TRIP?!

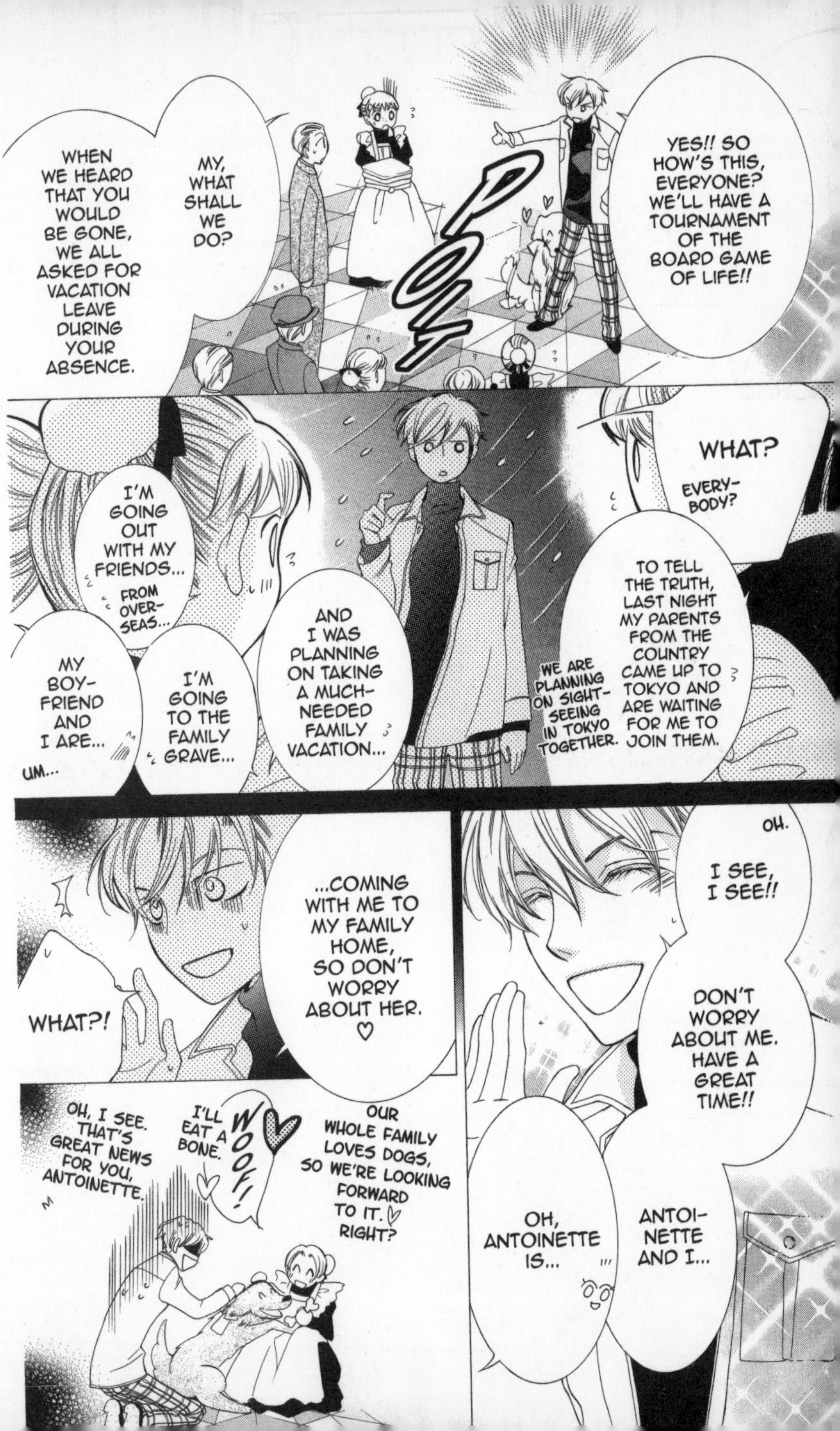
YES!! SO HOW'S THIS, EVERYONE? WE'LL HAVE A TOURNAMENT OF THE BOARD GAME OF LIFE!!
POOF
MY, WHAT SHALL WE DO?
WHEN WE HEARD THAT YOU WOULD BE GONE, WE ALL ASKED FOR VACATION LEAVE DURING YOUR ABSENCE.
WHAT?
EVERYBODY?
TO TELL THE TRUTH, LAST NIGHT MY PARENTS FROM THE COUNTRY CAME UP TO TOKYO AND ARE WAITING FOR ME TO JOIN THEM.
WE ARE PLANNING ON SIGHT-SEEING IN TOKYO TOGETHER.
AND I WAS PLANNING ON TAKING A MUCH-NEEDED FAMILY VACATION...
I'M GOING OUT WITH MY FRIENDS...
FROM OVER-SEAS...
I'M GOING TO THE FAMILY GRAVE...
MY BOY-FRIEND AND I ARE...
UM...
OH.
I SEE, I SEE!!
DON'T WORRY ABOUT ME. HAVE A GREAT TIME!!
ANTOI-NETTE AND I...
OH, ANTOINETTE IS...
...COMING WITH ME TO MY FAMILY HOME, SO DON'T WORRY ABOUT HER. ♡
WHAT?!
OUR WHOLE FAMILY LOVES DOGS, SO WE'RE LOOKING FORWARD TO IT. ♡ RIGHT?
WOOF!
I'LL EAT A BONE.
OH, I SEE. THAT'S GREAT NEWS FOR YOU, ANTOINETTE.

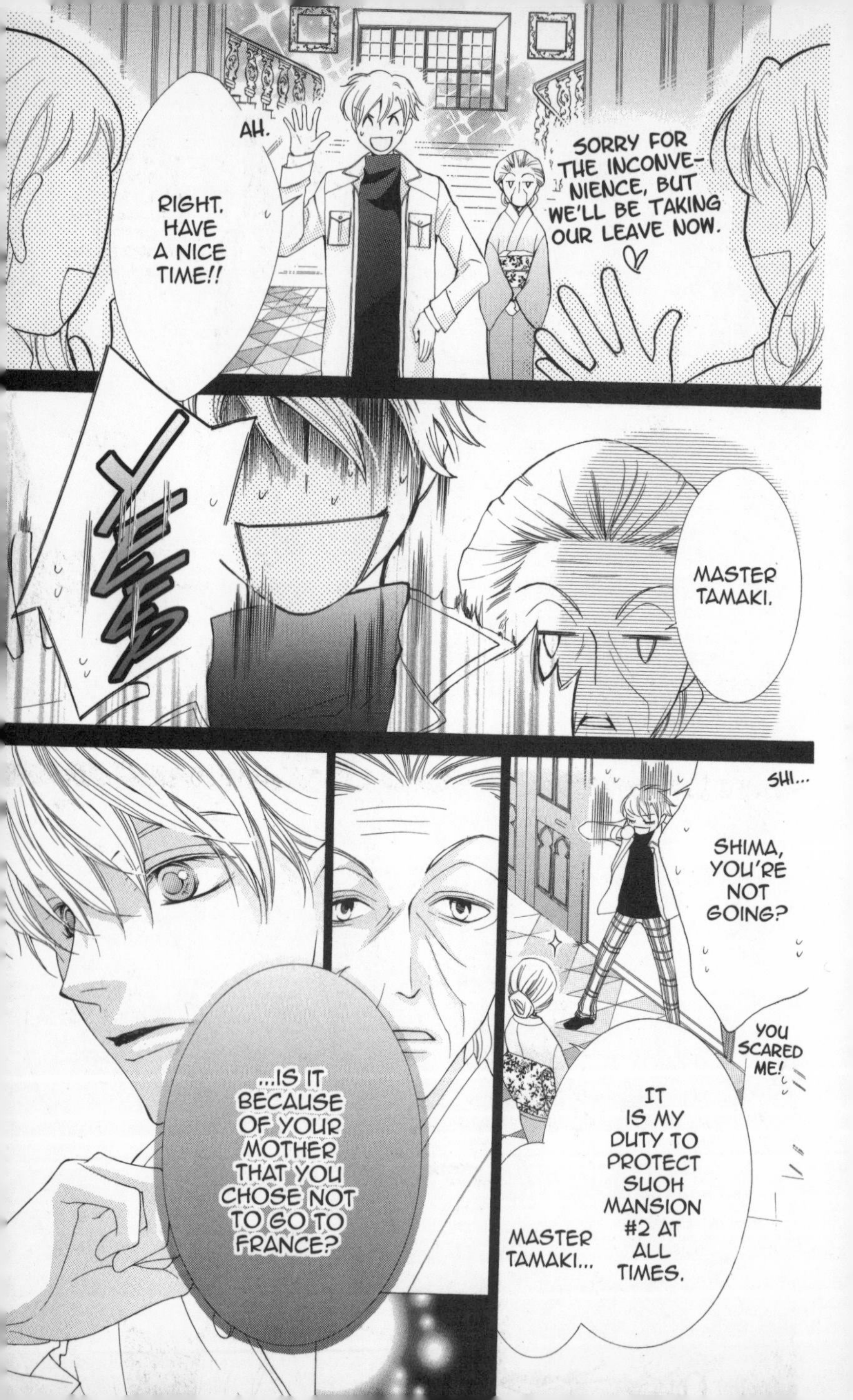
SORRY FOR THE INCONVE-NIENCE, BUT WE'LL BE TAKING OUR LEAVE NOW.
AH.
RIGHT. HAVE A NICE TIME!!
MASTER TAMAKI.
SHI...
SHIMA, YOU'RE NOT GOING?
YOU SCARED ME!
IT IS MY DUTY TO PROTECT SUOH MANSION #2 AT ALL TIMES.
MASTER TAMAKI...
...IS IT BECAUSE OF YOUR MOTHER THAT YOU CHOSE NOT TO GO TO FRANCE?

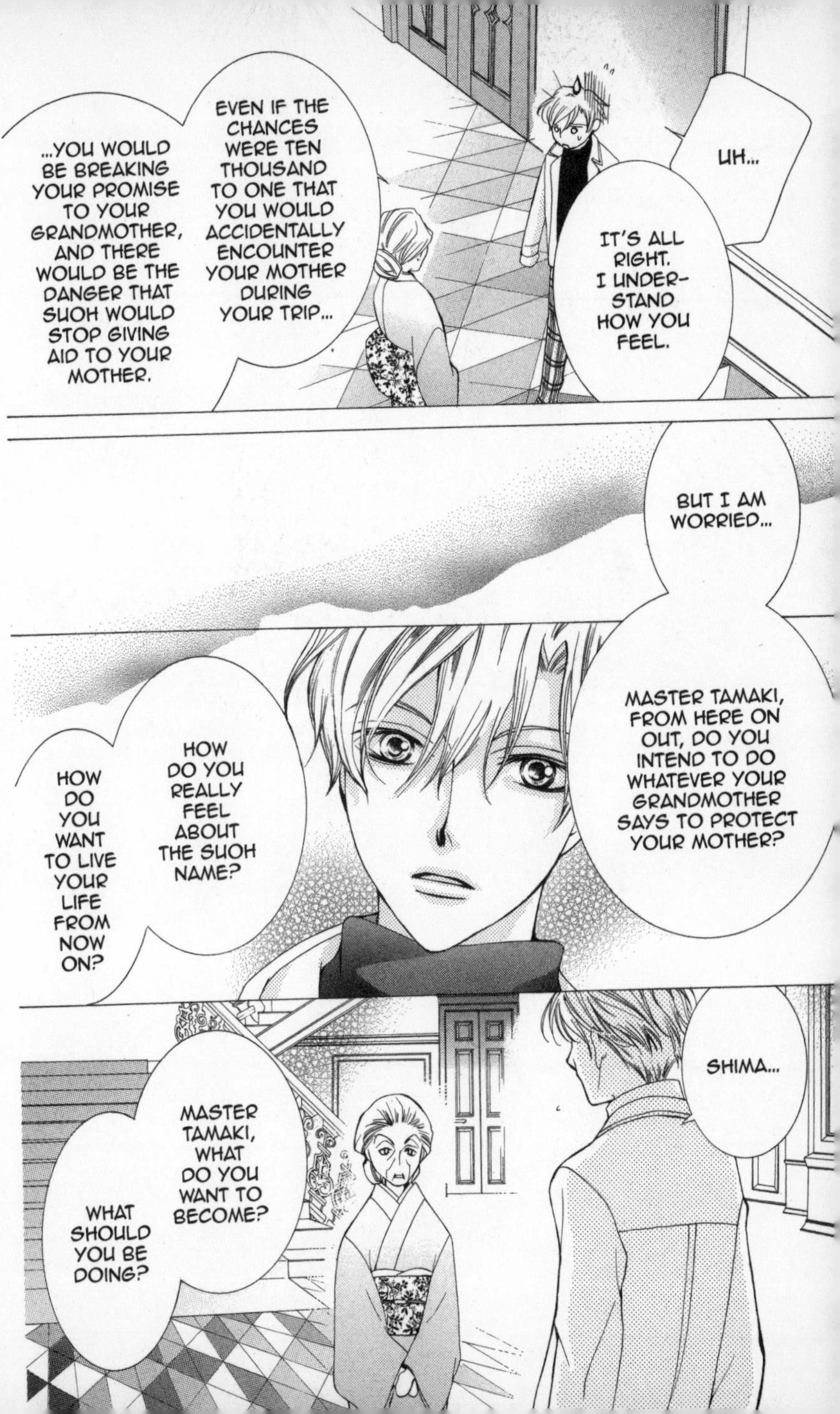
UH...
IT'S ALL RIGHT. I UNDERSTAND HOW YOU FEEL.
EVEN IF THE CHANCES WERE TEN THOUSAND TO ONE THAT YOU WOULD ACCIDENTALLY ENCOUNTER YOUR MOTHER DURING YOUR TRIP...
...YOU WOULD BE BREAKING YOUR PROMISE TO YOUR GRANDMOTHER, AND THERE WOULD BE THE DANGER THAT SUOH WOULD STOP GIVING AID TO YOUR MOTHER.
BUT I AM WORRIED...
MASTER TAMAKI, FROM HERE ON OUT, DO YOU INTEND TO DO WHATEVER YOUR GRANDMOTHER SAYS TO PROTECT YOUR MOTHER?
HOW DO YOU REALLY FEEL ABOUT THE SUOH NAME?
HOW DO YOU WANT TO LIVE YOUR LIFE FROM NOW ON?
SHIMA...
MASTER TAMAKI, WHAT DO YOU WANT TO BECOME?
WHAT SHOULD YOU BE DOING?

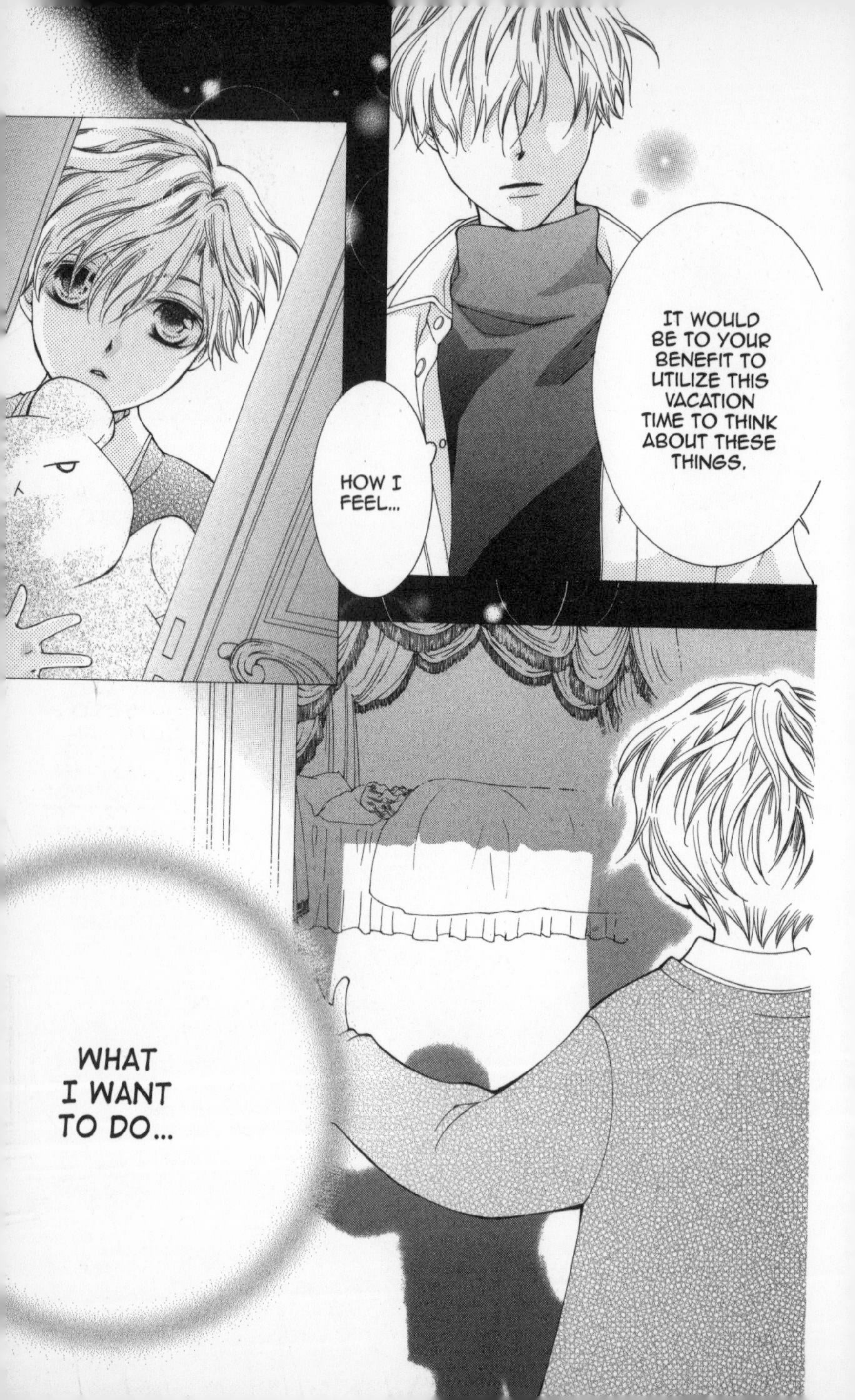
IT WOULD BE TO YOUR BENEFIT TO UTILIZE THIS VACATION TIME TO THINK ABOUT THESE THINGS.
HOW I FEEL...
WHAT I WANT TO DO...

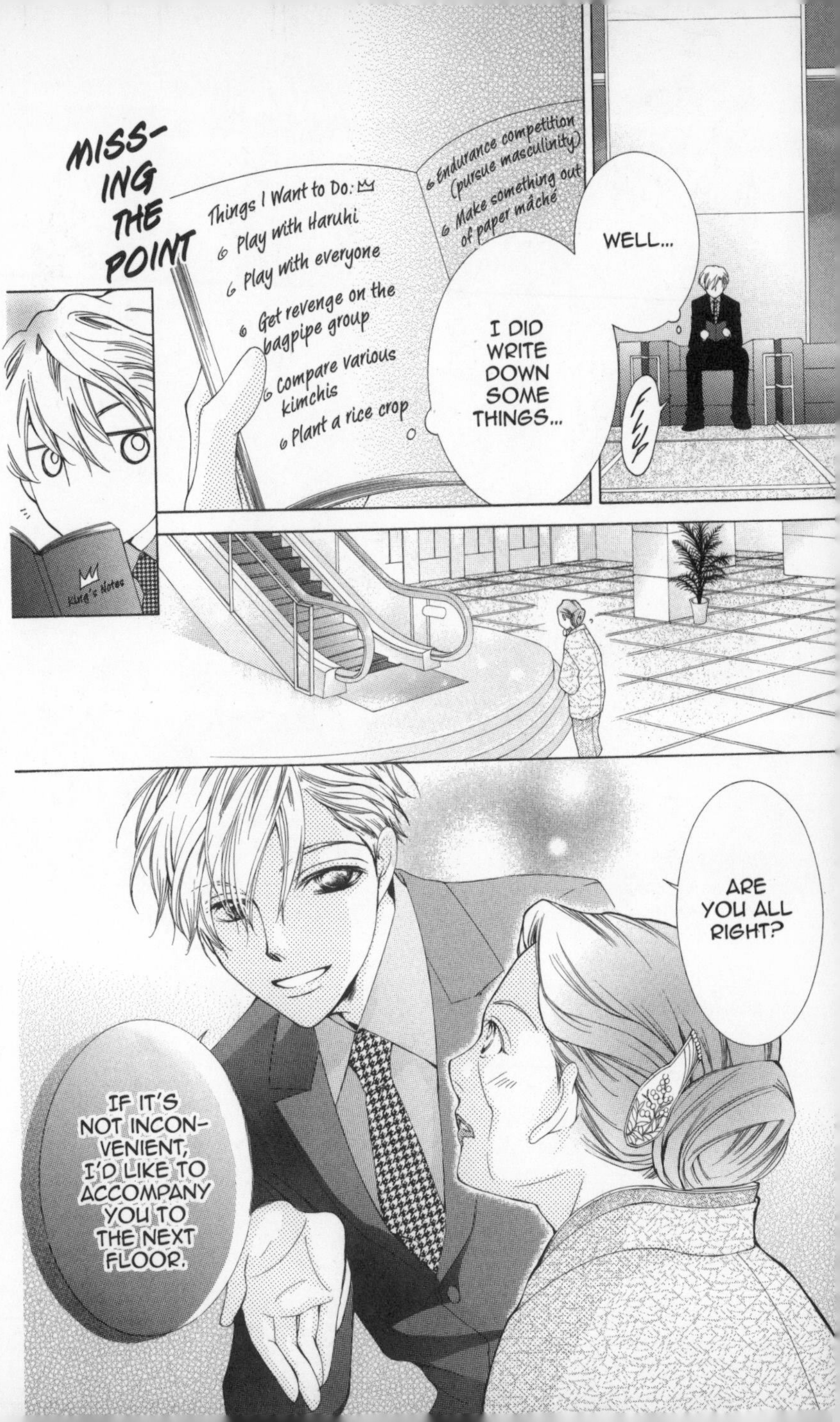
WELL...
FLIP
I DID WRITE DOWN SOME THINGS...
MISS-ING THE POINT
Things I Want to Do:
Play with Haruhi
Play with everyone
Get revenge on the bagpipe group
Compare various kimchis
Plant a rice crop
Endurance competition (pursue masculinity)
Make something out of paper mâché
King's Notes
ARE YOU ALL RIGHT?
IF IT'S NOT INCON-VENIENT, I'D LIKE TO ACCOMPANY YOU TO THE NEXT FLOOR.

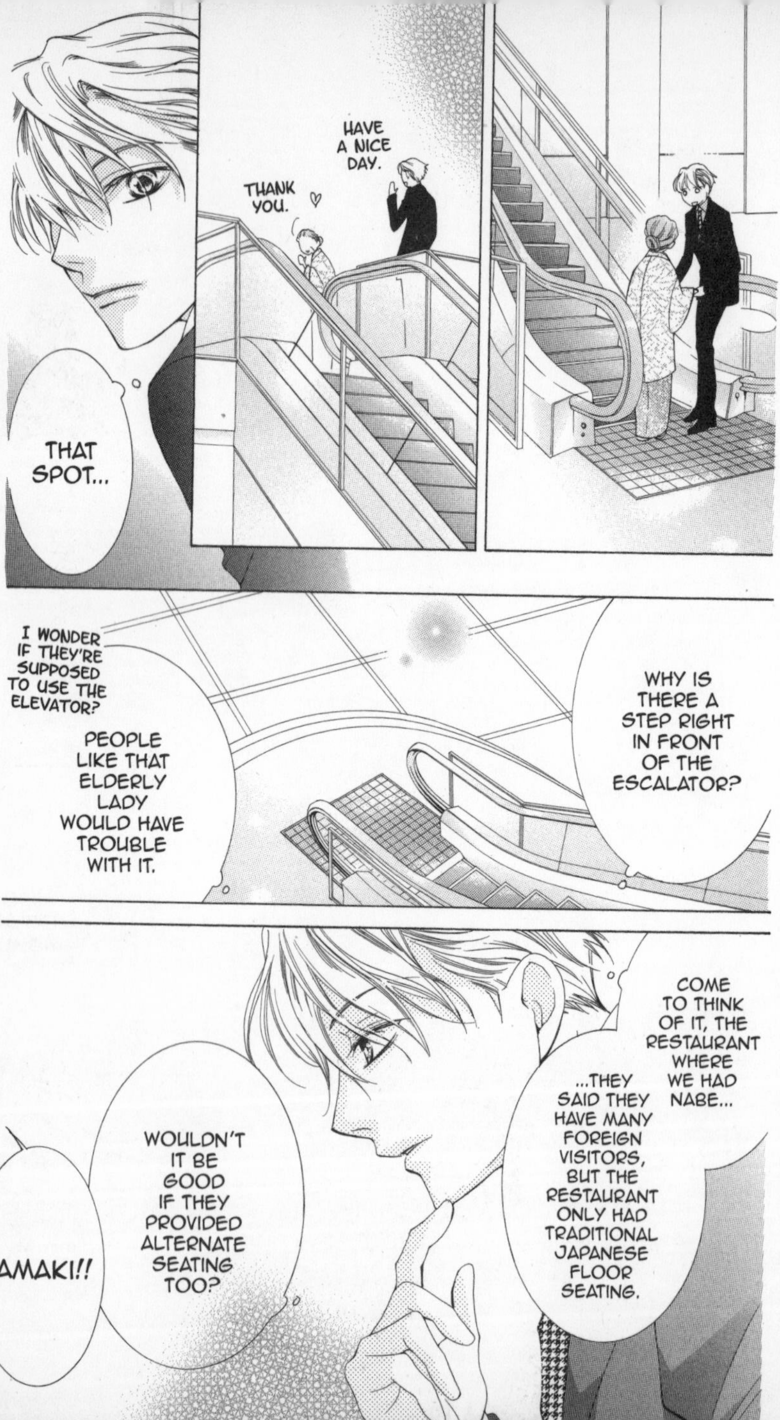

HAVE A NICE DAY.
THANK YOU.
THAT SPOT...
WHY IS THERE A STEP RIGHT IN FRONT OF THE ESCALATOR?
PEOPLE LIKE THAT ELDERLY LADY WOULD HAVE TROUBLE WITH IT.
I WONDER IF THEY'RE SUPPOSED TO USE THE ELEVATOR?
COME TO THINK OF IT, THE RESTAURANT WHERE WE HAD NABE...
...THEY SAID THEY HAVE MANY FOREIGN VISITORS, BUT THE RESTAURANT ONLY HAD TRADITIONAL JAPANESE FLOOR SEATING.
WOULDN'T IT BE GOOD IF THEY PROVIDED ALTERNATE SEATING TOO?
TAMAKI!!

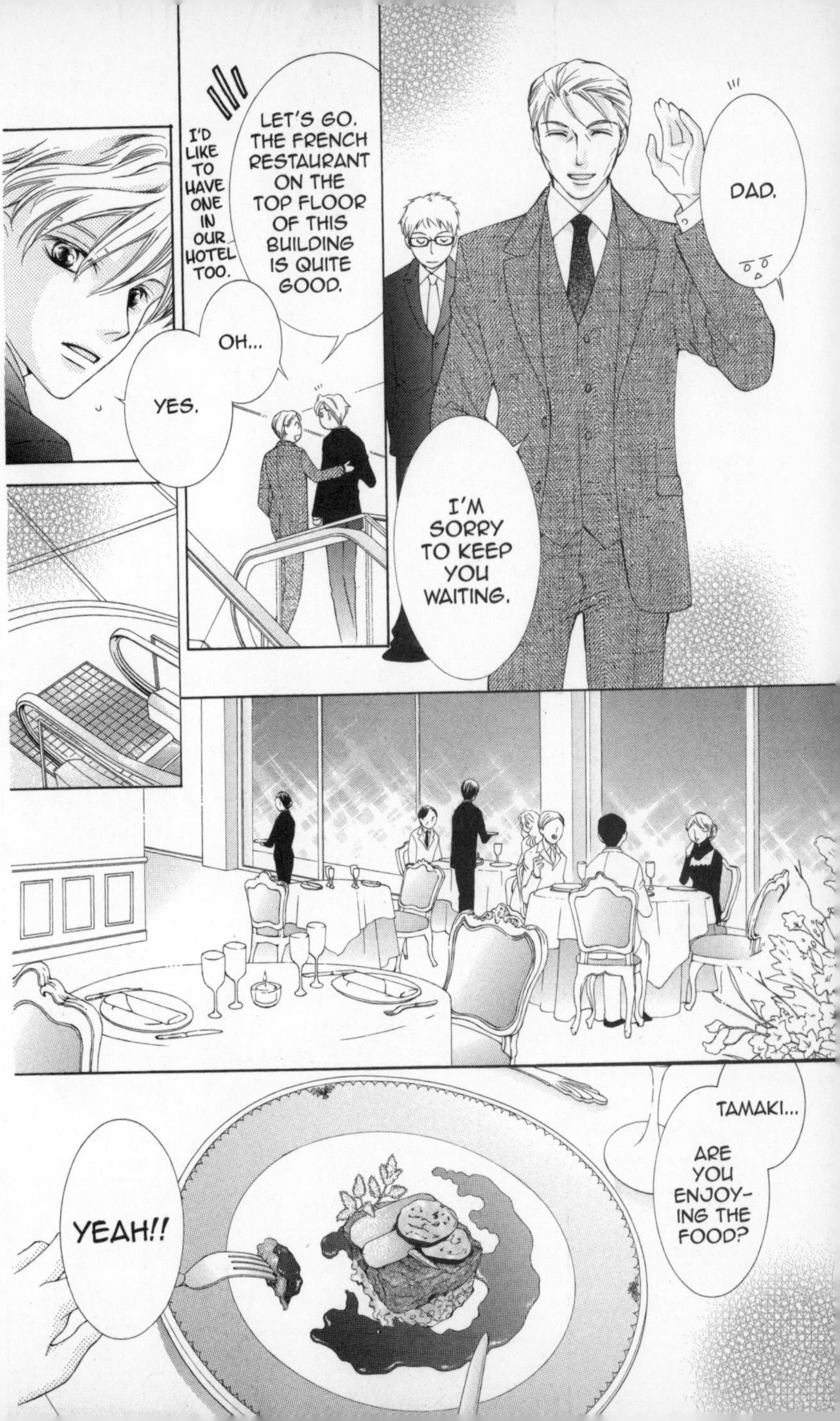
DAD.
I'M SORRY TO KEEP YOU WAITING.
LET'S GO. THE FRENCH RESTAURANT ON THE TOP FLOOR OF THIS BUILDING IS QUITE GOOD.
I'D LIKE TO HAVE ONE IN OUR HOTEL TOO.
OH... YES.
TAMAKI... ARE YOU ENJOYING THE FOOD?
YEAH!!

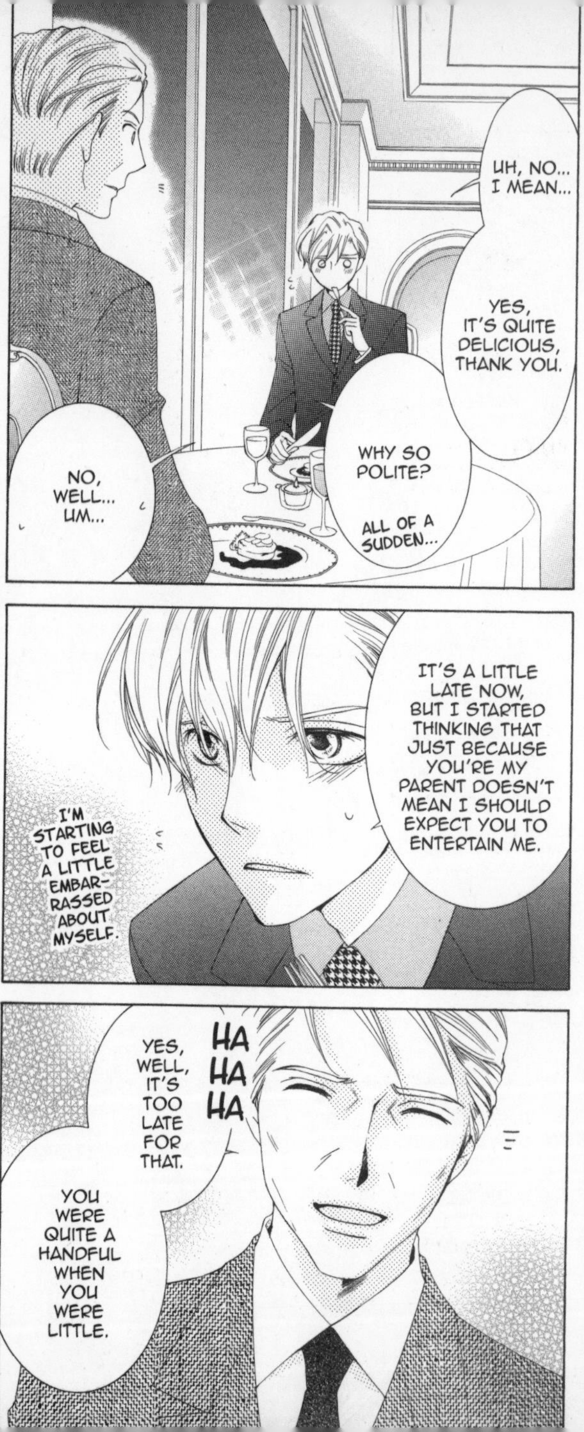
UH, NO... I MEAN...
YES, IT'S QUITE DELICIOUS, THANK YOU.
WHY SO POLITE?
ALL OF A SUDDEN...
NO, WELL... UM...
IT'S A LITTLE LATE NOW, BUT I STARTED THINKING THAT JUST BECAUSE YOU'RE MY PARENT DOESN'T MEAN I SHOULD EXPECT YOU TO ENTERTAIN ME.
I'M STARTING TO FEEL A LITTLE EMBARRASSED ABOUT MYSELF.
HA HA HA
YES, WELL, IT'S TOO LATE FOR THAT.
YOU WERE QUITE A HANDFUL WHEN YOU WERE LITTLE.

3

WHEN I LOOK AROUND MY DESK AND CAN'T FIND THINGS, I FIND THEM IN THE DRAWER IN THE KITCHEN, ON THE SHELF IN THE BATHROOM, OR ON MY SHOE RACK.

I WONDER WHY I CAN'T JUST PUT IT DOWN ON MY DESK BEFORE MOVING ON AND DOING SOMETHING ELSE.

BY THE WAY, WHEN I LOST MY WALLET, I LOOKED EVERYWHERE FOR IT. I THOUGHT TO MYSELF, "THERE'S NO WAY..." BUT I OVERTURNED THE TRASHCAN AND LOOKED INSIDE. THERE IT WAS. I'M TOO HORRIBLE...

MY MOTHER IS ALWAYS SAYING, "I HATE HOW YOUR FATHER IS ALWAYS FORGETTING HIS COAT (OR UMBRELLA OR WALLET OR BRIEFCASE) SOMEWHERE!!" I THINK I DEFINITELY SHARE A HEREDITARY TRAIT ON MY FATHER'S SIDE.

BUT AS MUCH AS I LOSE THINGS INSIDE MY HOUSE, I HAVE NEVER LOST SOMETHING WHILE I WAS OUT!!

ALTHOUGH I DID FORGET MY BACKPACK AT HOME TWICE WHEN I WAS IN SCHOOL.

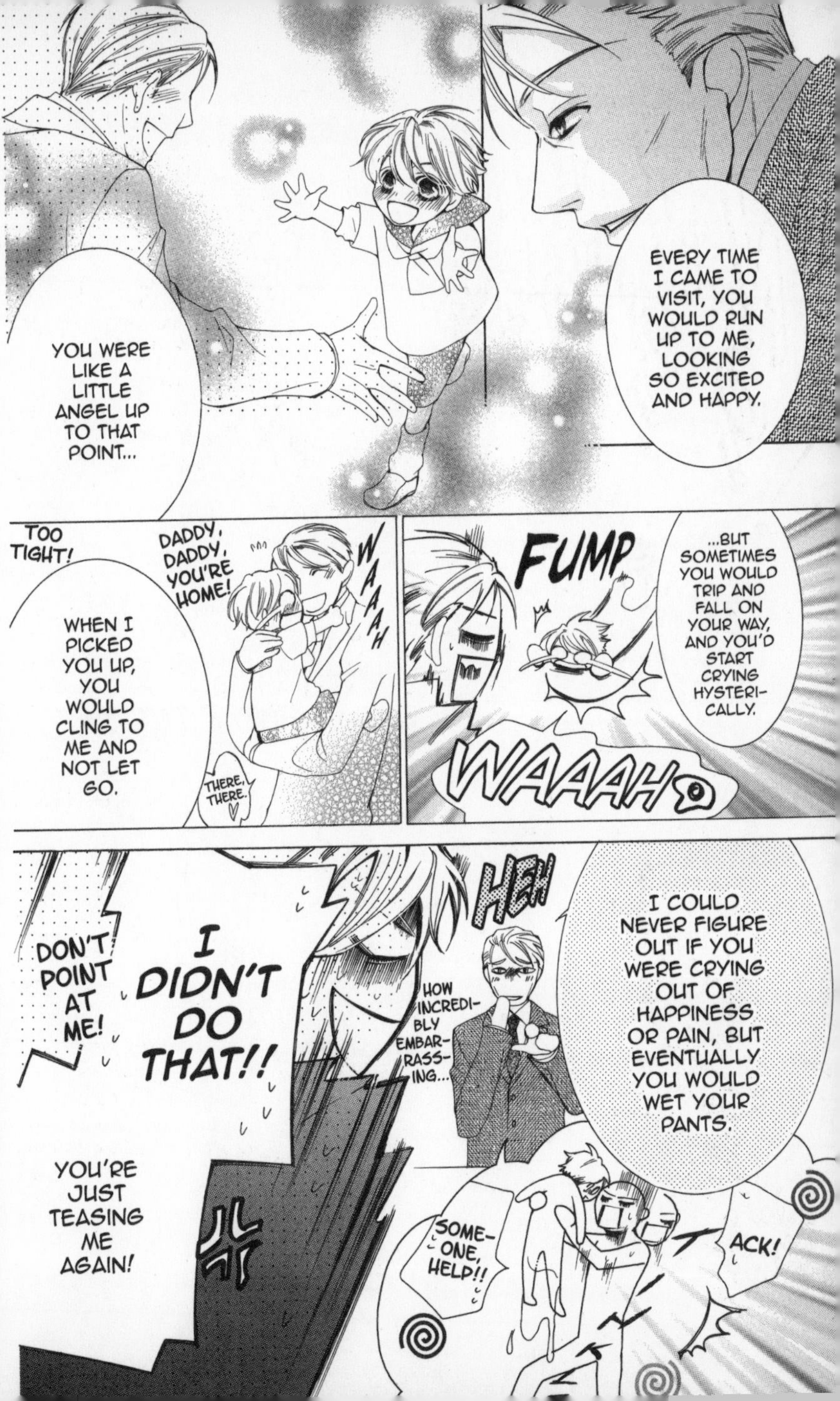
EVERY TIME I CAME TO VISIT, YOU WOULD RUN UP TO ME, LOOKING SO EXCITED AND HAPPY.
YOU WERE LIKE A LITTLE ANGEL UP TO THAT POINT...
...BUT SOMETIMES YOU WOULD TRIP AND FALL ON YOUR WAY, AND YOU'D START CRYING HYSTERICALLY.
FUMP
WAAAH
WAAAAH
DADDY, DADDY, YOU'RE HOME!
TOO TIGHT!
WHEN I PICKED YOU UP, YOU WOULD CLING TO ME AND NOT LET GO.
THERE, THERE.
I COULD NEVER FIGURE OUT IF YOU WERE CRYING OUT OF HAPPINESS OR PAIN, BUT EVENTUALLY YOU WOULD WET YOUR PANTS.
HEH
HOW INCREDIBLY EMBARRASSING...
ACK!
SOME-ONE, HELP!!
I DIDN'T DO THAT!!
DON'T POINT AT ME!
YOU'RE JUST TEASING ME AGAIN!

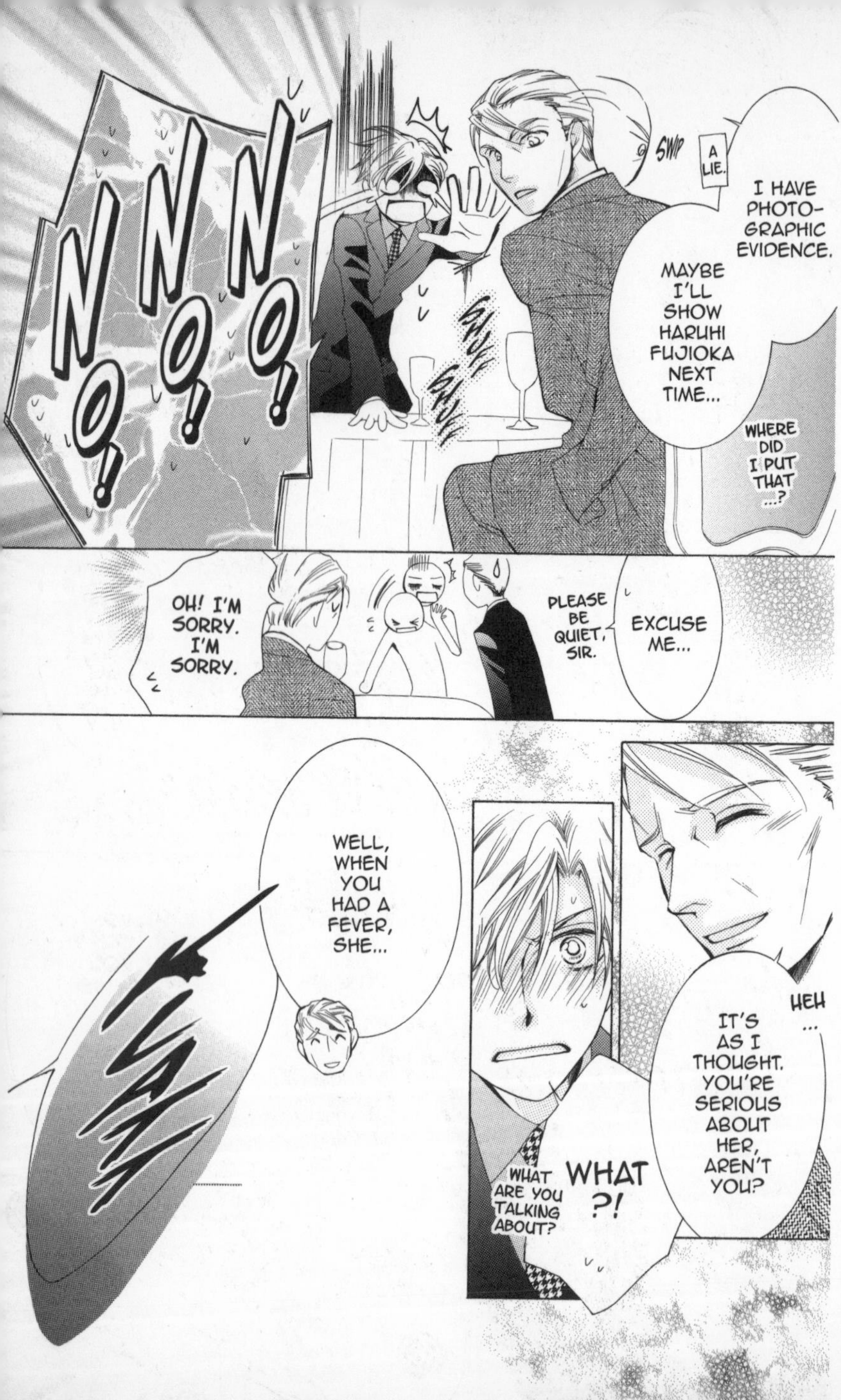
I HAVE PHOTOGRAPHIC EVIDENCE.
MAYBE I'LL SHOW HARUHI FUJIOKA NEXT TIME...
A LIE.
SWIP
WHERE DID I PUT THAT...?
NNNOOO!!!
EXCUSE ME...
PLEASE BE QUIET, SIR.
OH! I'M SORRY. I'M SORRY.
HEH...
IT'S AS I THOUGHT. YOU'RE SERIOUS ABOUT HER, AREN'T YOU?
WHAT?!
WHAT ARE YOU TALKING ABOUT?
WELL, WHEN YOU HAD A FEVER, SHE...

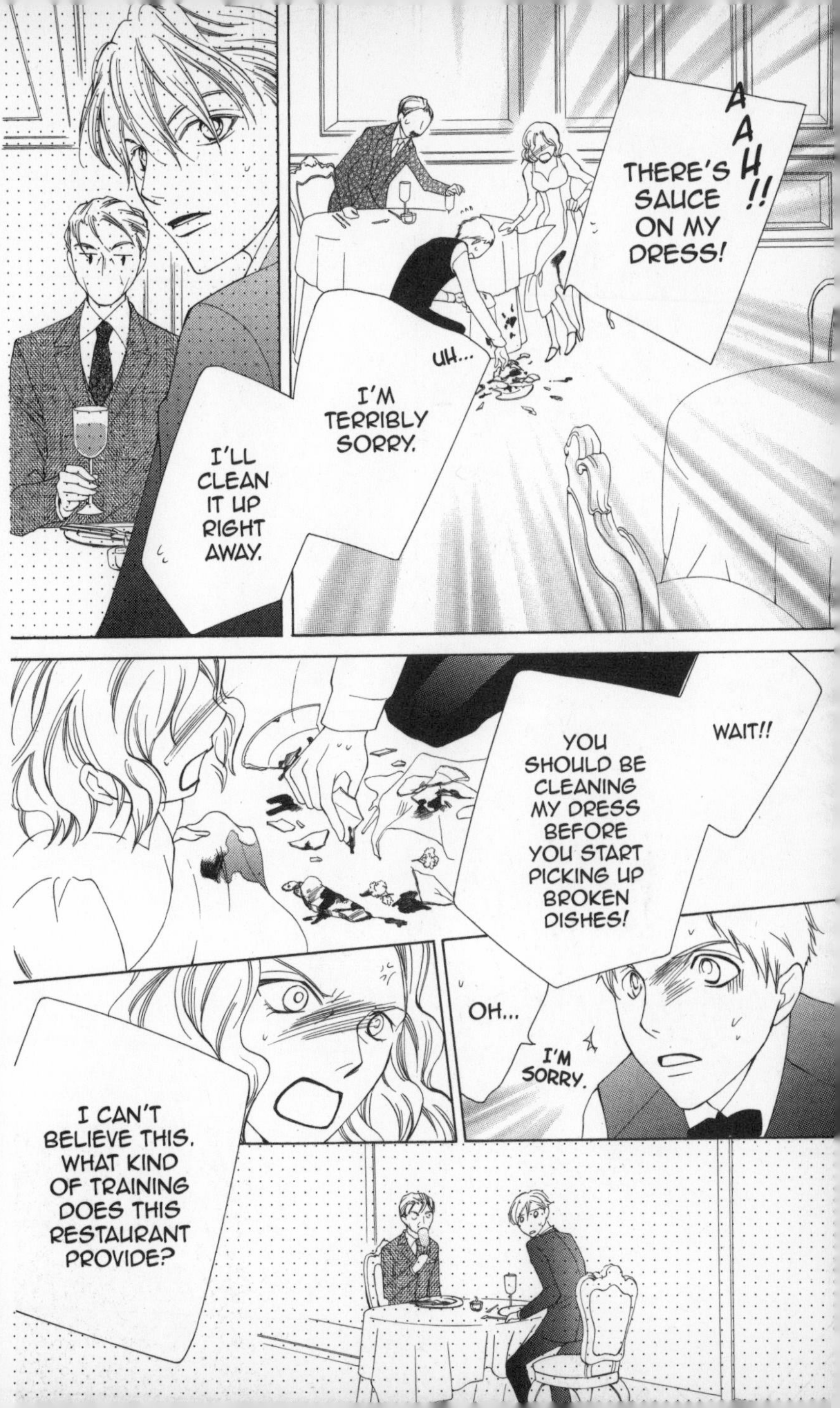
AAAH!!
THERE'S SAUCE ON MY DRESS!
UH...
I'M TERRIBLY SORRY.
I'LL CLEAN IT UP RIGHT AWAY.
WAIT!!
YOU SHOULD BE CLEANING MY DRESS BEFORE YOU START PICKING UP BROKEN DISHES!
OH...
I'M SORRY.
I CAN'T BELIEVE THIS. WHAT KIND OF TRAINING DOES THIS RESTAURANT PROVIDE?

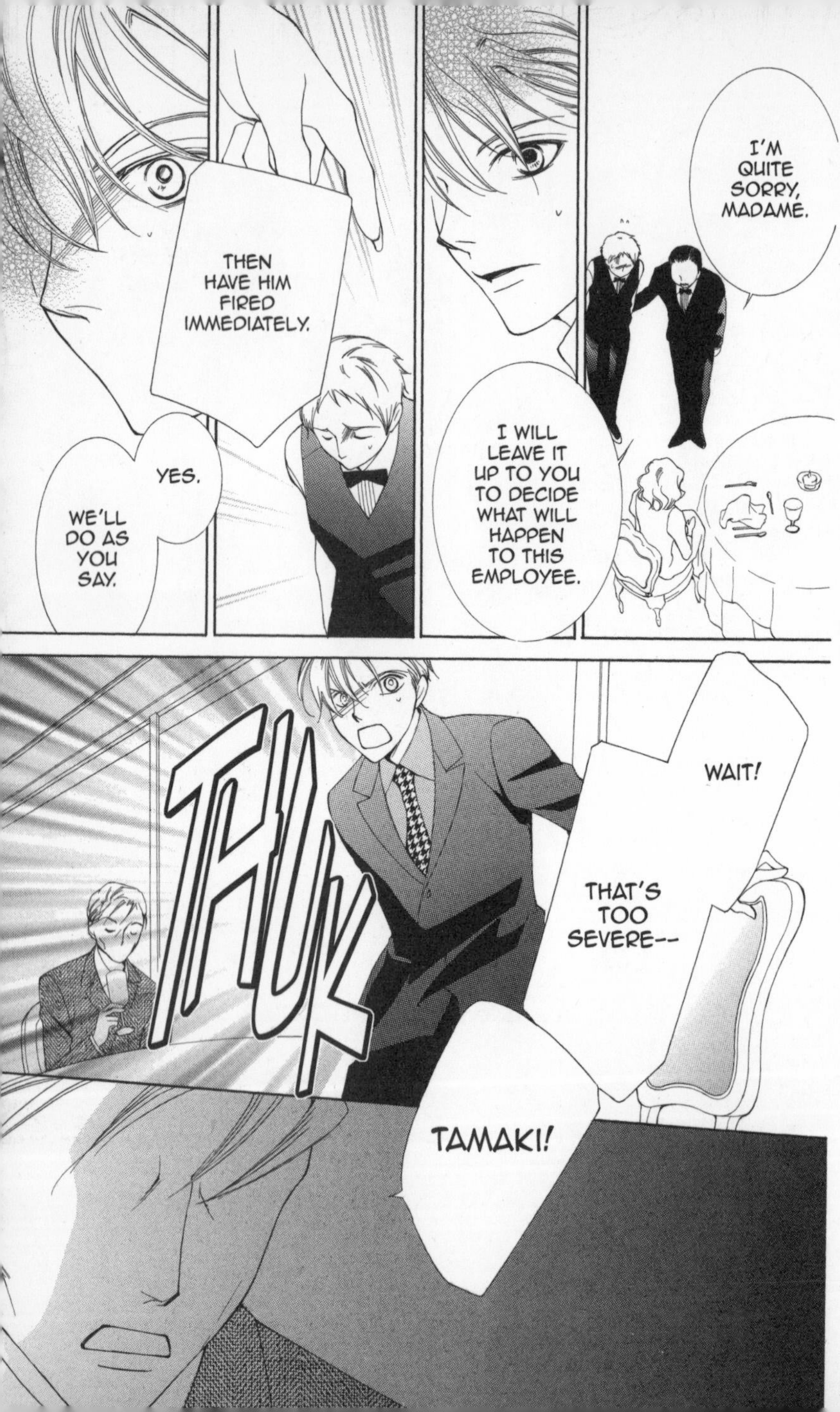
I'M QUITE SORRY, MADAME.
I WILL LEAVE IT UP TO YOU TO DECIDE WHAT WILL HAPPEN TO THIS EMPLOYEE.
THEN HAVE HIM FIRED IMMEDIATELY.
YES.
WE'LL DO AS YOU SAY.
WAIT!
THAT'S TOO SEVERE--
FLIP
TAMAKI!

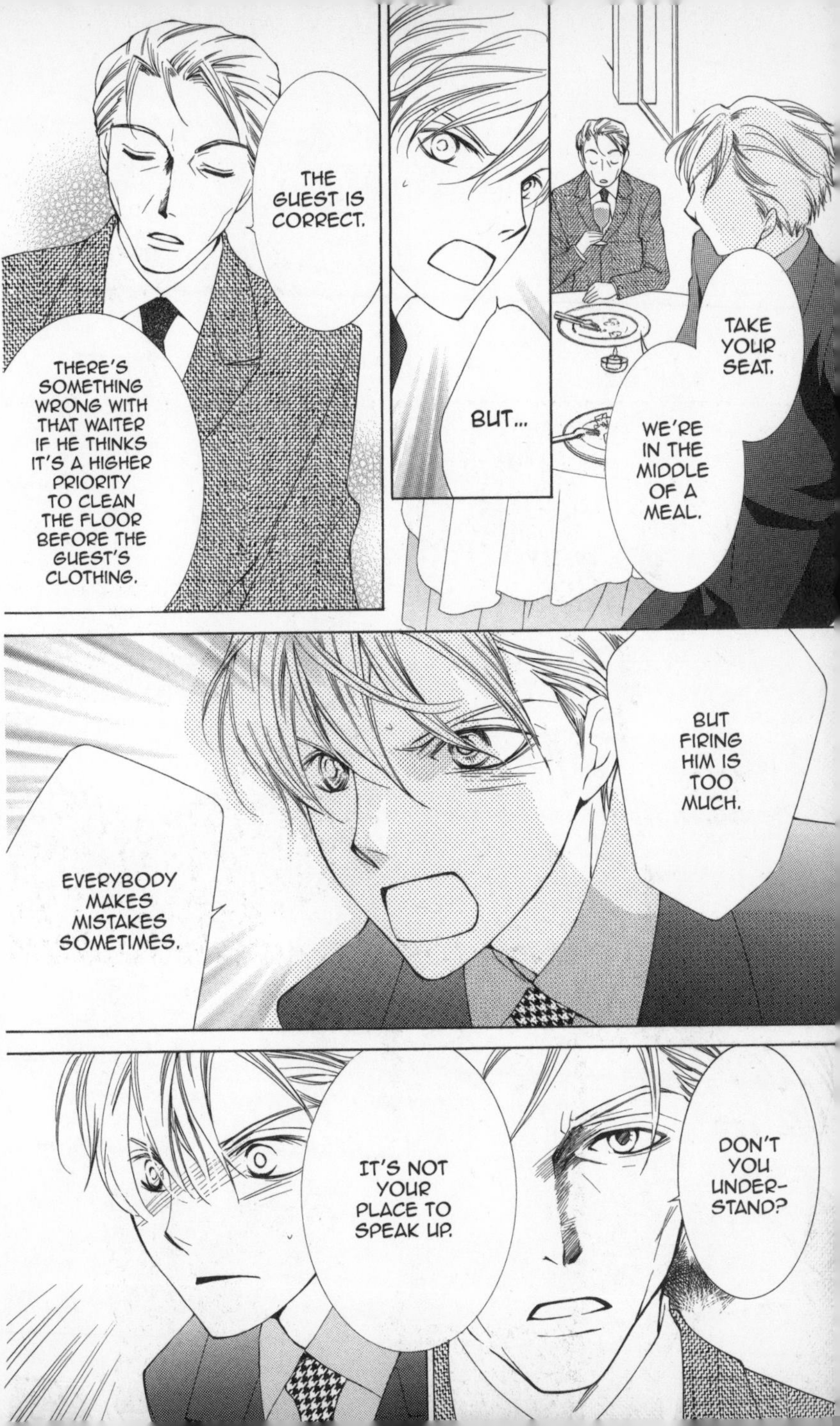
TAKE YOUR SEAT.
WE'RE IN THE MIDDLE OF A MEAL.
BUT...
THE GUEST IS CORRECT.
THERE'S SOMETHING WRONG WITH THAT WAITER IF HE THINKS IT'S A HIGHER PRIORITY TO CLEAN THE FLOOR BEFORE THE GUEST'S CLOTHING.
BUT FIRING HIM IS TOO MUCH.
EVERYBODY MAKES MISTAKES SOMETIMES.
DON'T YOU UNDER-STAND?
IT'S NOT YOUR PLACE TO SPEAK UP.

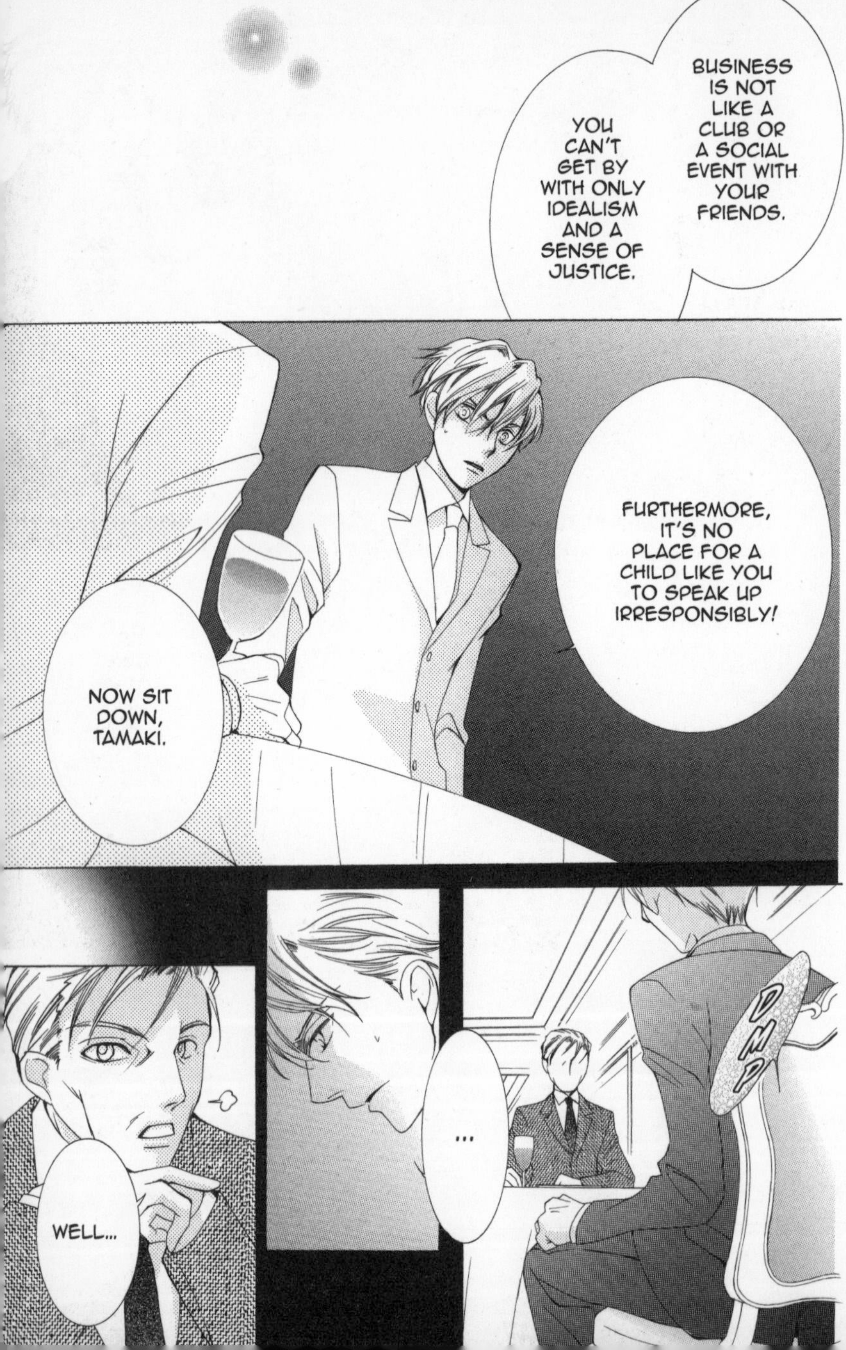
BUSINESS IS NOT LIKE A CLUB OR A SOCIAL EVENT WITH YOUR FRIENDS.
YOU CAN'T GET BY WITH ONLY IDEALISM AND A SENSE OF JUSTICE.
FURTHERMORE, IT'S NO PLACE FOR A CHILD LIKE YOU TO SPEAK UP IRRESPONSIBLY!
NOW SIT DOWN, TAMAKI.
DMP
...
WELL...

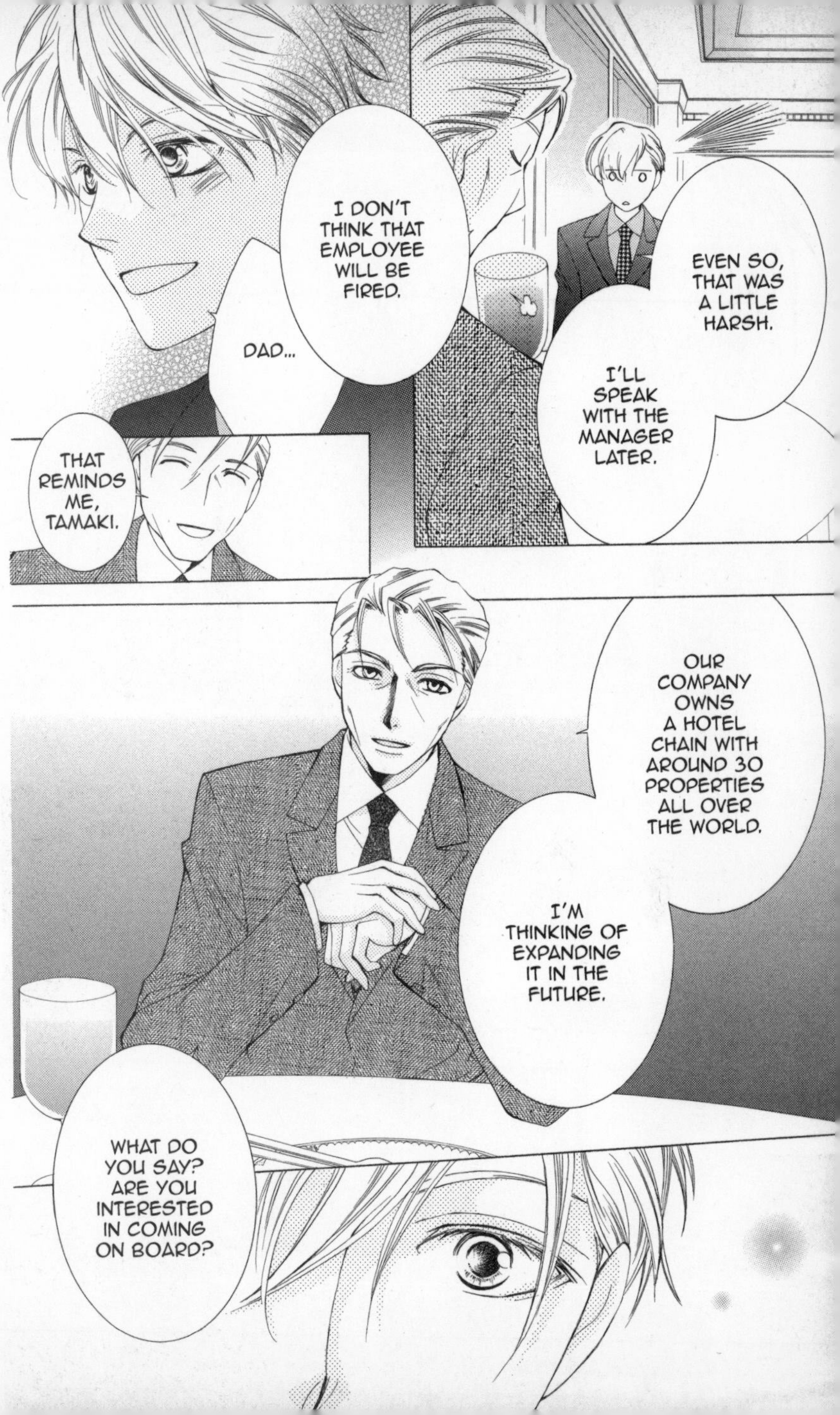
EVEN SO, THAT WAS A LITTLE HARSH.
I'LL SPEAK WITH THE MANAGER LATER.
I DON'T THINK THAT EMPLOYEE WILL BE FIRED.
DAD...
THAT REMINDS ME, TAMAKI.
OUR COMPANY OWNS A HOTEL CHAIN WITH AROUND 30 PROPERTIES ALL OVER THE WORLD.
I'M THINKING OF EXPANDING IT IN THE FUTURE.
WHAT DO YOU SAY? ARE YOU INTERESTED IN COMING ON BOARD?

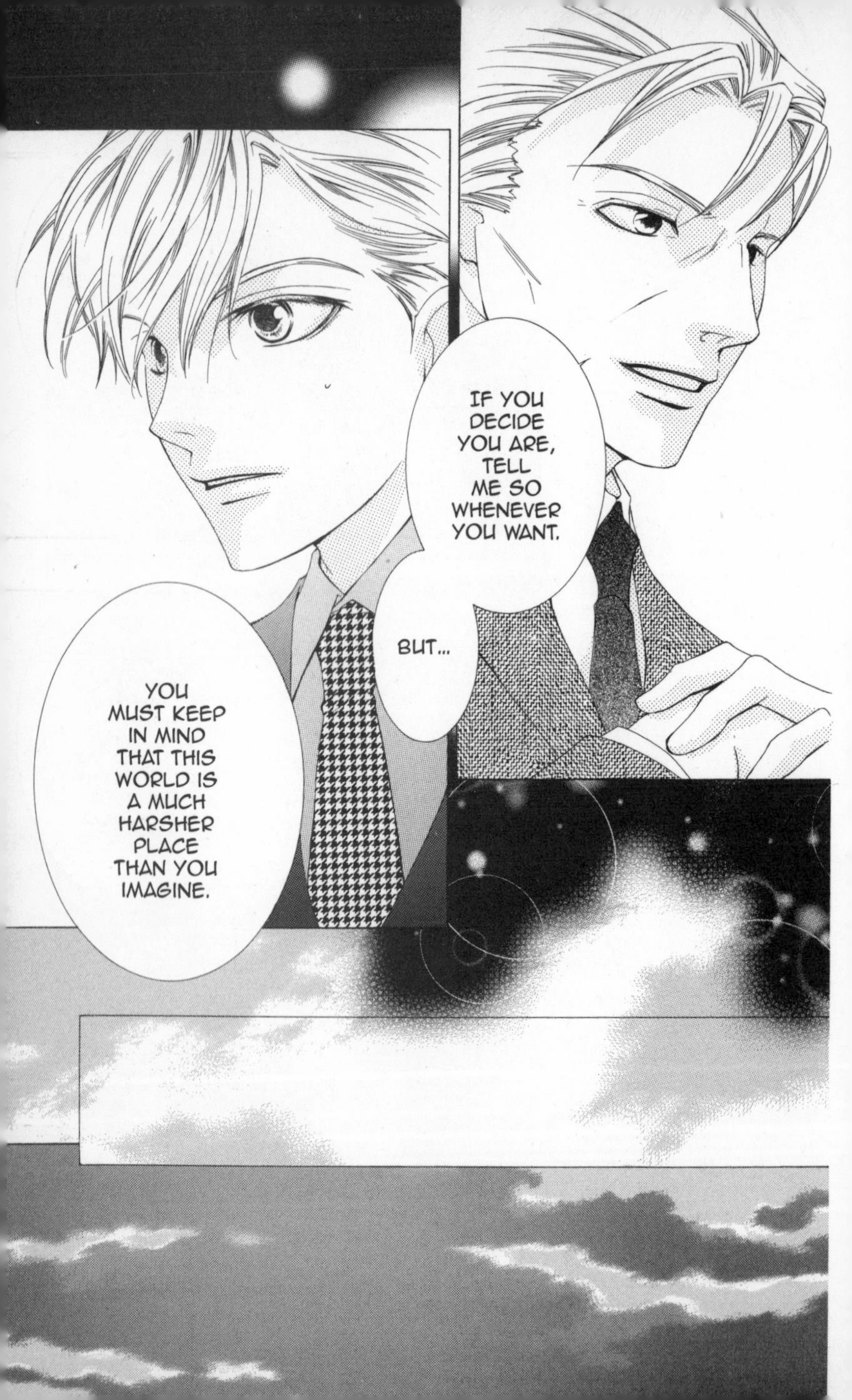
IF YOU DECIDE YOU ARE, TELL ME SO WHENEVER YOU WANT.
BUT...
YOU MUST KEEP IN MIND THAT THIS WORLD IS A MUCH HARSHER PLACE THAN YOU IMAGINE.

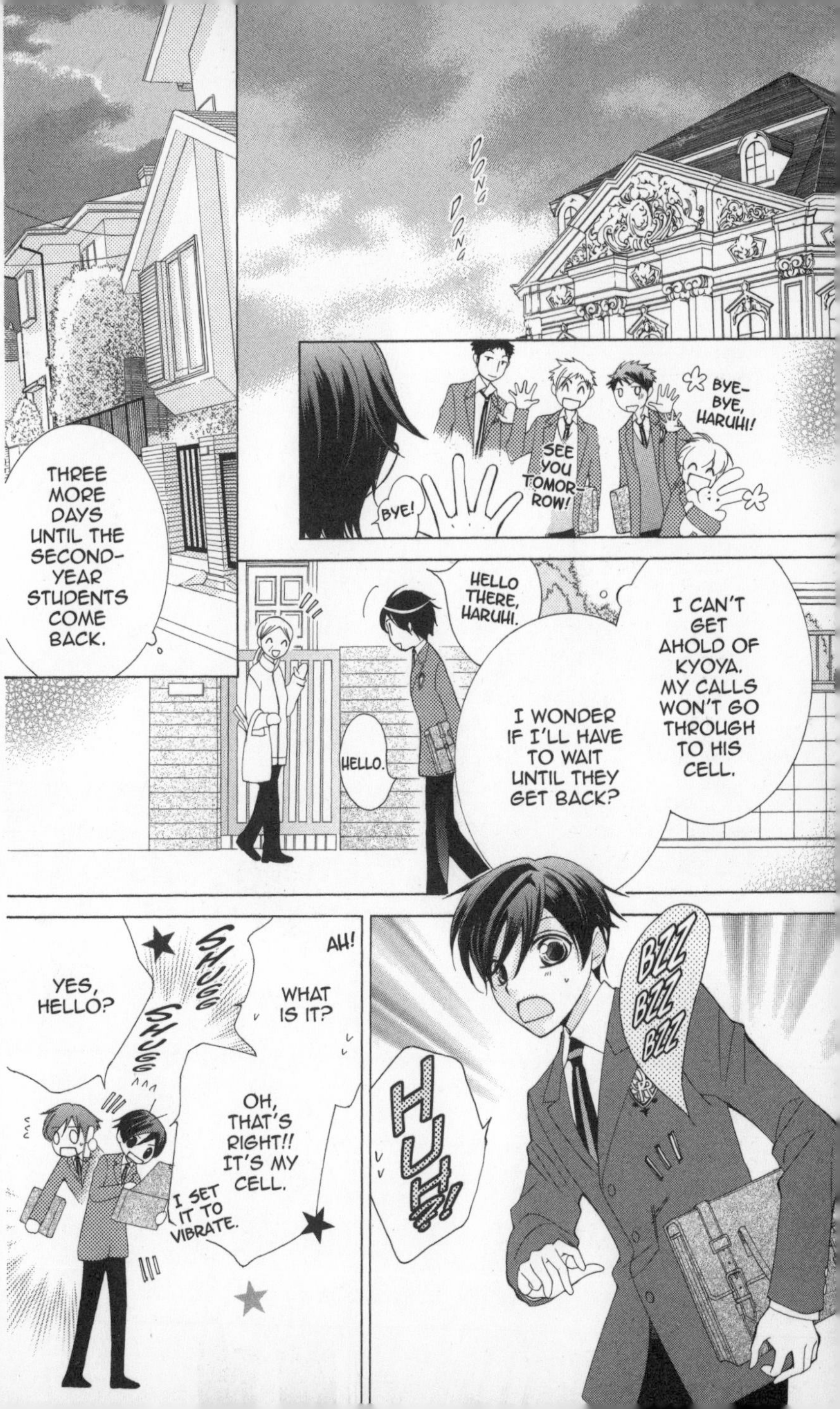
DONG
DONG
BYE-BYE, HARUHI!
SEE YOU TOMORROW!
BYE!
THREE MORE DAYS UNTIL THE SECOND-YEAR STUDENTS COME BACK.
HELLO THERE, HARUHI.
HELLO.
I CAN'T GET AHOLD OF KYOYA. MY CALLS WON'T GO THROUGH TO HIS CELL.
I WONDER IF I'LL HAVE TO WAIT UNTIL THEY GET BACK?
BZZ BZZ BZZ
HUH!
AH!
WHAT IS IT?
OH, THAT'S RIGHT!! IT'S MY CELL.
I SET IT TO VIBRATE.
SHUGG SHUGG
YES, HELLO?

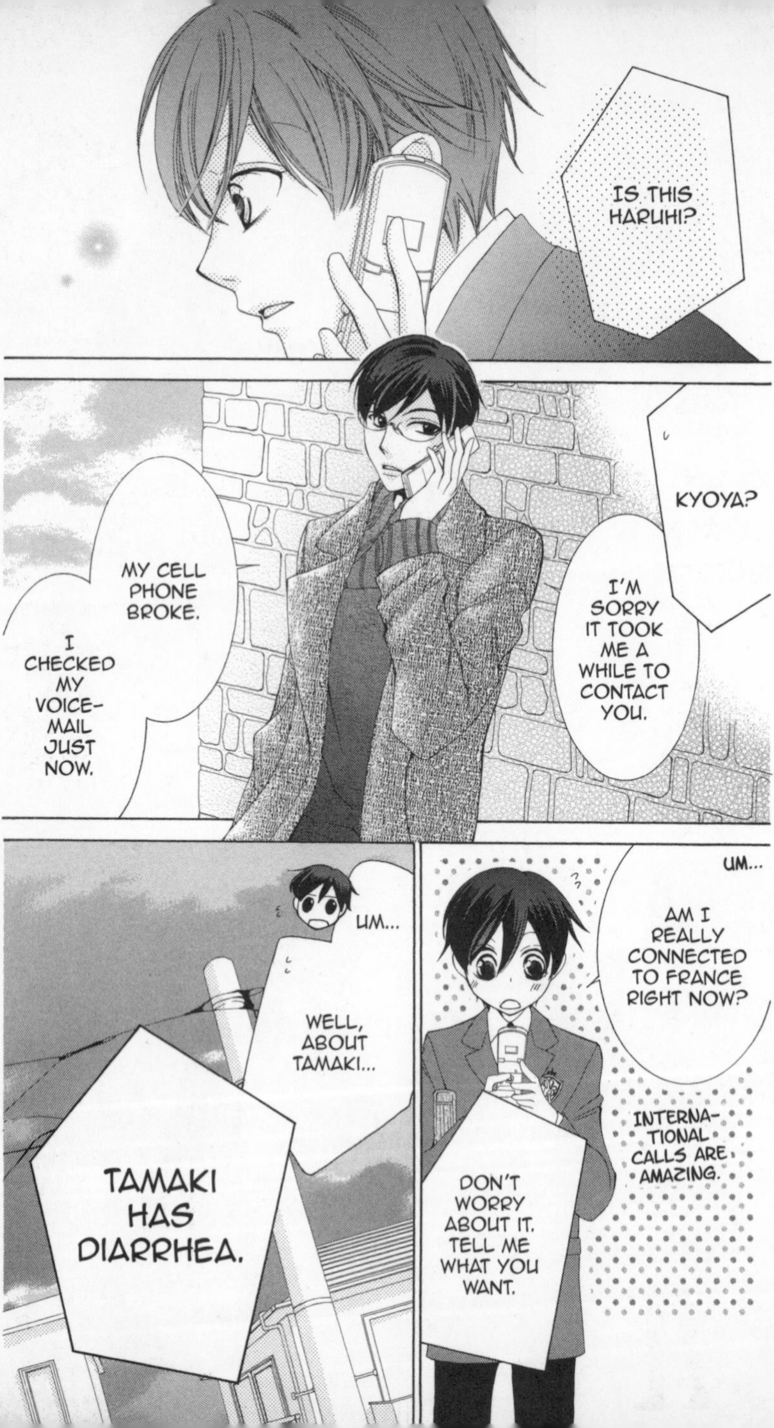
IS THIS HARUHI?
KYOYA?
I'M SORRY IT TOOK ME A WHILE TO CONTACT YOU.
MY CELL PHONE BROKE.
I CHECKED MY VOICE-MAIL JUST NOW.
UM...
AM I REALLY CONNECTED TO FRANCE RIGHT NOW?
INTERNATIONAL CALLS ARE AMAZING.
DON'T WORRY ABOUT IT. TELL ME WHAT YOU WANT.
UM...
WELL, ABOUT TAMAKI...
TAMAKI HAS DIARRHEA.

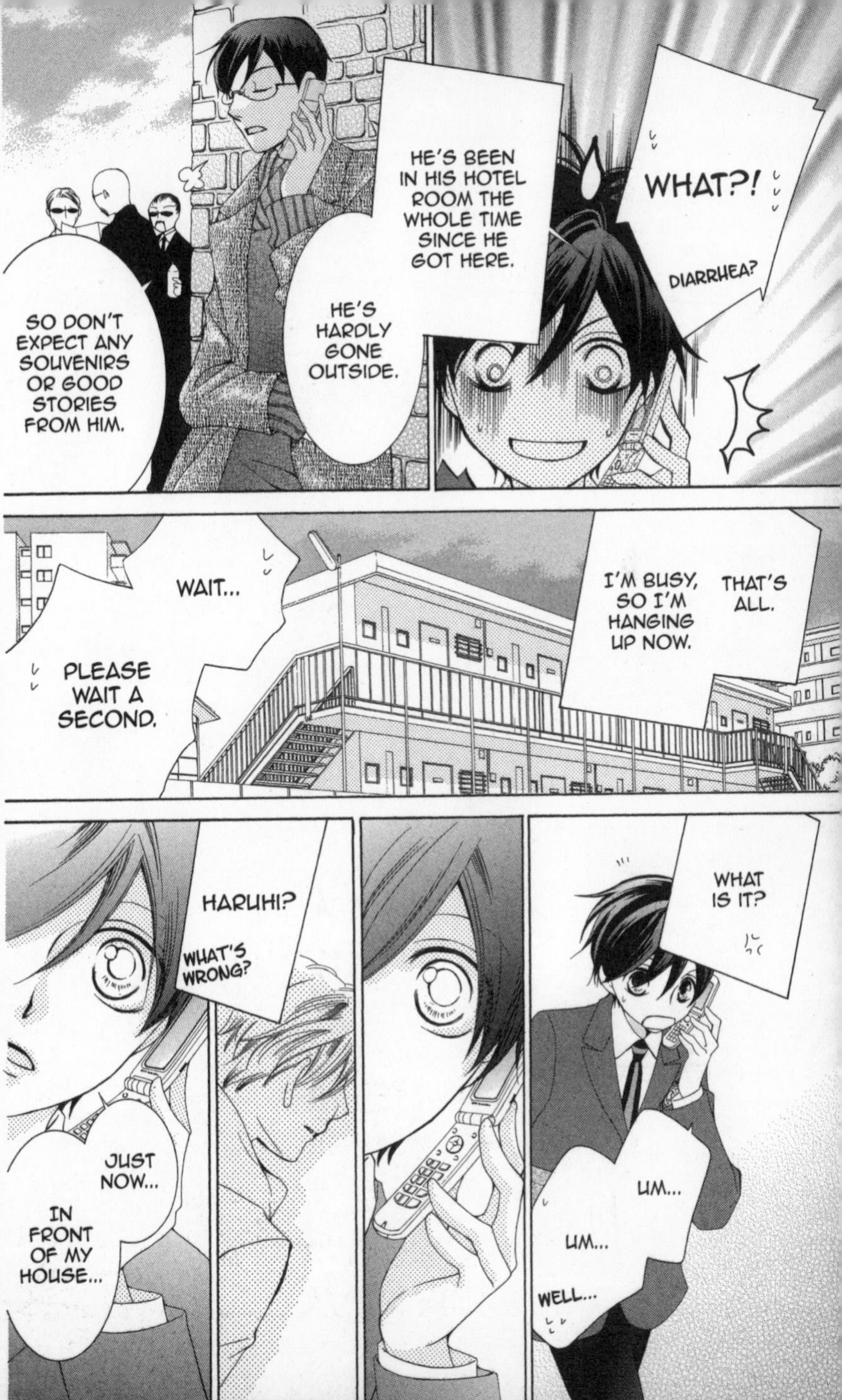
WHAT?!
DIARRHEA?
HE'S BEEN IN HIS HOTEL ROOM THE WHOLE TIME SINCE HE GOT HERE.
HE'S HARDLY GONE OUTSIDE.
SO DON'T EXPECT ANY SOUVENIRS OR GOOD STORIES FROM HIM.
THAT'S ALL.
I'M BUSY, SO I'M HANGING UP NOW.
WAIT...
PLEASE WAIT A SECOND.
WHAT IS IT?
UM...
UM...
WELL...
HARUHI?
WHAT'S WRONG?
JUST NOW...
IN FRONT OF MY HOUSE...

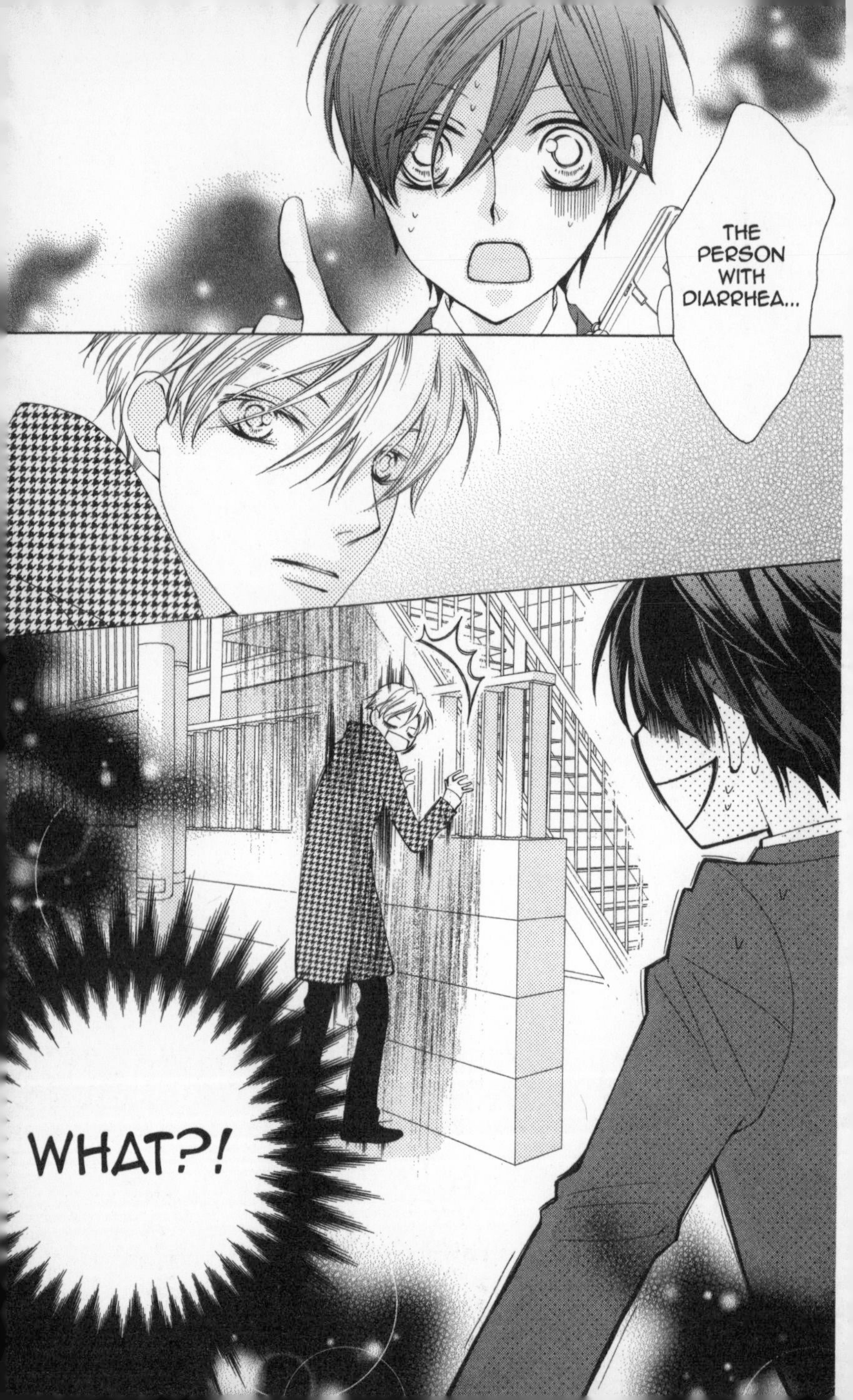
THE PERSON WITH DIARRHEA...
WHAT?!

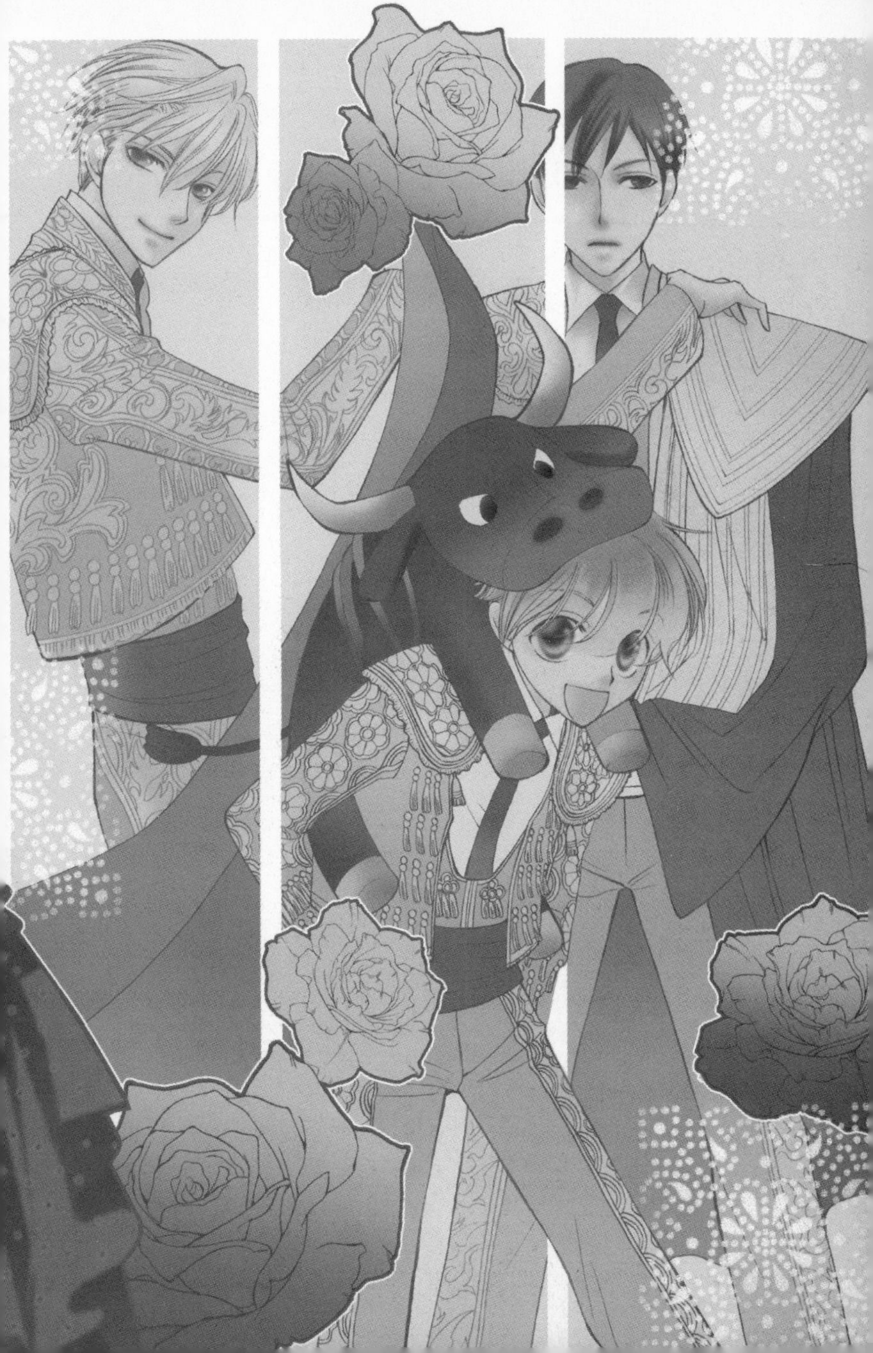

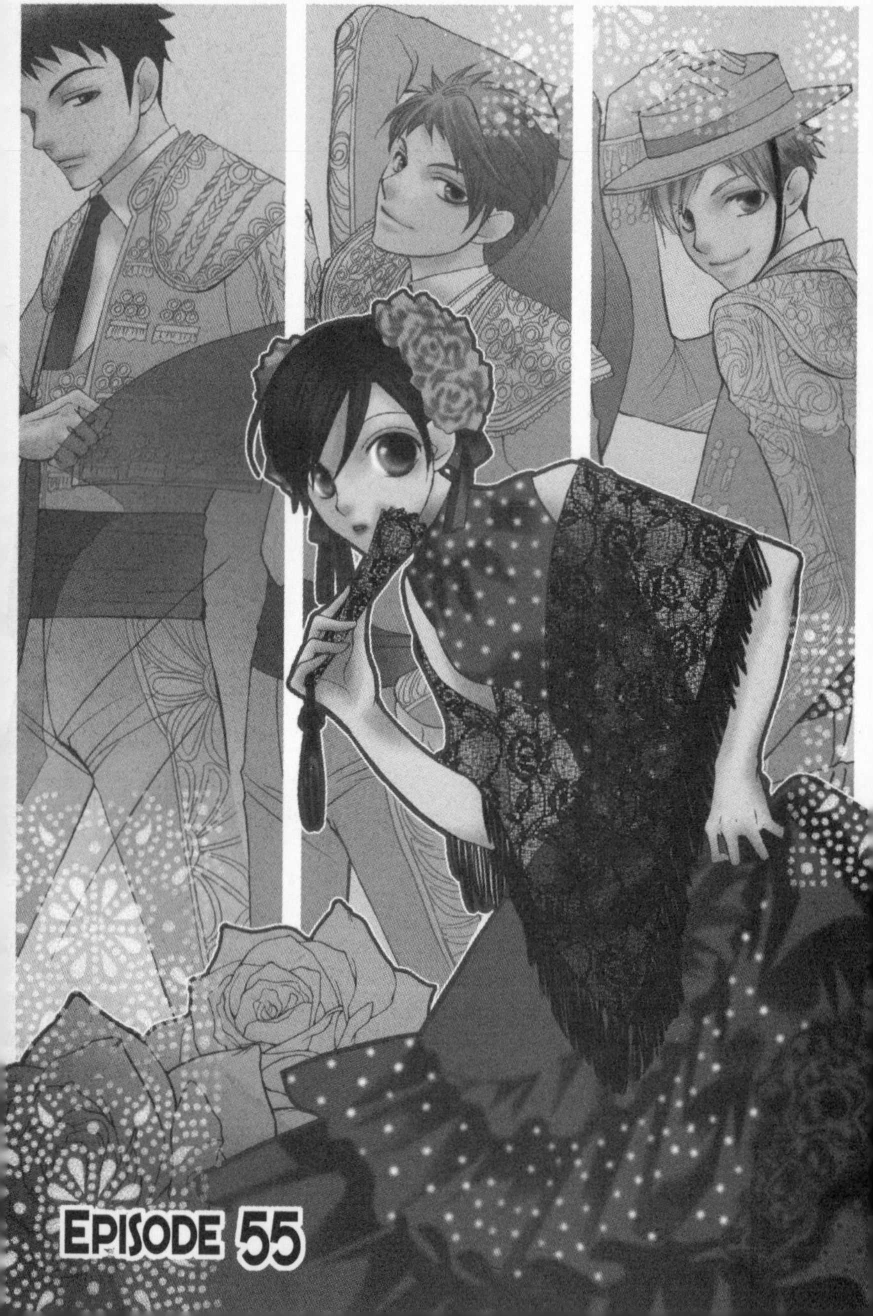
EPISODE 55

GUEST ROOM: FAXES

SPECIAL THANKS TO
MOMOE EZAKI!!

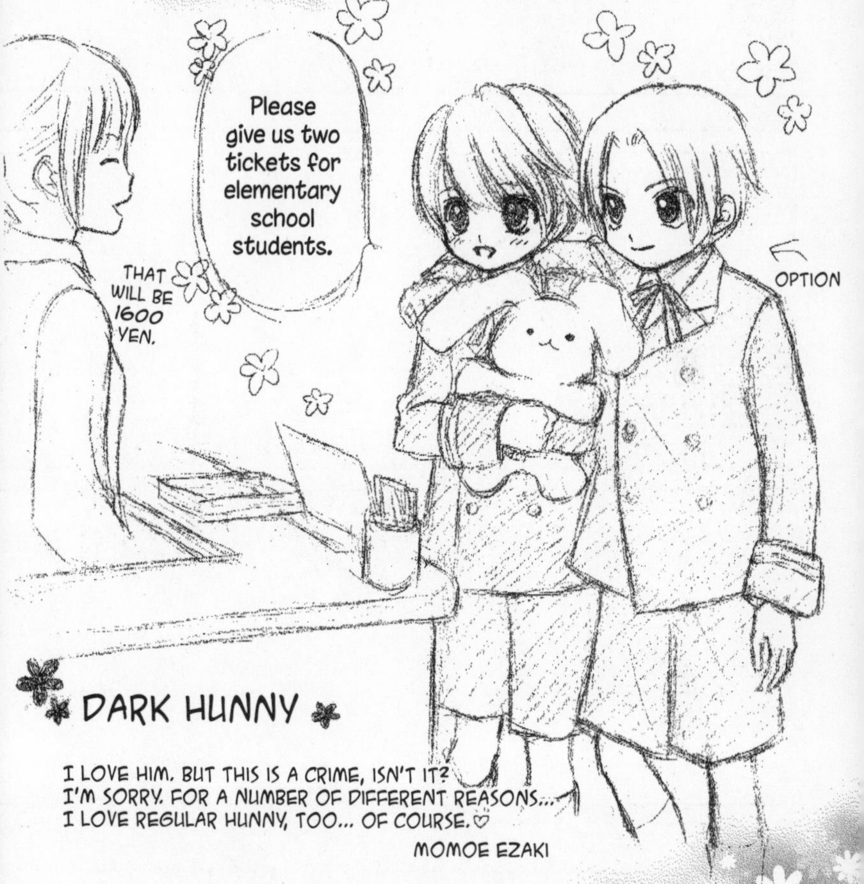
Please give us two tickets for elementary school students.
THAT WILL BE 1600 YEN.
OPTION

DARK HUNNY

I LOVE HIM. BUT THIS IS A CRIME, ISN'T IT?
I'M SORRY. FOR A NUMBER OF DIFFERENT REASONS...
I LOVE REGULAR HUNNY, TOO... OF COURSE.♡

MOMOE EZAKI

EZAKI-SAN, WHO HAS A FIRM GRIP ON HATORI'S HEART BECAUSE OF HER UNIQUE STYLE OF WORK, DREW AN IMAGE FOR US!! HUNNY IS TOO BLACK...THE WAY HE'S STANDING, SLIGHTLY KNOCK-KNEED, IS THE KEY. IT'S VERY CUTE, BUT PLEASE DON'T IMITATE IT!!! (TRULY!!) EZAKI-SAN IS CHILDHOOD FRIENDS WITH MY SUPER STAFF MEMBER YUI. WHEN I HEARD ABOUT IT FROM YUI, I REALLY FELT THAT THE WORLD IS SUCH A SMALL PLACE! YOU CAN ALSO READ A WEB-ONLY COMIC BY EZAKI-SAN ON THE HAKUSENSHA WEBSITE. YOU MUST CHECK IT OUT!!!

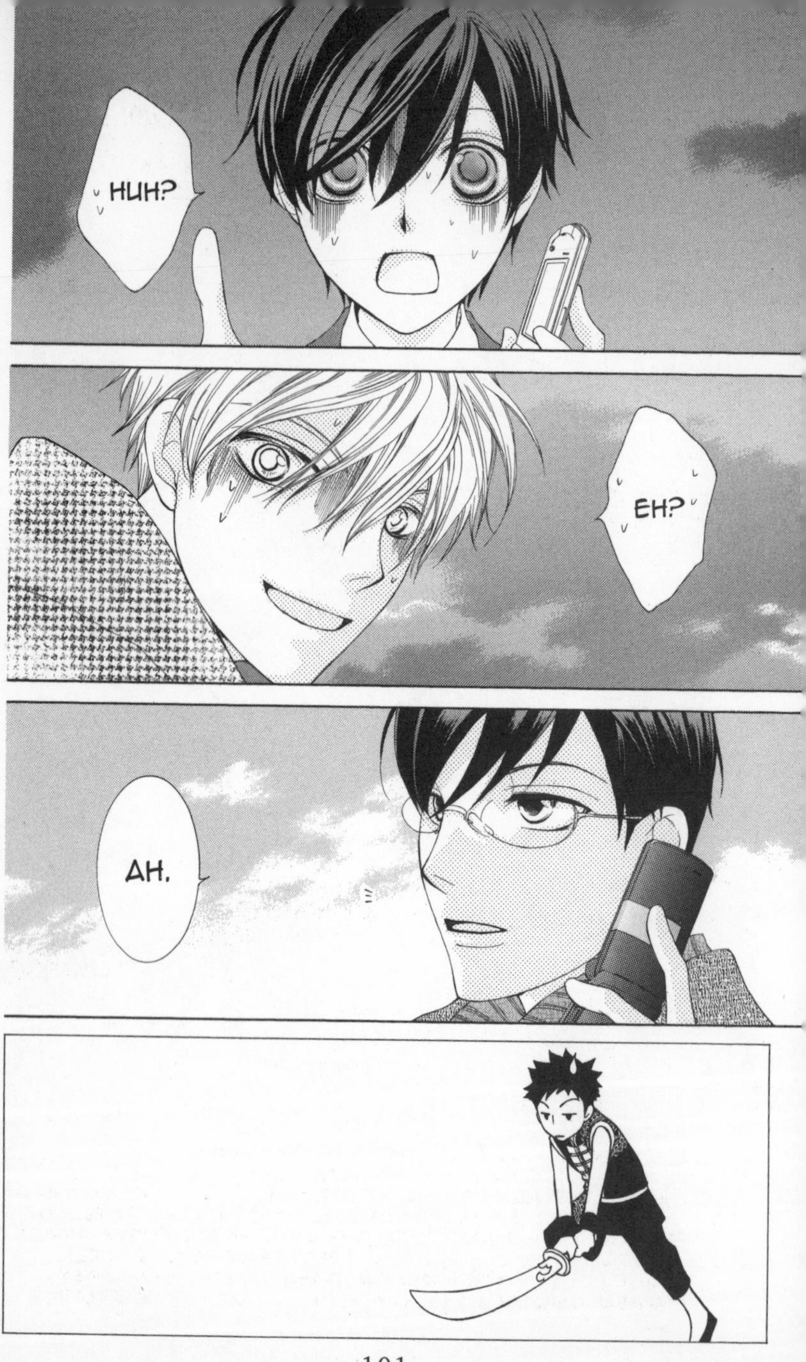
HUH?
EH?
AH.

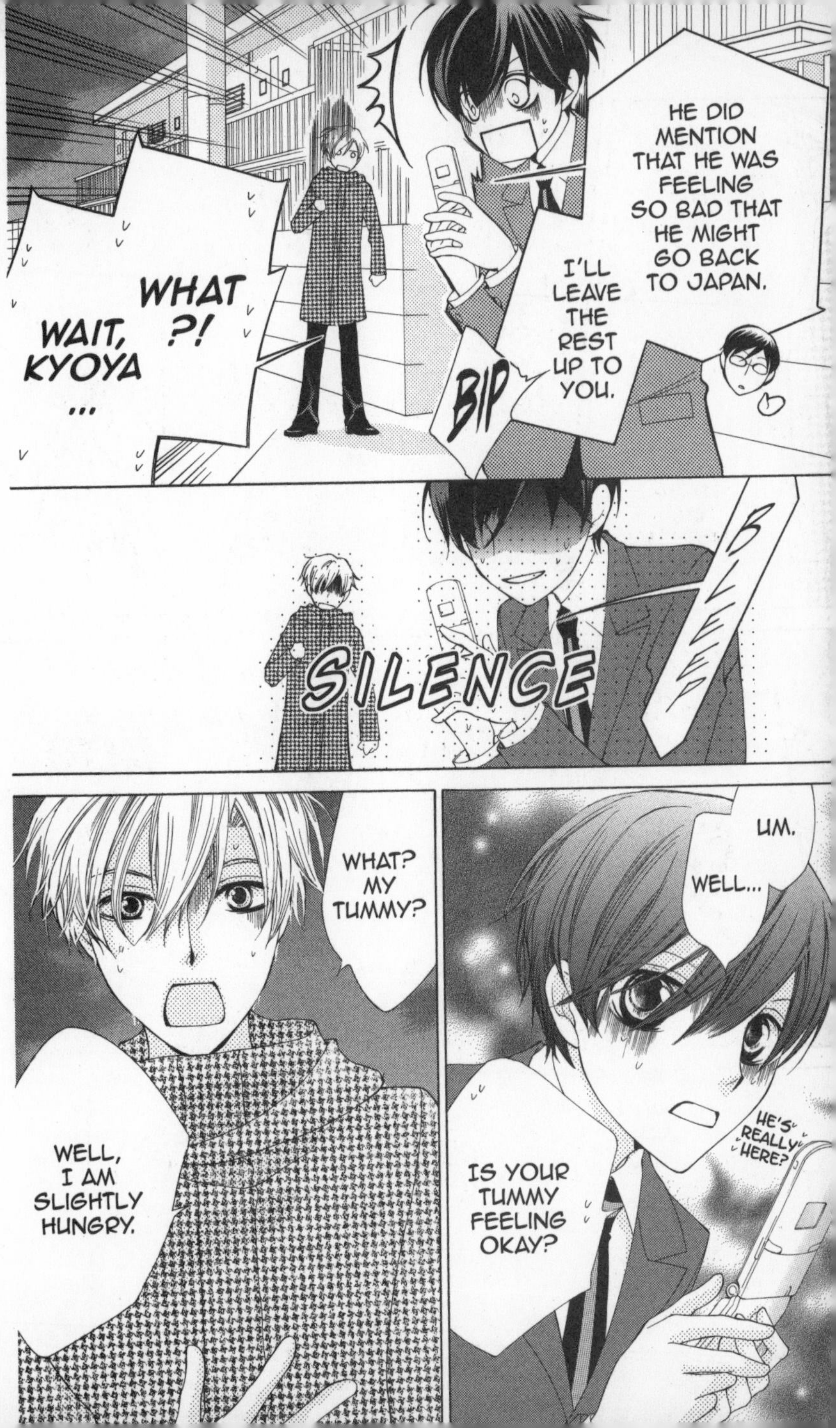
HE DID MENTION THAT HE WAS FEELING SO BAD THAT HE MIGHT GO BACK TO JAPAN.
I'LL LEAVE THE REST UP TO YOU.
BIP
WHAT ?!
WAIT, KYOYA ...
SILENCE
UM.
WELL...
HE'S REALLY HERE?
IS YOUR TUMMY FEELING OKAY?
WHAT? MY TUMMY?
WELL, I AM SLIGHTLY HUNGRY.

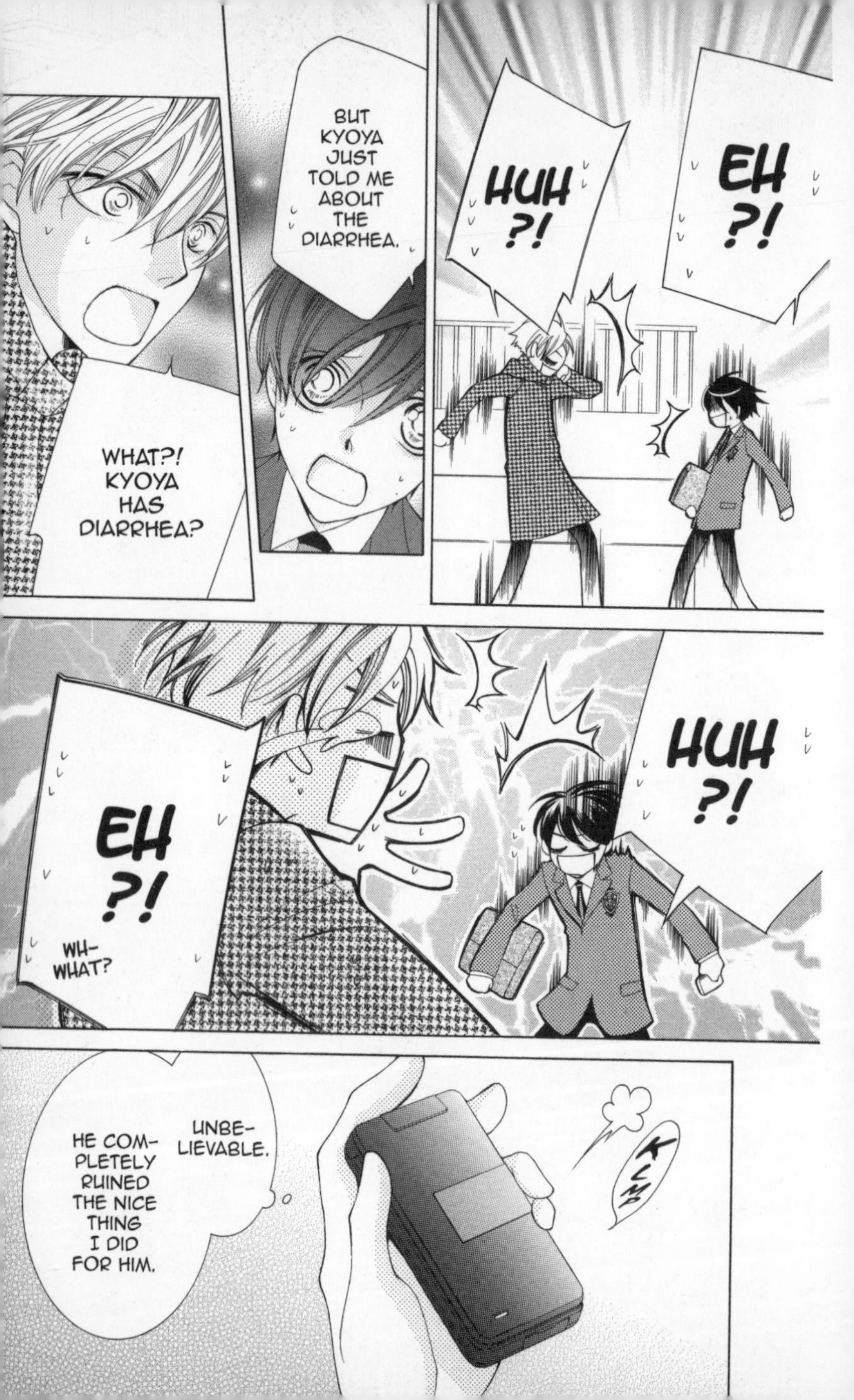
EH ?!
HUH ?!
BUT KYOYA JUST TOLD ME ABOUT THE DIARRHEA.
WHAT?! KYOYA HAS DIARRHEA?
HUH ?!
EH ?!
WH-WHAT?
KUMP
UNBE-LIEVABLE.
HE COM-PLETELY RUINED THE NICE THING I DID FOR HIM.

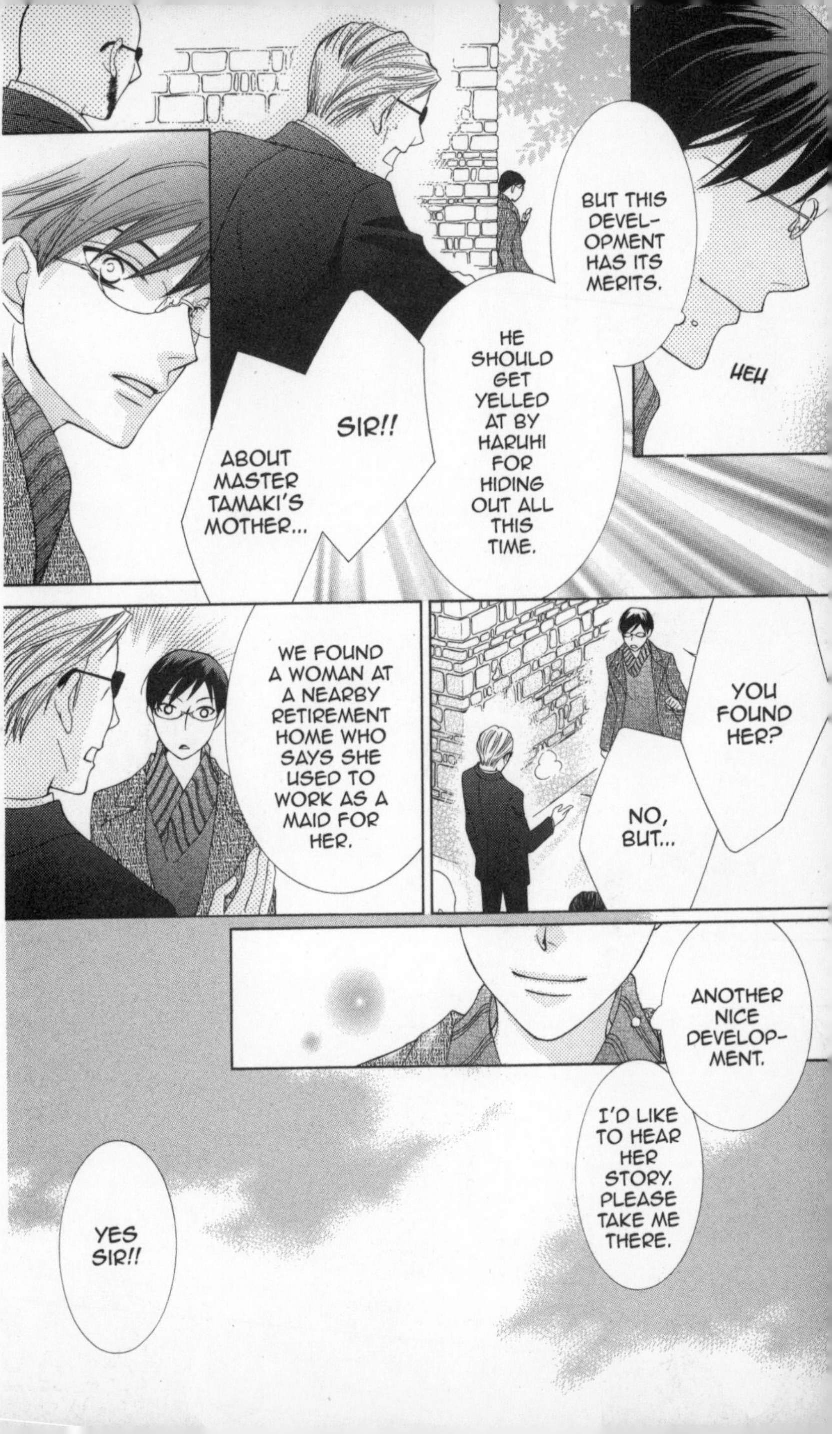
BUT THIS DEVEL- OPMENT HAS ITS MERITS.
HEH
HE SHOULD GET YELLED AT BY HARUHI FOR HIDING OUT ALL THIS TIME.
SIR!!
ABOUT MASTER TAMAKI'S MOTHER...
YOU FOUND HER?
NO, BUT...
WE FOUND A WOMAN AT A NEARBY RETIREMENT HOME WHO SAYS SHE USED TO WORK AS A MAID FOR HER.
ANOTHER NICE DEVELOP- MENT.
I'D LIKE TO HEAR HER STORY. PLEASE TAKE ME THERE.
YES SIR!!

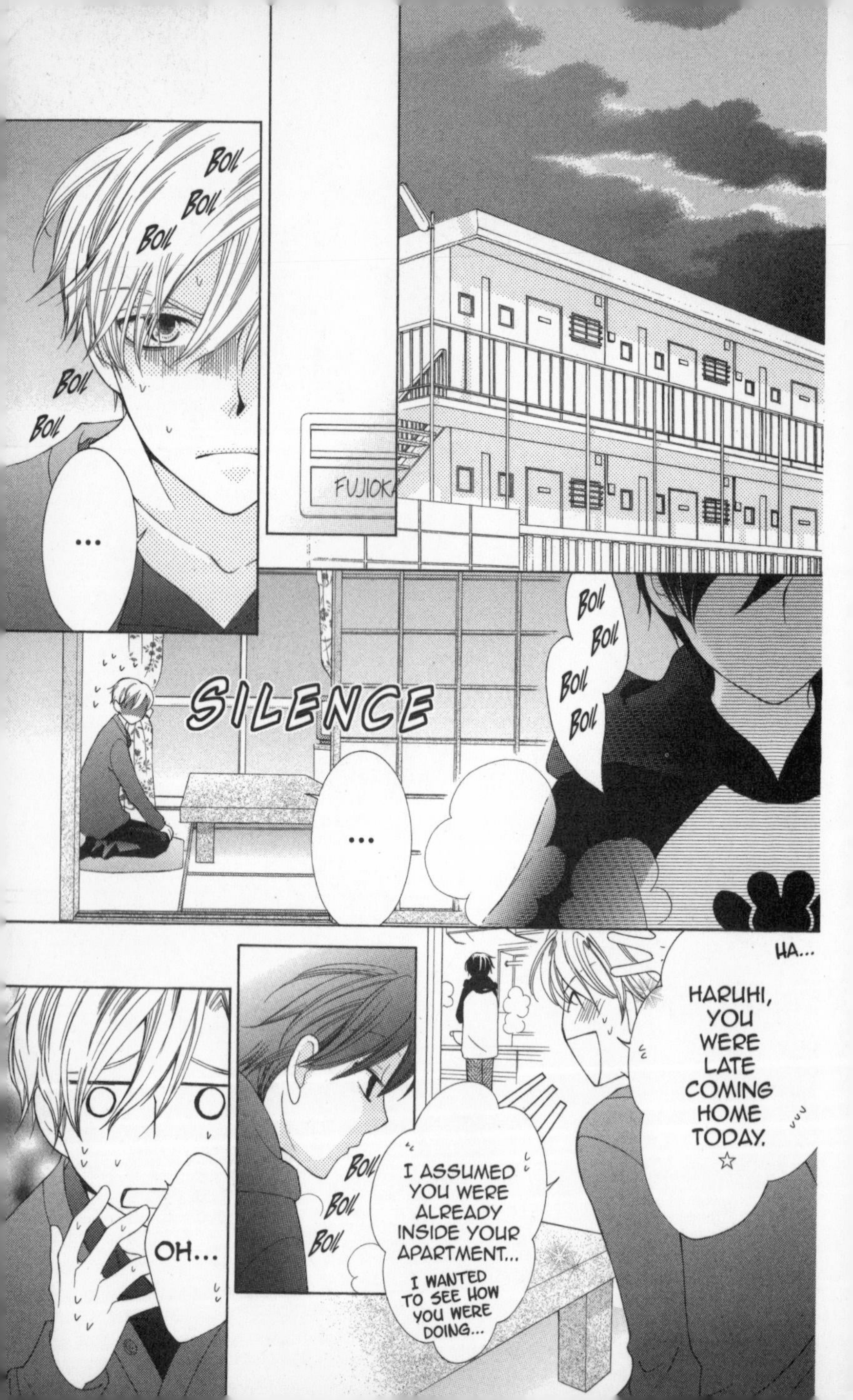
FUJIOKA
BOIL
BOIL
BOIL
BOIL
BOIL
...
BOIL
BOIL
BOIL
BOIL
...
SILENCE
HA...
HARUHI, YOU WERE LATE COMING HOME TODAY. ☆
BOIL
BOIL
BOIL
I ASSUMED YOU WERE ALREADY INSIDE YOUR APARTMENT...
I WANTED TO SEE HOW YOU WERE DOING...
OH...

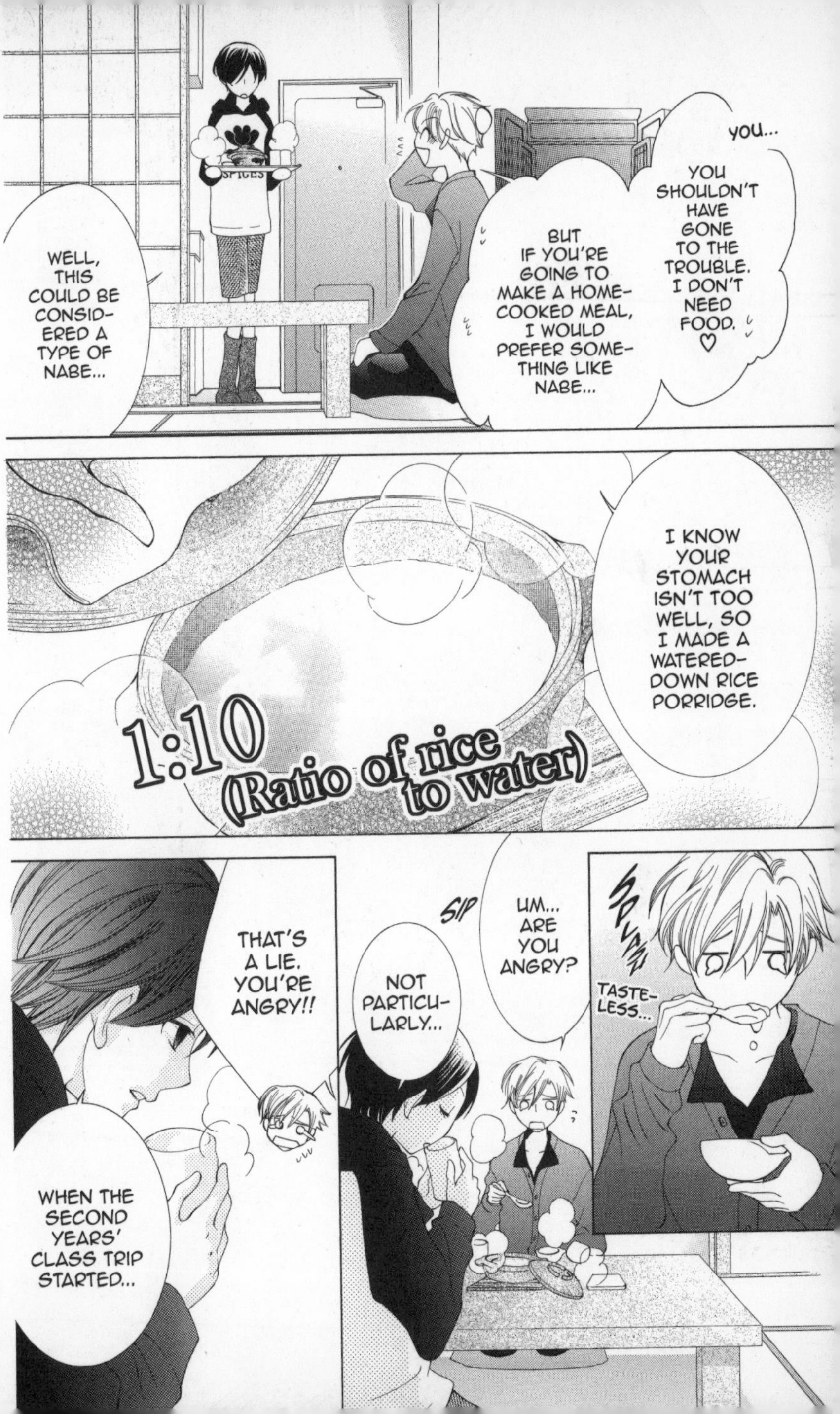
YOU...
YOU SHOULDN'T HAVE GONE TO THE TROUBLE. I DON'T NEED FOOD. ♡
BUT IF YOU'RE GOING TO MAKE A HOME-COOKED MEAL, I WOULD PREFER SOMETHING LIKE NABE...
WELL, THIS COULD BE CONSIDERED A TYPE OF NABE...
I KNOW YOUR STOMACH ISN'T TOO WELL, SO I MADE A WATERED-DOWN RICE PORRIDGE.
1:10 (Ratio of rice to water)
TASTE-LESS...
UM... ARE YOU ANGRY?
SIP
NOT PARTICU-LARLY...
THAT'S A LIE. YOU'RE ANGRY!!
WHEN THE SECOND YEARS' CLASS TRIP STARTED...

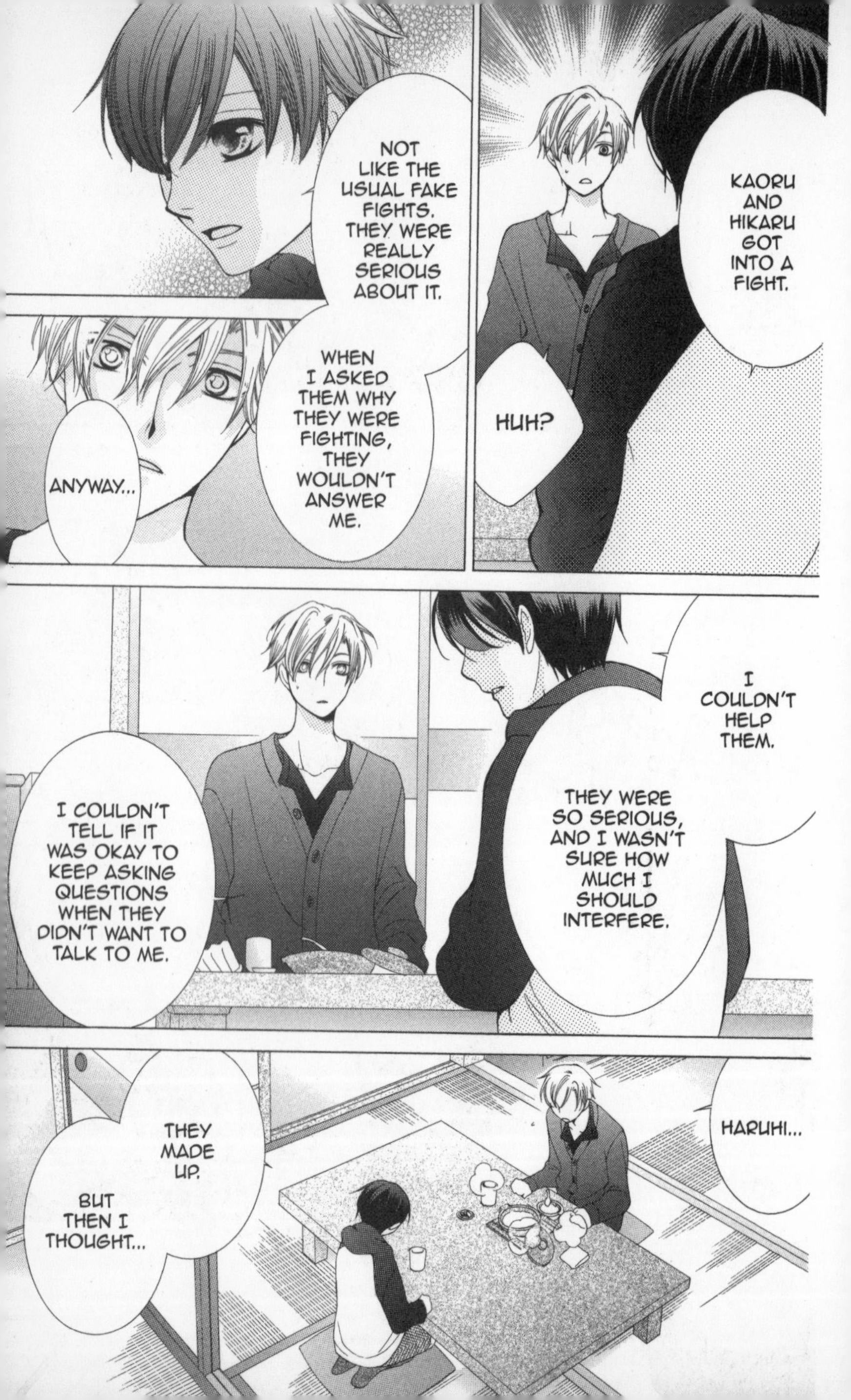
KAORU AND HIKARU GOT INTO A FIGHT.
HUH?
NOT LIKE THE USUAL FAKE FIGHTS. THEY WERE REALLY SERIOUS ABOUT IT.
WHEN I ASKED THEM WHY THEY WERE FIGHTING, THEY WOULDN'T ANSWER ME.
ANYWAY...
I COULDN'T HELP THEM.
THEY WERE SO SERIOUS, AND I WASN'T SURE HOW MUCH I SHOULD INTERFERE.
I COULDN'T TELL IF IT WAS OKAY TO KEEP ASKING QUESTIONS WHEN THEY DIDN'T WANT TO TALK TO ME.
HARUHI...
THEY MADE UP.
BUT THEN I THOUGHT...

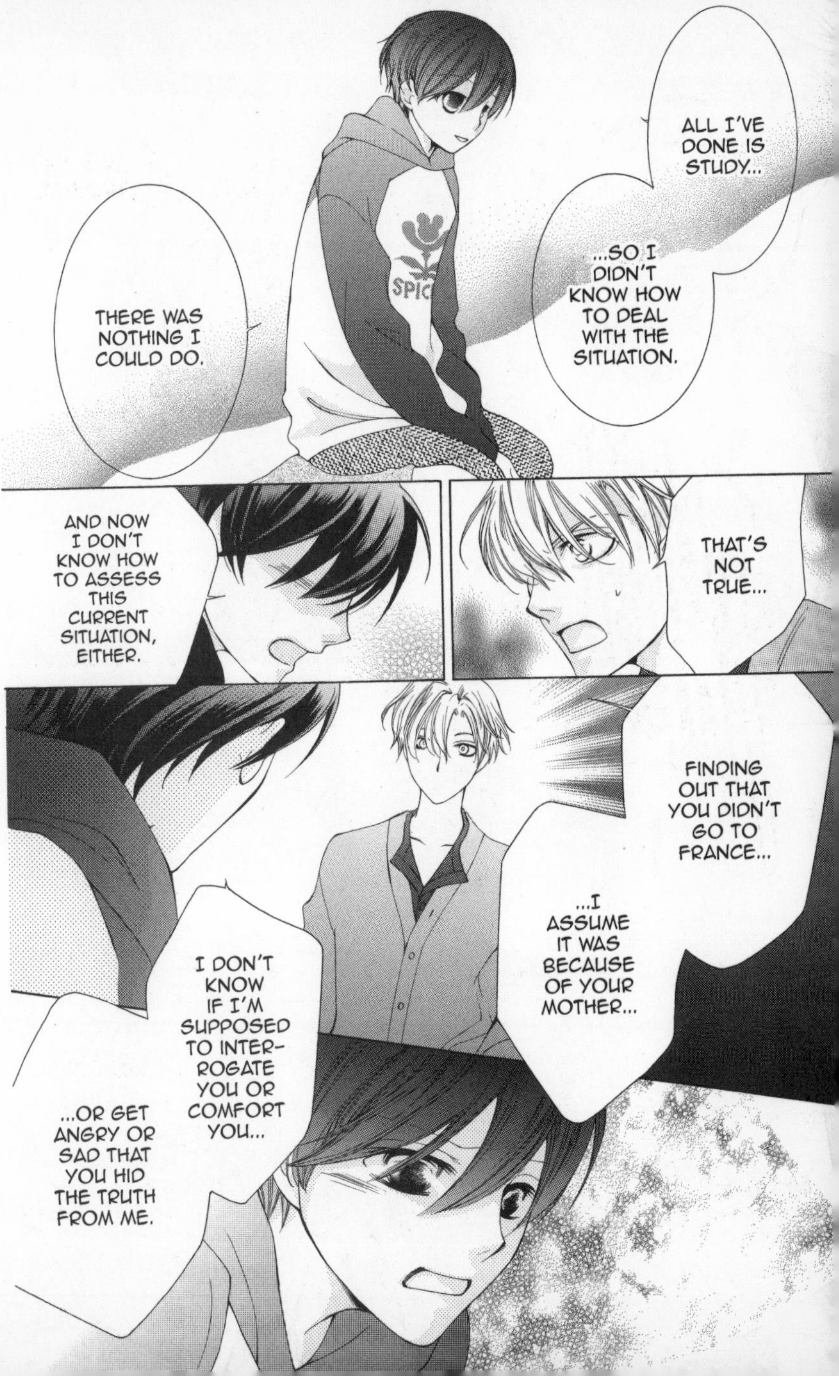
ALL I'VE DONE IS STUDY...
...SO I DIDN'T KNOW HOW TO DEAL WITH THE SITUATION.
THERE WAS NOTHING I COULD DO.
THAT'S NOT TRUE...
AND NOW I DON'T KNOW HOW TO ASSESS THIS CURRENT SITUATION, EITHER.
FINDING OUT THAT YOU DIDN'T GO TO FRANCE...
...I ASSUME IT WAS BECAUSE OF YOUR MOTHER...
I DON'T KNOW IF I'M SUPPOSED TO INTER-ROGATE YOU OR COMFORT YOU...
...OR GET ANGRY OR SAD THAT YOU HID THE TRUTH FROM ME.

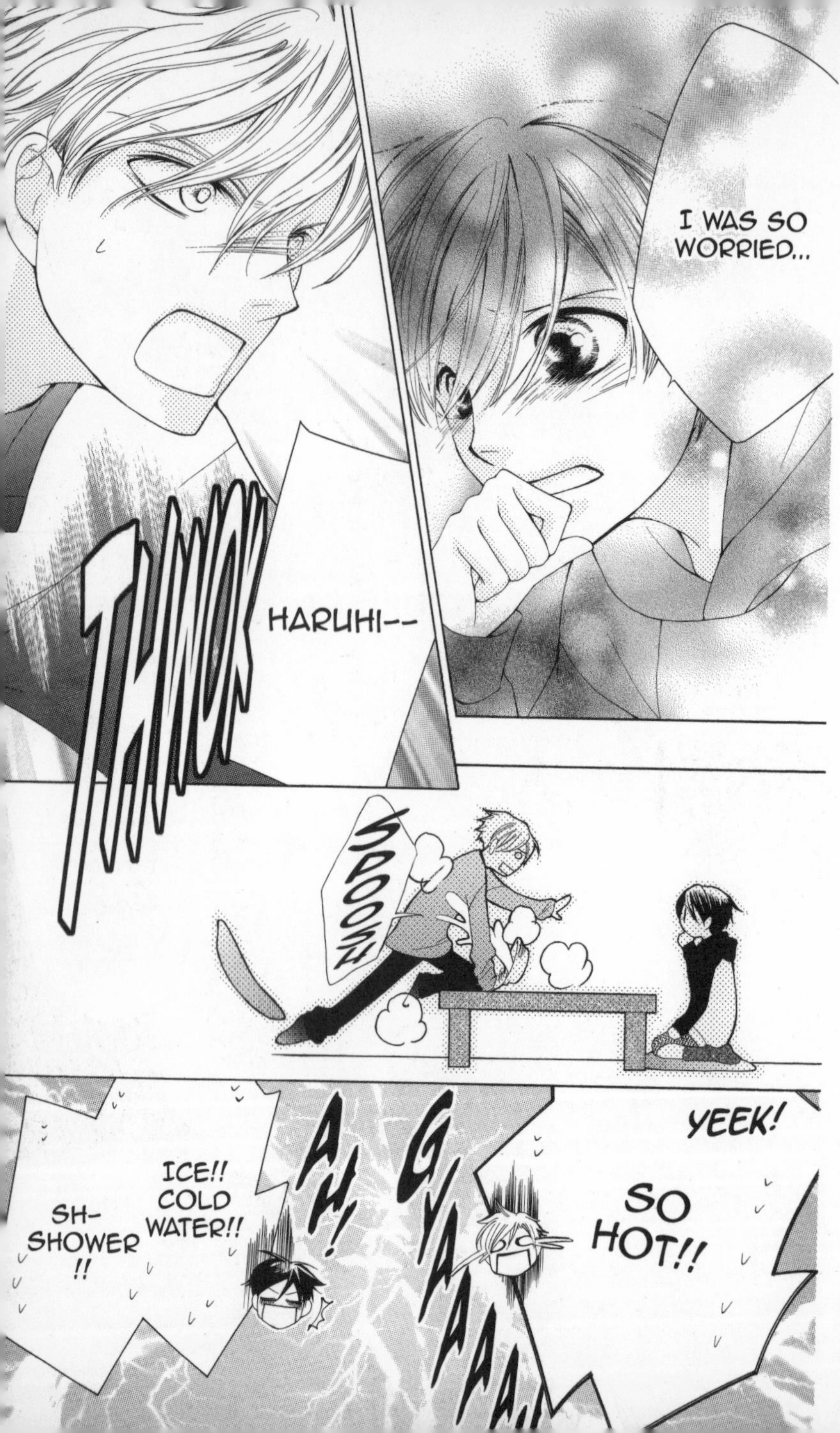
I WAS SO WORRIED...
HARUHI--
THWOK
SPOOSH
YEEK!
SO HOT!!
GYAAAAA
AH!
ICE!! COLD WATER!!
SH-SHOWER!!

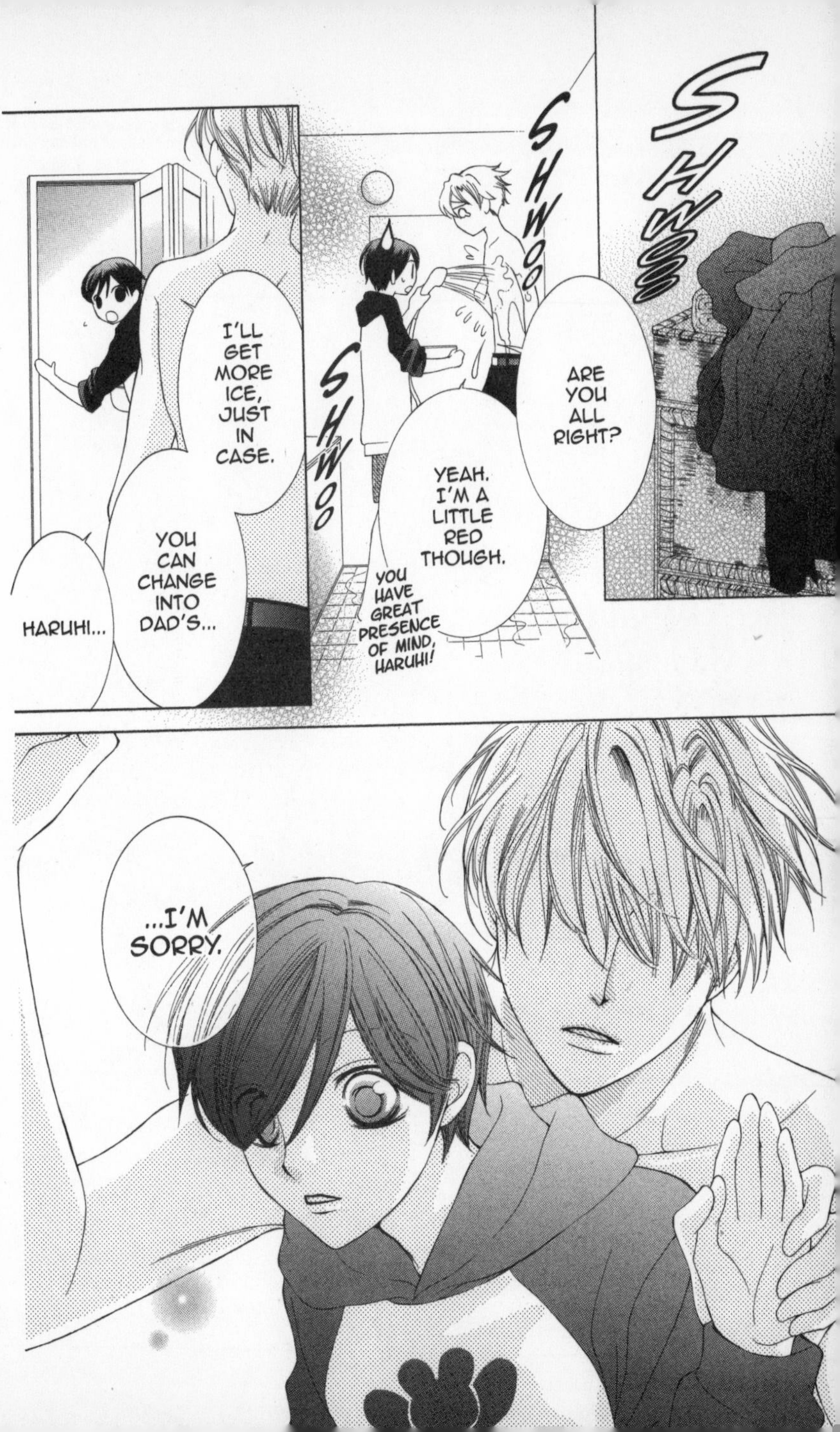
SHWOOO
SHWOO
ARE YOU ALL RIGHT?
YEAH. I'M A LITTLE RED THOUGH.
SHWOO
YOU HAVE GREAT PRESENCE OF MIND, HARUHI!
I'LL GET MORE ICE, JUST IN CASE.
YOU CAN CHANGE INTO DAD'S...
HARUHI...
...I'M SORRY.

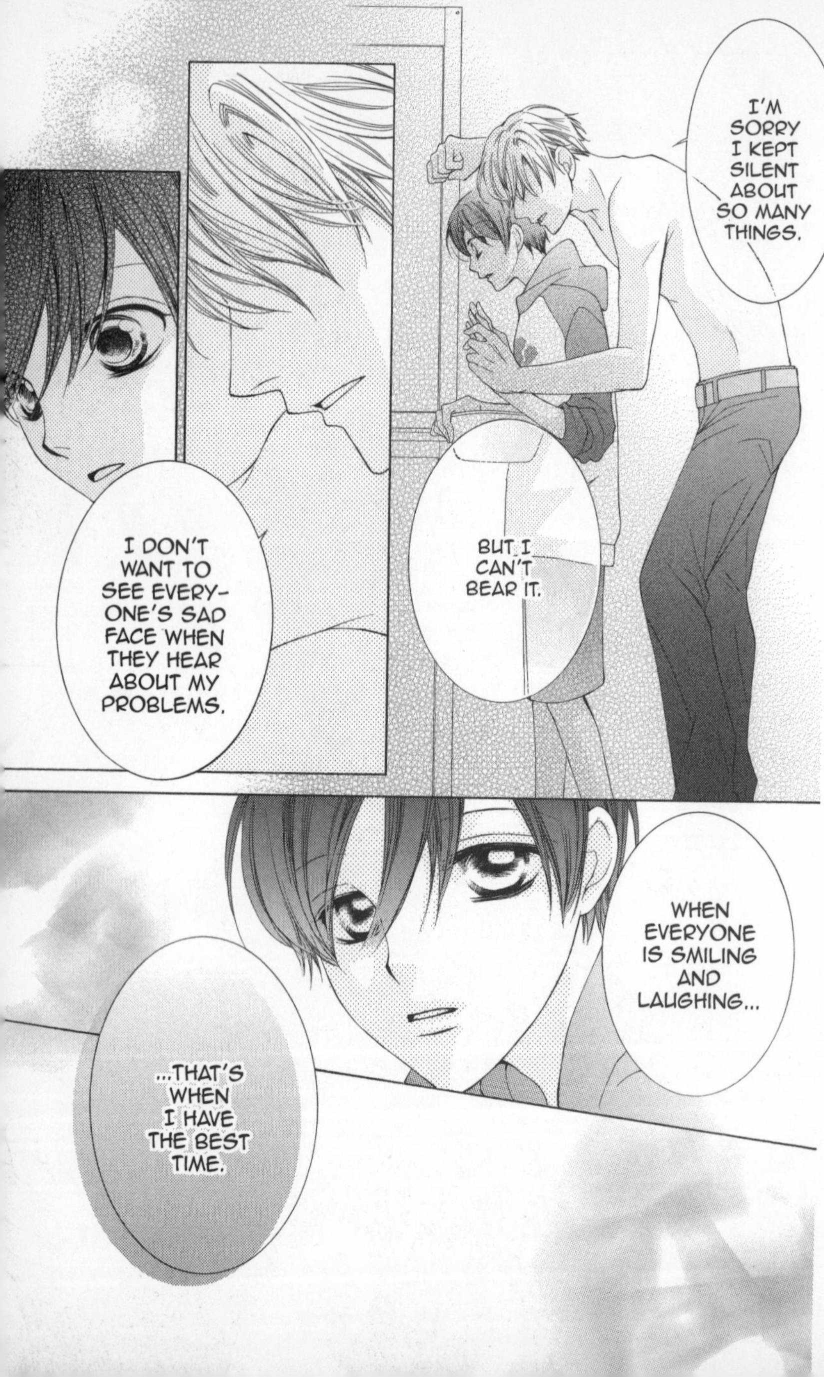
I'M SORRY I KEPT SILENT ABOUT SO MANY THINGS.
BUT I CAN'T BEAR IT.
I DON'T WANT TO SEE EVERY-ONE'S SAD FACE WHEN THEY HEAR ABOUT MY PROBLEMS.
WHEN EVERYONE IS SMILING AND LAUGHING...
...THAT'S WHEN I HAVE THE BEST TIME.

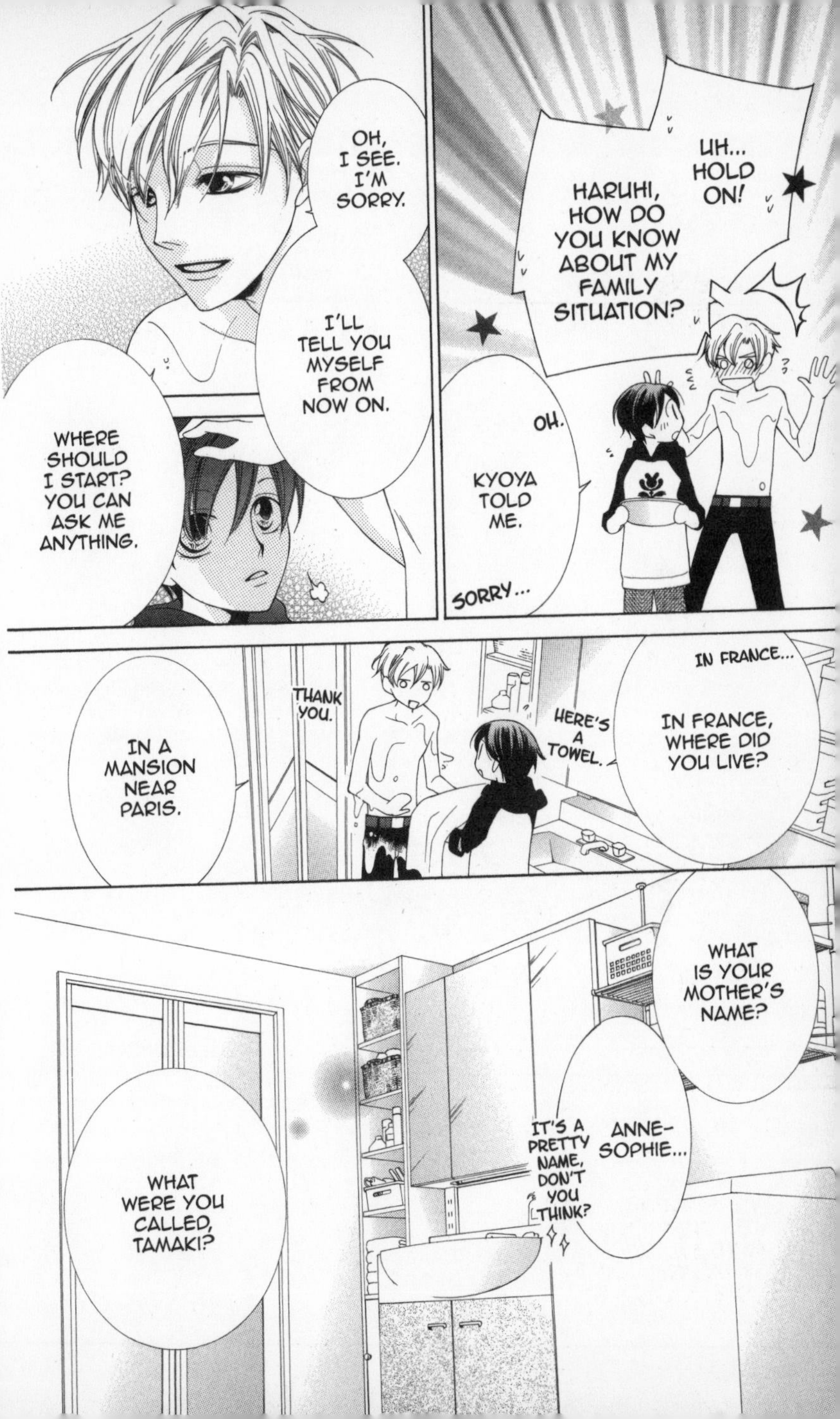
UH... HOLD ON!
HARUHI, HOW DO YOU KNOW ABOUT MY FAMILY SITUATION?
OH.
KYOYA TOLD ME.
SORRY...
OH, I SEE. I'M SORRY.
I'LL TELL YOU MYSELF FROM NOW ON.
WHERE SHOULD I START? YOU CAN ASK ME ANYTHING.
IN FRANCE...
IN FRANCE, WHERE DID YOU LIVE?
HERE'S A TOWEL.
THANK YOU.
IN A MANSION NEAR PARIS.
WHAT IS YOUR MOTHER'S NAME?
ANNE-SOPHIE...
IT'S A PRETTY NAME, DON'T YOU THINK?
WHAT WERE YOU CALLED, TAMAKI?

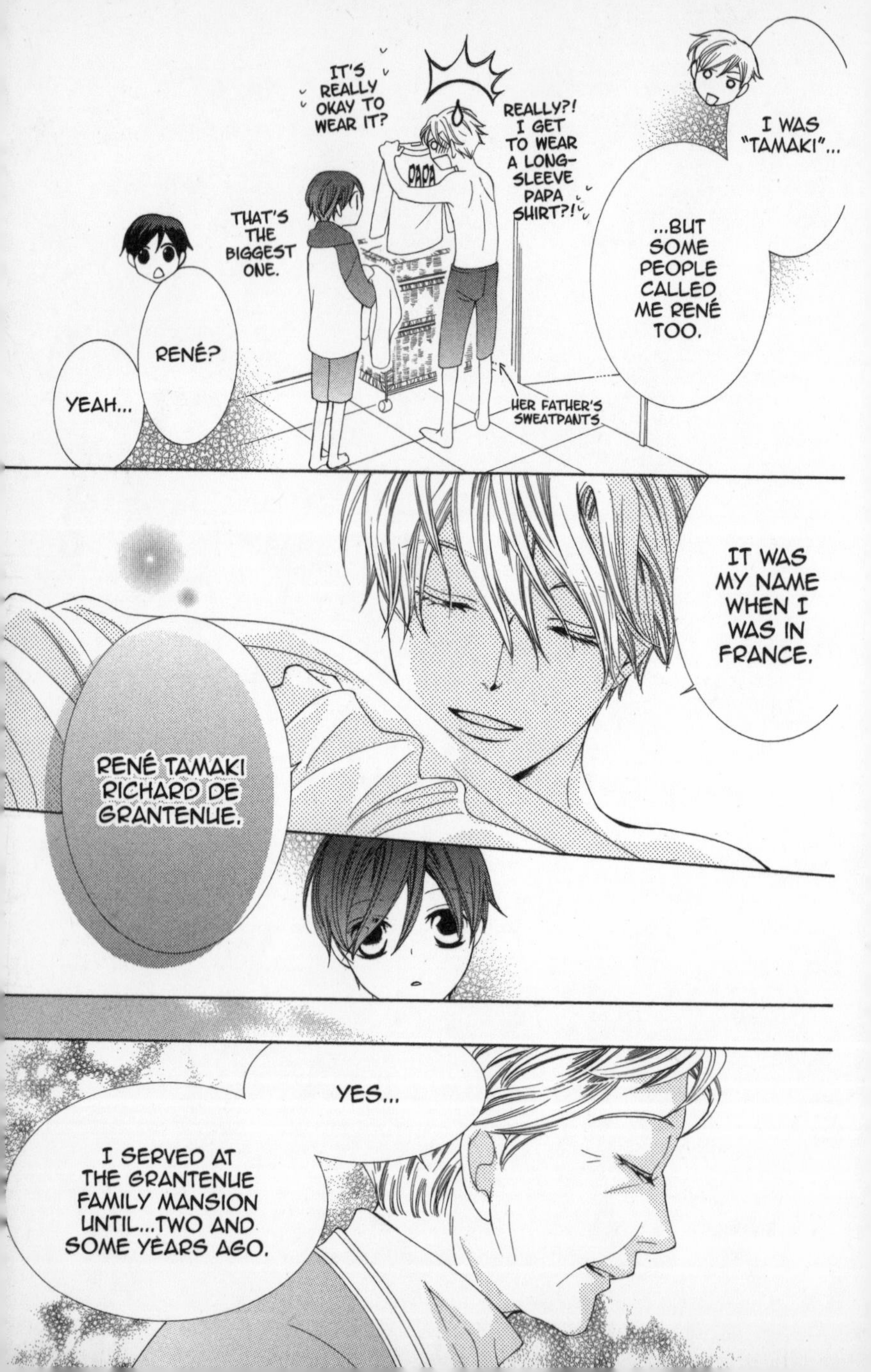
I WAS "TAMAKI"...
...BUT SOME PEOPLE CALLED ME RENÉ TOO.
REALLY?! I GET TO WEAR A LONG-SLEEVE PAPA SHIRT?!
IT'S REALLY OKAY TO WEAR IT?
PAPA
HER FATHER'S SWEATPANTS
THAT'S THE BIGGEST ONE.
RENÉ?
YEAH...
IT WAS MY NAME WHEN I WAS IN FRANCE.
RENÉ TAMAKI RICHARD DE GRANTENUE.
YES...
I SERVED AT THE GRANTENUE FAMILY MANSION UNTIL...TWO AND SOME YEARS AGO.

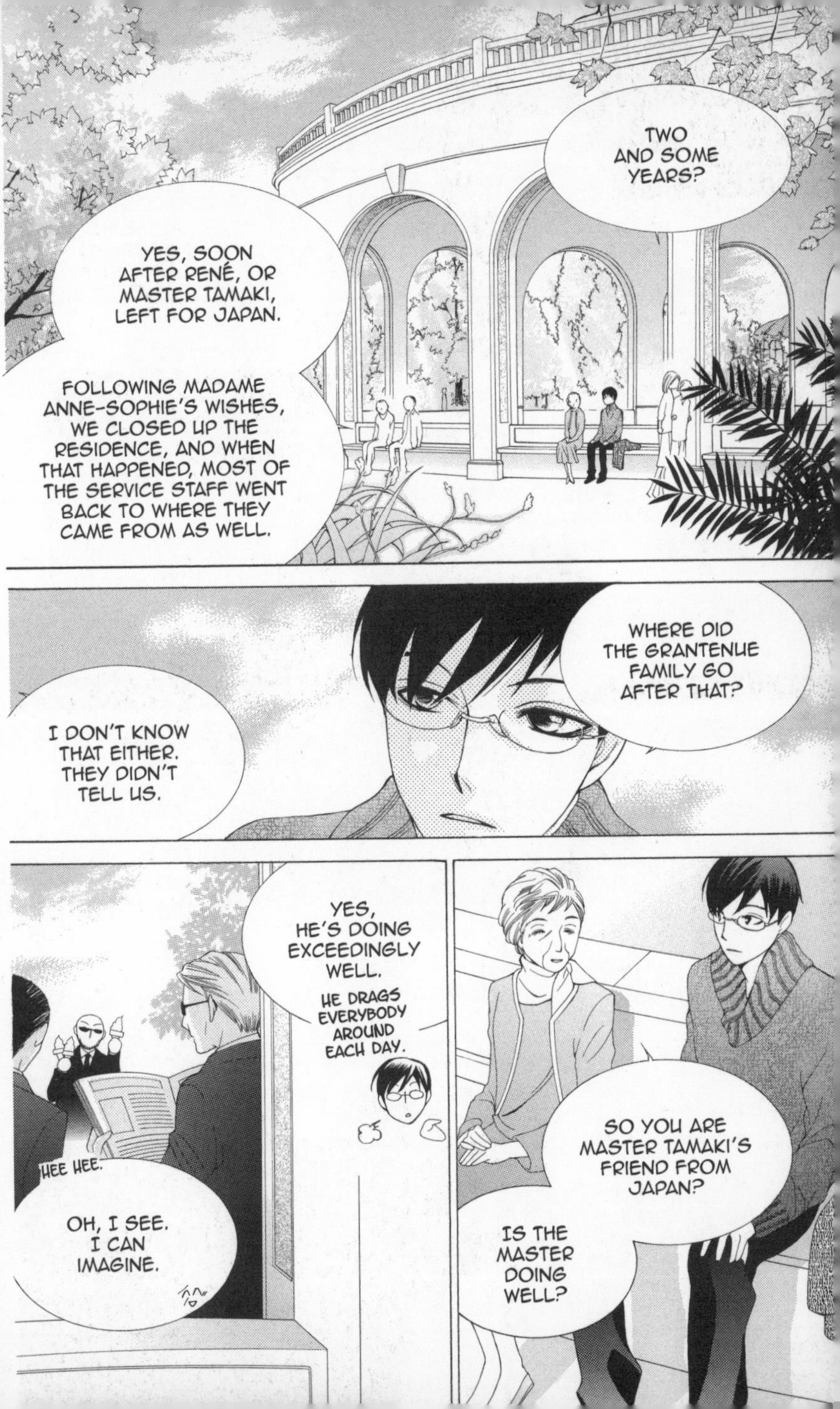
TWO AND SOME YEARS?
YES, SOON AFTER RENÉ, OR MASTER TAMAKI, LEFT FOR JAPAN.
FOLLOWING MADAME ANNE-SOPHIE'S WISHES, WE CLOSED UP THE RESIDENCE, AND WHEN THAT HAPPENED, MOST OF THE SERVICE STAFF WENT BACK TO WHERE THEY CAME FROM AS WELL.
WHERE DID THE GRANTENUE FAMILY GO AFTER THAT?
I DON'T KNOW THAT EITHER. THEY DIDN'T TELL US.
SO YOU ARE MASTER TAMAKI'S FRIEND FROM JAPAN?
IS THE MASTER DOING WELL?
YES, HE'S DOING EXCEEDINGLY WELL.
HE DRAGS EVERYBODY AROUND EACH DAY.
HEE HEE.
OH, I SEE. I CAN IMAGINE.

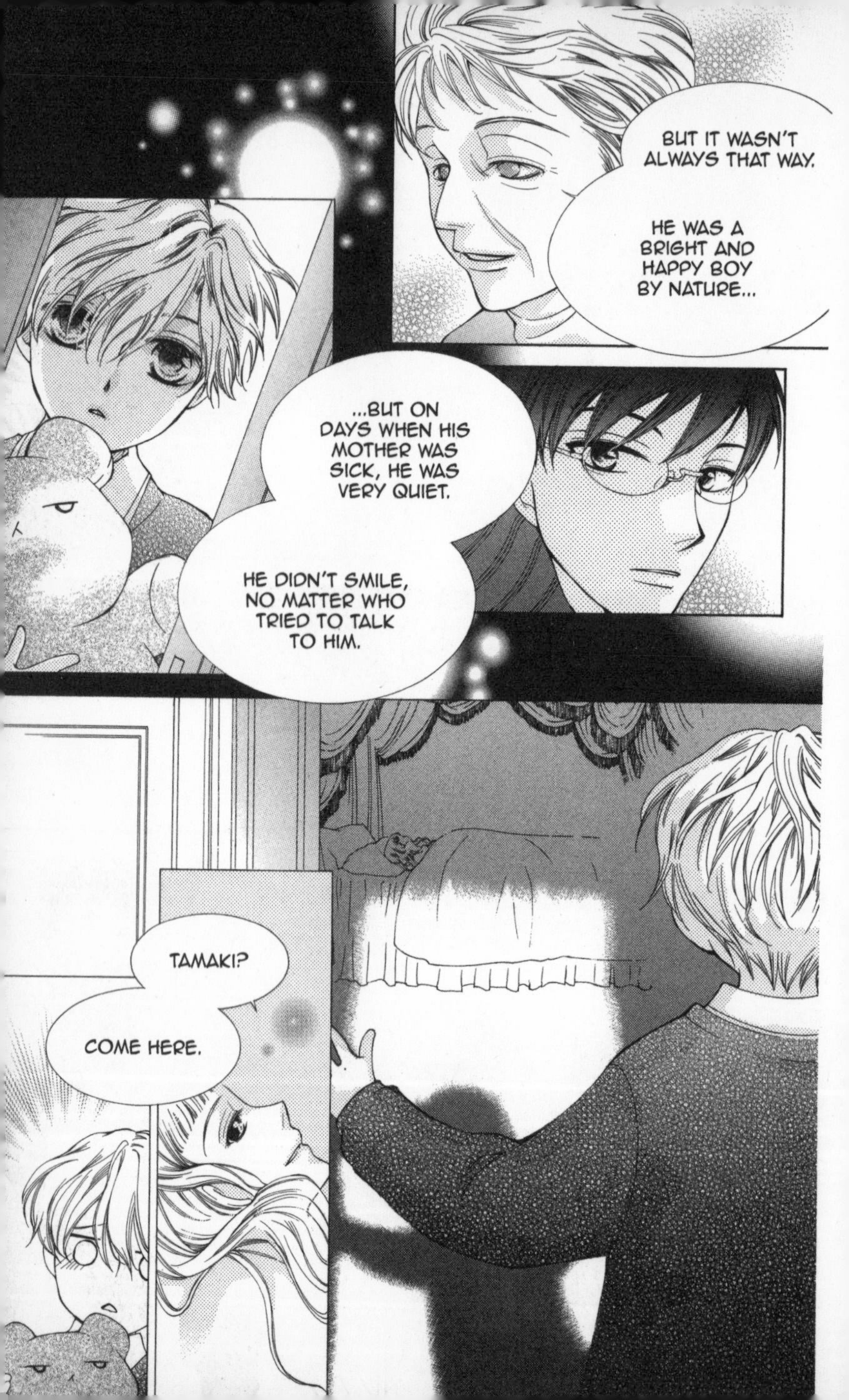
BUT IT WASN'T ALWAYS THAT WAY.
HE WAS A BRIGHT AND HAPPY BOY BY NATURE...
...BUT ON DAYS WHEN HIS MOTHER WAS SICK, HE WAS VERY QUIET.
HE DIDN'T SMILE, NO MATTER WHO TRIED TO TALK TO HIM.
TAMAKI?
COME HERE.

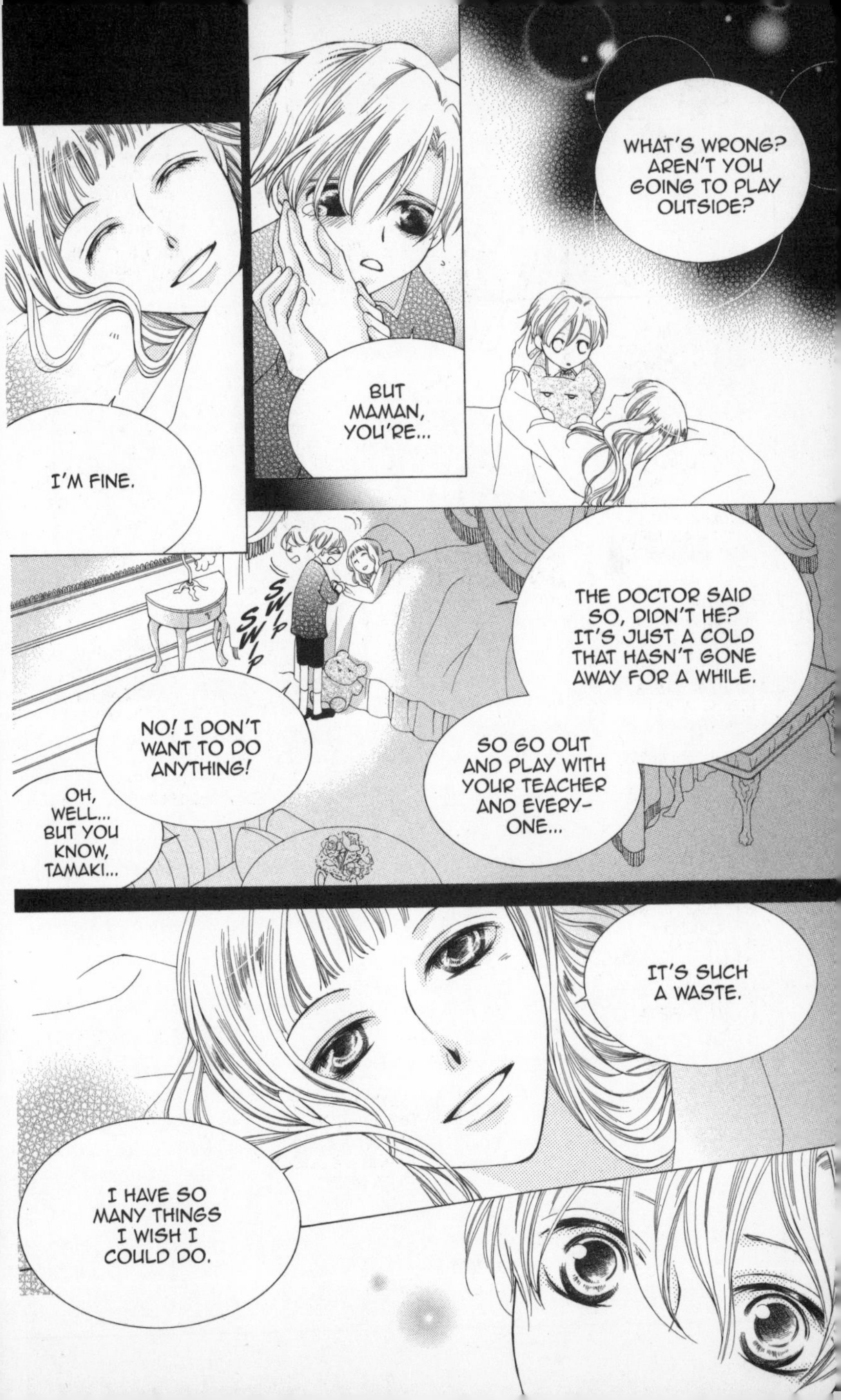
WHAT'S WRONG? AREN'T YOU GOING TO PLAY OUTSIDE?
BUT MAMAN, YOU'RE...
I'M FINE.
THE DOCTOR SAID SO, DIDN'T HE? IT'S JUST A COLD THAT HASN'T GONE AWAY FOR A WHILE.
SO GO OUT AND PLAY WITH YOUR TEACHER AND EVERY-ONE...
SWIP SWIP
NO! I DON'T WANT TO DO ANYTHING!
OH, WELL... BUT YOU KNOW, TAMAKI...
IT'S SUCH A WASTE.
I HAVE SO MANY THINGS I WISH I COULD DO.

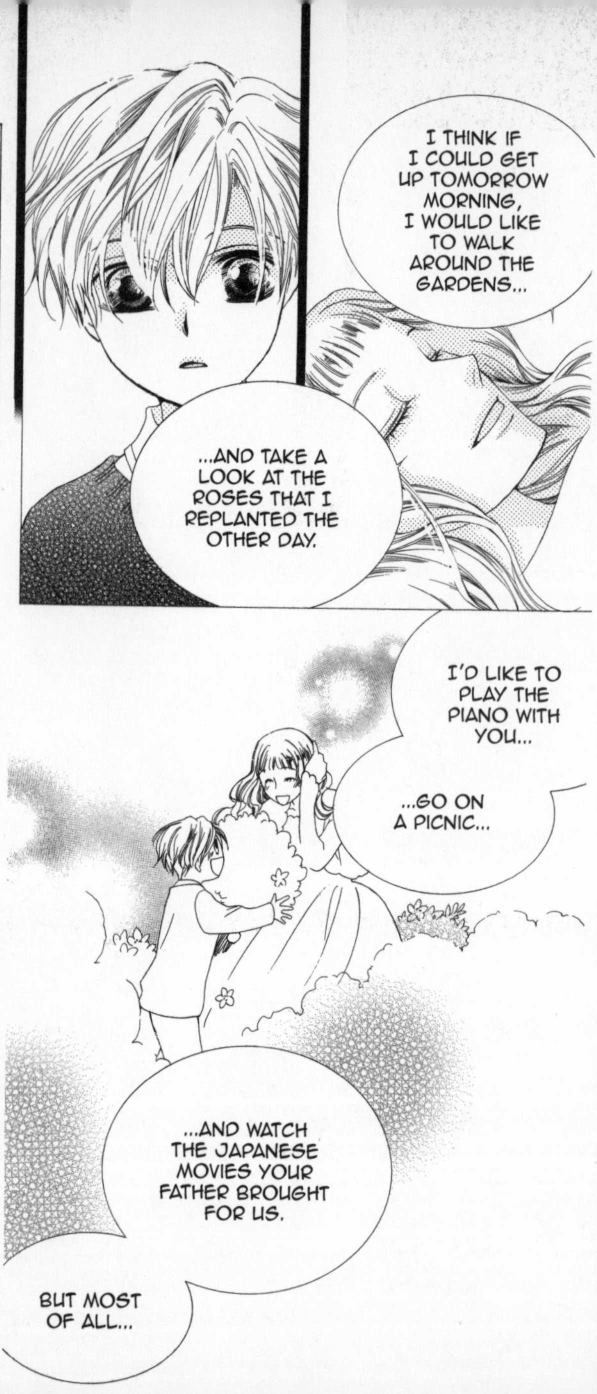
I THINK IF I COULD GET UP TOMORROW MORNING, I WOULD LIKE TO WALK AROUND THE GARDENS...
...AND TAKE A LOOK AT THE ROSES THAT I REPLANTED THE OTHER DAY.
I'D LIKE TO PLAY THE PIANO WITH YOU...
...GO ON A PICNIC...
...AND WATCH THE JAPANESE MOVIES YOUR FATHER BROUGHT FOR US.
BUT MOST OF ALL...

4

✿ CHANGING THE SUBJECT...

MANY READERS HAVE ASKED WHAT KIND OF DRAWING MATERIALS I USE, SO I WILL INTRODUCE A FEW OF THEM HERE. I'M STILL IN THE MIDST OF EXPERIMENTING, SO I URGE EVERYONE TO CONTINUE LOOKING FOR MATERIALS THAT SUIT THEM BEST.

✿ PEN NIB: NIKKOUMARU PEN (BUT IN THE PAST I USED ZEBRA PENS.)

✿ BORDER IMAGES [FRAME LINES]: PIGMA 0.4

✿ BRUSH PEN: KURETAKE FOUNTAIN BRUSH PEN, NO. 8

✿ INK: PILOT FOR DRAFTING

✿ RULER: MY FAVORITE IS THE LETTER GRID RULER, BUT THERE ARE VERY FEW PLACES THAT SELL THEM.

✿ DRAFTING PAPER: IC MANGA PAPER, 135 KG

✿ WHITE OUT: DOCTOR MARTIN BLEED PROOF WHITE

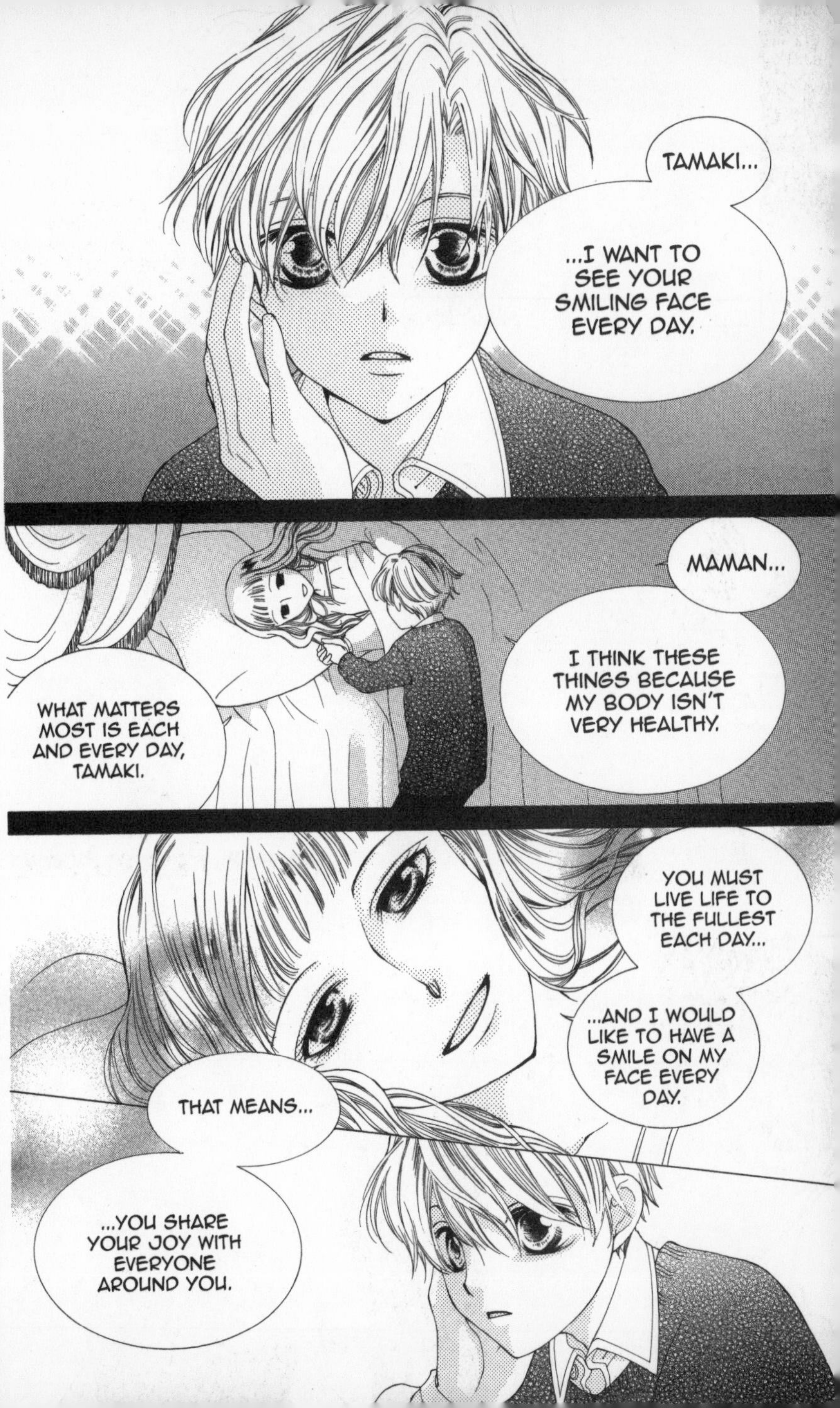
TAMAKI...
...I WANT TO SEE YOUR SMILING FACE EVERY DAY.
MAMAN...
I THINK THESE THINGS BECAUSE MY BODY ISN'T VERY HEALTHY.
WHAT MATTERS MOST IS EACH AND EVERY DAY, TAMAKI.
YOU MUST LIVE LIFE TO THE FULLEST EACH DAY...
...AND I WOULD LIKE TO HAVE A SMILE ON MY FACE EVERY DAY.
THAT MEANS...
...YOU SHARE YOUR JOY WITH EVERYONE AROUND YOU.

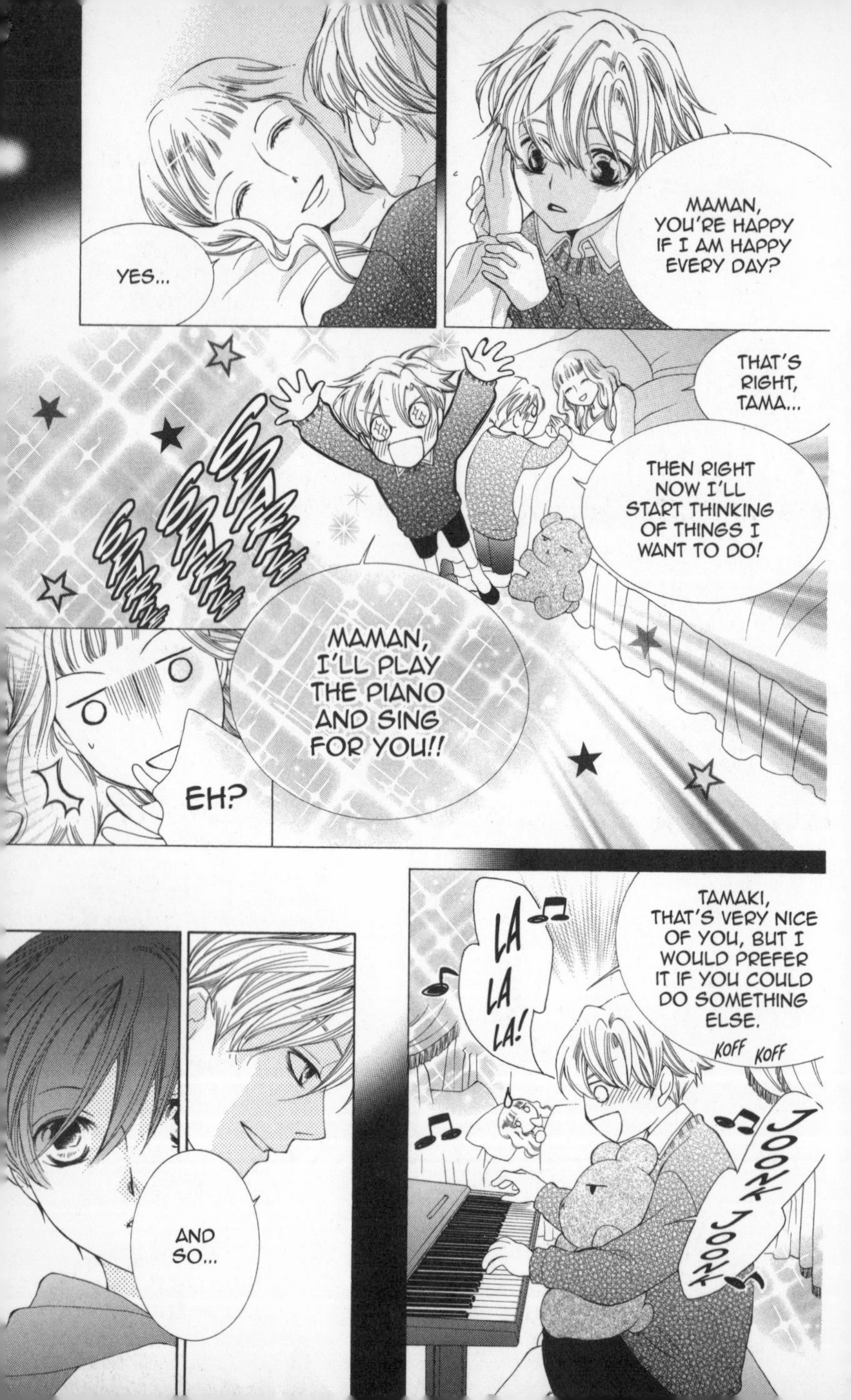
MAMAN, YOU'RE HAPPY IF I AM HAPPY EVERY DAY?
YES...
THAT'S RIGHT, TAMA...
THEN RIGHT NOW I'LL START THINKING OF THINGS I WANT TO DO!
MAMAN, I'LL PLAY THE PIANO AND SING FOR YOU!!
EH?
TAMAKI, THAT'S VERY NICE OF YOU, BUT I WOULD PREFER IT IF YOU COULD DO SOMETHING ELSE.
KOFF KOFF
LA LA LA!
JOONK JOONK JOONK
AND SO...

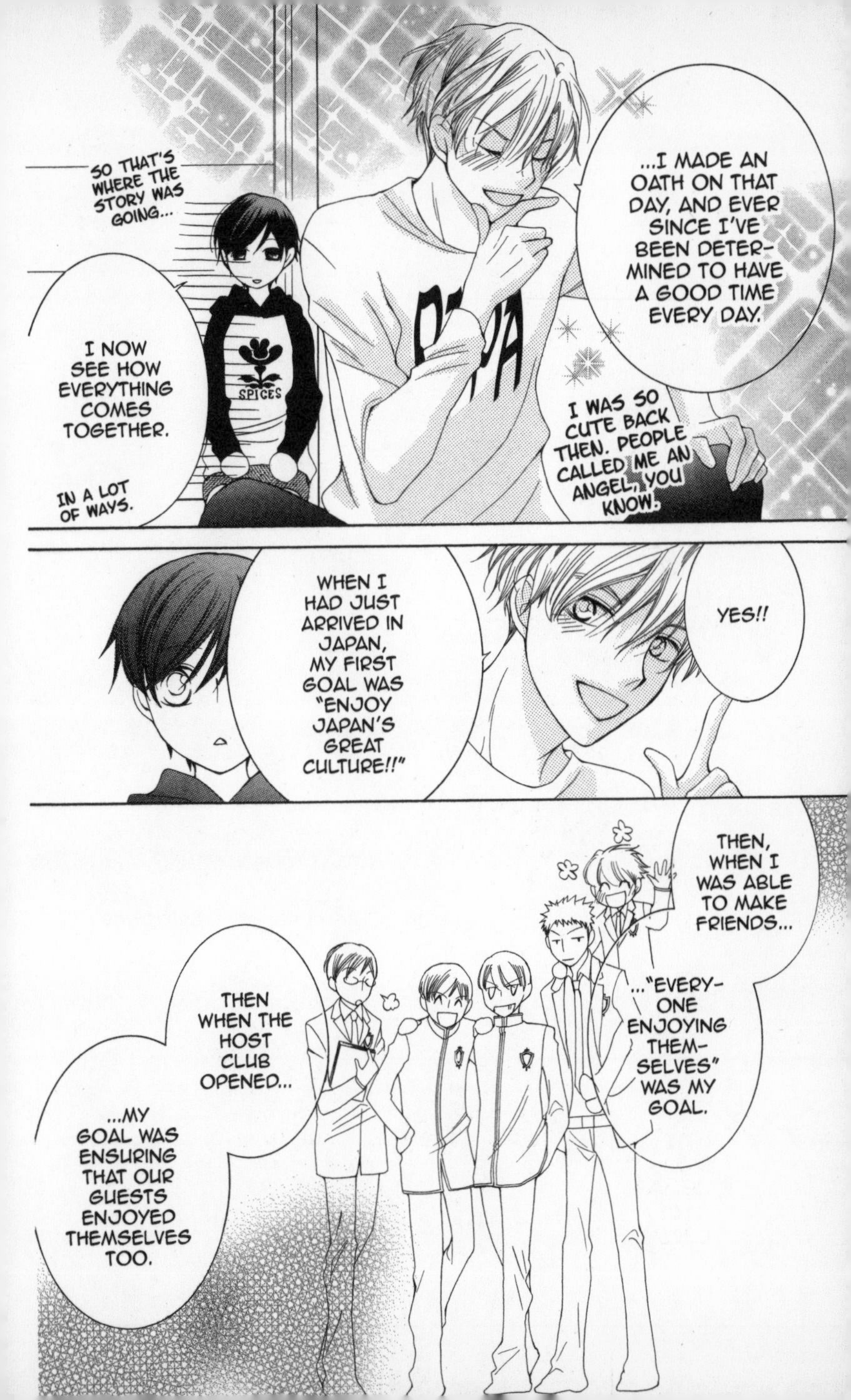
...I MADE AN OATH ON THAT DAY, AND EVER SINCE I'VE BEEN DETERMINED TO HAVE A GOOD TIME EVERY DAY.
I WAS SO CUTE BACK THEN. PEOPLE CALLED ME AN ANGEL, YOU KNOW.
SO THAT'S WHERE THE STORY WAS GOING...
I NOW SEE HOW EVERYTHING COMES TOGETHER.
IN A LOT OF WAYS.
YES!!
WHEN I HAD JUST ARRIVED IN JAPAN, MY FIRST GOAL WAS "ENJOY JAPAN'S GREAT CULTURE!!"
THEN, WHEN I WAS ABLE TO MAKE FRIENDS...
..."EVERYONE ENJOYING THEMSELVES" WAS MY GOAL.
THEN WHEN THE HOST CLUB OPENED...
...MY GOAL WAS ENSURING THAT OUR GUESTS ENJOYED THEMSELVES TOO.

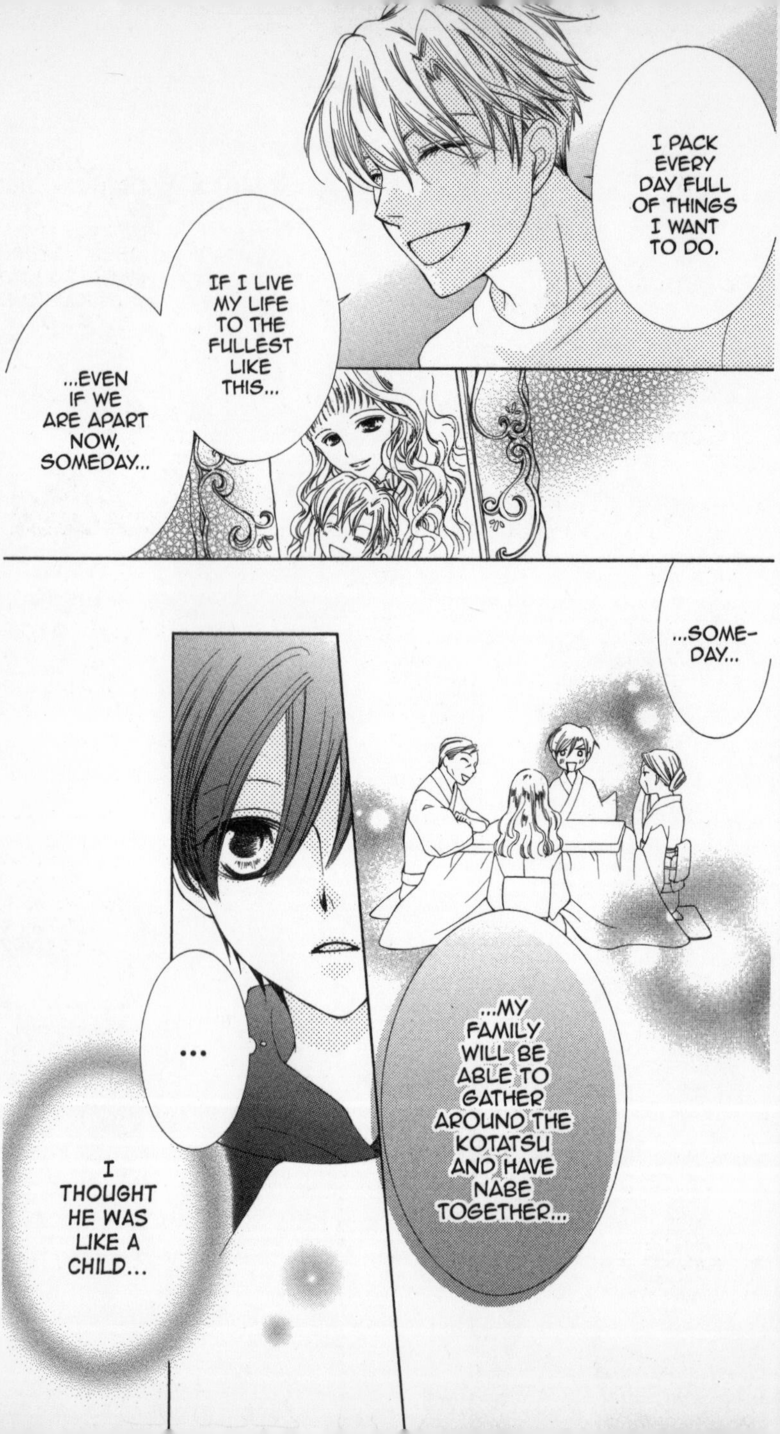
I PACK EVERY DAY FULL OF THINGS I WANT TO DO.
IF I LIVE MY LIFE TO THE FULLEST LIKE THIS...
...EVEN IF WE ARE APART NOW, SOMEDAY...
...SOME-DAY...
...MY FAMILY WILL BE ABLE TO GATHER AROUND THE KOTATSU AND HAVE NABE TOGETHER...
...
I THOUGHT HE WAS LIKE A CHILD...

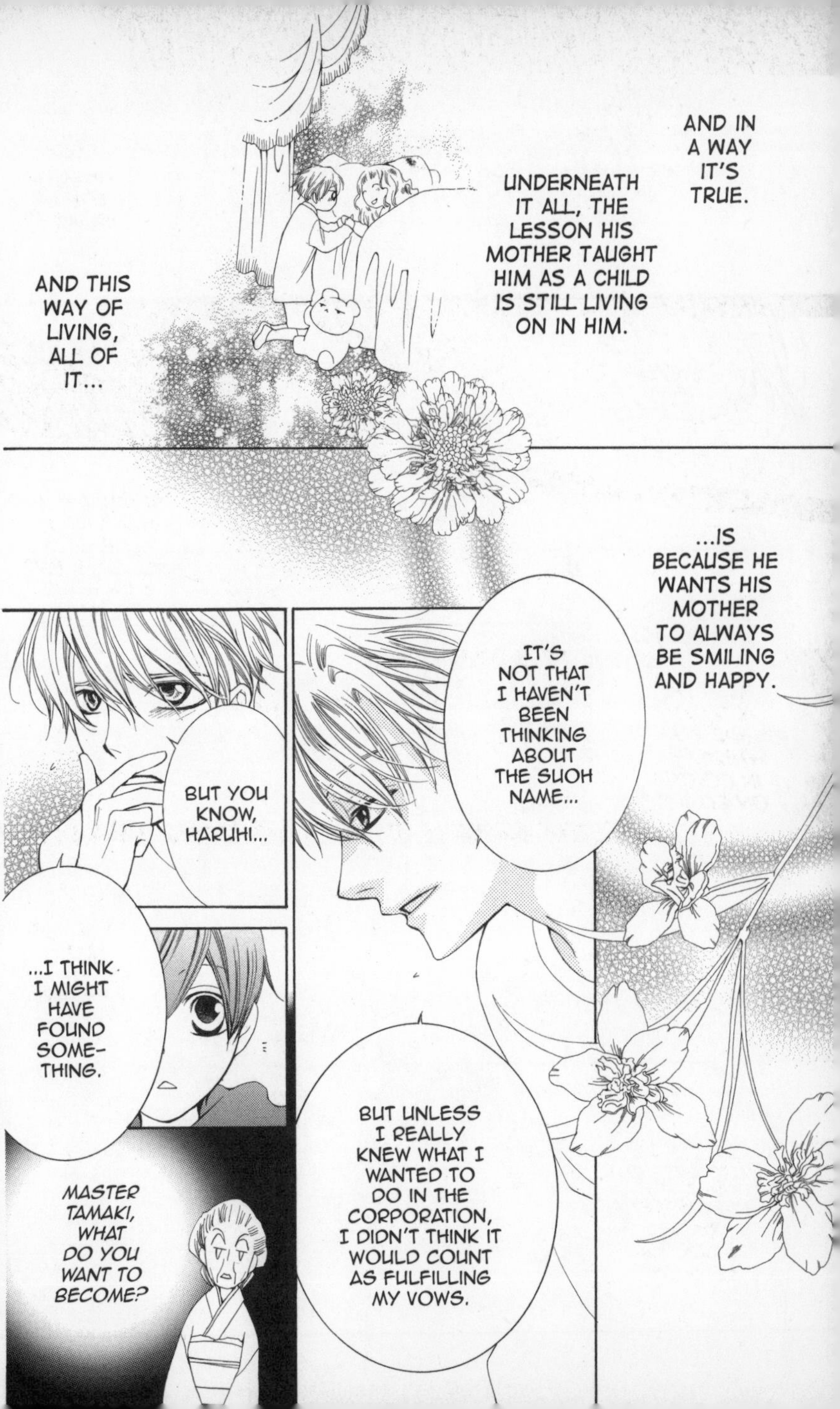
AND IN A WAY IT'S TRUE.
UNDERNEATH IT ALL, THE LESSON HIS MOTHER TAUGHT HIM AS A CHILD IS STILL LIVING ON IN HIM.
AND THIS WAY OF LIVING, ALL OF IT...
...IS BECAUSE HE WANTS HIS MOTHER TO ALWAYS BE SMILING AND HAPPY.
IT'S NOT THAT I HAVEN'T BEEN THINKING ABOUT THE SUOH NAME...
BUT UNLESS I REALLY KNEW WHAT I WANTED TO DO IN THE CORPORATION, I DIDN'T THINK IT WOULD COUNT AS FULFILLING MY VOWS.
BUT YOU KNOW, HARUHI...
...I THINK I MIGHT HAVE FOUND SOME-THING.
MASTER TAMAKI, WHAT DO YOU WANT TO BECOME?

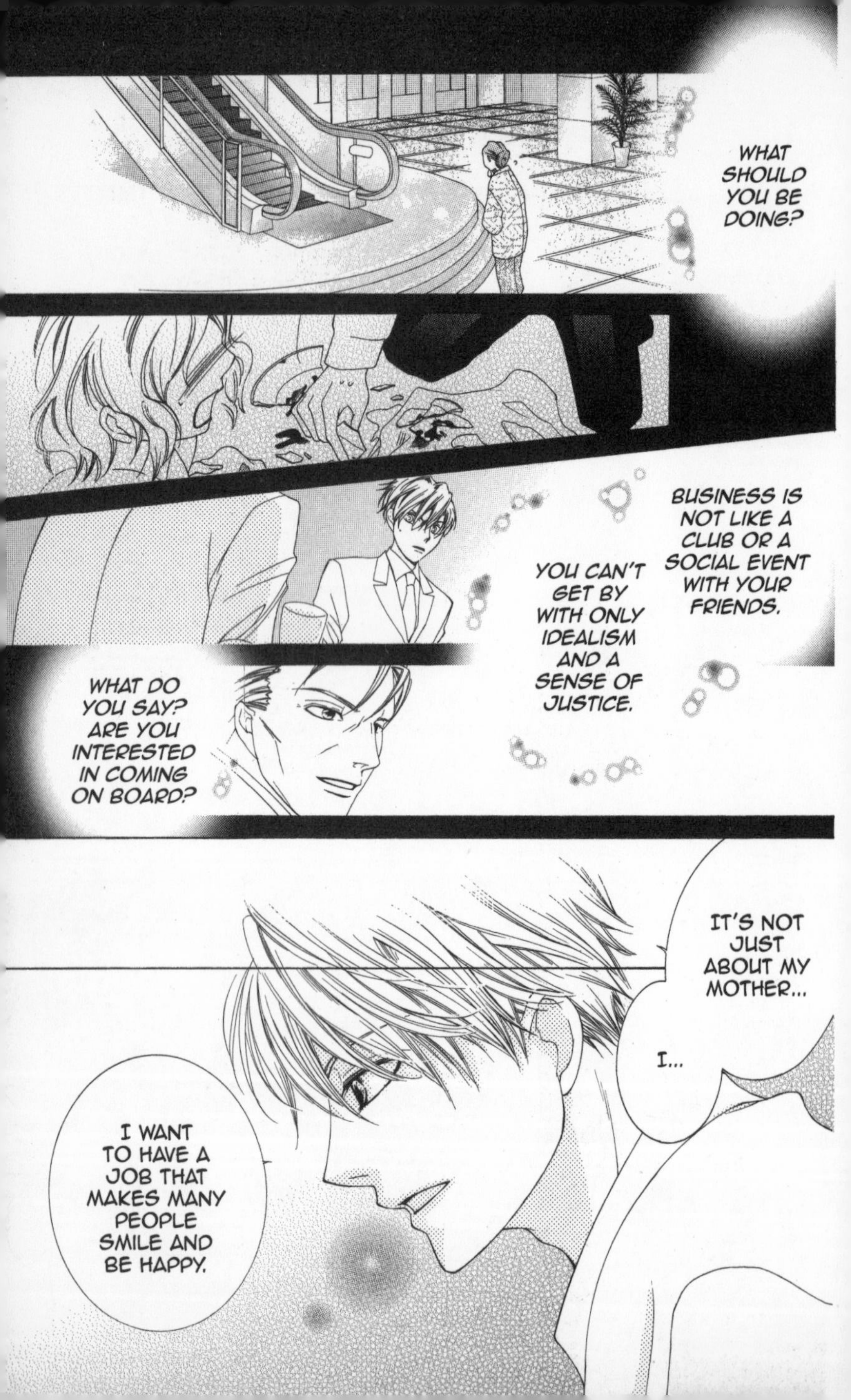
WHAT SHOULD YOU BE DOING?
BUSINESS IS NOT LIKE A CLUB OR A SOCIAL EVENT WITH YOUR FRIENDS.
YOU CAN'T GET BY WITH ONLY IDEALISM AND A SENSE OF JUSTICE.
WHAT DO YOU SAY? ARE YOU INTERESTED IN COMING ON BOARD?
IT'S NOT JUST ABOUT MY MOTHER...
I...
I WANT TO HAVE A JOB THAT MAKES MANY PEOPLE SMILE AND BE HAPPY.

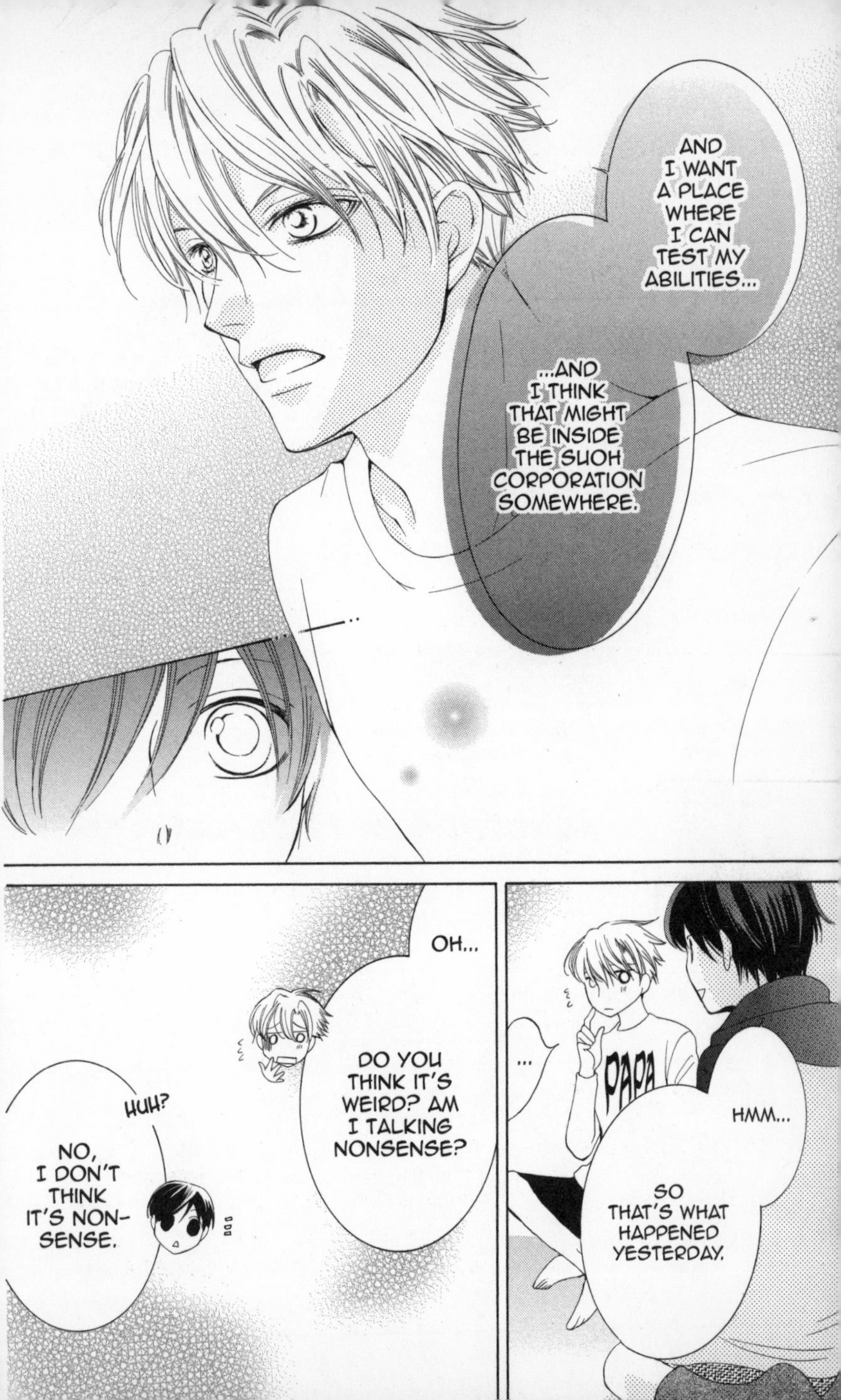
AND I WANT A PLACE WHERE I CAN TEST MY ABILITIES...
...AND I THINK THAT MIGHT BE INSIDE THE SUOH CORPORATION SOMEWHERE.
HMM...
SO THAT'S WHAT HAPPENED YESTERDAY.
...
OH...
DO YOU THINK IT'S WEIRD? AM I TALKING NONSENSE?
HUH?
NO, I DON'T THINK IT'S NON-SENSE.

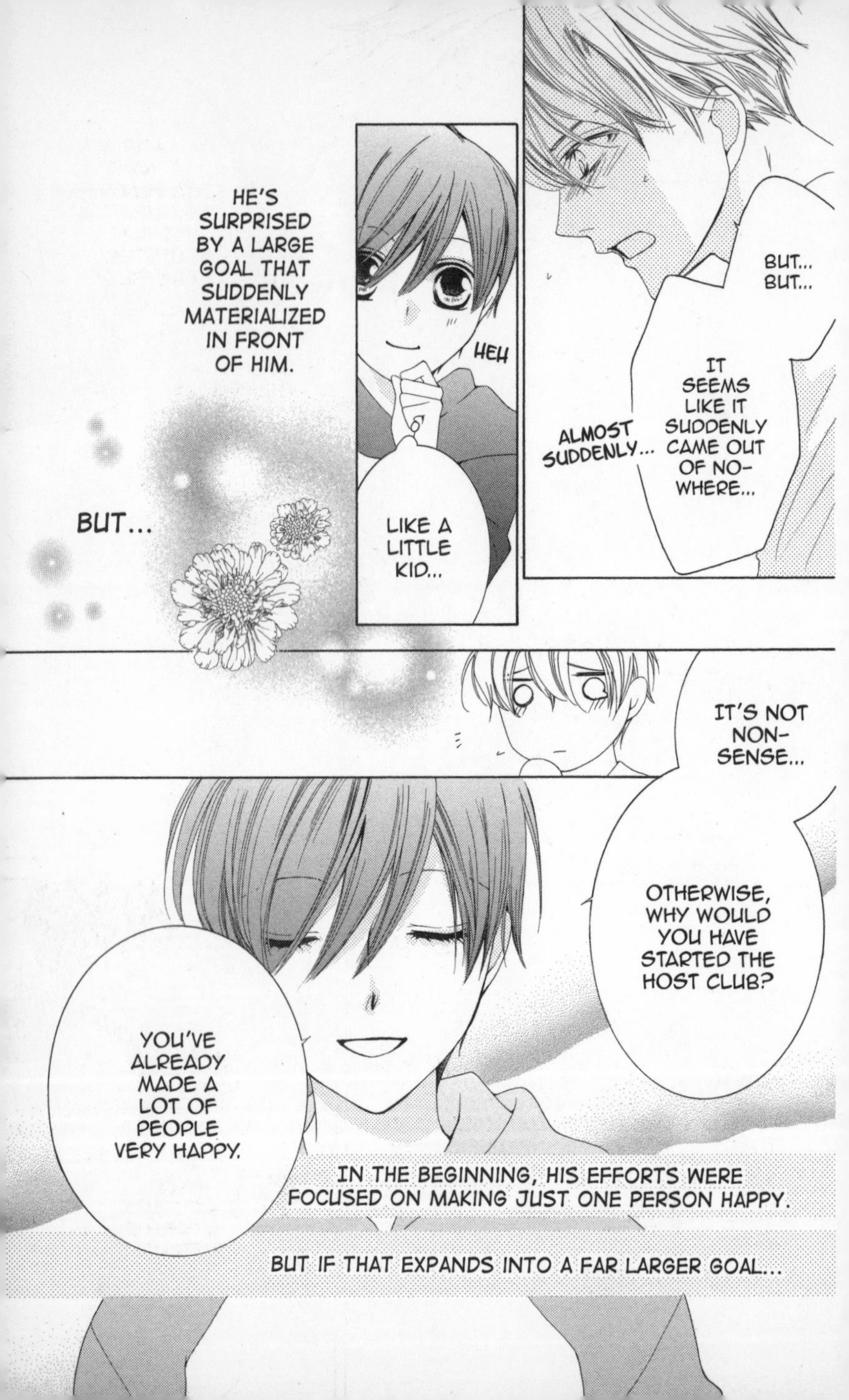
BUT... BUT...
IT SEEMS LIKE IT SUDDENLY CAME OUT OF NO-WHERE...
ALMOST SUDDENLY...
HEH
LIKE A LITTLE KID...
HE'S SURPRISED BY A LARGE GOAL THAT SUDDENLY MATERIALIZED IN FRONT OF HIM.
BUT...
IT'S NOT NON-SENSE...
OTHERWISE, WHY WOULD YOU HAVE STARTED THE HOST CLUB?
YOU'VE ALREADY MADE A LOT OF PEOPLE VERY HAPPY.
IN THE BEGINNING, HIS EFFORTS WERE FOCUSED ON MAKING JUST ONE PERSON HAPPY.
BUT IF THAT EXPANDS INTO A FAR LARGER GOAL...

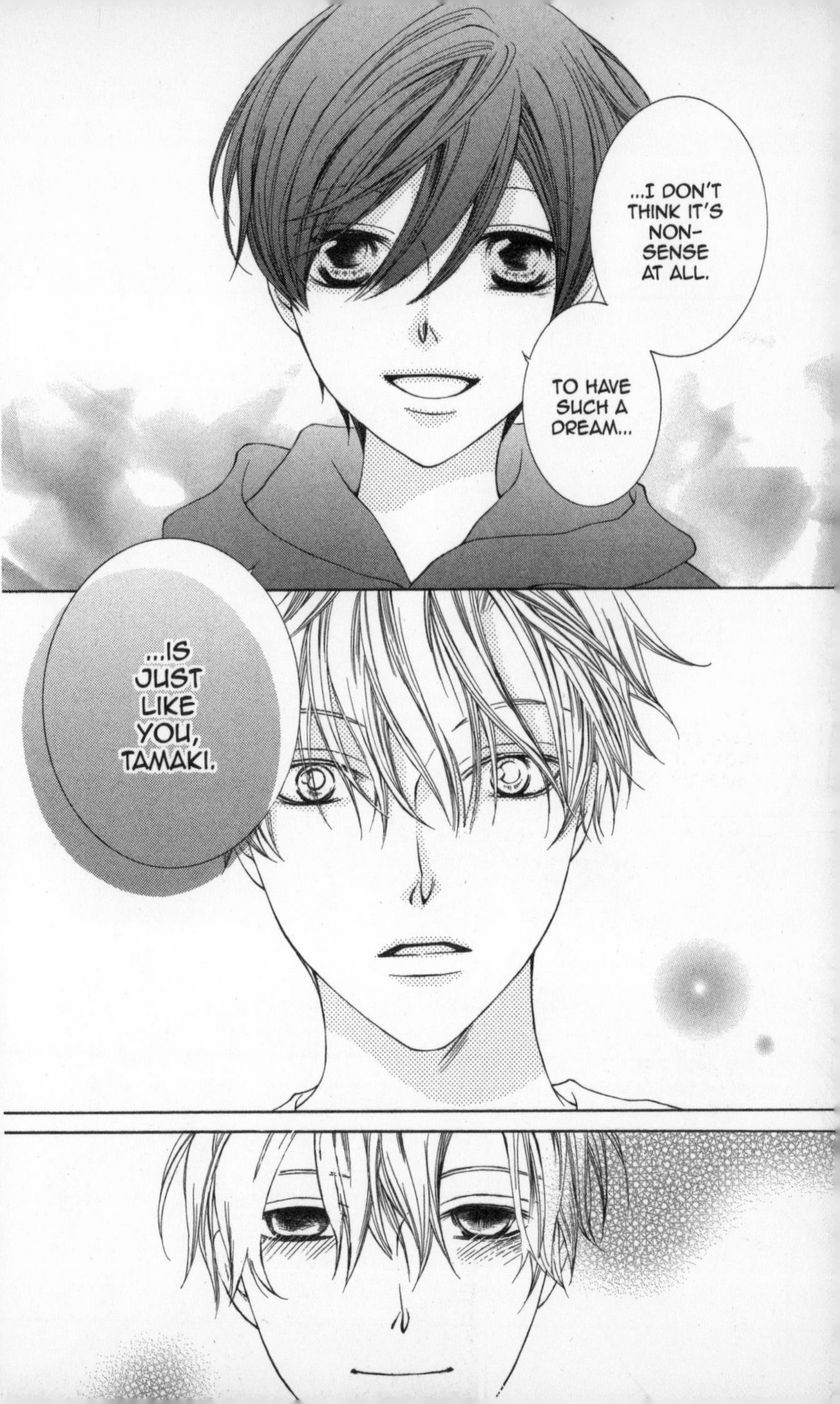
...I DON'T THINK IT'S NON-SENSE AT ALL.
TO HAVE SUCH A DREAM...
...IS JUST LIKE YOU, TAMAKI.

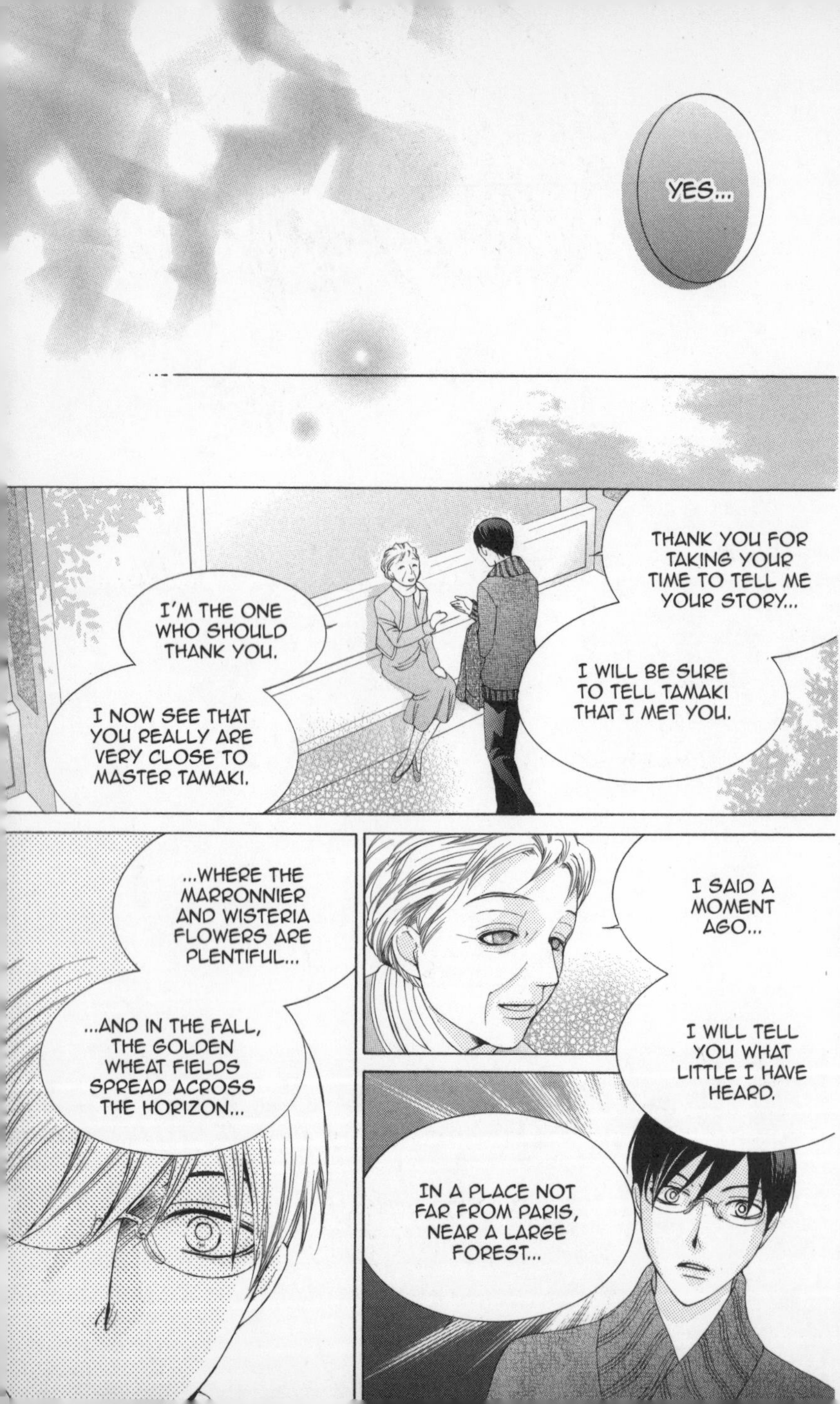
YES...
THANK YOU FOR TAKING YOUR TIME TO TELL ME YOUR STORY...
I WILL BE SURE TO TELL TAMAKI THAT I MET YOU.
I'M THE ONE WHO SHOULD THANK YOU.
I NOW SEE THAT YOU REALLY ARE VERY CLOSE TO MASTER TAMAKI.
I SAID A MOMENT AGO...
I WILL TELL YOU WHAT LITTLE I HAVE HEARD.
IN A PLACE NOT FAR FROM PARIS, NEAR A LARGE FOREST...
...WHERE THE MARRONNIER AND WISTERIA FLOWERS ARE PLENTIFUL...
...AND IN THE FALL, THE GOLDEN WHEAT FIELDS SPREAD ACROSS THE HORIZON...

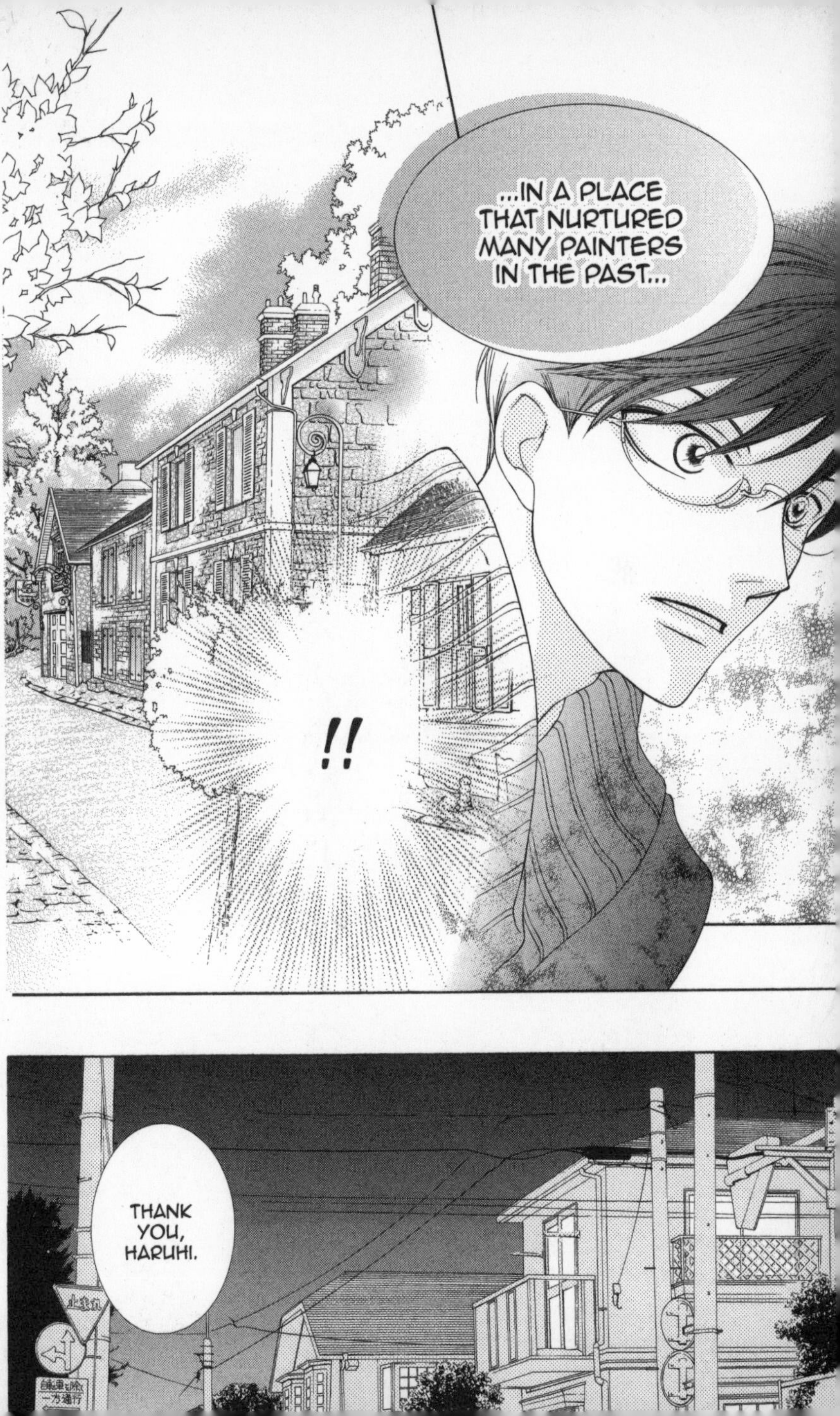
...IN A PLACE THAT NURTURED MANY PAINTERS IN THE PAST...
!!
THANK YOU, HARUHI.

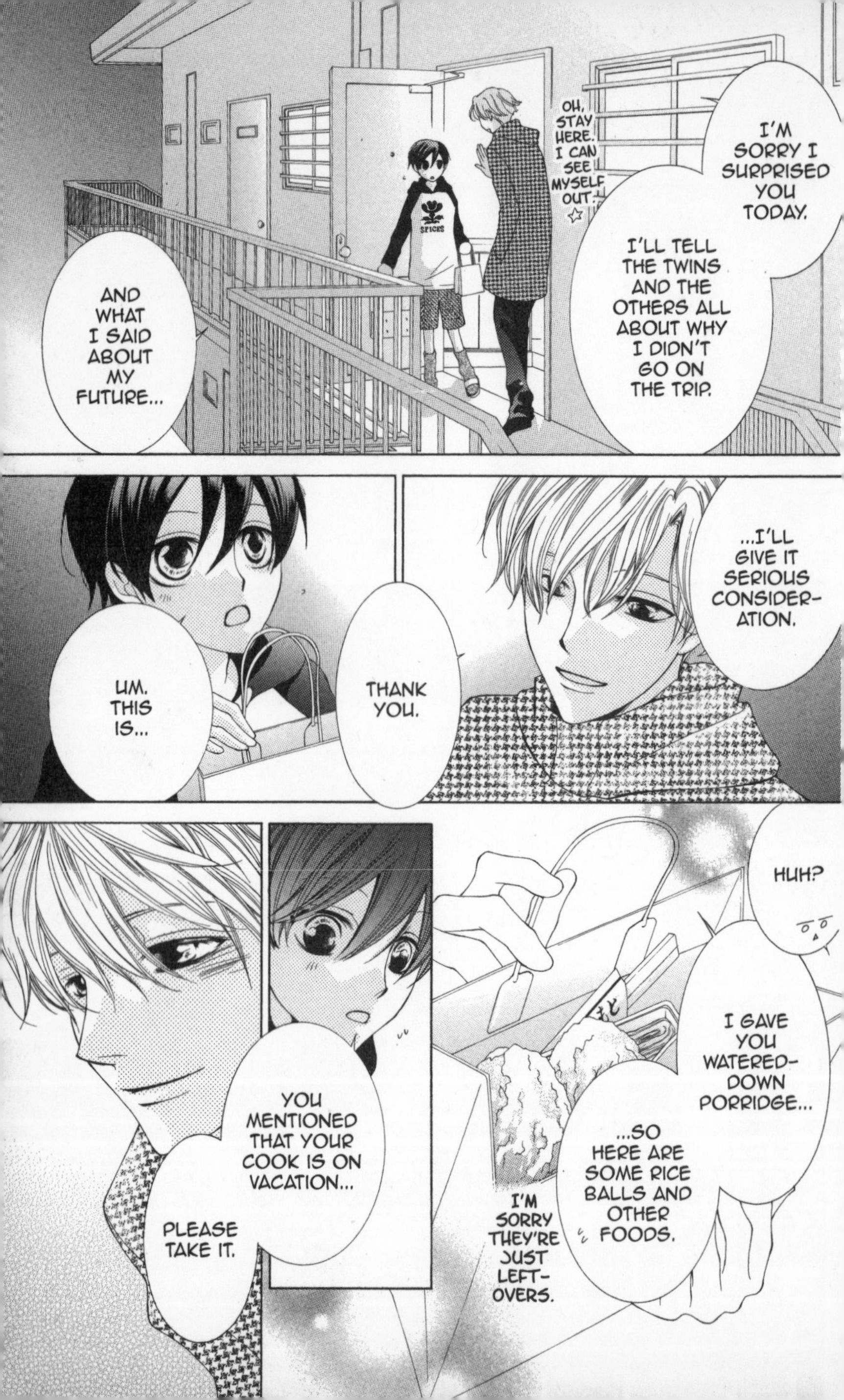
I'M SORRY I SURPRISED YOU TODAY.
OH, STAY HERE. I CAN SEE MYSELF OUT. ☆
I'LL TELL THE TWINS AND THE OTHERS ALL ABOUT WHY I DIDN'T GO ON THE TRIP.
AND WHAT I SAID ABOUT MY FUTURE...
...I'LL GIVE IT SERIOUS CONSIDER-ATION.
THANK YOU.
UM. THIS IS...
HUH?
I GAVE YOU WATERED-DOWN PORRIDGE...
...SO HERE ARE SOME RICE BALLS AND OTHER FOODS.
I'M SORRY THEY'RE JUST LEFT-OVERS.
YOU MENTIONED THAT YOUR COOK IS ON VACATION...
PLEASE TAKE IT.

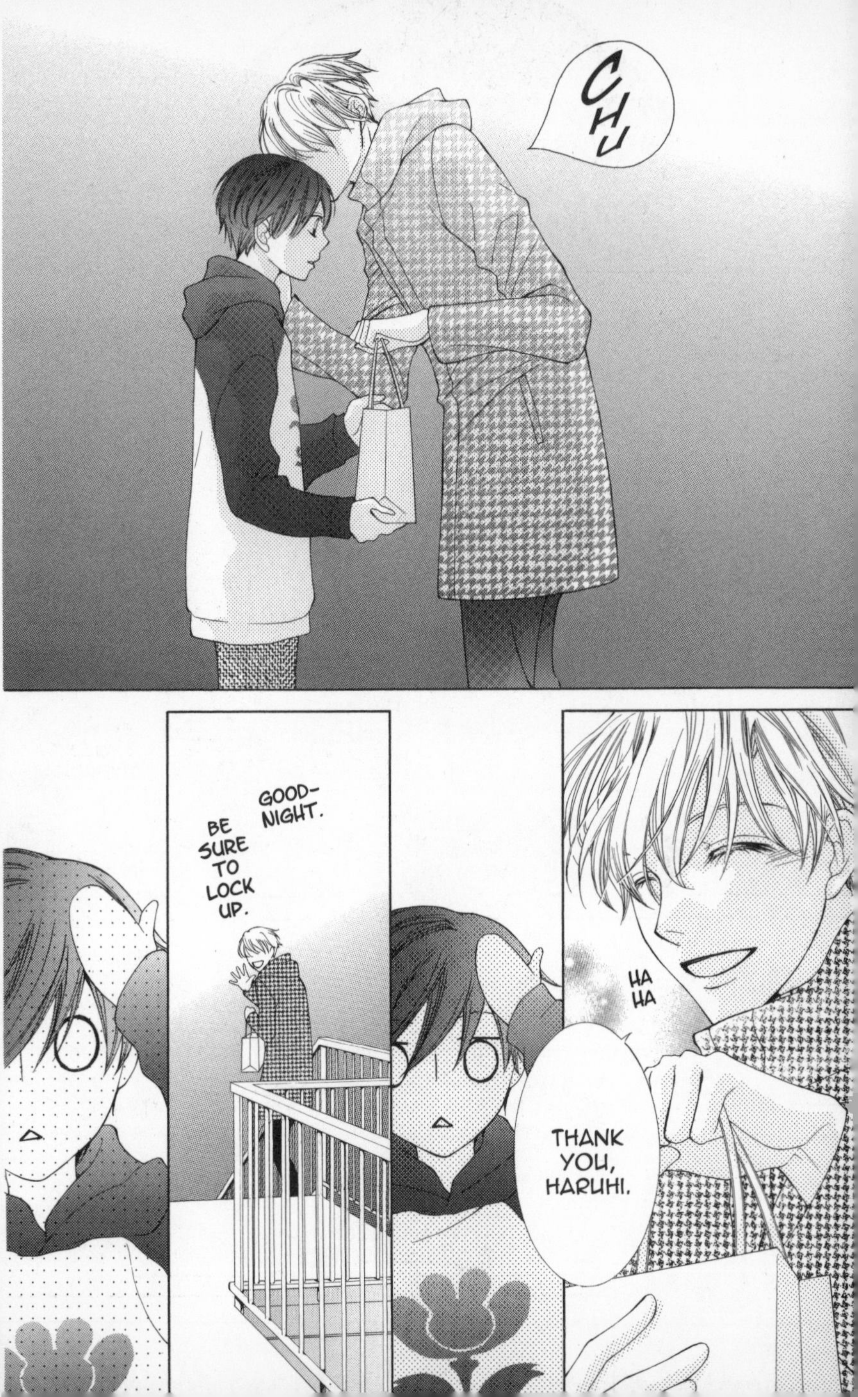
CHU
HA HA
THANK YOU, HARUHI.
GOOD-NIGHT.
BE SURE TO LOCK UP.

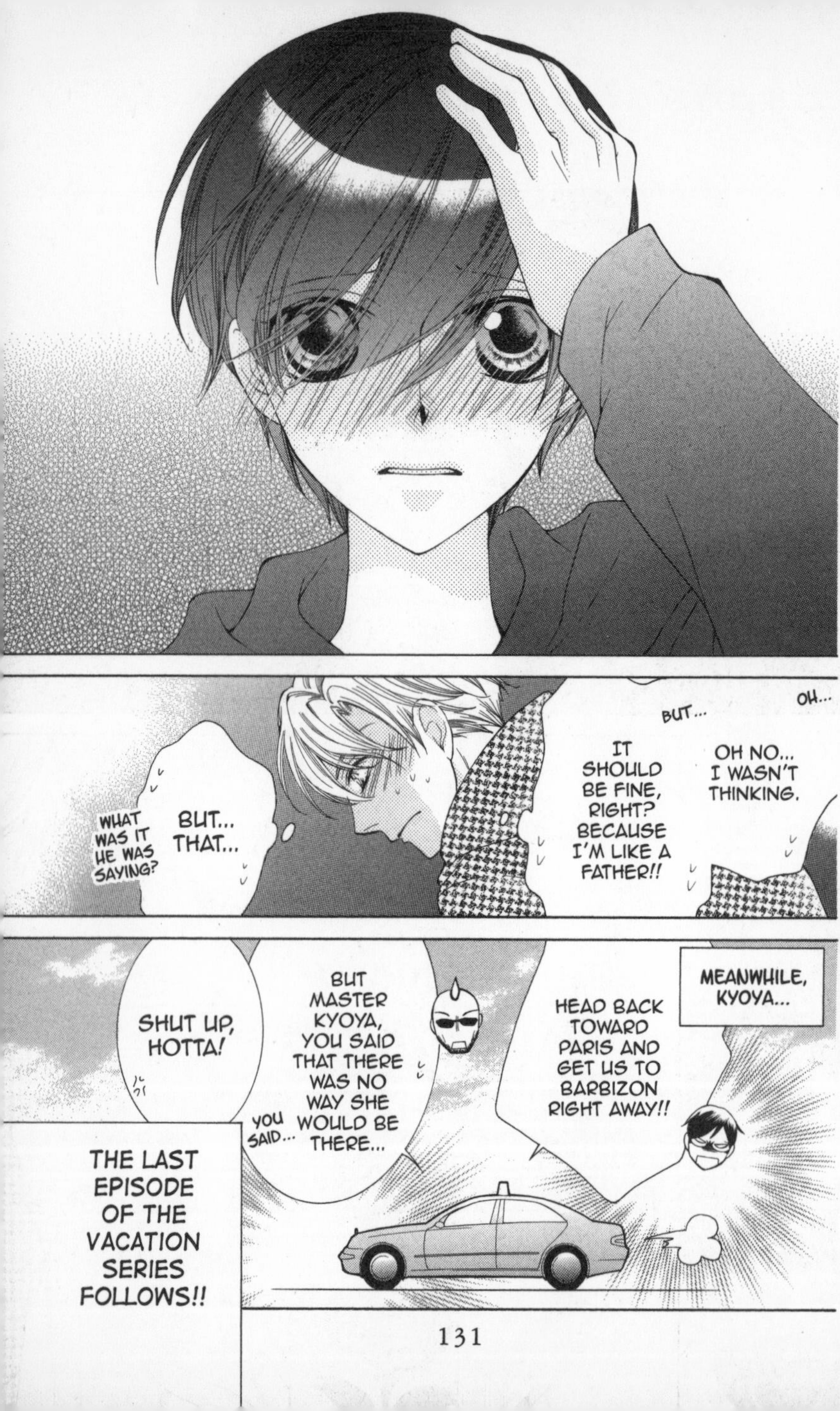
OH...
OH NO... I WASN'T THINKING.
BUT...
IT SHOULD BE FINE, RIGHT? BECAUSE I'M LIKE A FATHER!!
BUT... THAT...
WHAT WAS IT HE WAS SAYING?
MEANWHILE, KYOYA...
HEAD BACK TOWARD PARIS AND GET US TO BARBIZON RIGHT AWAY!!
BUT MASTER KYOYA, YOU SAID THAT THERE WAS NO WAY SHE WOULD BE THERE...
YOU SAID...
SHUT UP, HOTTA!
THE LAST EPISODE OF THE VACATION SERIES FOLLOWS!!

GUEST ROOM: FAXES

SPECIAL THANKS TO AKIRA HAGIO!!

SEXY KAORU + DANDY HIKARU

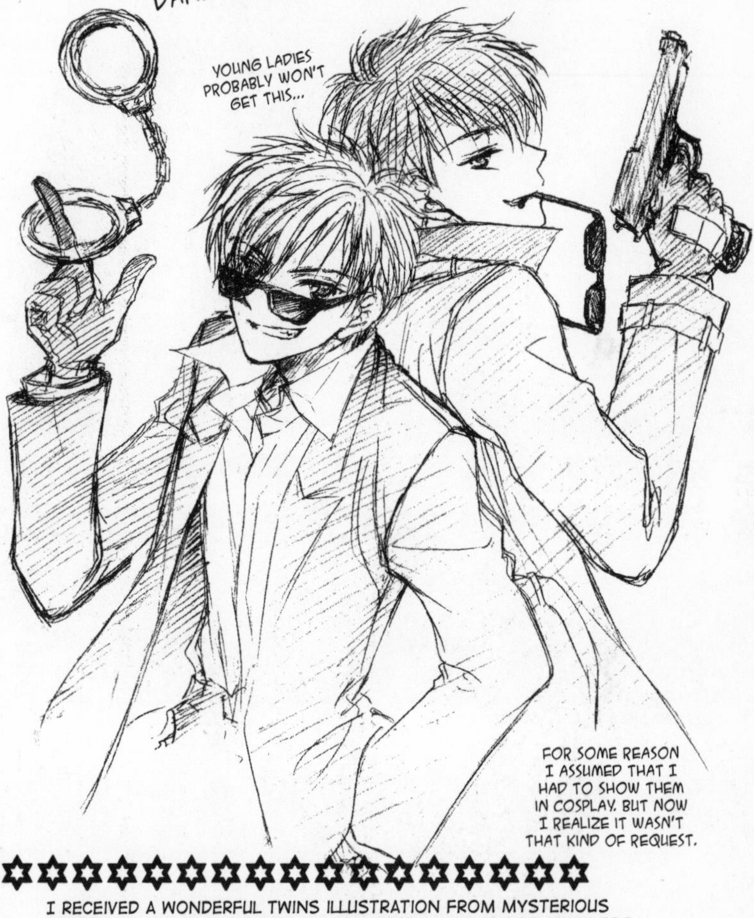
YOUNG LADIES PROBABLY WON'T GET THIS...

FOR SOME REASON I ASSUMED THAT I HAD TO SHOW THEM IN COSPLAY. BUT NOW I REALIZE IT WASN'T THAT KIND OF REQUEST.

I RECEIVED A WONDERFUL TWINS ILLUSTRATION FROM MYSTERIOUS BEAUTY AKI, OTHERWISE KNOWN AS HAGIO!! THANK YOU SO MUCH FOR GOING AS FAR AS HAVING THEM IN COSPLAY!! AT FIRST THE IDEA WAS TO HAVE MAI DRESSED AS A POLICEWOMAN IN A MINISKIRT (BECAUSE HARUHI'S BREASTS AREN'T LARGE ENOUGH). BUT IN THE END, IT WAS THE TWINS. I UNDERSTAND...YOU WERE STUMPED BY THE LIPS WITH MAI. (LAUGH) BY THE WAY, THE COSPLAY IS FROM *ABU○I DEKA*. ☆ OF COURSE, I'M OF AN AGE THAT UNDERSTANDS THE REFERENCE.♡ (BUT I'VE ACTUALLY NEVER SEEN THE SERIES.)

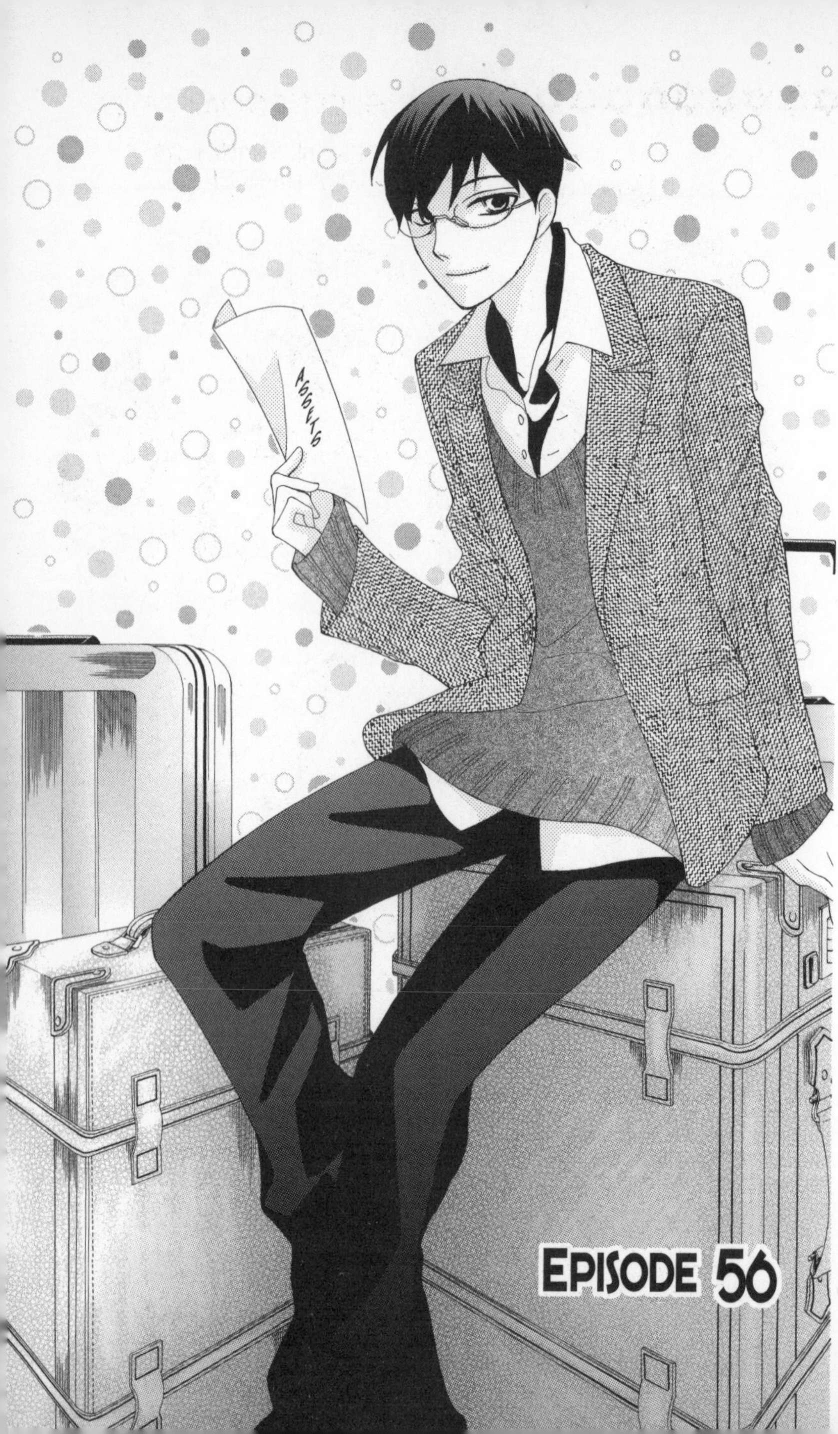
ASSETS

EPISODE 56

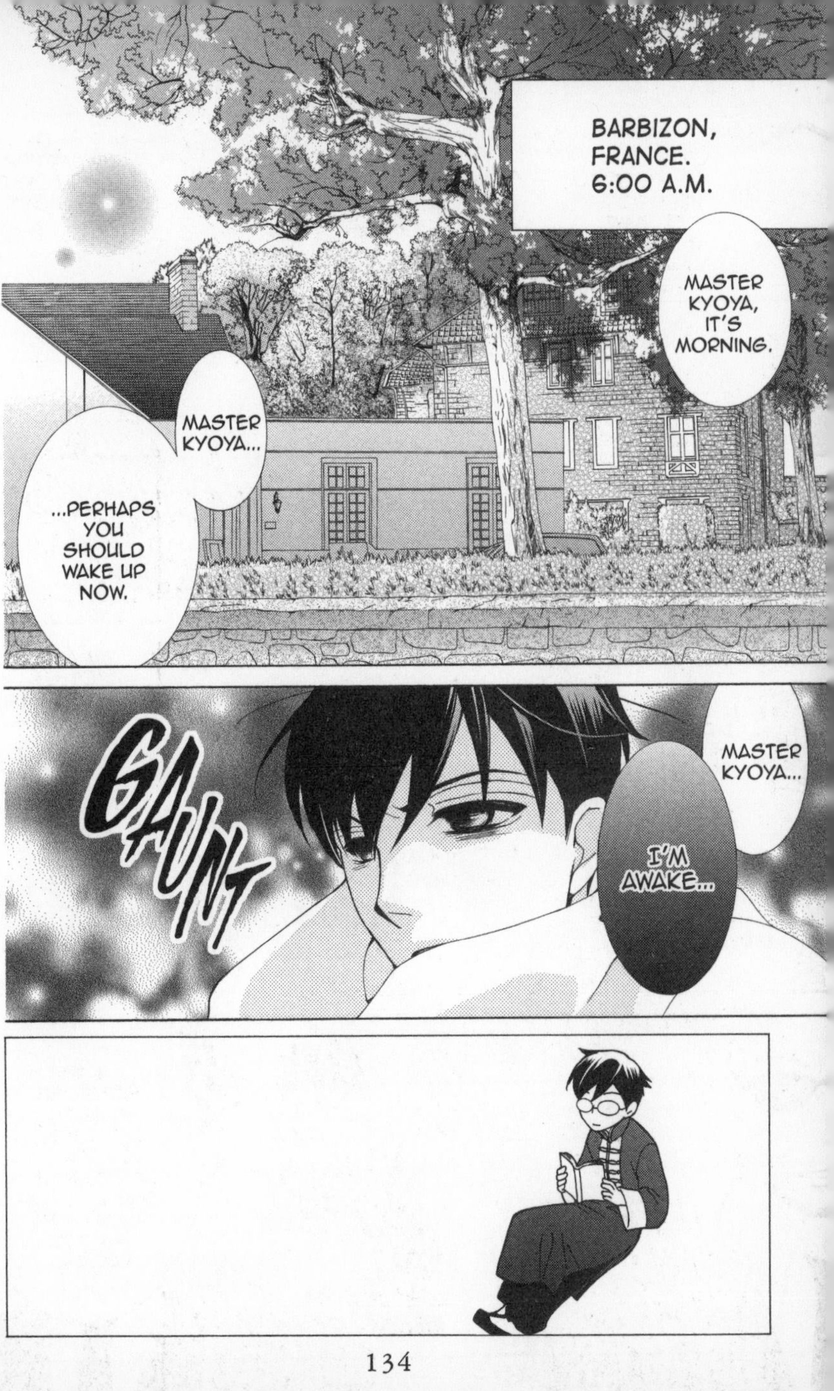
BARBIZON, FRANCE. 6:00 A.M.
MASTER KYOYA, IT'S MORNING.
MASTER KYOYA...
...PERHAPS YOU SHOULD WAKE UP NOW.
MASTER KYOYA...
I'M AWAKE...
GAUNT

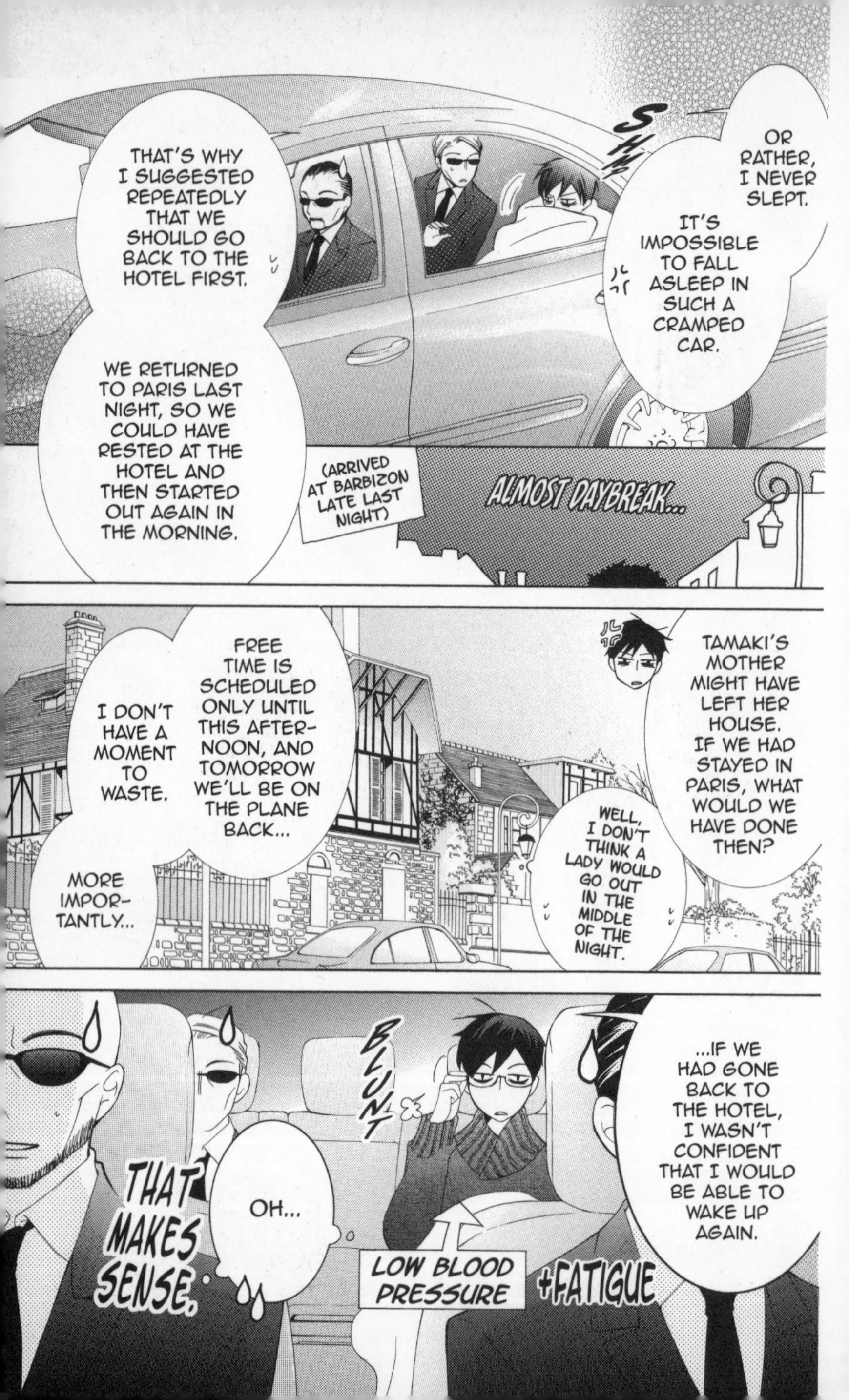
SHIMP
OR RATHER, I NEVER SLEPT.
IT'S IMPOSSIBLE TO FALL ASLEEP IN SUCH A CRAMPED CAR.
THAT'S WHY I SUGGESTED REPEATEDLY THAT WE SHOULD GO BACK TO THE HOTEL FIRST.
ALMOST DAYBREAK...
(ARRIVED AT BARBIZON LATE LAST NIGHT)
WE RETURNED TO PARIS LAST NIGHT, SO WE COULD HAVE RESTED AT THE HOTEL AND THEN STARTED OUT AGAIN IN THE MORNING.
TAMAKI'S MOTHER MIGHT HAVE LEFT HER HOUSE. IF WE HAD STAYED IN PARIS, WHAT WOULD WE HAVE DONE THEN?
WELL, I DON'T THINK A LADY WOULD GO OUT IN THE MIDDLE OF THE NIGHT.
FREE TIME IS SCHEDULED ONLY UNTIL THIS AFTERNOON, AND TOMORROW WE'LL BE ON THE PLANE BACK...
I DON'T HAVE A MOMENT TO WASTE.
MORE IMPORTANTLY...
...IF WE HAD GONE BACK TO THE HOTEL, I WASN'T CONFIDENT THAT I WOULD BE ABLE TO WAKE UP AGAIN.
+FATIGUE
LOW BLOOD PRESSURE
BLUNT
OH...
THAT MAKES SENSE.

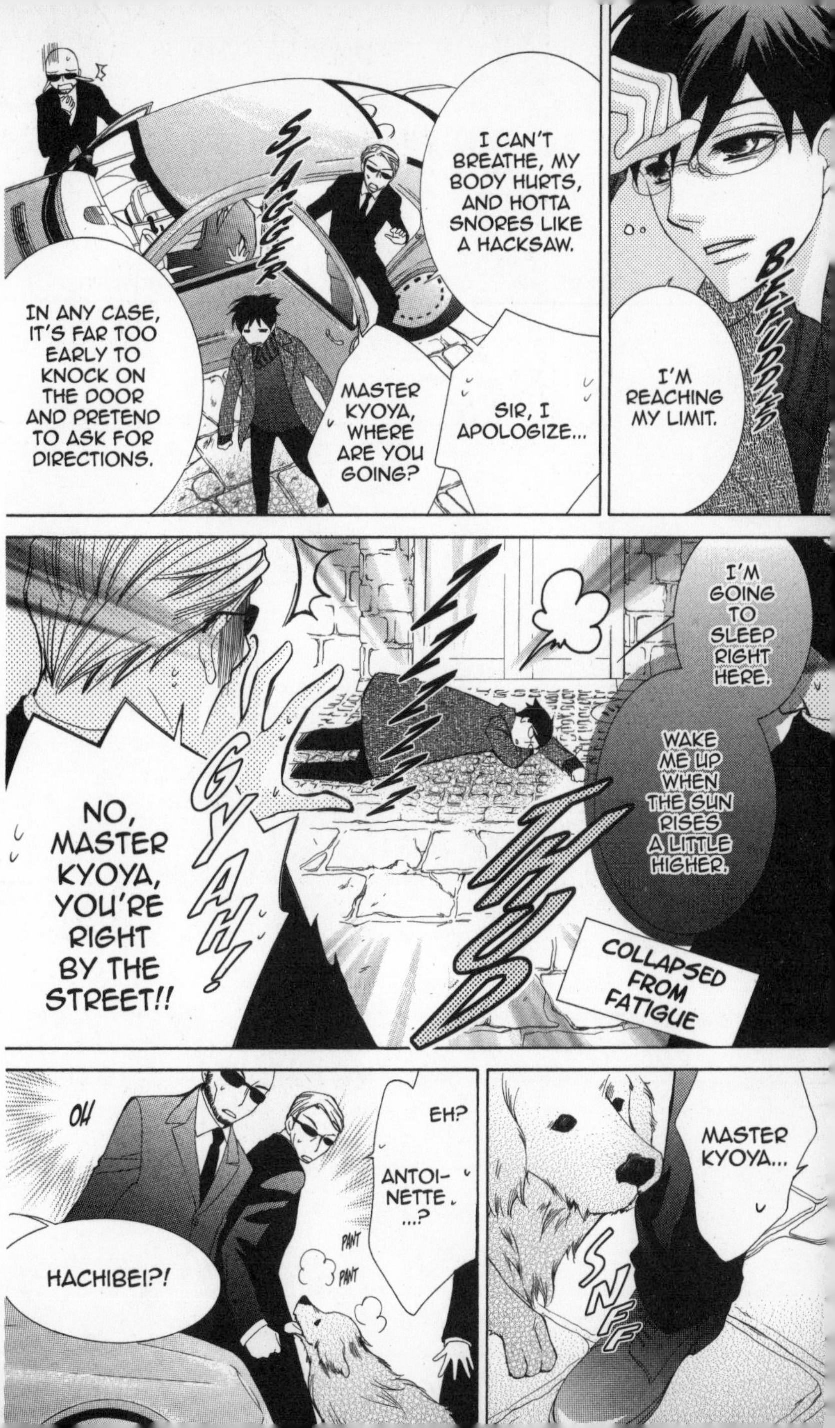

I'M REACHING MY LIMIT.
I CAN'T BREATHE, MY BODY HURTS, AND HOTTA SNORES LIKE A HACKSAW.
SIR, I APOLOGIZE...
MASTER KYOYA, WHERE ARE YOU GOING?
STAGGER
IN ANY CASE, IT'S FAR TOO EARLY TO KNOCK ON THE DOOR AND PRETEND TO ASK FOR DIRECTIONS.
I'M GOING TO SLEEP RIGHT HERE.
WAKE ME UP WHEN THE SUN RISES A LITTLE HIGHER.
COLLAPSED FROM FATIGUE
GYAAH!
NO, MASTER KYOYA, YOU'RE RIGHT BY THE STREET!!
MASTER KYOYA...
SNFF
EH?
ANTOINETTE...?
OH
PANT
PANT
HACHIBEI?!

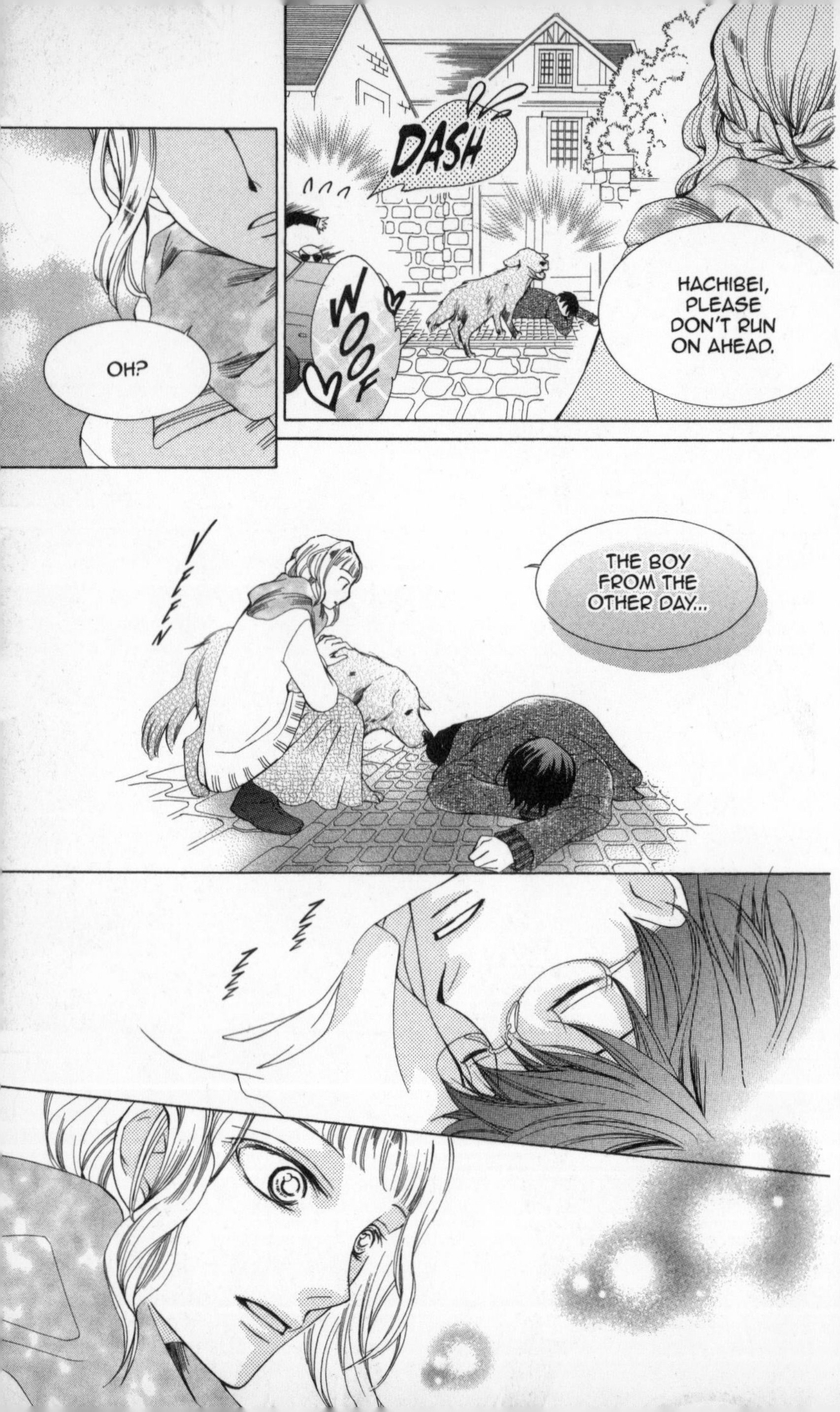
HACHIBEI, PLEASE DON'T RUN ON AHEAD.
DASH
WOOF
OH?
VEEN
THE BOY FROM THE OTHER DAY...
ZZZ
ZZZ

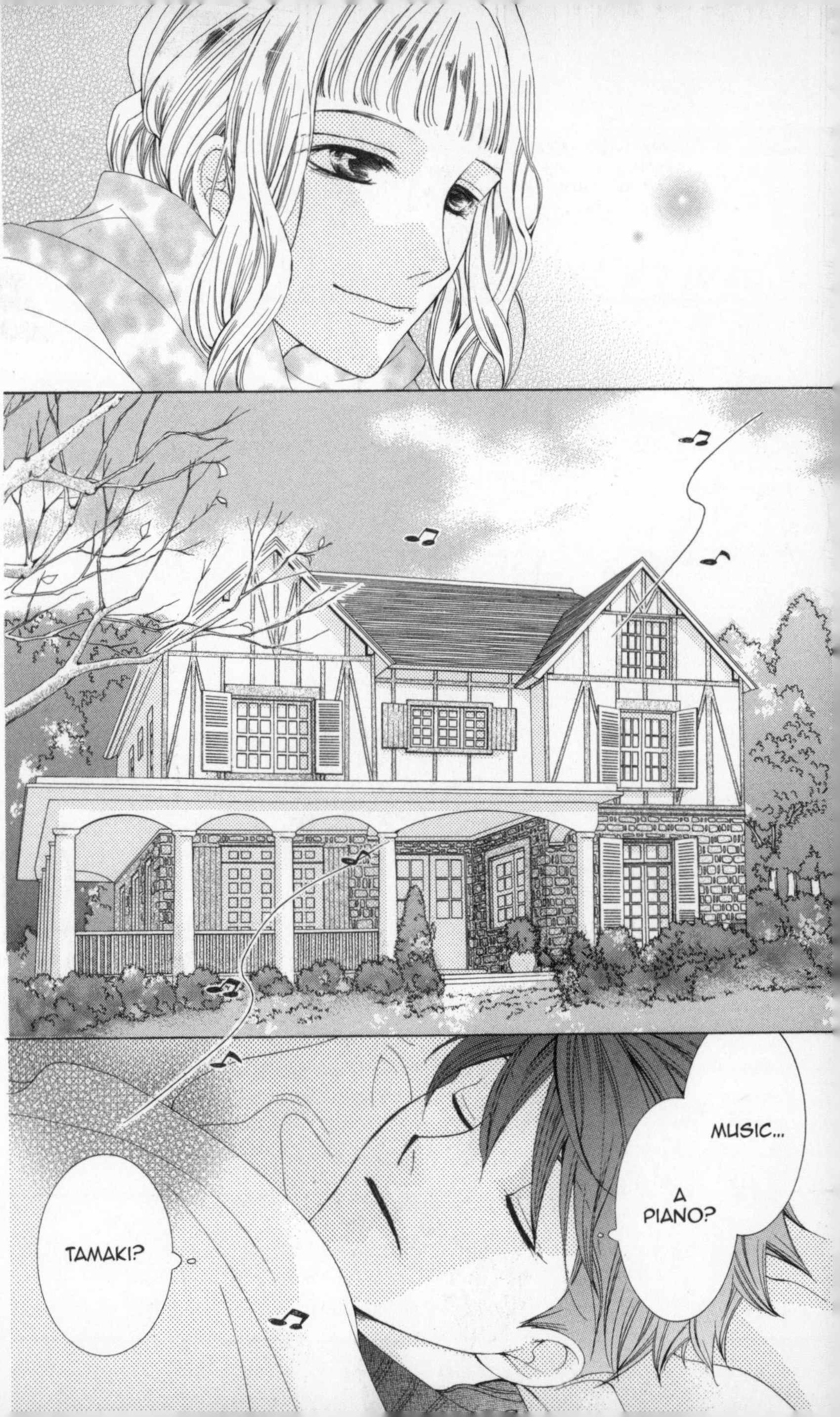
MUSIC... A PIANO?
TAMAKI?

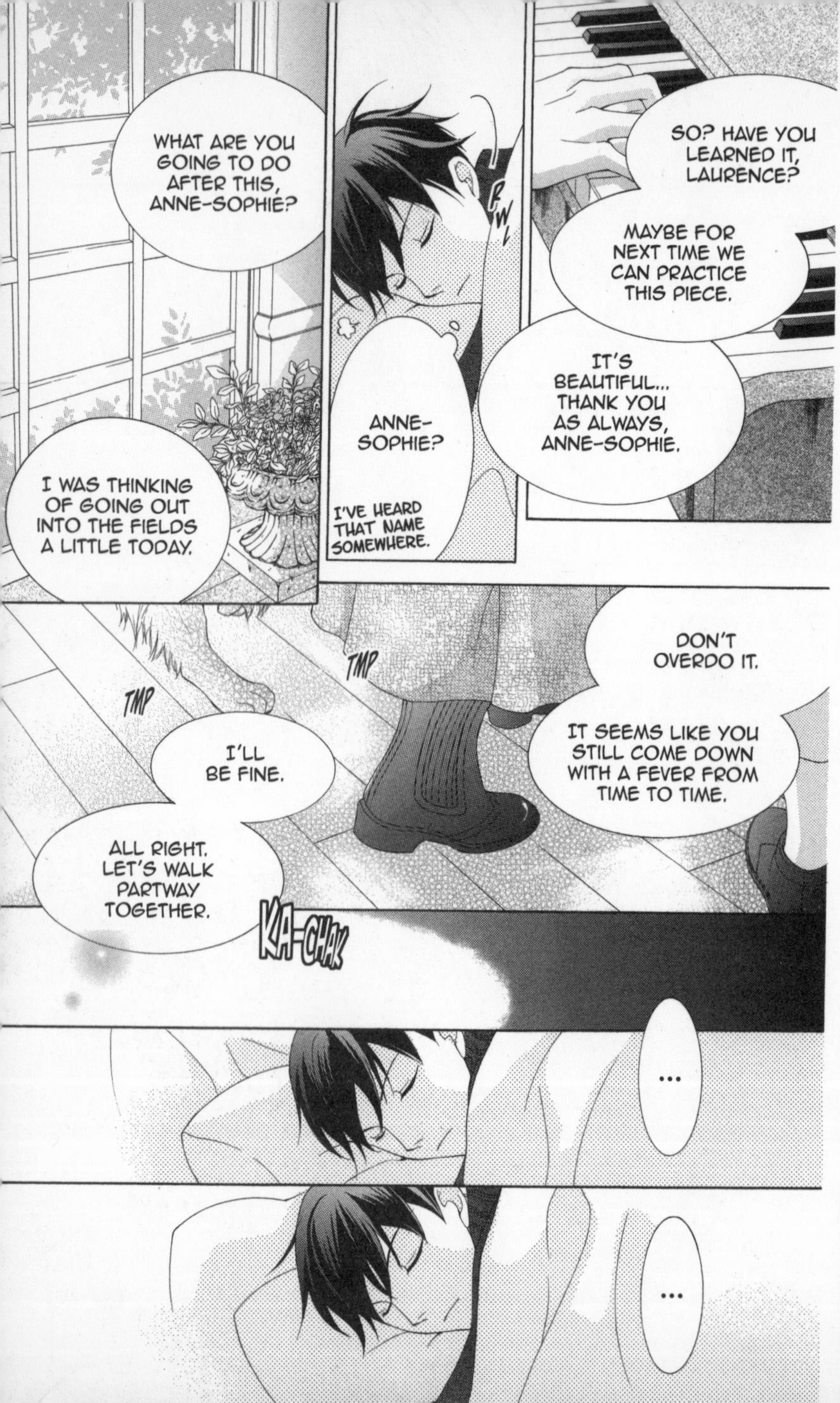
SO? HAVE YOU LEARNED IT, LAURENCE?
MAYBE FOR NEXT TIME WE CAN PRACTICE THIS PIECE.
IT'S BEAUTIFUL... THANK YOU AS ALWAYS, ANNE-SOPHIE.
ANNE-SOPHIE?
I'VE HEARD THAT NAME SOMEWHERE.
WHAT ARE YOU GOING TO DO AFTER THIS, ANNE-SOPHIE?
I WAS THINKING OF GOING OUT INTO THE FIELDS A LITTLE TODAY.
DON'T OVERDO IT.
IT SEEMS LIKE YOU STILL COME DOWN WITH A FEVER FROM TIME TO TIME.
TMP
TMP
I'LL BE FINE.
ALL RIGHT. LET'S WALK PARTWAY TOGETHER.
KA-CHAK
...
...

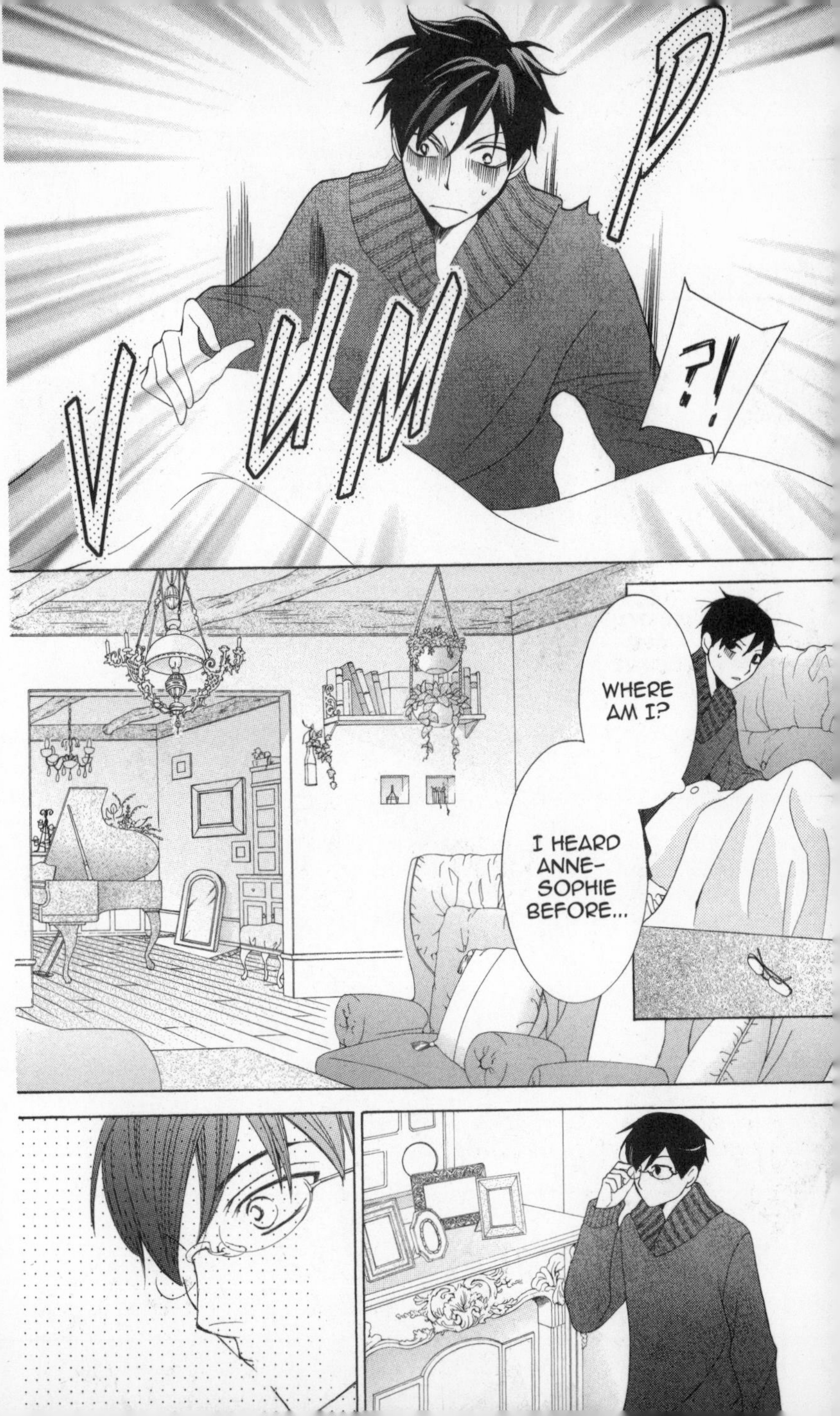
VUMP
?!
WHERE AM I?
I HEARD ANNE-SOPHIE BEFORE...

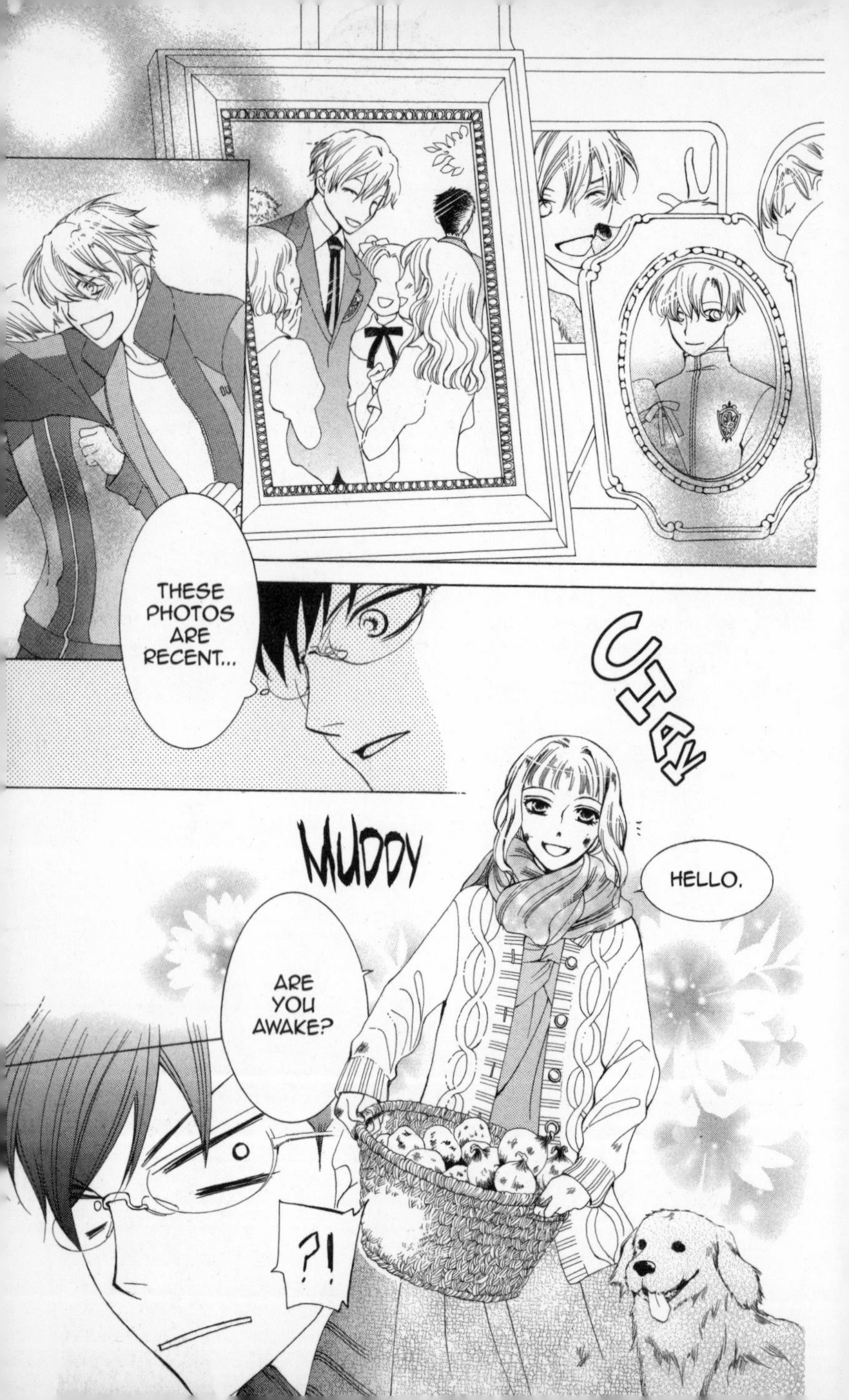
THESE PHOTOS ARE RECENT...
HELLO.
MUDDY
ARE YOU AWAKE?
?!

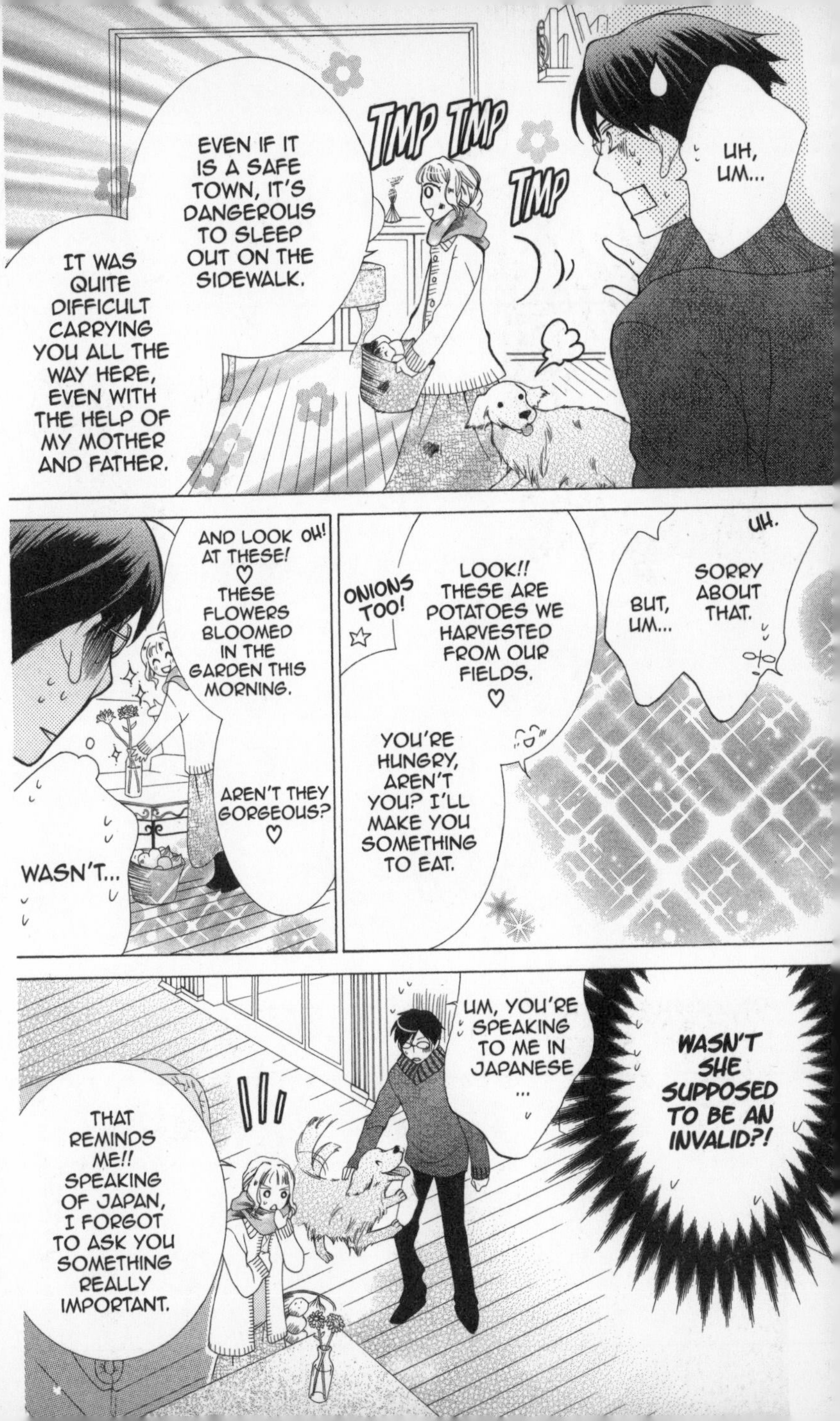
UH, UM...
TMP TMP
TMP
EVEN IF IT IS A SAFE TOWN, IT'S DANGEROUS TO SLEEP OUT ON THE SIDEWALK.
IT WAS QUITE DIFFICULT CARRYING YOU ALL THE WAY HERE, EVEN WITH THE HELP OF MY MOTHER AND FATHER.
UH.
SORRY ABOUT THAT.
BUT, UM...
LOOK!! THESE ARE POTATOES WE HARVESTED FROM OUR FIELDS. ♡
ONIONS TOO!
YOU'RE HUNGRY, AREN'T YOU? I'LL MAKE YOU SOMETHING TO EAT.
OH!
AND LOOK AT THESE! ♡ THESE FLOWERS BLOOMED IN THE GARDEN THIS MORNING.
AREN'T THEY GORGEOUS? ♡
WASN'T...
WASN'T SHE SUPPOSED TO BE AN INVALID?!
UM, YOU'RE SPEAKING TO ME IN JAPANESE ...
THAT REMINDS ME!! SPEAKING OF JAPAN, I FORGOT TO ASK YOU SOMETHING REALLY IMPORTANT.

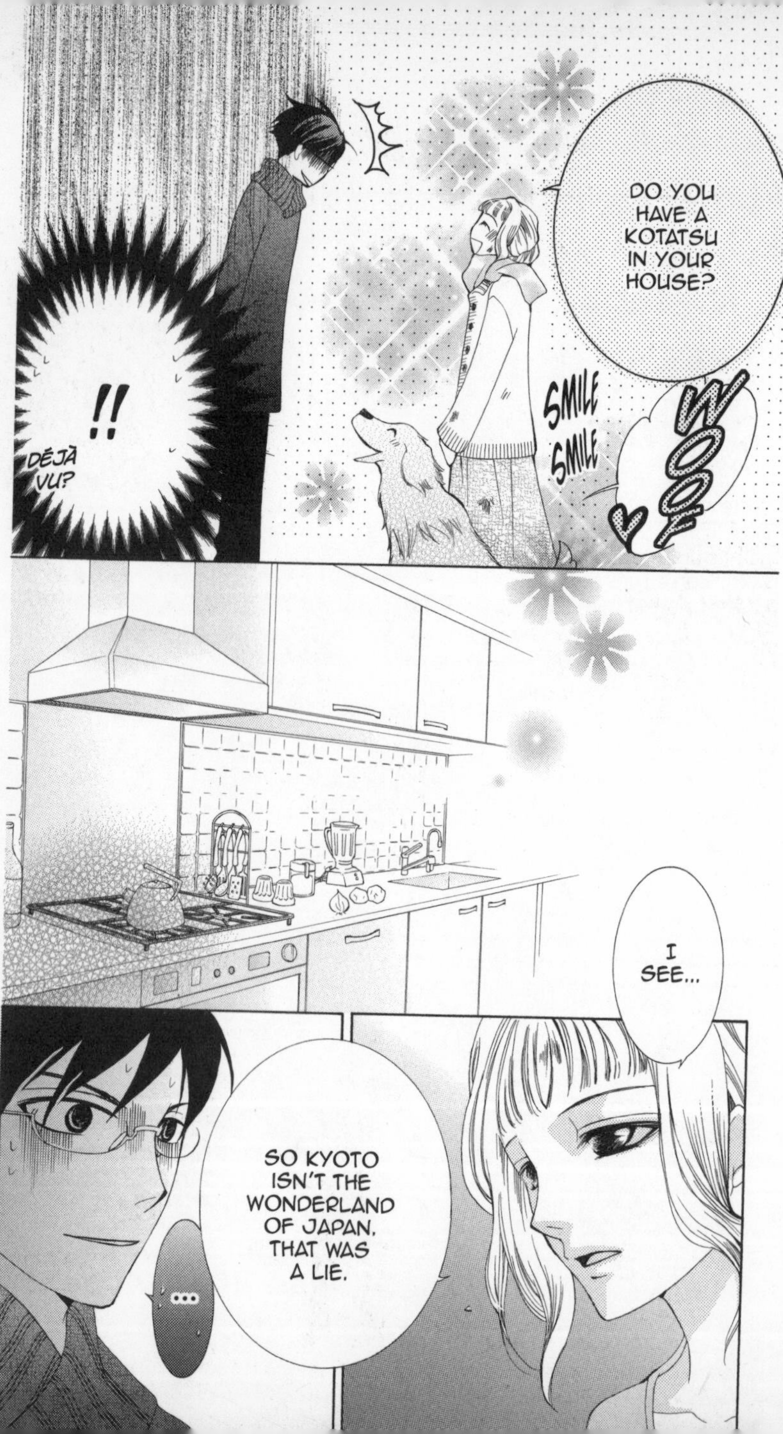
DO YOU HAVE A KOTATSU IN YOUR HOUSE?
WOOF
SMILE SMILE
!!
DÉJÀ VU?
I SEE...
SO KYOTO ISN'T THE WONDERLAND OF JAPAN. THAT WAS A LIE.
...

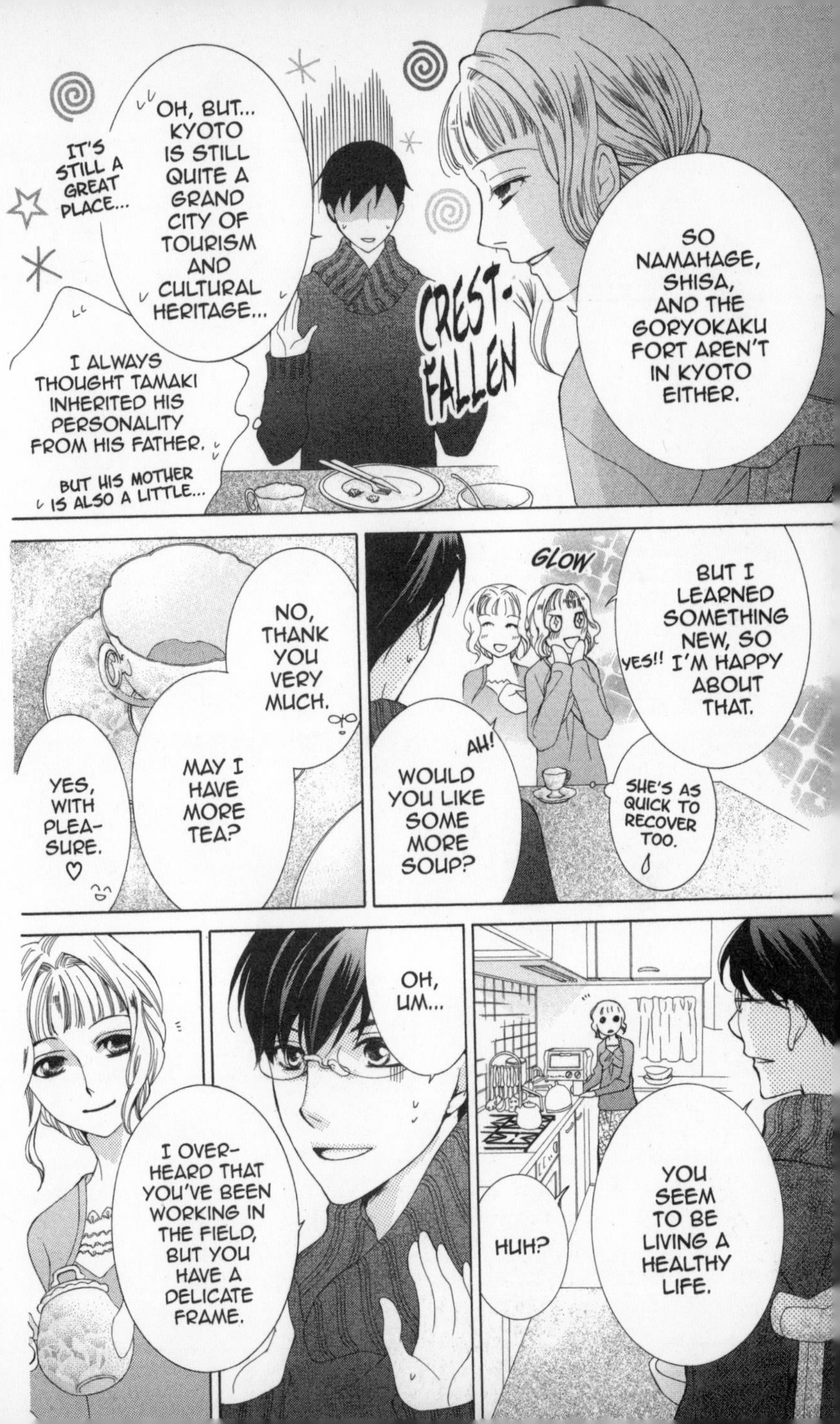
SO NAMAHAGE, SHISA, AND THE GORYOKAKU FORT AREN'T IN KYOTO EITHER.
CREST-FALLEN
OH, BUT... KYOTO IS STILL QUITE A GRAND CITY OF TOURISM AND CULTURAL HERITAGE...
IT'S STILL A GREAT PLACE...
I ALWAYS THOUGHT TAMAKI INHERITED HIS PERSONALITY FROM HIS FATHER.
BUT HIS MOTHER IS ALSO A LITTLE...
GLOW
BUT I LEARNED SOMETHING NEW, SO I'M HAPPY ABOUT THAT.
YES!!
SHE'S AS QUICK TO RECOVER TOO.
AH!
WOULD YOU LIKE SOME MORE SOUP?
NO, THANK YOU VERY MUCH.
MAY I HAVE MORE TEA?
YES, WITH PLEA-SURE. ♡
YOU SEEM TO BE LIVING A HEALTHY LIFE.
HUH?
OH, UM...
I OVER-HEARD THAT YOU'VE BEEN WORKING IN THE FIELD, BUT YOU HAVE A DELICATE FRAME.

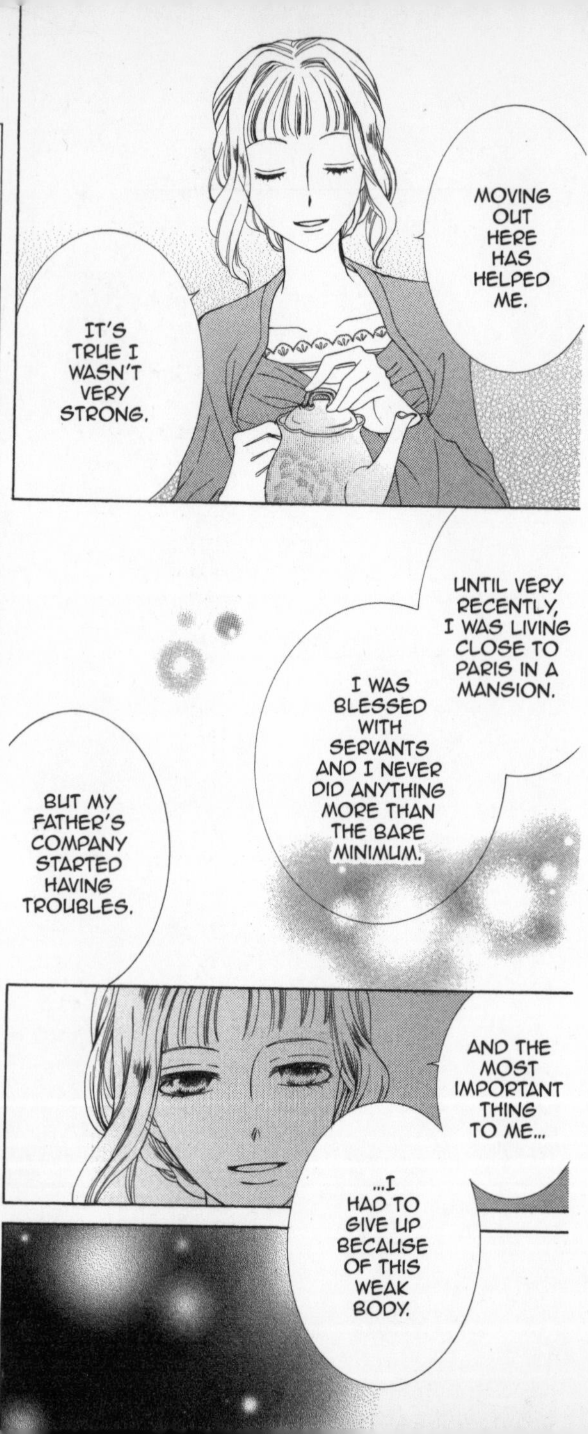
MOVING OUT HERE HAS HELPED ME.
IT'S TRUE I WASN'T VERY STRONG.
UNTIL VERY RECENTLY, I WAS LIVING CLOSE TO PARIS IN A MANSION.
I WAS BLESSED WITH SERVANTS AND I NEVER DID ANYTHING MORE THAN THE BARE MINIMUM.
BUT MY FATHER'S COMPANY STARTED HAVING TROUBLES.
AND THE MOST IMPORTANT THING TO ME...
...I HAD TO GIVE UP BECAUSE OF THIS WEAK BODY.

5

✿ AND THIS ISN'T DRAWING EQUIPMENT, BUT...

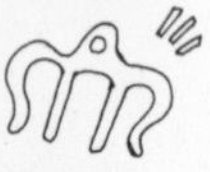

THERE'S A CLIP SHAPED LIKE THIS TO KEEP PAGES OPEN FOR PLAYING MUSIC. IF YOU HAVE A THIN RESOURCE BOOK, I'D RECOMMEND KEEPING IT OPEN WITH THIS.

✿ ALSO, I DRAW MY ROUGH DRAFTS USING AN ORANGE MECHANICAL PENCIL, AND THEN I DRAW OVER THAT USING A BLACK MECHANICAL PENCIL.

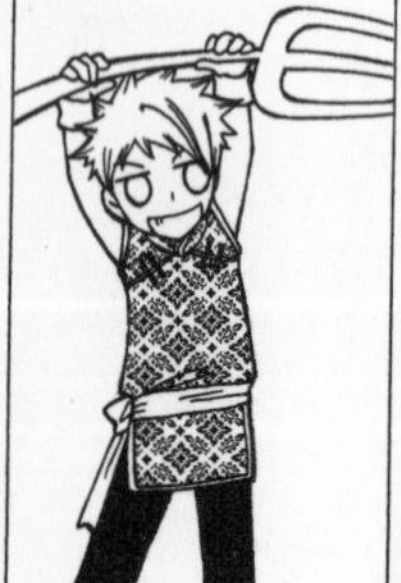

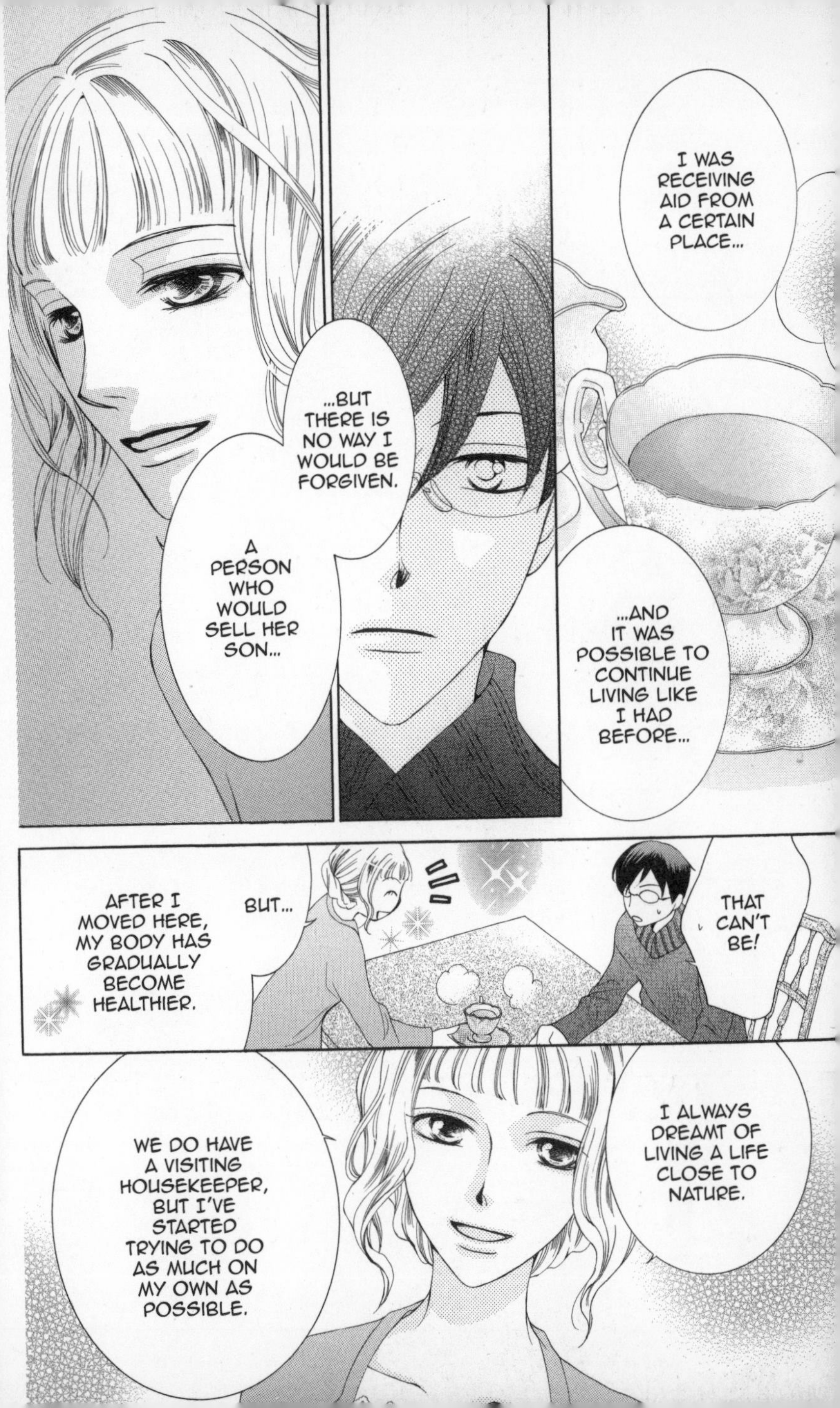
I WAS RECEIVING AID FROM A CERTAIN PLACE...
...AND IT WAS POSSIBLE TO CONTINUE LIVING LIKE I HAD BEFORE...
A PERSON WHO WOULD SELL HER SON...
...BUT THERE IS NO WAY I WOULD BE FORGIVEN.
THAT CAN'T BE!
BUT...
AFTER I MOVED HERE, MY BODY HAS GRADUALLY BECOME HEALTHIER.
I ALWAYS DREAMT OF LIVING A LIFE CLOSE TO NATURE.
WE DO HAVE A VISITING HOUSEKEEPER, BUT I'VE STARTED TRYING TO DO AS MUCH ON MY OWN AS POSSIBLE.

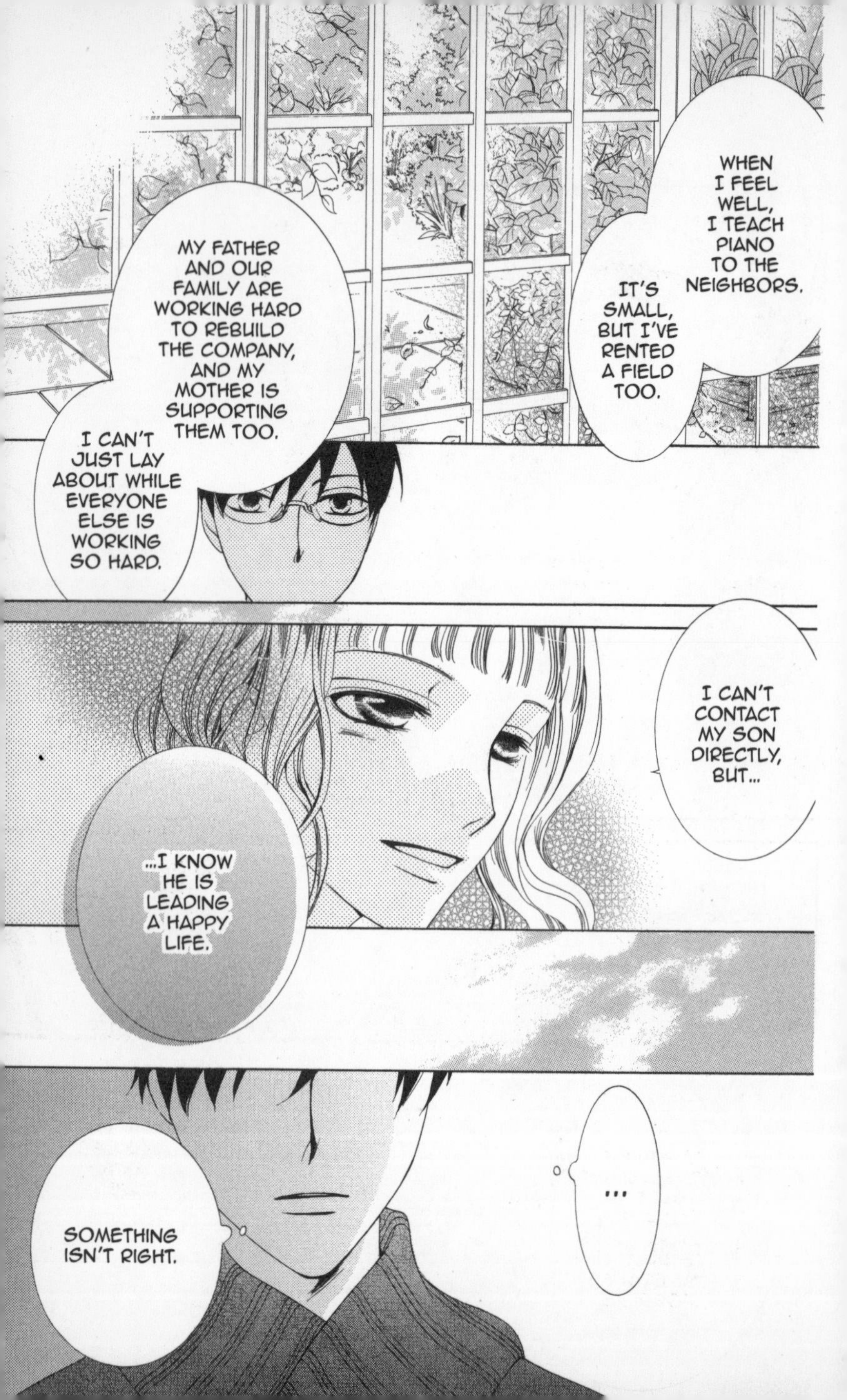
WHEN I FEEL WELL, I TEACH PIANO TO THE NEIGHBORS.
IT'S SMALL, BUT I'VE RENTED A FIELD TOO.
MY FATHER AND OUR FAMILY ARE WORKING HARD TO REBUILD THE COMPANY, AND MY MOTHER IS SUPPORTING THEM TOO.
I CAN'T JUST LAY ABOUT WHILE EVERYONE ELSE IS WORKING SO HARD.
I CAN'T CONTACT MY SON DIRECTLY, BUT...
...I KNOW HE IS LEADING A HAPPY LIFE.
...
SOMETHING ISN'T RIGHT.

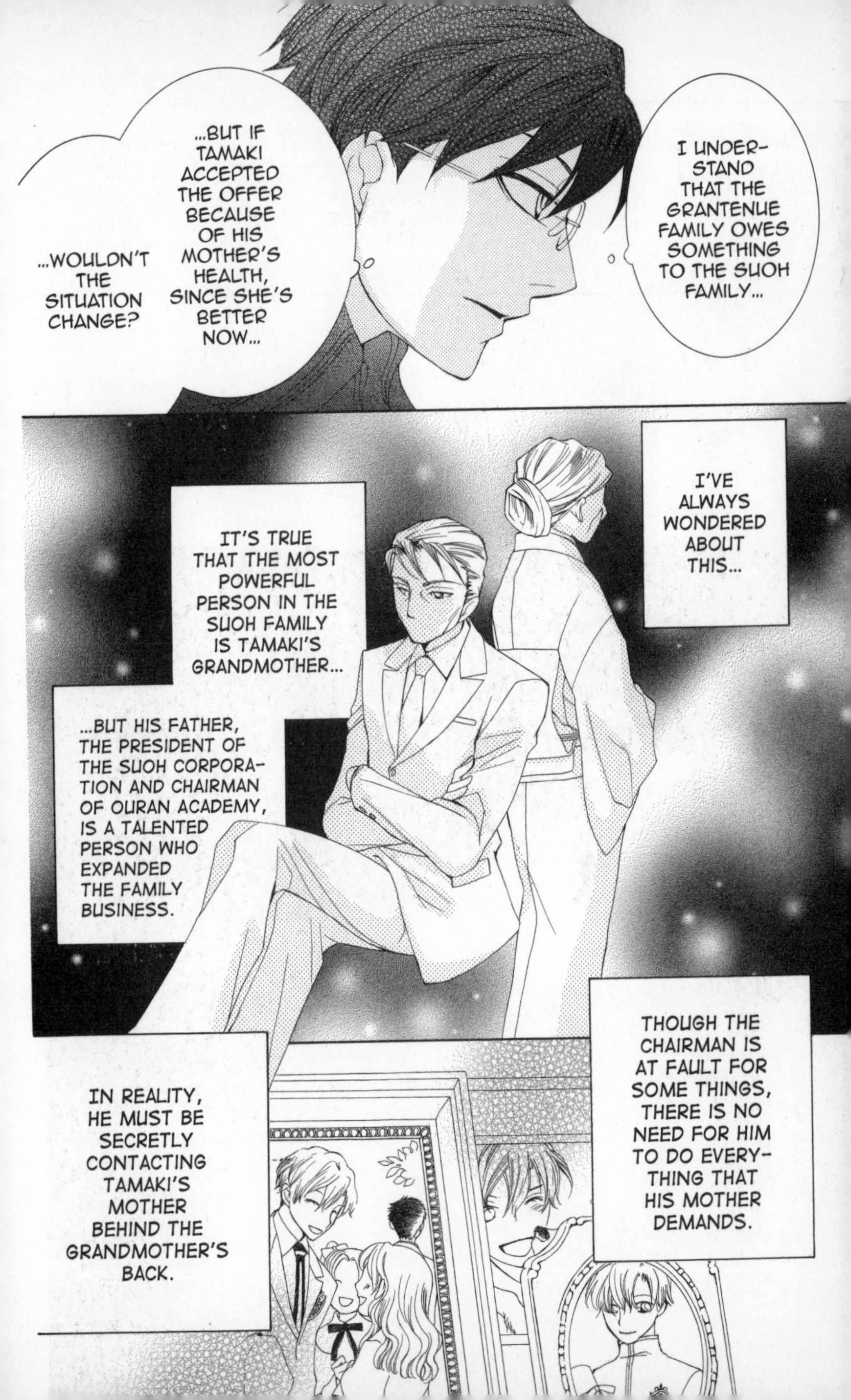
I UNDER-STAND THAT THE GRANTENUE FAMILY OWES SOMETHING TO THE SUOH FAMILY...
...BUT IF TAMAKI ACCEPTED THE OFFER BECAUSE OF HIS MOTHER'S HEALTH, SINCE SHE'S BETTER NOW...
...WOULDN'T THE SITUATION CHANGE?
I'VE ALWAYS WONDERED ABOUT THIS...
IT'S TRUE THAT THE MOST POWERFUL PERSON IN THE SUOH FAMILY IS TAMAKI'S GRANDMOTHER...
...BUT HIS FATHER, THE PRESIDENT OF THE SUOH CORPORA-TION AND CHAIRMAN OF OURAN ACADEMY, IS A TALENTED PERSON WHO EXPANDED THE FAMILY BUSINESS.
THOUGH THE CHAIRMAN IS AT FAULT FOR SOME THINGS, THERE IS NO NEED FOR HIM TO DO EVERY-THING THAT HIS MOTHER DEMANDS.
IN REALITY, HE MUST BE SECRETLY CONTACTING TAMAKI'S MOTHER BEHIND THE GRANDMOTHER'S BACK.

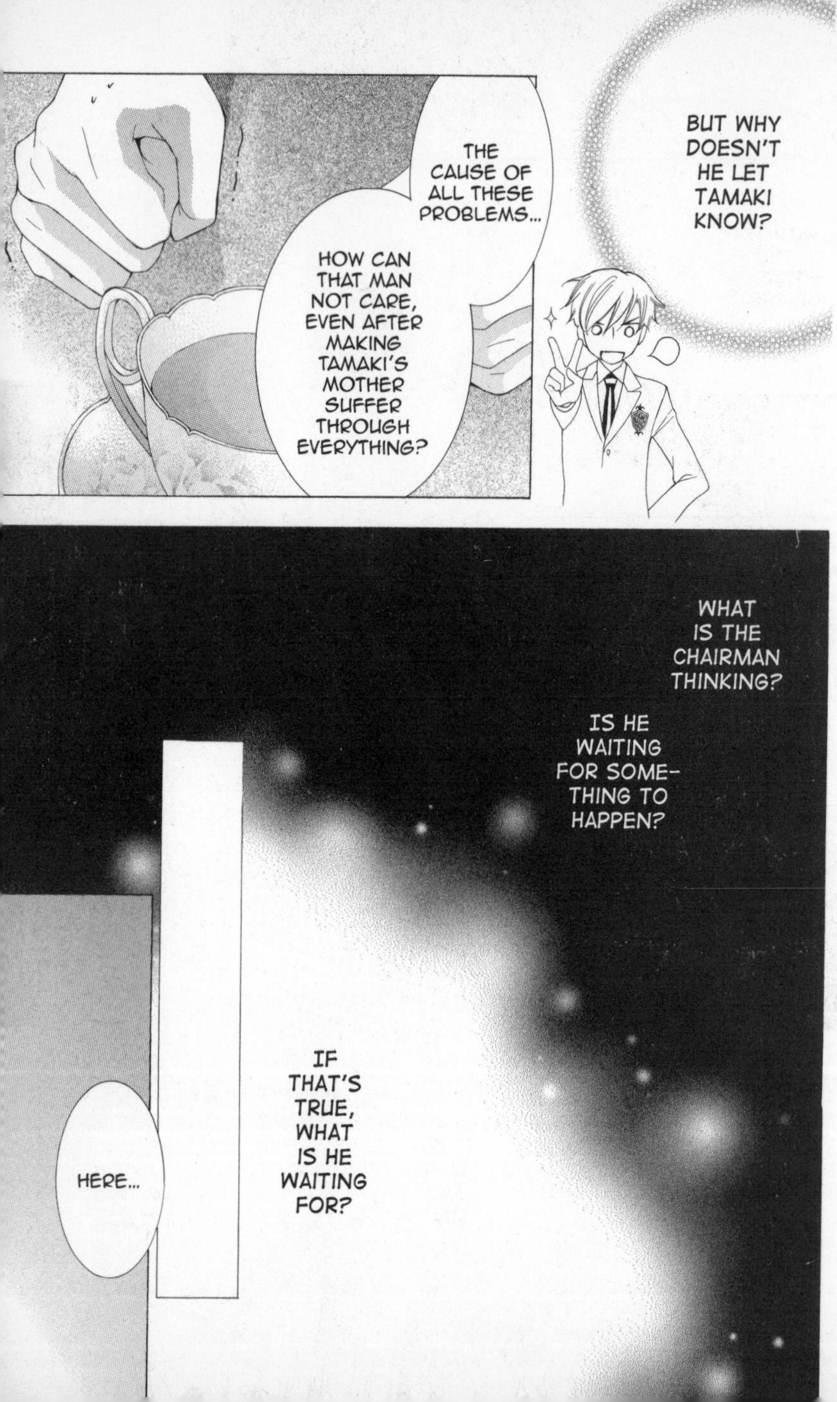
BUT WHY DOESN'T HE LET TAMAKI KNOW?
THE CAUSE OF ALL THESE PROBLEMS...
HOW CAN THAT MAN NOT CARE, EVEN AFTER MAKING TAMAKI'S MOTHER SUFFER THROUGH EVERYTHING?
WHAT IS THE CHAIRMAN THINKING?
IS HE WAITING FOR SOME-THING TO HAPPEN?
IF THAT'S TRUE, WHAT IS HE WAITING FOR?
HERE...

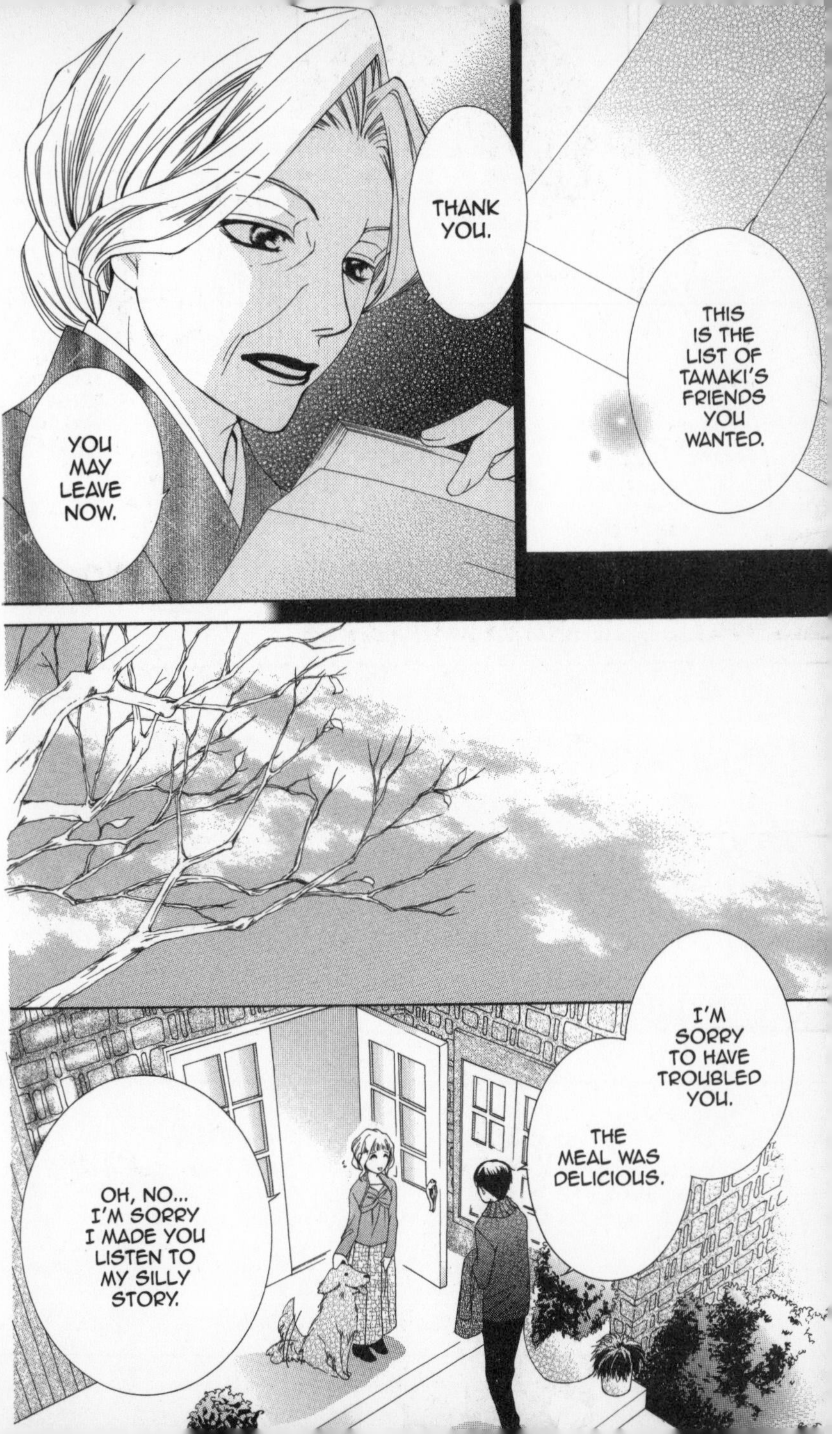
THIS IS THE LIST OF TAMAKI'S FRIENDS YOU WANTED.
THANK YOU.
YOU MAY LEAVE NOW.
I'M SORRY TO HAVE TROUBLED YOU.
THE MEAL WAS DELICIOUS.
OH, NO... I'M SORRY I MADE YOU LISTEN TO MY SILLY STORY.

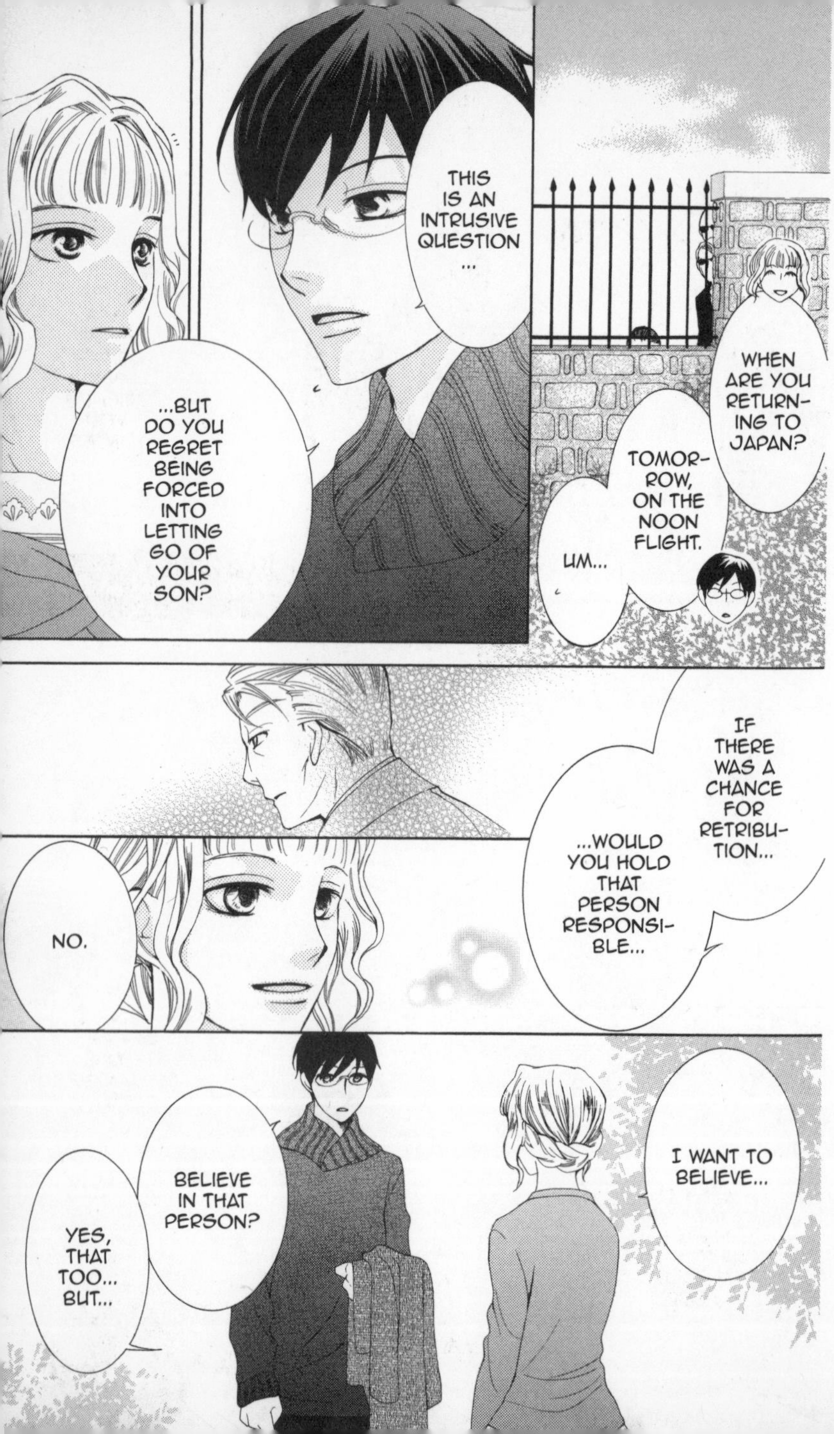
WHEN ARE YOU RETURN-ING TO JAPAN?
TOMOR-ROW, ON THE NOON FLIGHT.
UM...
THIS IS AN INTRUSIVE QUESTION ...
...BUT DO YOU REGRET BEING FORCED INTO LETTING GO OF YOUR SON?
IF THERE WAS A CHANCE FOR RETRIBU-TION...
...WOULD YOU HOLD THAT PERSON RESPONSI-BLE...
NO.
I WANT TO BELIEVE...
BELIEVE IN THAT PERSON?
YES, THAT TOO... BUT...

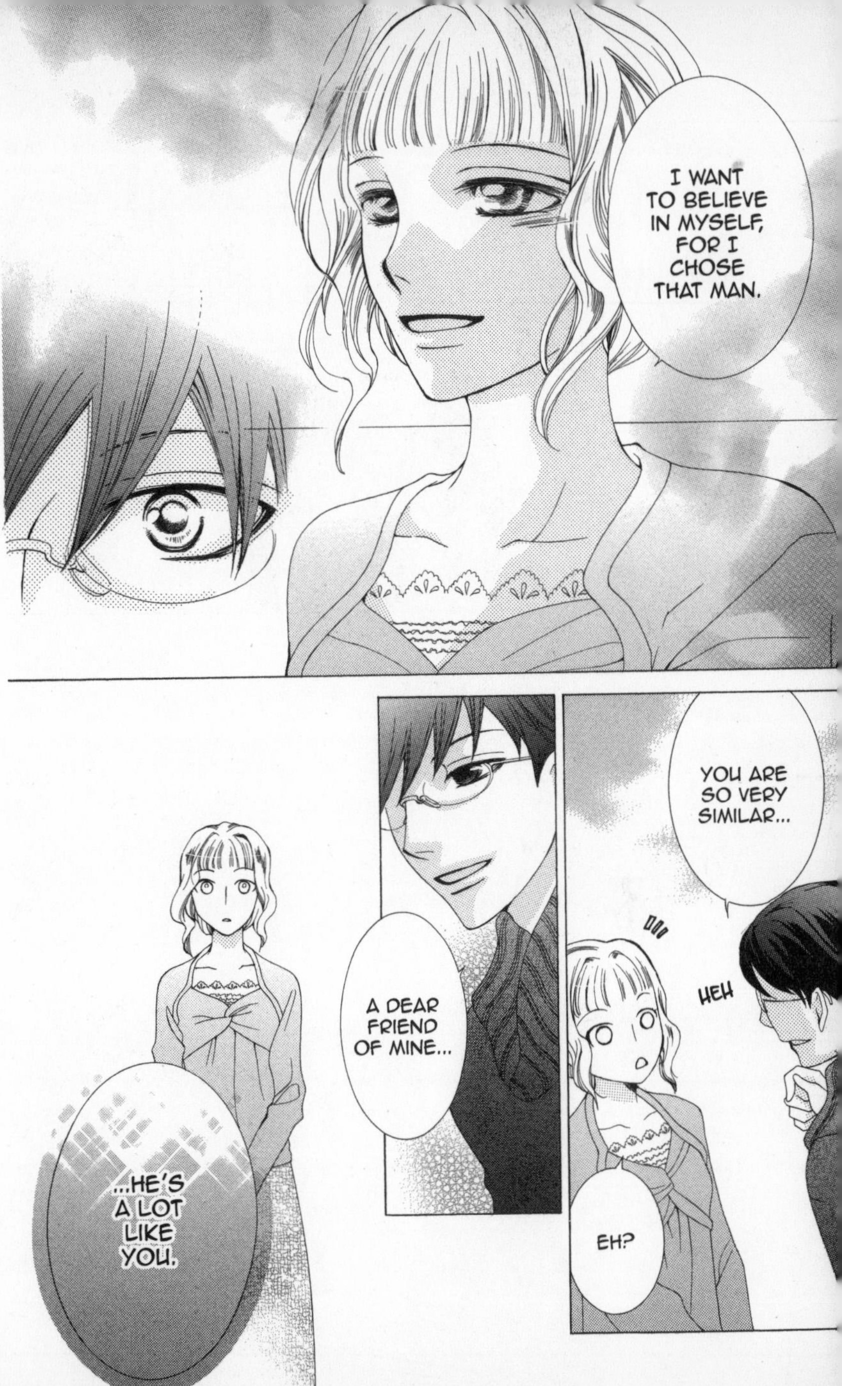
I WANT TO BELIEVE IN MYSELF, FOR I CHOSE THAT MAN.
YOU ARE SO VERY SIMILAR...
HEH
EH?
A DEAR FRIEND OF MINE...
...HE'S A LOT LIKE YOU.

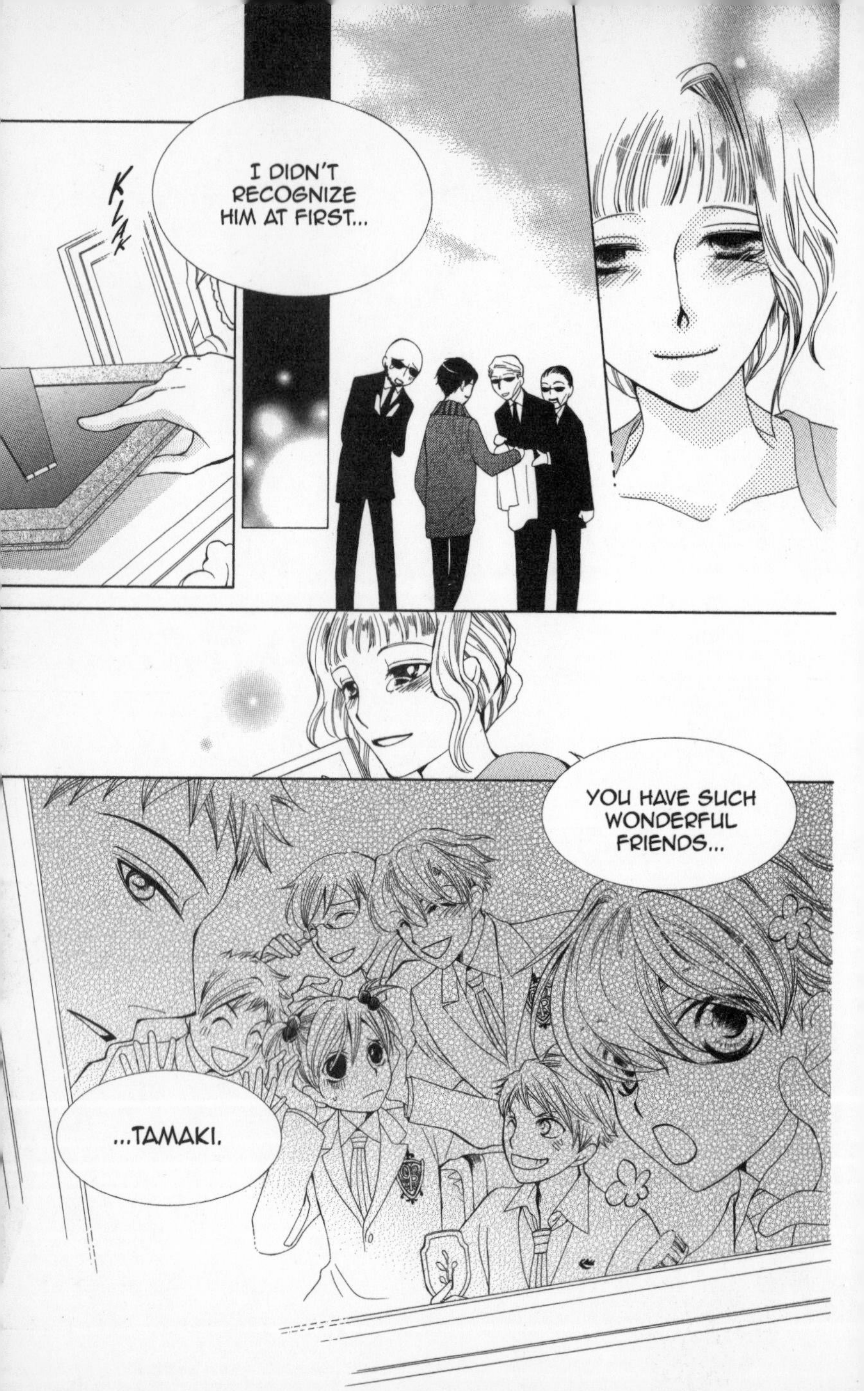
I DIDN'T RECOGNIZE HIM AT FIRST...
KLAK
YOU HAVE SUCH WONDERFUL FRIENDS...
...TAMAKI.

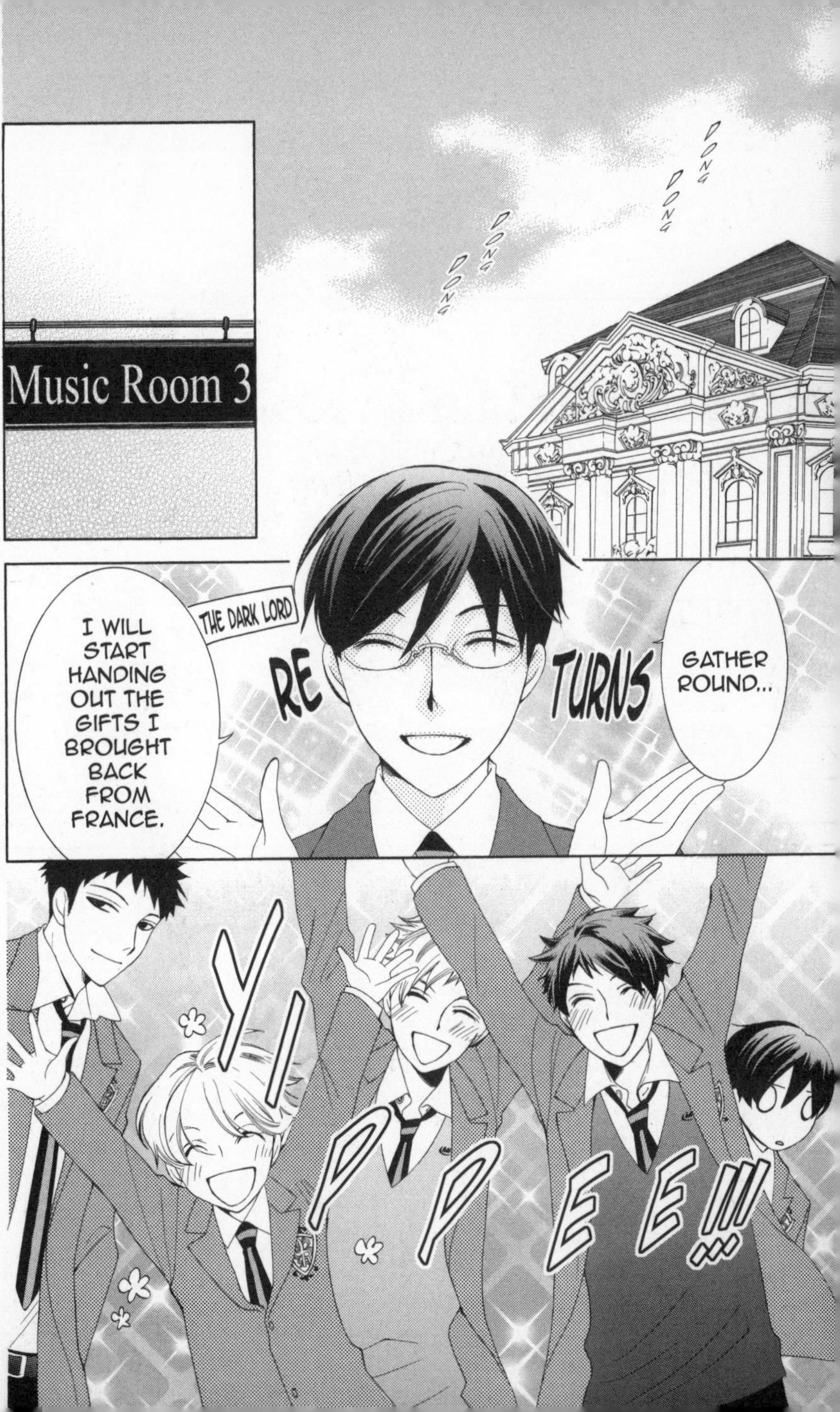
DONG DONG
DONG DONG
Music Room 3
GATHER ROUND...
THE DARK LORD
RE TURNS
I WILL START HANDING OUT THE GIFTS I BROUGHT BACK FROM FRANCE.
YIPPEE!!!

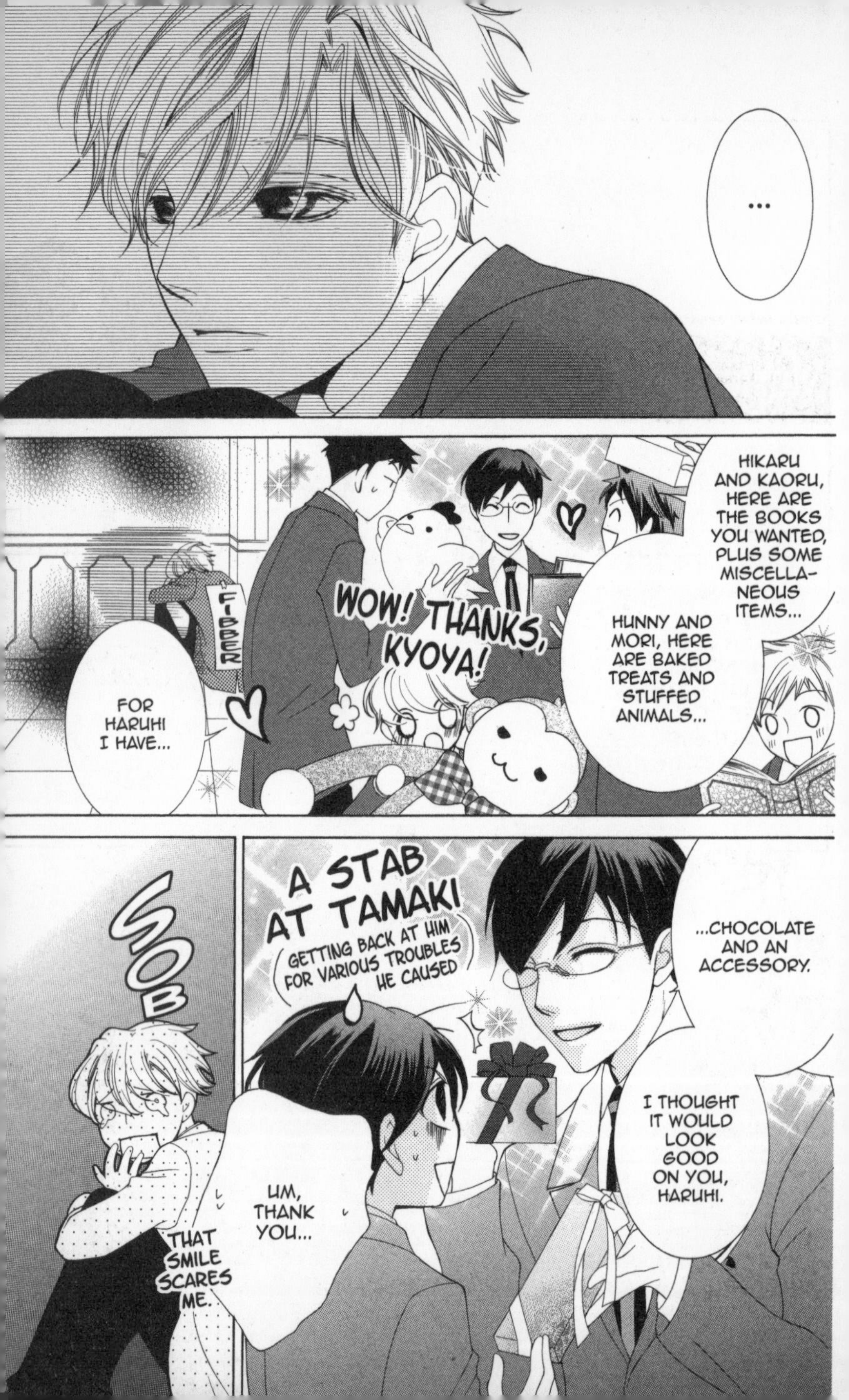
...
HIKARU AND KAORU, HERE ARE THE BOOKS YOU WANTED, PLUS SOME MISCELLA-NEOUS ITEMS...
HUNNY AND MORI, HERE ARE BAKED TREATS AND STUFFED ANIMALS...
WOW! THANKS, KYOYA!
FIBBER
FOR HARUHI I HAVE...
...CHOCOLATE AND AN ACCESSORY.
A STAB AT TAMAKI
(GETTING BACK AT HIM FOR VARIOUS TROUBLES HE CAUSED)
I THOUGHT IT WOULD LOOK GOOD ON YOU, HARUHI.
UM, THANK YOU...
SOB
THAT SMILE SCARES ME.

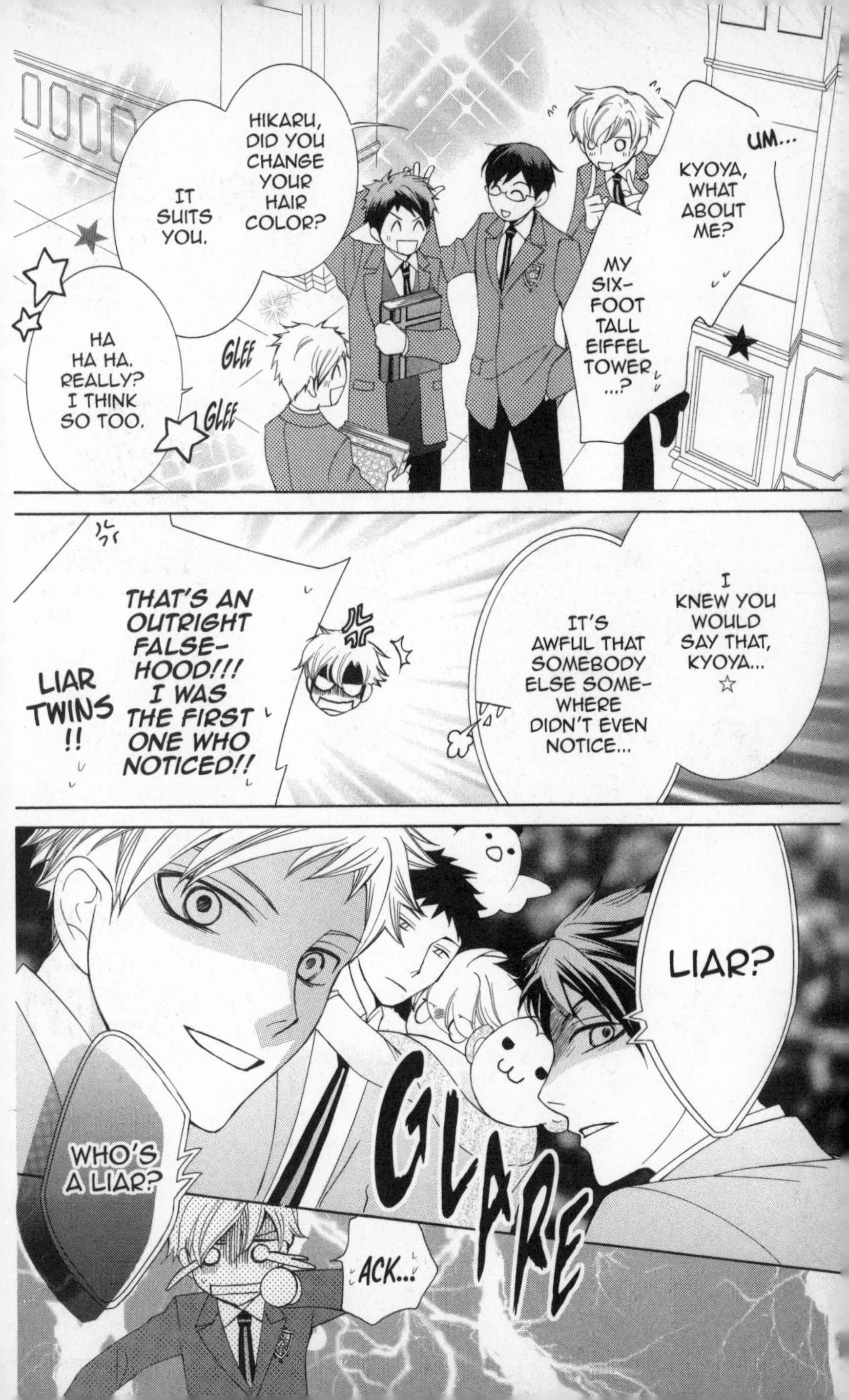
UM...
KYOYA, WHAT ABOUT ME?
MY SIX-FOOT TALL EIFFEL TOWER ...?
HIKARU, DID YOU CHANGE YOUR HAIR COLOR?
IT SUITS YOU.
GLEE
GLEE
HA HA HA. REALLY? I THINK SO TOO.
I KNEW YOU WOULD SAY THAT, KYOYA... ☆
IT'S AWFUL THAT SOMEBODY ELSE SOME-WHERE DIDN'T EVEN NOTICE...
THAT'S AN OUTRIGHT FALSE-HOOD!!! I WAS THE FIRST ONE WHO NOTICED!!
LIAR TWINS !!
LIAR?
WHO'S A LIAR?
GLARE
ACK...

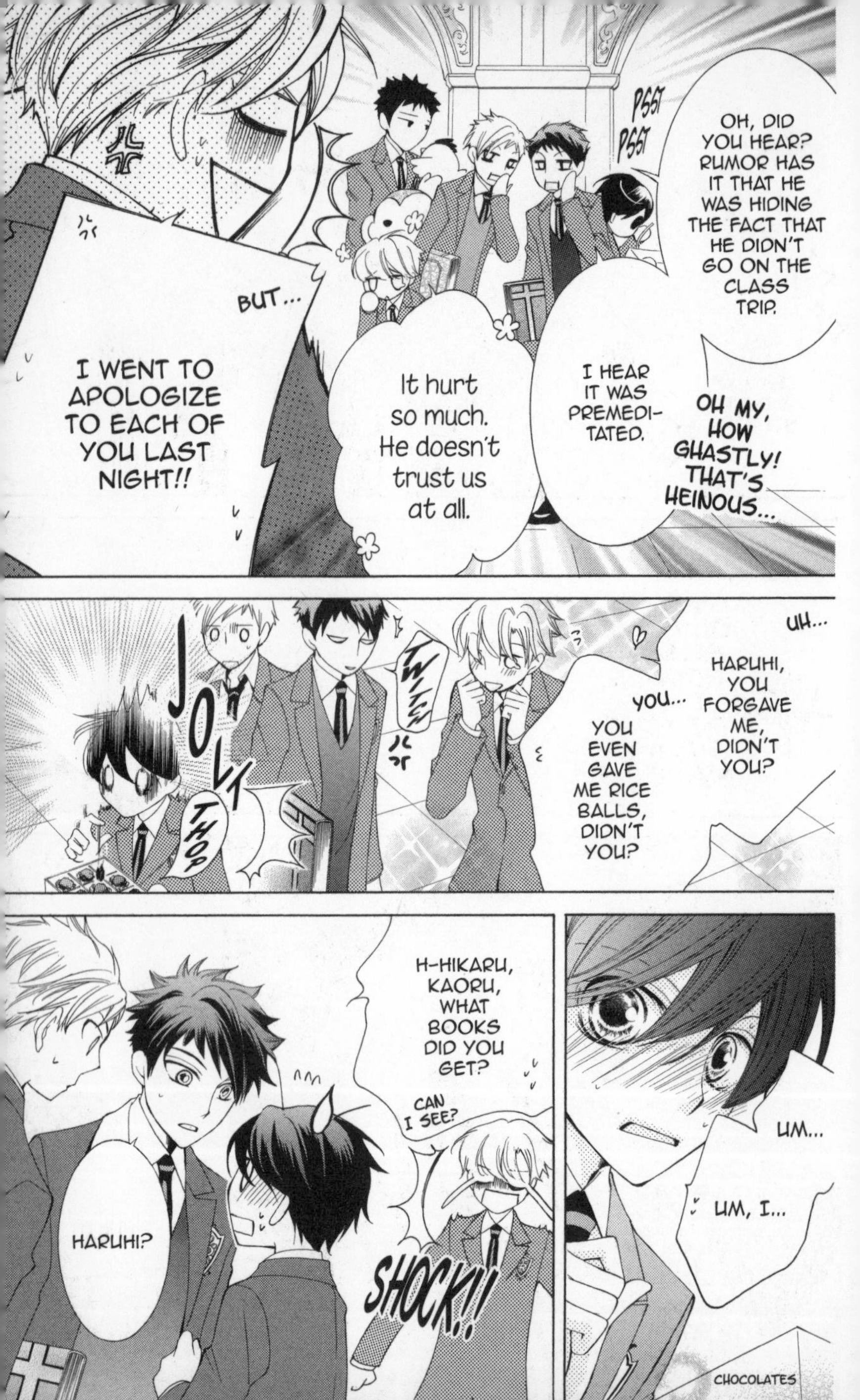
PSST
PSST
OH, DID YOU HEAR? RUMOR HAS IT THAT HE WAS HIDING THE FACT THAT HE DIDN'T GO ON THE CLASS TRIP.
OH MY, HOW GHASTLY! THAT'S HEINOUS...
I HEAR IT WAS PREMEDITATED.
It hurt so much. He doesn't trust us at all.
BUT...
I WENT TO APOLOGIZE TO EACH OF YOU LAST NIGHT!!
UH...
HARUHI, YOU FORGAVE ME, DIDN'T YOU?
YOU...
YOU EVEN GAVE ME RICE BALLS, DIDN'T YOU?
TWITCH
JOLT
THOP
UM...
UM, I...
CHOCOLATES
H-HIKARU, KAORU, WHAT BOOKS DID YOU GET?
CAN I SEE?
SHOCK!!
HARUHI?

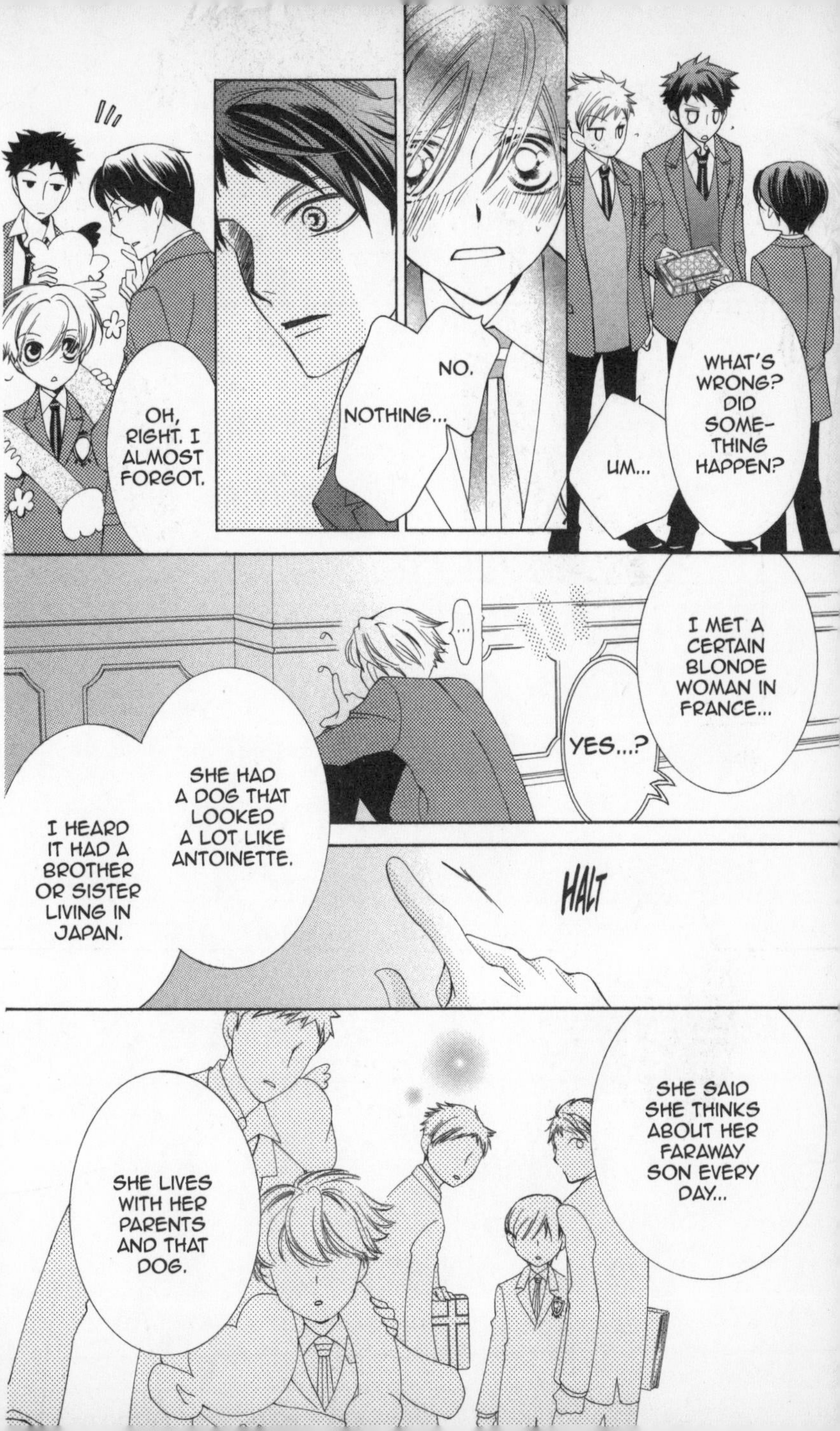
WHAT'S WRONG? DID SOME-THING HAPPEN?
UM...
NO.
NOTHING...
OH, RIGHT. I ALMOST FORGOT.
I MET A CERTAIN BLONDE WOMAN IN FRANCE...
YES...?
...
HALT
SHE HAD A DOG THAT LOOKED A LOT LIKE ANTOINETTE.
I HEARD IT HAD A BROTHER OR SISTER LIVING IN JAPAN.
SHE SAID SHE THINKS ABOUT HER FARAWAY SON EVERY DAY...
SHE LIVES WITH HER PARENTS AND THAT DOG.

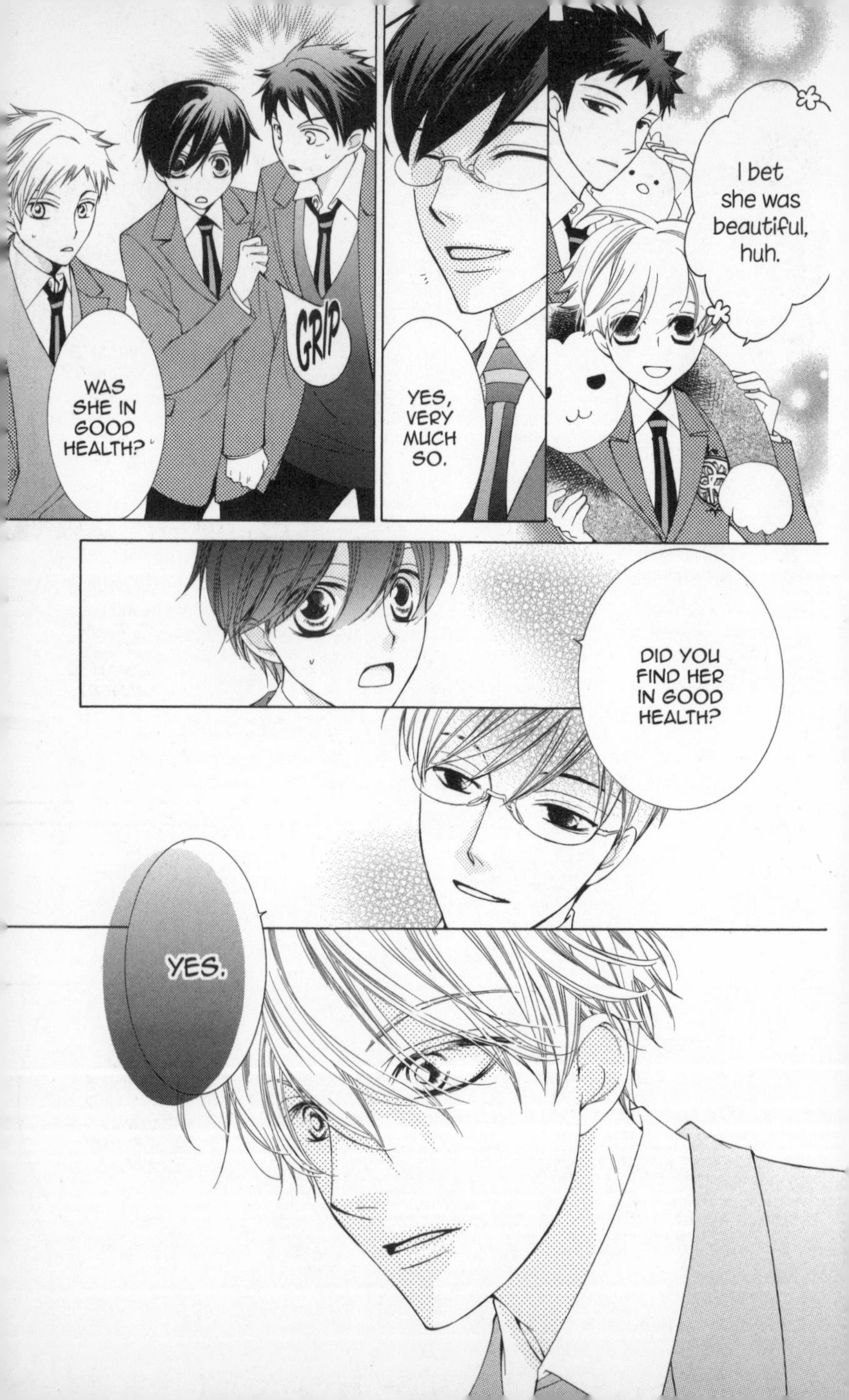

I bet she was beautiful, huh.
YES, VERY MUCH SO.
GRIP
WAS SHE IN GOOD HEALTH?
DID YOU FIND HER IN GOOD HEALTH?
YES.

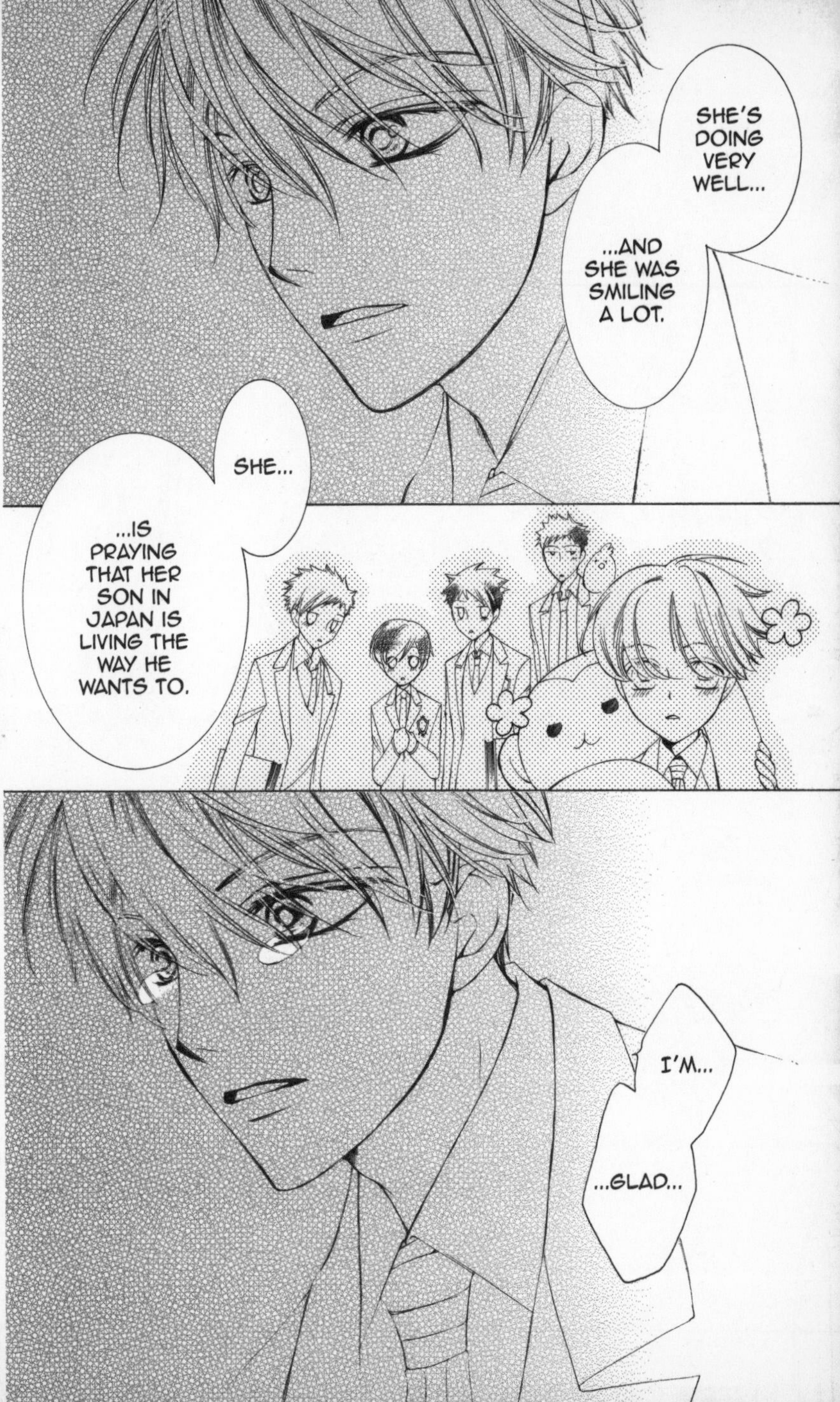
SHE'S DOING VERY WELL...
...AND SHE WAS SMILING A LOT.
SHE...
...IS PRAYING THAT HER SON IN JAPAN IS LIVING THE WAY HE WANTS TO.
I'M...
...GLAD...

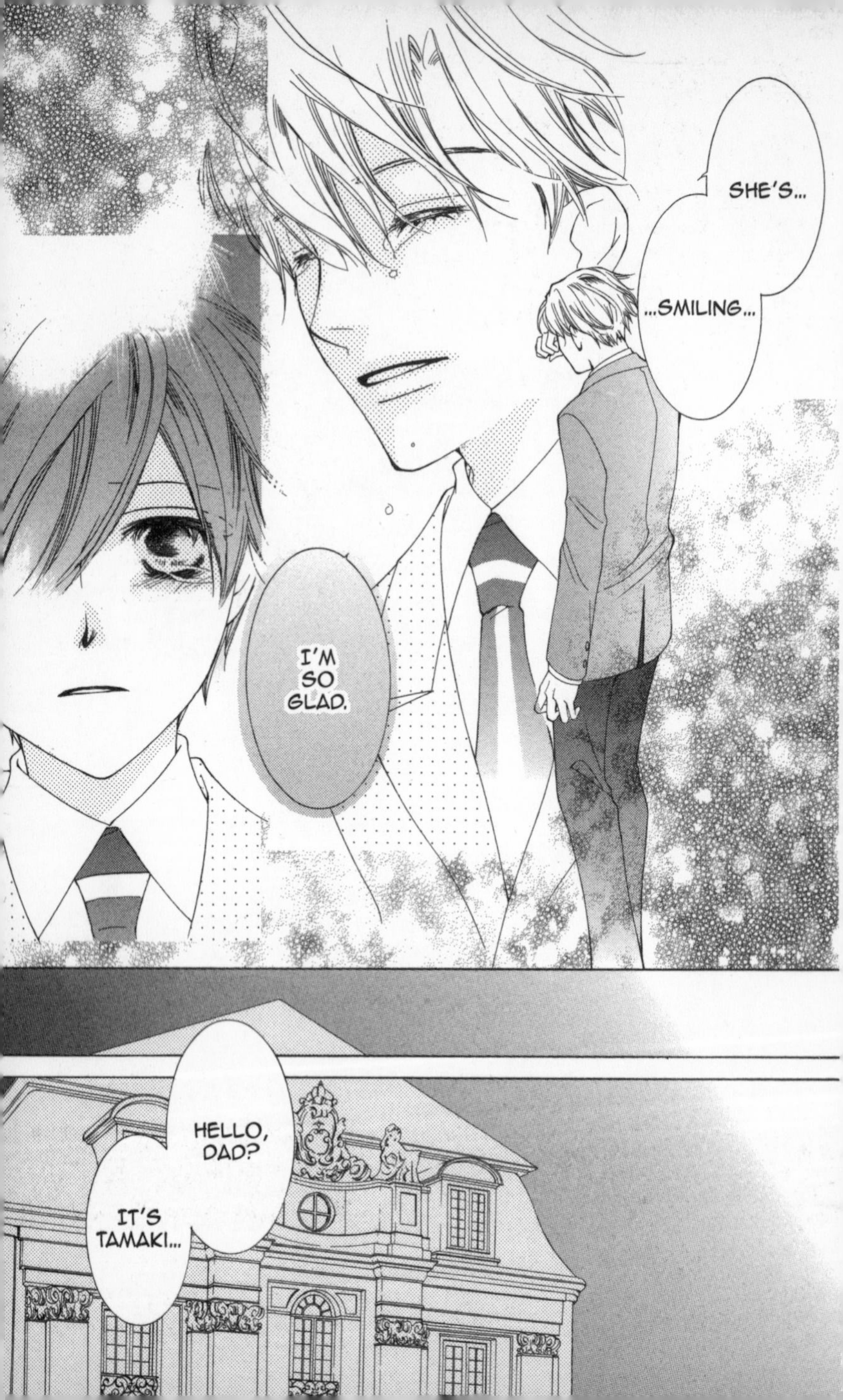
SHE'S...
...SMILING...
I'M SO GLAD.
HELLO, DAD?
IT'S TAMAKI...

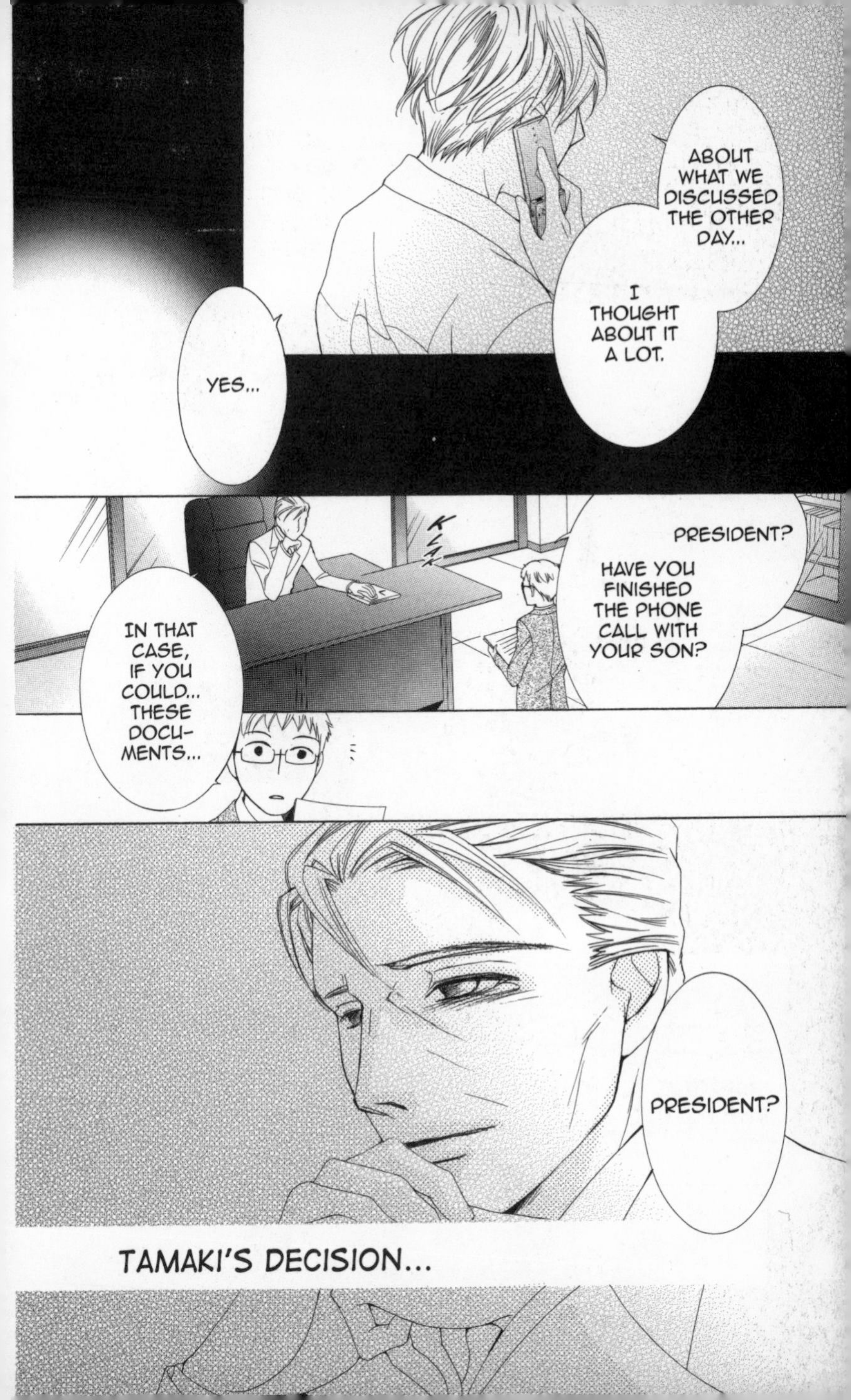
ABOUT WHAT WE DISCUSSED THE OTHER DAY...
I THOUGHT ABOUT IT A LOT.
YES...
PRESIDENT? HAVE YOU FINISHED THE PHONE CALL WITH YOUR SON?
KLAK
IN THAT CASE, IF YOU COULD... THESE DOCU-MENTS...
PRESIDENT?
TAMAKI'S DECISION...

...LOOKING BACK, IT MIGHT HAVE BEEN THE BEGINNING OF THE END FOR THE HOST CLUB.

WHAT'S WRONG WITH ME?

WHAT'S WRONG WITH ME?

FOR SOME REASON, I CAN'T MAKE EYE CONTACT WITH TAMAKI...

pillow

...MY HEART RACES SO MUCH THAT I CAN'T BREATHE.

OH

BUT NO ONE KNOWS THAT YET...

IT'S SOMETHING THAT HAPPENS IN THE FUTURE.

IT'S A COLD! I SHOULD REST.

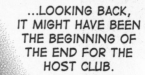

OURAN HIGH SCHOOL HOST CLUB, VOL. 12/THE END

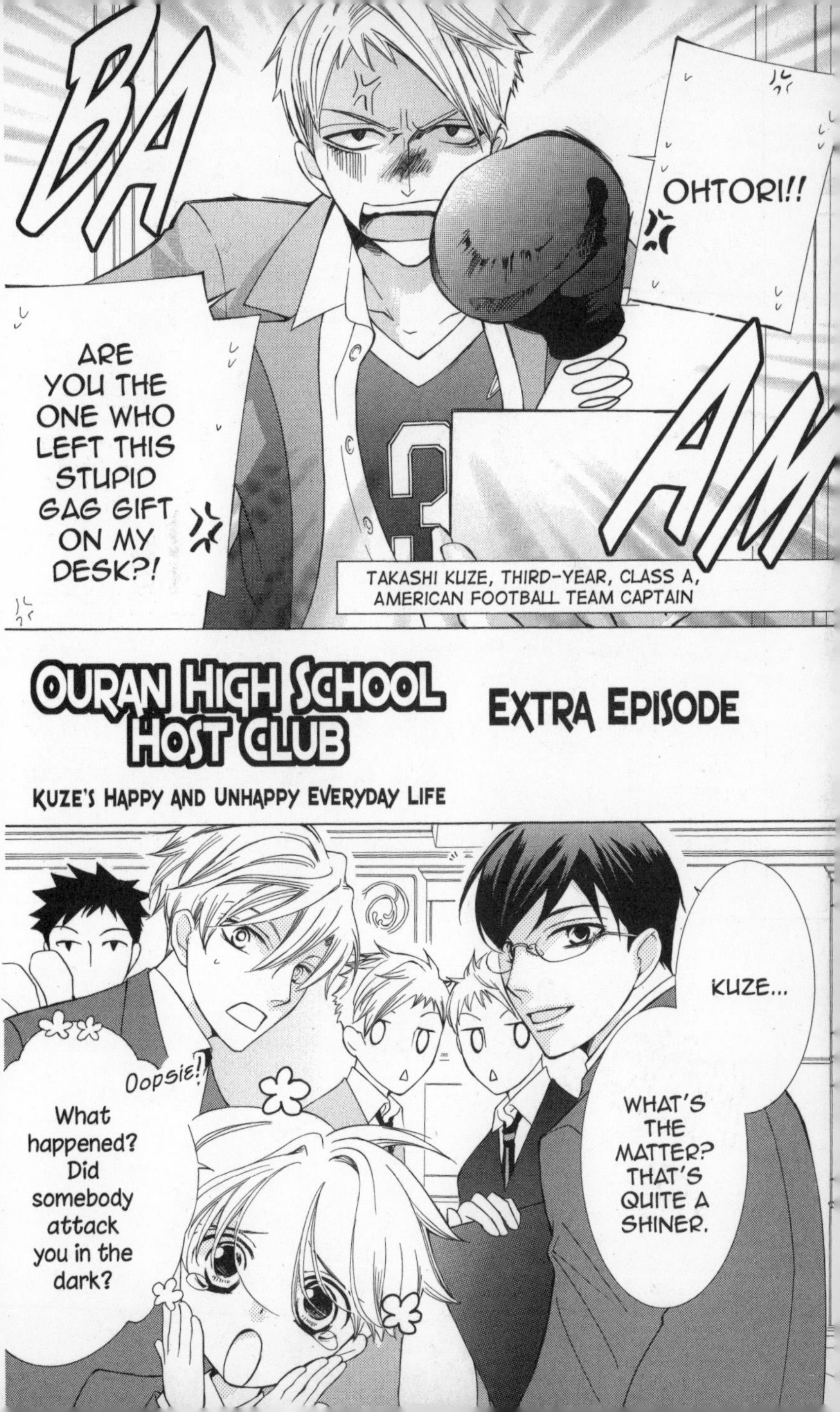
BAM
OHTORI!!
ARE YOU THE ONE WHO LEFT THIS STUPID GAG GIFT ON MY DESK?!
TAKASHI KUZE, THIRD-YEAR, CLASS A, AMERICAN FOOTBALL TEAM CAPTAIN
OURAN HIGH SCHOOL HOST CLUB
EXTRA EPISODE
KUZE'S HAPPY AND UNHAPPY EVERYDAY LIFE
KUZE...
WHAT'S THE MATTER? THAT'S QUITE A SHINER.
Oopsie!
What happened? Did somebody attack you in the dark?

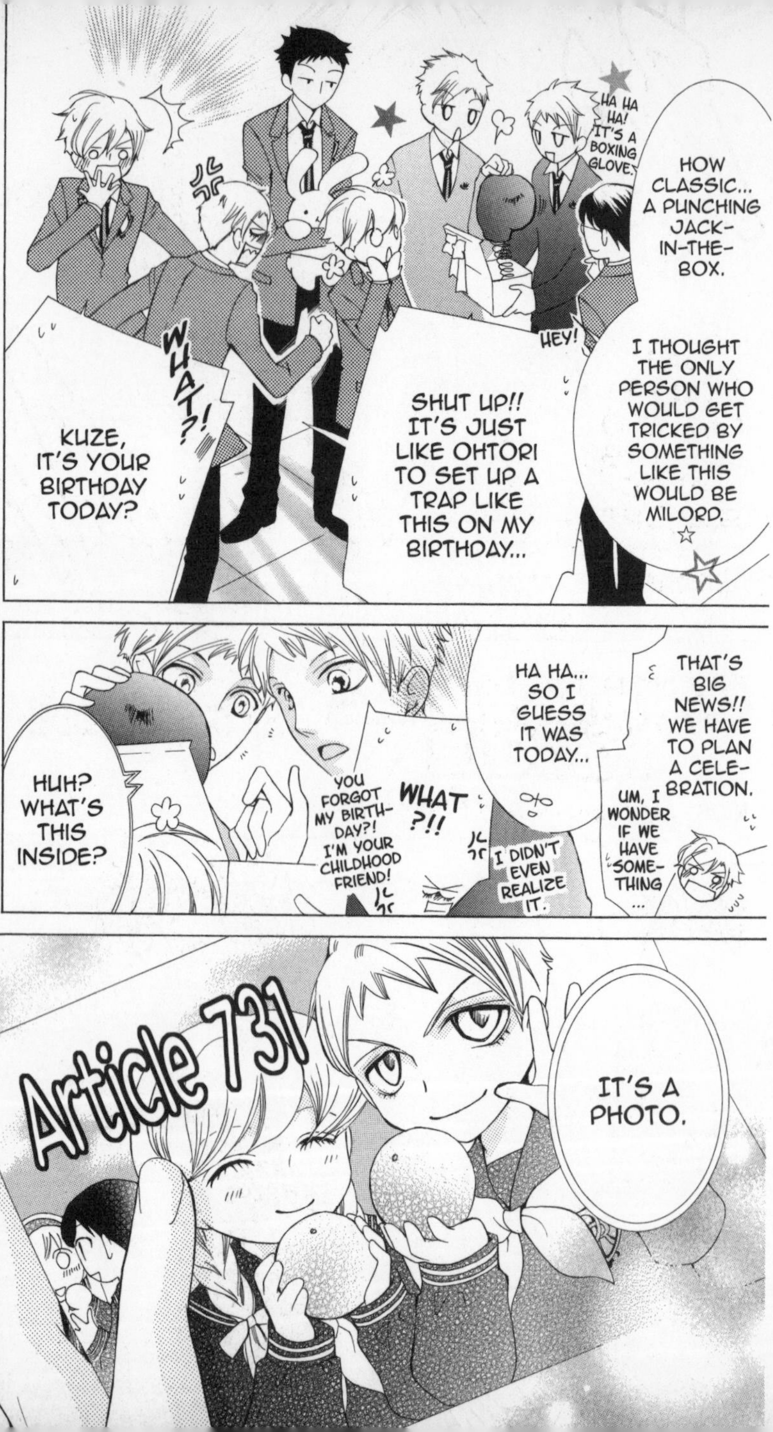
HA HA HA! IT'S A BOXING GLOVE.
HOW CLASSIC... A PUNCHING JACK-IN-THE-BOX.
I THOUGHT THE ONLY PERSON WHO WOULD GET TRICKED BY SOMETHING LIKE THIS WOULD BE MILORD.
HEY!
SHUT UP!! IT'S JUST LIKE OHTORI TO SET UP A TRAP LIKE THIS ON MY BIRTHDAY...
WHAT?!
KUZE, IT'S YOUR BIRTHDAY TODAY?
THAT'S BIG NEWS!! WE HAVE TO PLAN A CELEBRATION.
UM, I WONDER IF WE HAVE SOMETHING...
HA HA... SO I GUESS IT WAS TODAY...
I DIDN'T EVEN REALIZE IT.
WHAT?!!
YOU FORGOT MY BIRTHDAY?! I'M YOUR CHILDHOOD FRIEND!
HUH? WHAT'S THIS INSIDE?
IT'S A PHOTO.
Article 731

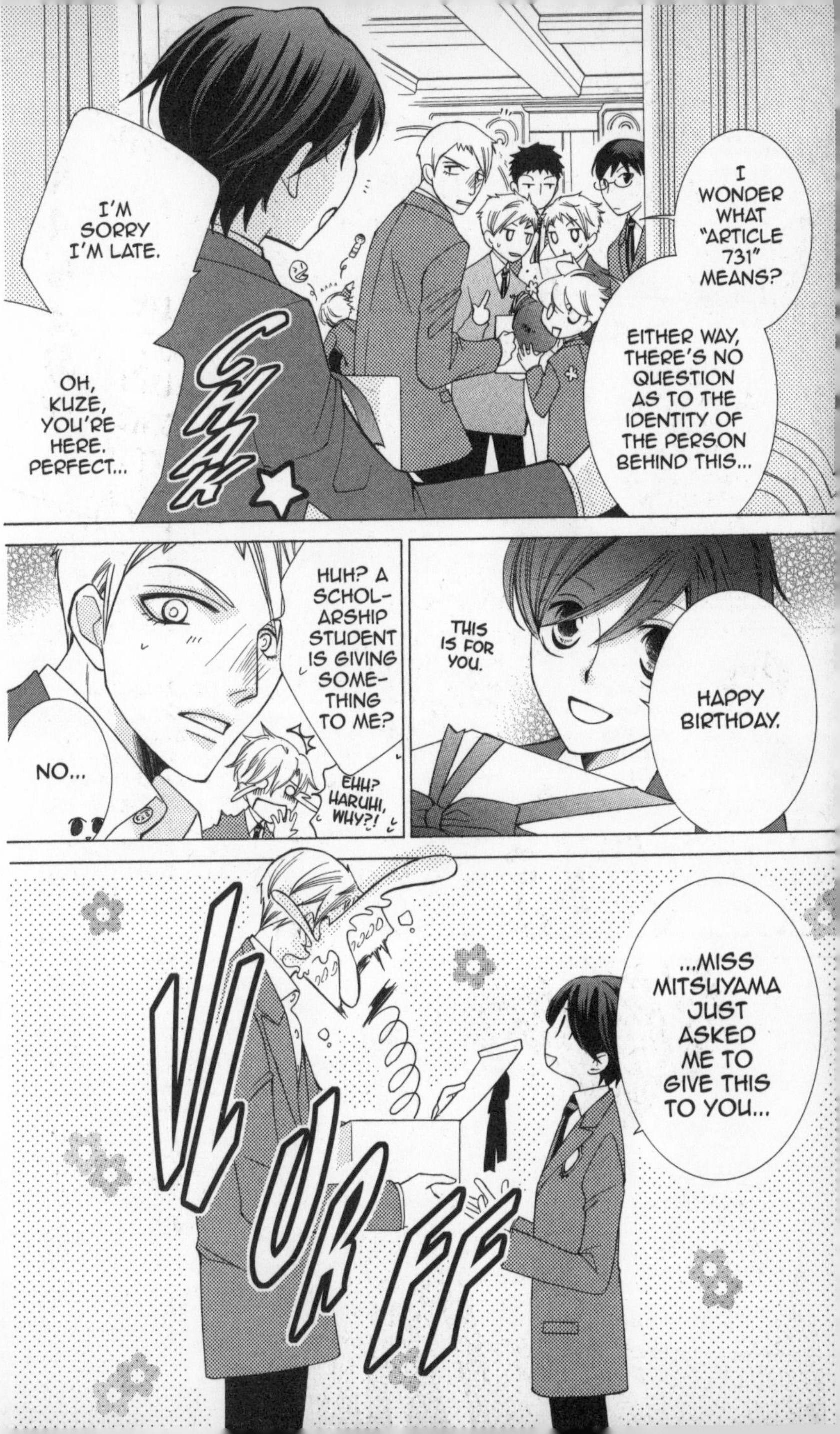
I WONDER WHAT "ARTICLE 731" MEANS?
EITHER WAY, THERE'S NO QUESTION AS TO THE IDENTITY OF THE PERSON BEHIND THIS...
I'M SORRY I'M LATE.
CHAK
OH, KUZE, YOU'RE HERE. PERFECT...
HAPPY BIRTHDAY.
THIS IS FOR YOU.
HUH? A SCHOL-ARSHIP STUDENT IS GIVING SOME-THING TO ME?
EHH? HARUHI, WHY?!
NO...
...MISS MITSUYAMA JUST ASKED ME TO GIVE THIS TO YOU...
VWORFF

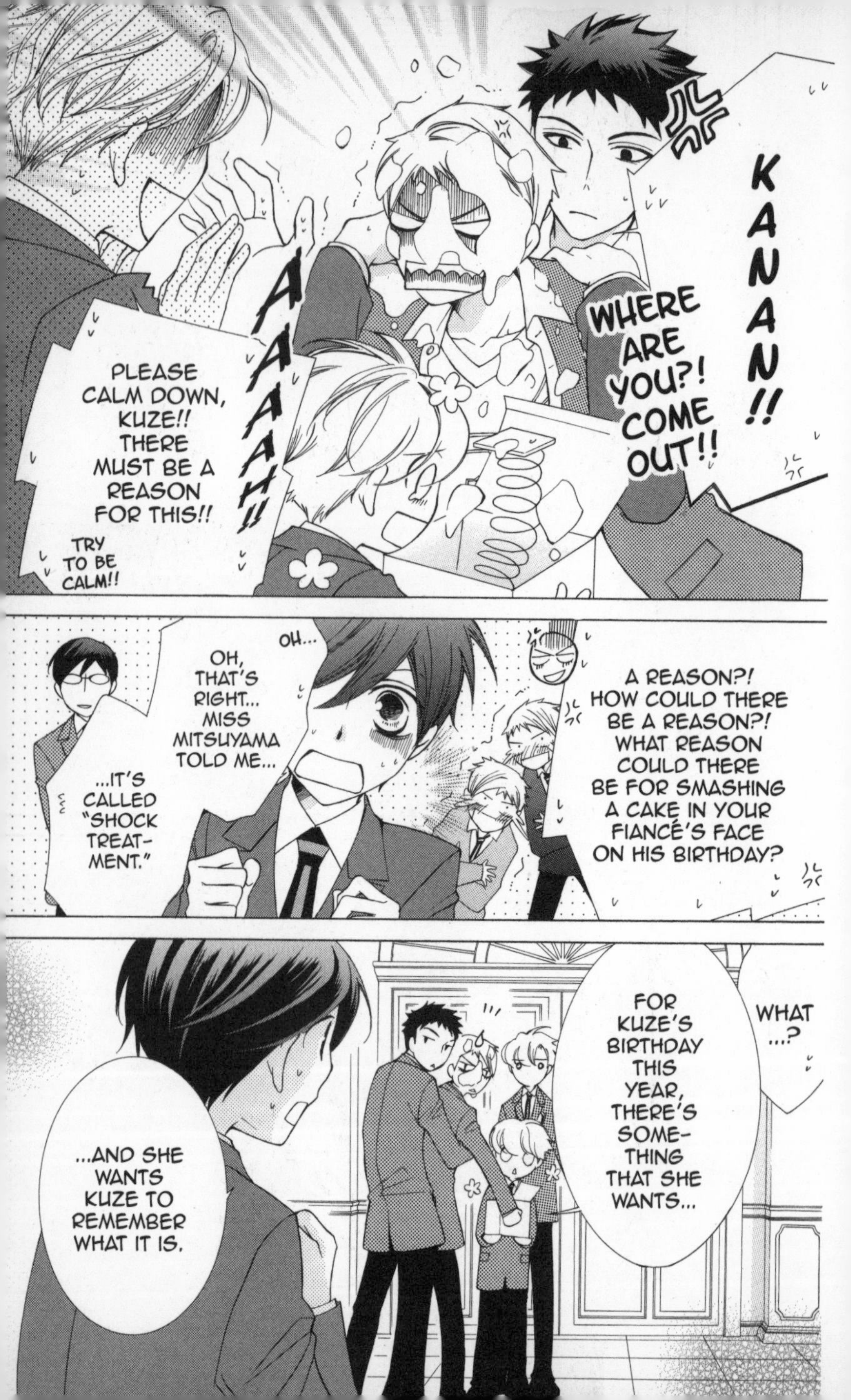
KANAN!!
WHERE ARE YOU?! COME OUT!!
AAAAAH!!
PLEASE CALM DOWN, KUZE!! THERE MUST BE A REASON FOR THIS!!
TRY TO BE CALM!!
A REASON?! HOW COULD THERE BE A REASON?! WHAT REASON COULD THERE BE FOR SMASHING A CAKE IN YOUR FIANCÉ'S FACE ON HIS BIRTHDAY?
OH...
OH, THAT'S RIGHT... MISS MITSUYAMA TOLD ME...
...IT'S CALLED "SHOCK TREATMENT."
WHAT ...?
FOR KUZE'S BIRTHDAY THIS YEAR, THERE'S SOME-THING THAT SHE WANTS...
...AND SHE WANTS KUZE TO REMEMBER WHAT IT IS.

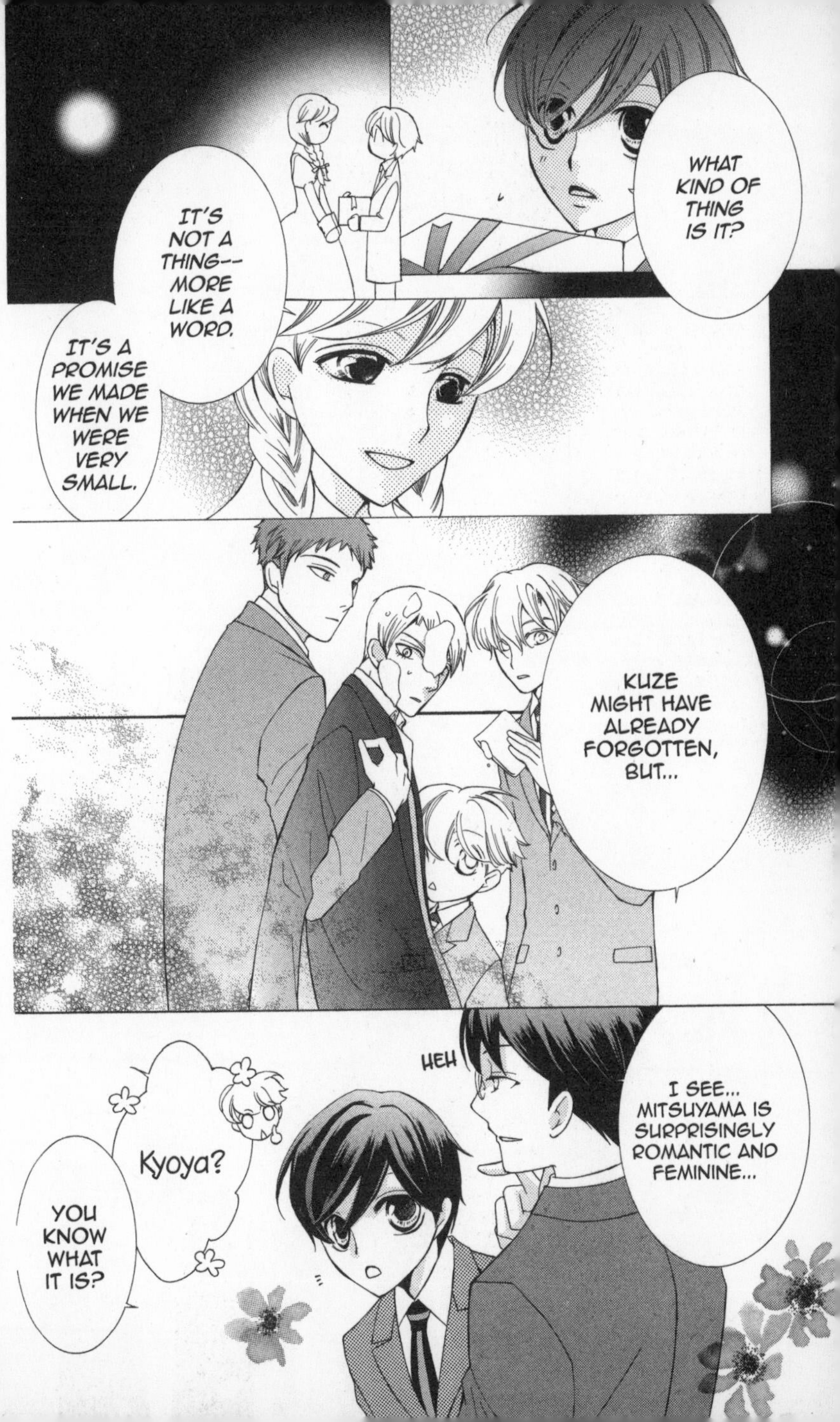
WHAT KIND OF THING IS IT?
IT'S NOT A THING-- MORE LIKE A WORD.
IT'S A PROMISE WE MADE WHEN WE WERE VERY SMALL.
KUZE MIGHT HAVE ALREADY FORGOTTEN, BUT...
HEH
I SEE... MITSUYAMA IS SURPRISINGLY ROMANTIC AND FEMININE...
Kyoya?
YOU KNOW WHAT IT IS?

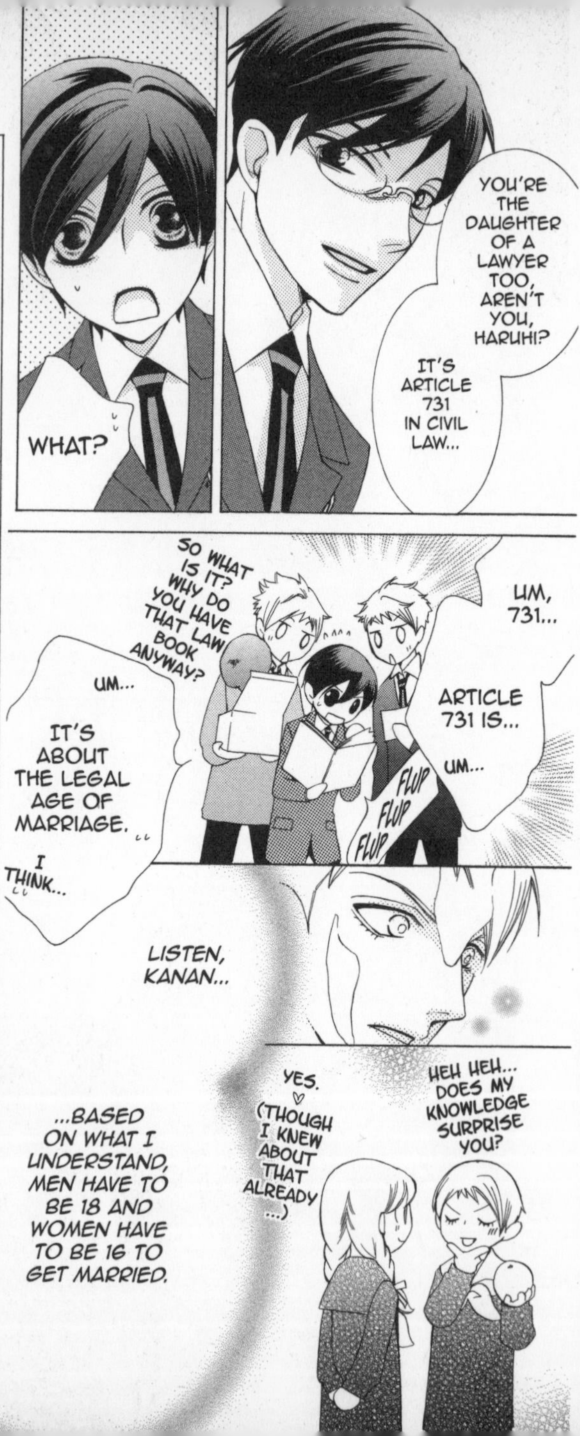

YOU'RE THE DAUGHTER OF A LAWYER TOO, AREN'T YOU, HARUHI?
IT'S ARTICLE 731 IN CIVIL LAW...
WHAT?
UM, 731...
ARTICLE 731 IS...
UM...
SO WHAT IS IT? WHY DO YOU HAVE THAT LAW BOOK ANYWAY?
FLUP FLUP FLUP
UM...
IT'S ABOUT THE LEGAL AGE OF MARRIAGE.
I THINK...
LISTEN, KANAN...
...BASED ON WHAT I UNDERSTAND, MEN HAVE TO BE 18 AND WOMEN HAVE TO BE 16 TO GET MARRIED.
HEH HEH... DOES MY KNOWLEDGE SURPRISE YOU?
YES. ♡ (THOUGH I KNEW ABOUT THAT ALREADY...)

6

I USED TO USE BLUE, BUT ORANGE IS EASIER ON THE EYES, I FOUND OUT (THIS IS STRICTLY SPEAKING FROM PERSONAL EXPERIENCE ONLY). NOW I BUY WHOLE BOXES OF THOSE PENCILS AT A TIME. IT'S SOMETHING I DEFINITELY CAN'T DO WITHOUT.

IT MIGHT NOT HAVE HELPED VERY MUCH, BUT I RECEIVE MANY LETTERS FROM PEOPLE TRYING TO BECOME MANGAKA.♡ MANGA NEEDS ◊ PERSEVERANCE ◊. LET'S KEEP TRYING HARD TOGETHER!!!

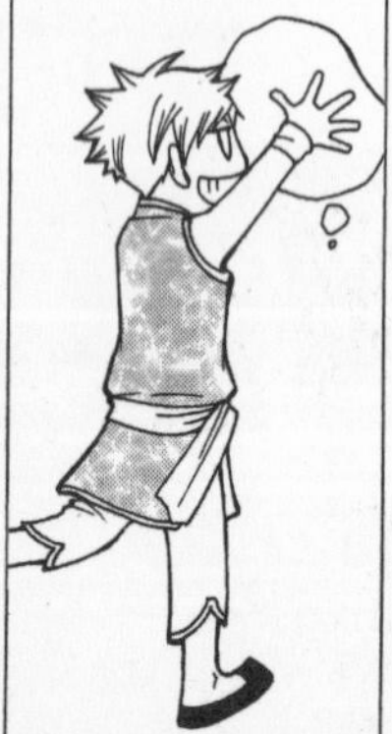

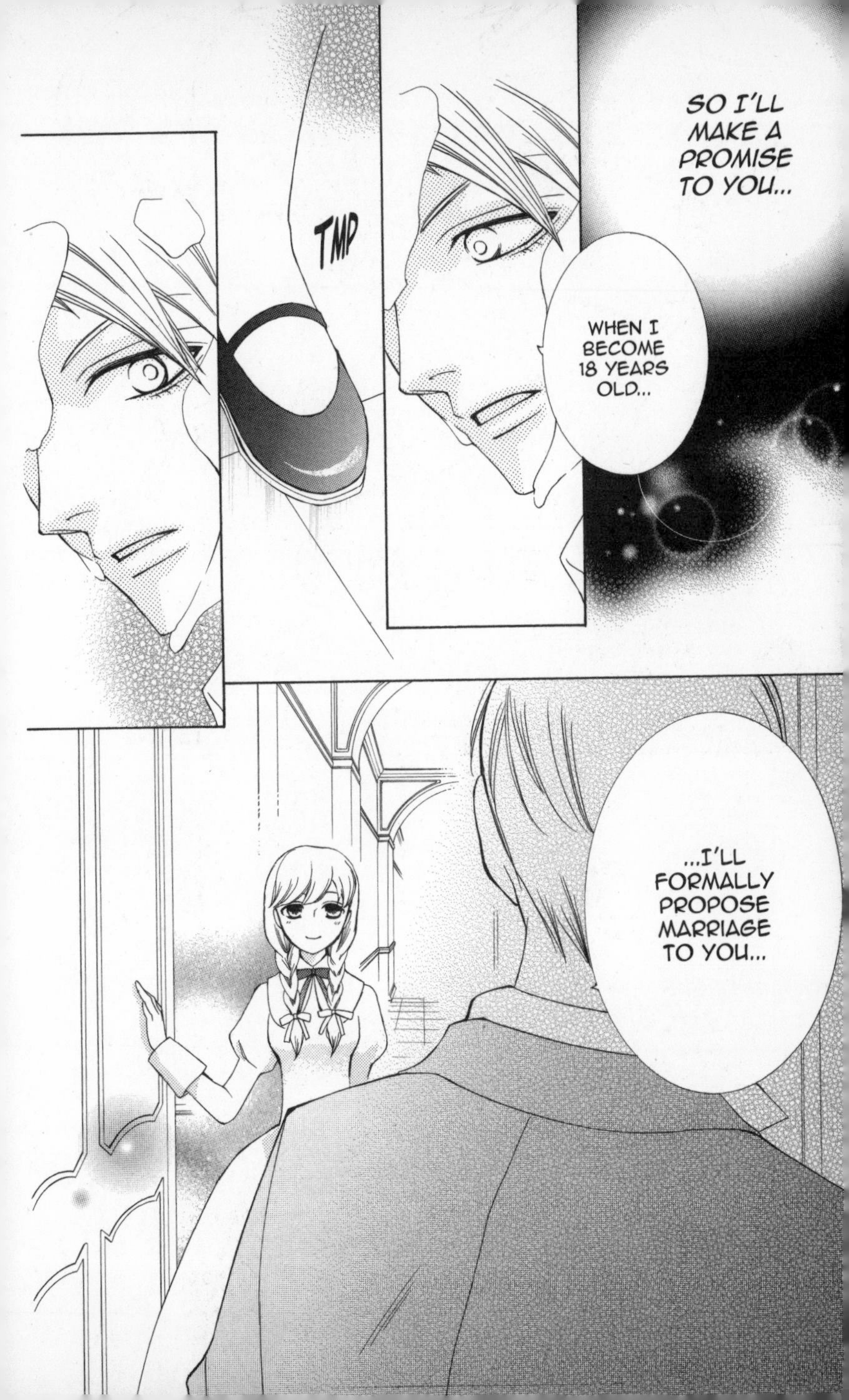
SO I'LL MAKE A PROMISE TO YOU...
WHEN I BECOME 18 YEARS OLD...
TMP
...I'LL FORMALLY PROPOSE MARRIAGE TO YOU...

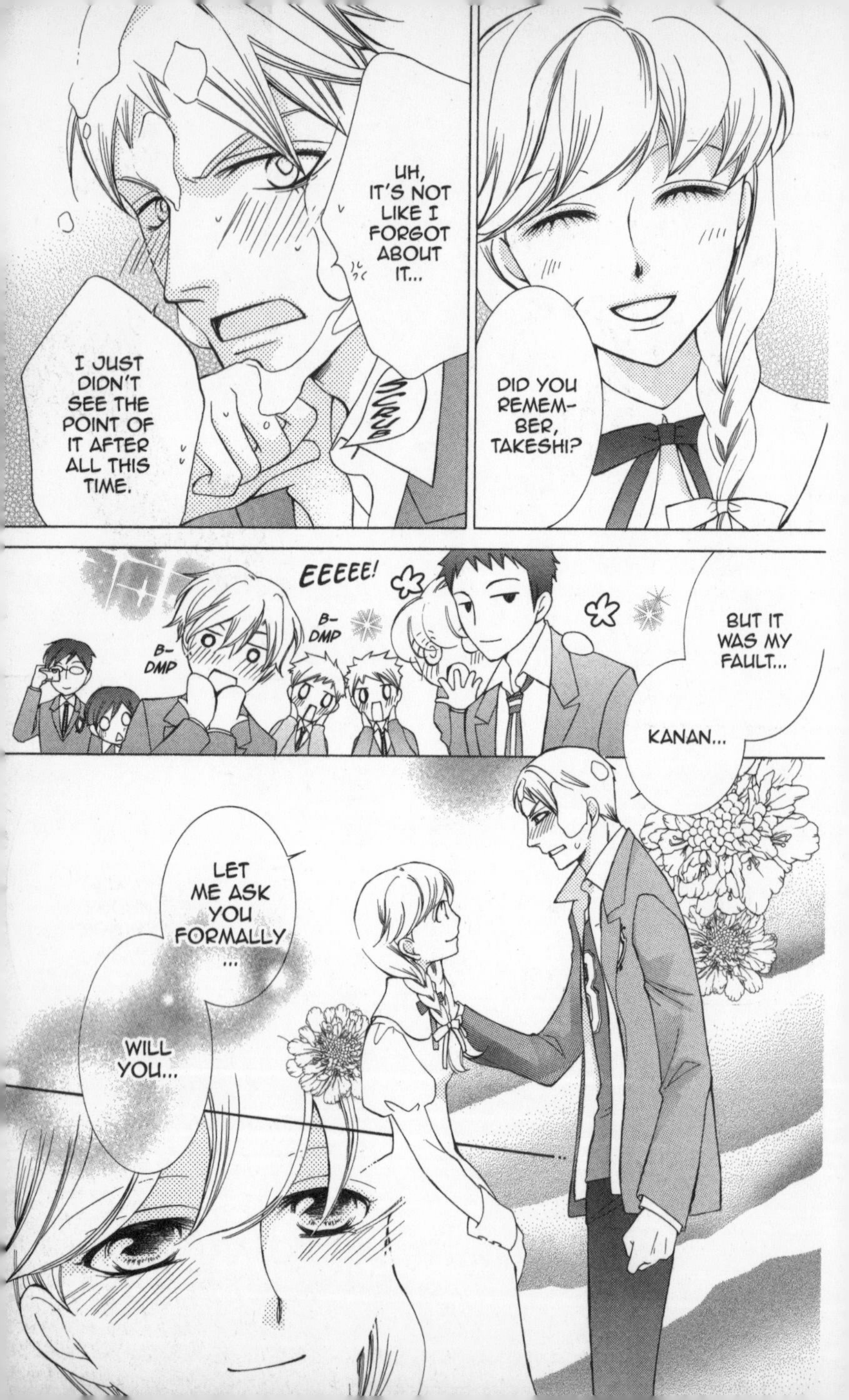
DID YOU REMEMBER, TAKESHI?
UH, IT'S NOT LIKE I FORGOT ABOUT IT...
SCRUB
I JUST DIDN'T SEE THE POINT OF IT AFTER ALL THIS TIME.
BUT IT WAS MY FAULT...
EEEEE!
B-DMP
B-DMP
KANAN...
LET ME ASK YOU FORMALLY...
WILL YOU...
...

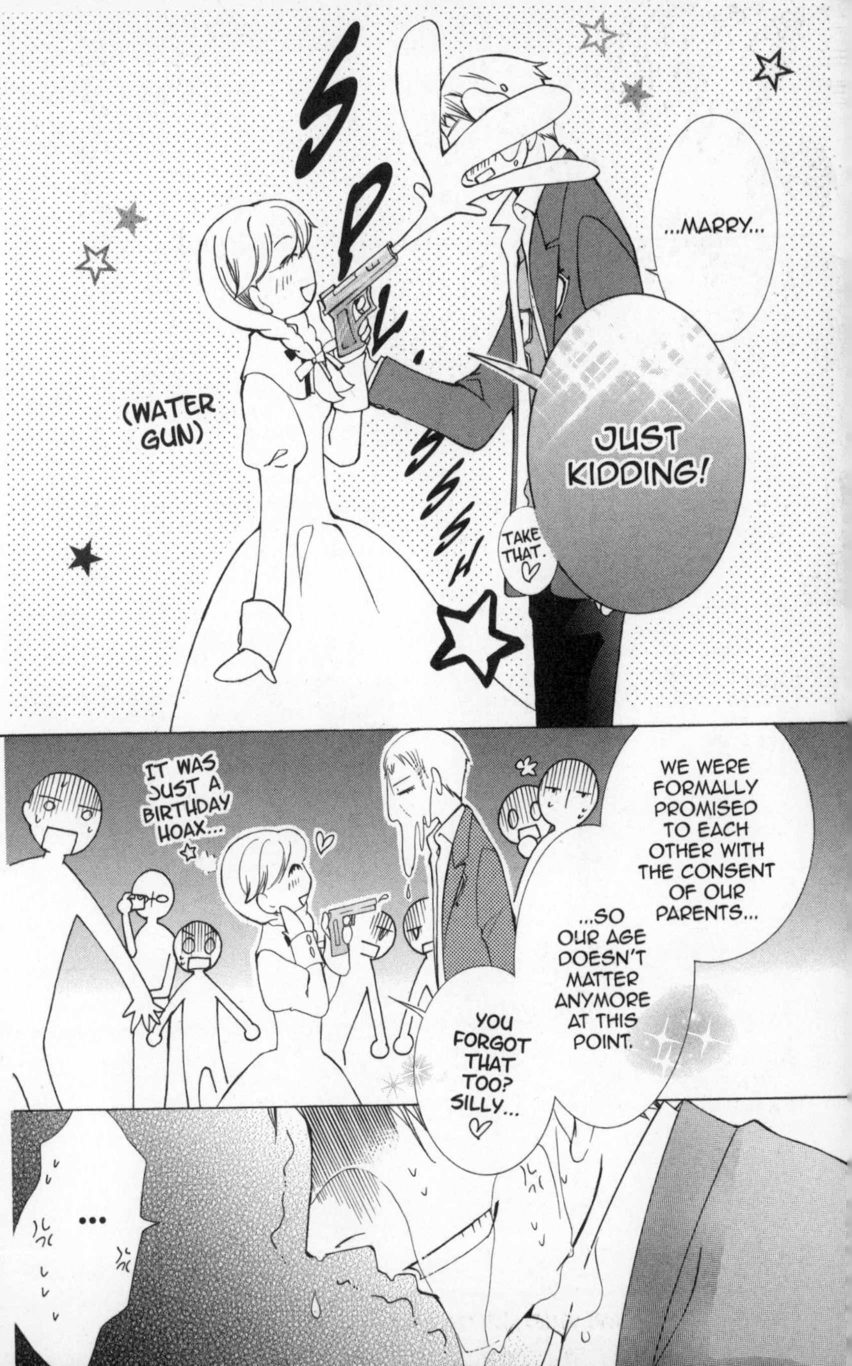
...MARRY...
JUST KIDDING!
TAKE THAT. ♡
SPLASSSH
(WATER GUN)
WE WERE FORMALLY PROMISED TO EACH OTHER WITH THE CONSENT OF OUR PARENTS...
...SO OUR AGE DOESN'T MATTER ANYMORE AT THIS POINT.
YOU FORGOT THAT TOO? SILLY... ♡
IT WAS JUST A BIRTHDAY HOAX...
...

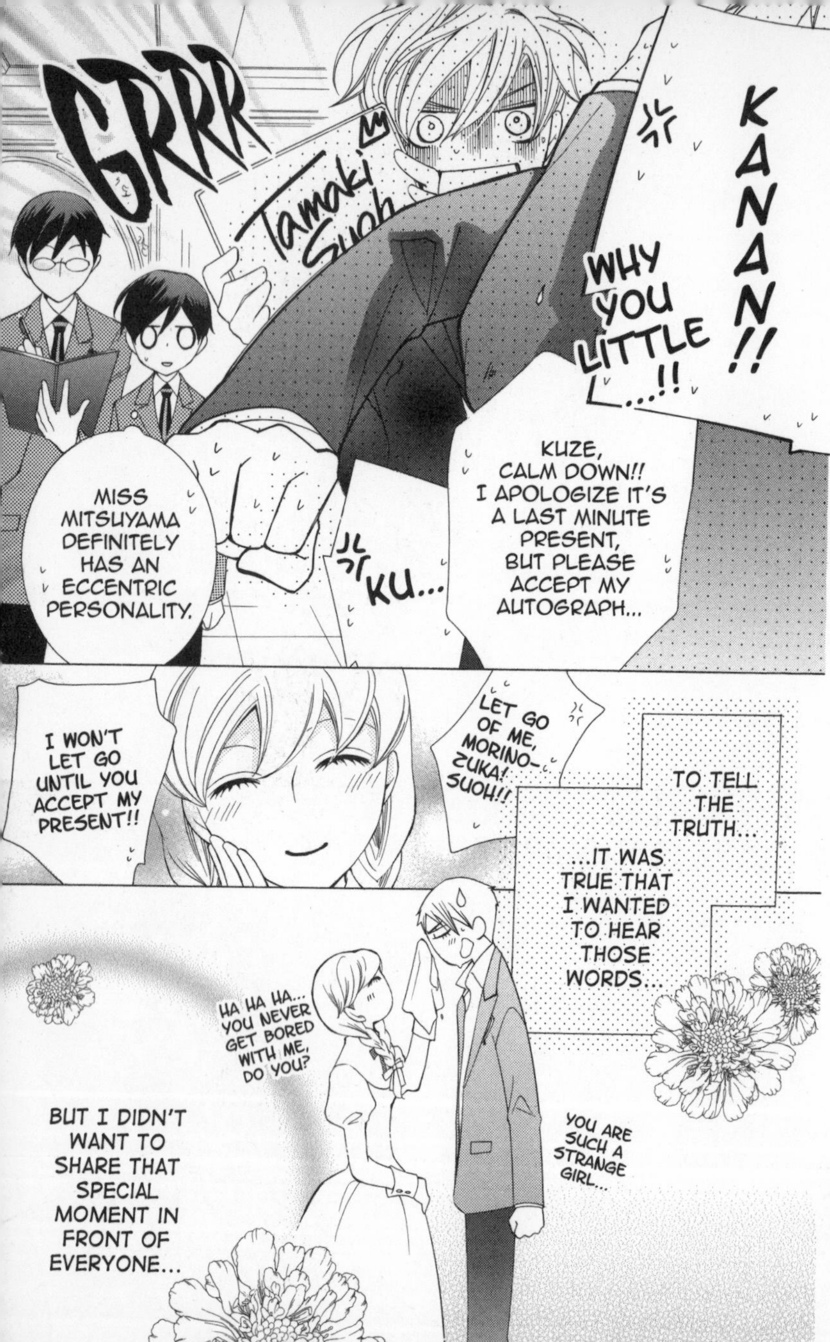
KANAN!!
WHY YOU LITTLE ...!!
GRRR
Tamaki Suoh
KUZE, CALM DOWN!! I APOLOGIZE IT'S A LAST MINUTE PRESENT, BUT PLEASE ACCEPT MY AUTOGRAPH...
KU...
MISS MITSUYAMA DEFINITELY HAS AN ECCENTRIC PERSONALITY.
TO TELL THE TRUTH...
LET GO OF ME, MORINOZUKA! SUOH!!
I WON'T LET GO UNTIL YOU ACCEPT MY PRESENT!!
...IT WAS TRUE THAT I WANTED TO HEAR THOSE WORDS...
YOU ARE SUCH A STRANGE GIRL...
HA HA HA... YOU NEVER GET BORED WITH ME, DO YOU?
BUT I DIDN'T WANT TO SHARE THAT SPECIAL MOMENT IN FRONT OF EVERYONE...

Extra Episode: Kuze's Happy and Unhappy Everyday Life/The End

Egoistic Club

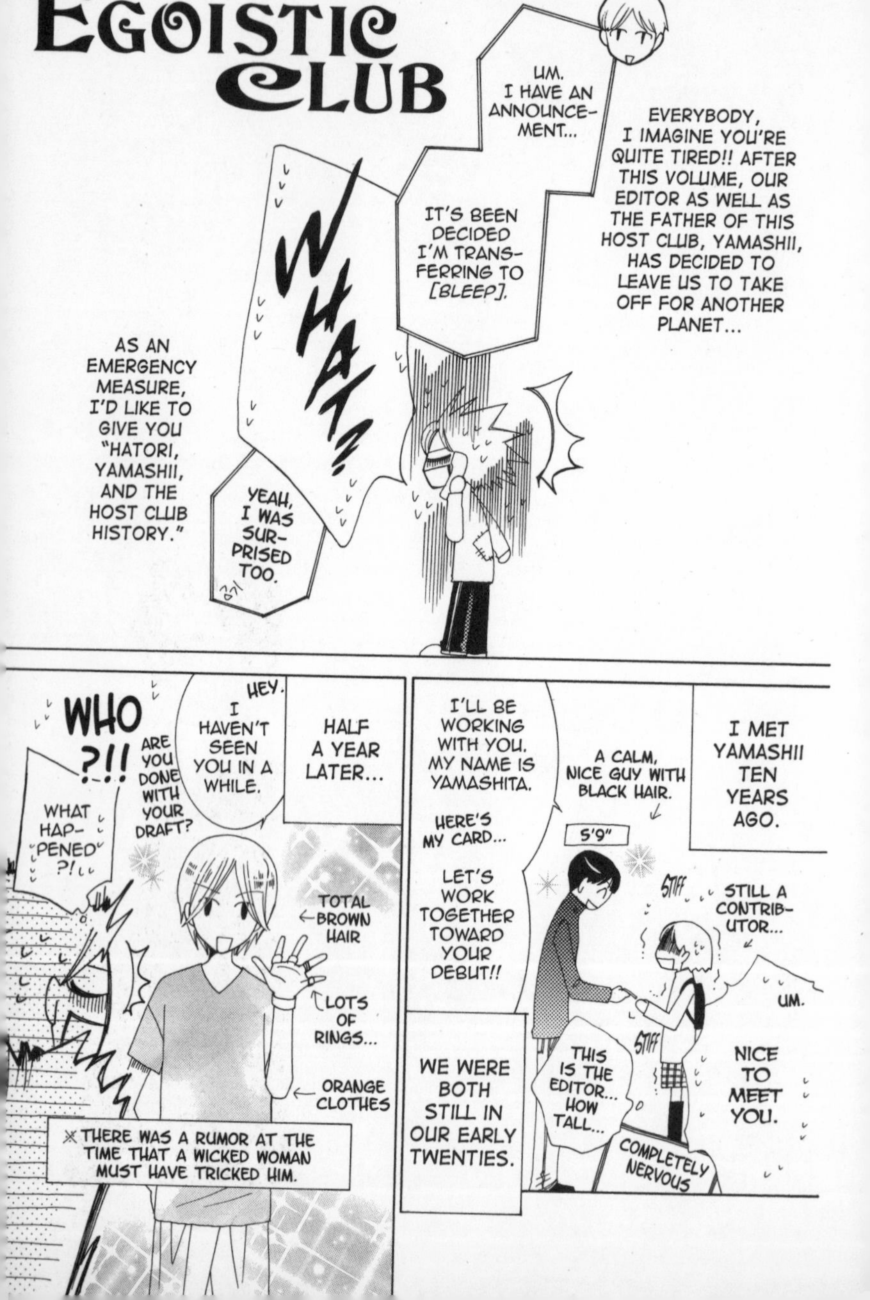
EVERYBODY, I IMAGINE YOU'RE QUITE TIRED!! AFTER THIS VOLUME, OUR EDITOR AS WELL AS THE FATHER OF THIS HOST CLUB, YAMASHII, HAS DECIDED TO LEAVE US TO TAKE OFF FOR ANOTHER PLANET...
UM. I HAVE AN ANNOUNCE-MENT...
IT'S BEEN DECIDED I'M TRANS-FERRING TO [BLEEP].
WHAA!
YEAH, I WAS SUR-PRISED TOO.
AS AN EMERGENCY MEASURE, I'D LIKE TO GIVE YOU "HATORI, YAMASHII, AND THE HOST CLUB HISTORY."
I MET YAMASHII TEN YEARS AGO.
A CALM, NICE GUY WITH BLACK HAIR.
5'9"
I'LL BE WORKING WITH YOU. MY NAME IS YAMASHITA.
HERE'S MY CARD...
LET'S WORK TOGETHER TOWARD YOUR DEBUT!!
STILL A CONTRIB-UTOR...
STIFF
UM.
STIFF
NICE TO MEET YOU.
THIS IS THE EDITOR... HOW TALL...
COMPLETELY NERVOUS
WE WERE BOTH STILL IN OUR EARLY TWENTIES.
HALF A YEAR LATER...
HEY. I HAVEN'T SEEN YOU IN A WHILE.
ARE YOU DONE WITH YOUR DRAFT?
TOTAL BROWN HAIR
LOTS OF RINGS...
ORANGE CLOTHES
WHO ?!!
WHAT HAP-PENED ?!
※THERE WAS A RUMOR AT THE TIME THAT A WICKED WOMAN MUST HAVE TRICKED HIM.

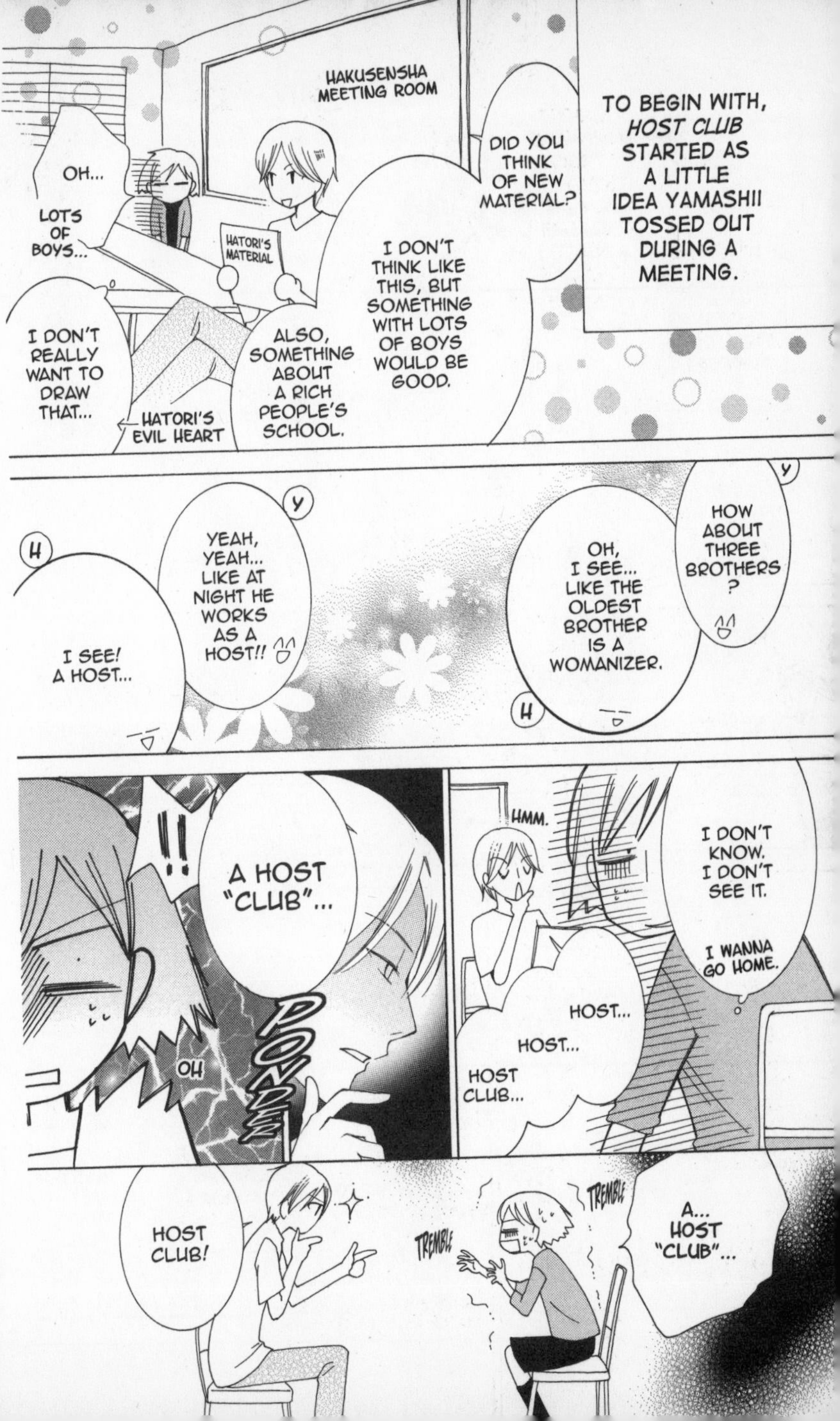
TO BEGIN WITH, *HOST CLUB* STARTED AS A LITTLE IDEA YAMASHII TOSSED OUT DURING A MEETING.
DID YOU THINK OF NEW MATERIAL?
HAKUSENSHA MEETING ROOM
I DON'T THINK LIKE THIS, BUT SOMETHING WITH LOTS OF BOYS WOULD BE GOOD.
ALSO, SOMETHING ABOUT A RICH PEOPLE'S SCHOOL.
HATORI'S MATERIAL
OH...
LOTS OF BOYS...
I DON'T REALLY WANT TO DRAW THAT...
HATORI'S EVIL HEART
Y
HOW ABOUT THREE BROTHERS?
H
OH, I SEE... LIKE THE OLDEST BROTHER IS A WOMANIZER.
Y
YEAH, YEAH... LIKE AT NIGHT HE WORKS AS A HOST!!
H
I SEE! A HOST...
I DON'T KNOW. I DON'T SEE IT.
HMM.
I WANNA GO HOME.
HOST...
HOST...
HOST CLUB...
A HOST "CLUB"...
!!
PON
OH
A... HOST "CLUB"...
TREMBLE
TREMBLE
HOST CLUB!

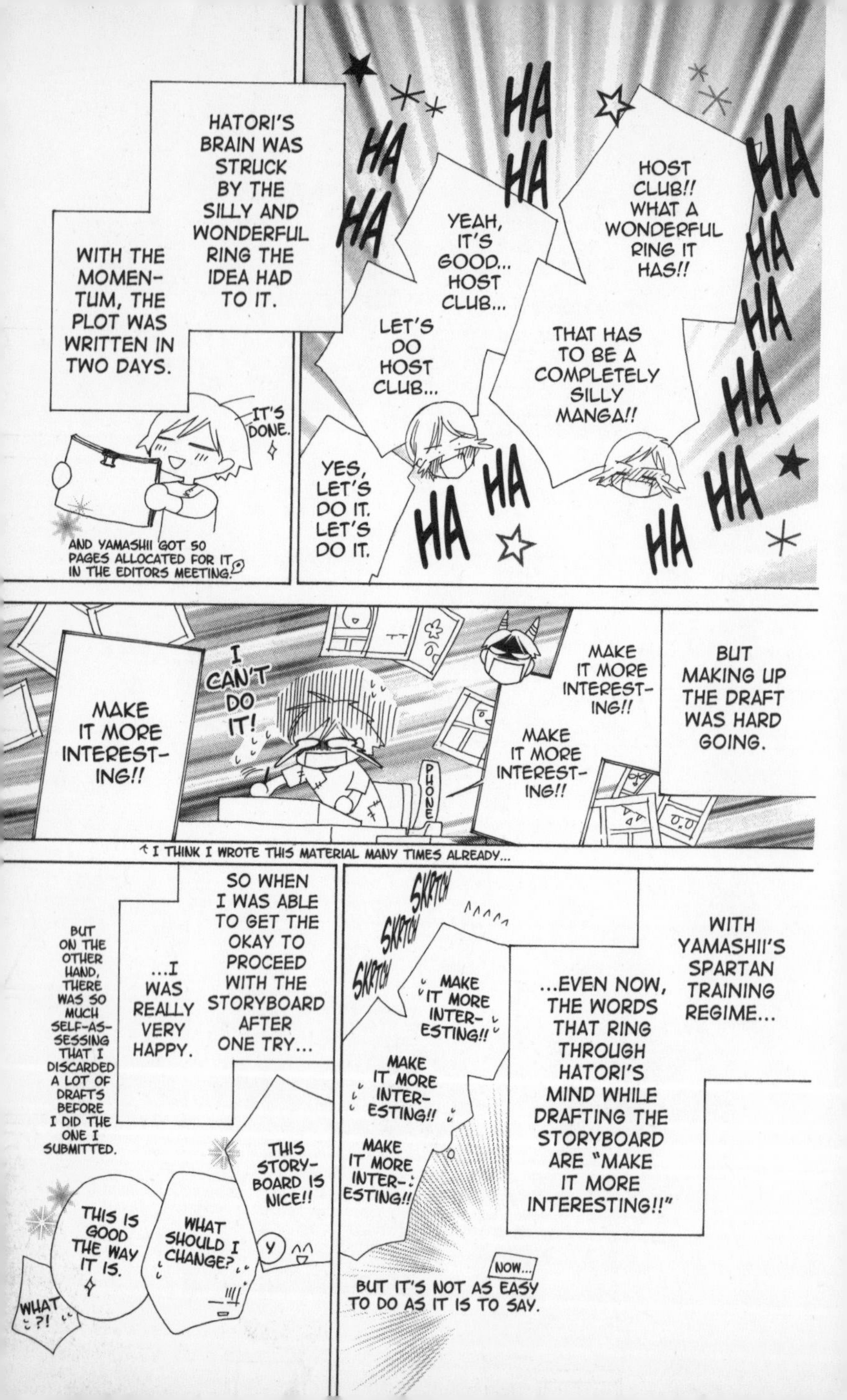
HA HA HA HA HA HA
HOST CLUB!! WHAT A WONDERFUL RING IT HAS!!
HA HA
THAT HAS TO BE A COMPLETELY SILLY MANGA!!
YEAH, IT'S GOOD... HOST CLUB...
HA HA
LET'S DO HOST CLUB...
YES, LET'S DO IT. LET'S DO IT.
HA HA
HATORI'S BRAIN WAS STRUCK BY THE SILLY AND WONDERFUL RING THE IDEA HAD TO IT.
WITH THE MOMENTUM, THE PLOT WAS WRITTEN IN TWO DAYS.
IT'S DONE.
AND YAMASHII GOT 50 PAGES ALLOCATED FOR IT IN THE EDITORS MEETING.
BUT MAKING UP THE DRAFT WAS HARD GOING.
MAKE IT MORE INTERESTING!!
MAKE IT MORE INTERESTING!!
PHONE
I CAN'T DO IT!
MAKE IT MORE INTERESTING!!
I THINK I WROTE THIS MATERIAL MANY TIMES ALREADY...
WITH YAMASHII'S SPARTAN TRAINING REGIME...
...EVEN NOW, THE WORDS THAT RING THROUGH HATORI'S MIND WHILE DRAFTING THE STORYBOARD ARE "MAKE IT MORE INTERESTING!!"
SKRTCH SKRTCH SKRTCH
MAKE IT MORE INTERESTING!!
MAKE IT MORE INTERESTING!!
MAKE IT MORE INTERESTING!!
NOW...
BUT IT'S NOT AS EASY TO DO AS IT IS TO SAY.
SO WHEN I WAS ABLE TO GET THE OKAY TO PROCEED WITH THE STORYBOARD AFTER ONE TRY...
...I WAS REALLY VERY HAPPY.
BUT ON THE OTHER HAND, THERE WAS SO MUCH SELF-ASSESSING THAT I DISCARDED A LOT OF DRAFTS BEFORE I DID THE ONE I SUBMITTED.
THIS STORYBOARD IS NICE!!
Y
WHAT SHOULD I CHANGE?
THIS IS GOOD THE WAY IT IS.
WHAT?!

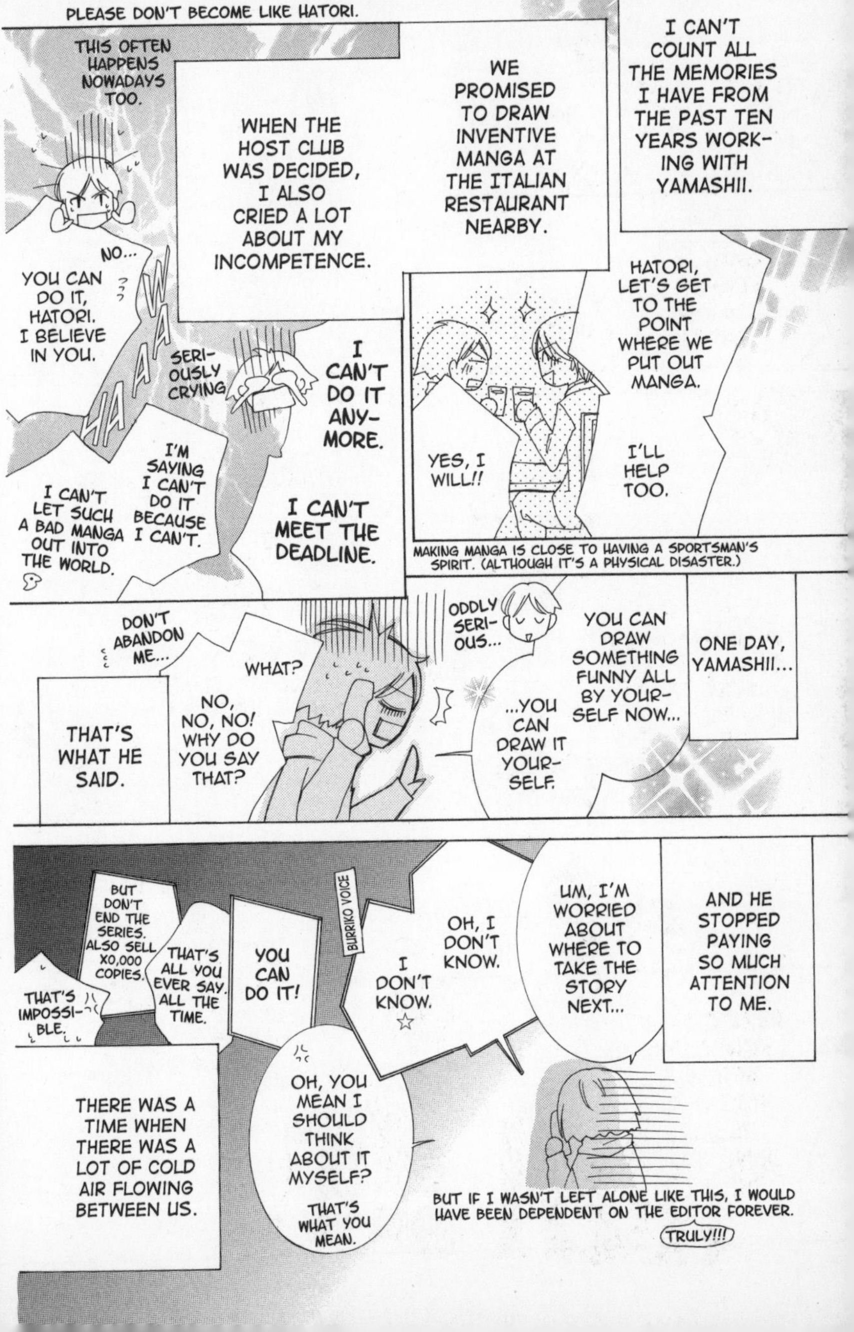
PLEASE DON'T BECOME LIKE HATORI.
I CAN'T COUNT ALL THE MEMORIES I HAVE FROM THE PAST TEN YEARS WORKING WITH YAMASHII.
WE PROMISED TO DRAW INVENTIVE MANGA AT THE ITALIAN RESTAURANT NEARBY.
HATORI, LET'S GET TO THE POINT WHERE WE PUT OUT MANGA.
I'LL HELP TOO.
YES, I WILL!!
MAKING MANGA IS CLOSE TO HAVING A SPORTSMAN'S SPIRIT. (ALTHOUGH IT'S A PHYSICAL DISASTER.)
WHEN THE HOST CLUB WAS DECIDED, I ALSO CRIED A LOT ABOUT MY INCOMPETENCE.
THIS OFTEN HAPPENS NOWADAYS TOO.
I CAN'T DO IT ANYMORE.
I CAN'T MEET THE DEADLINE.
SERIOUSLY CRYING
I'M SAYING I CAN'T DO IT BECAUSE I CAN'T.
NO...
YOU CAN DO IT, HATORI. I BELIEVE IN YOU.
I CAN'T LET SUCH A BAD MANGA OUT INTO THE WORLD.
ONE DAY, YAMASHII...
YOU CAN DRAW SOMETHING FUNNY ALL BY YOURSELF NOW...
...YOU CAN DRAW IT YOURSELF.
ODDLY SERIOUS...
WHAT?
NO, NO, NO! WHY DO YOU SAY THAT?
DON'T ABANDON ME...
THAT'S WHAT HE SAID.
AND HE STOPPED PAYING SO MUCH ATTENTION TO ME.
UM, I'M WORRIED ABOUT WHERE TO TAKE THE STORY NEXT...
OH, I DON'T KNOW.
I DON'T KNOW. ☆
BURRIKO VOICE
YOU CAN DO IT!
THAT'S ALL YOU EVER SAY. ALL THE TIME.
BUT DON'T END THE SERIES. ALSO SELL X0,000 COPIES.
THAT'S IMPOSSIBLE.
OH, YOU MEAN I SHOULD THINK ABOUT IT MYSELF?
THAT'S WHAT YOU MEAN.
BUT IF I WASN'T LEFT ALONE LIKE THIS, I WOULD HAVE BEEN DEPENDENT ON THE EDITOR FOREVER.
TRULY!!!
THERE WAS A TIME WHEN THERE WAS A LOT OF COLD AIR FLOWING BETWEEN US.

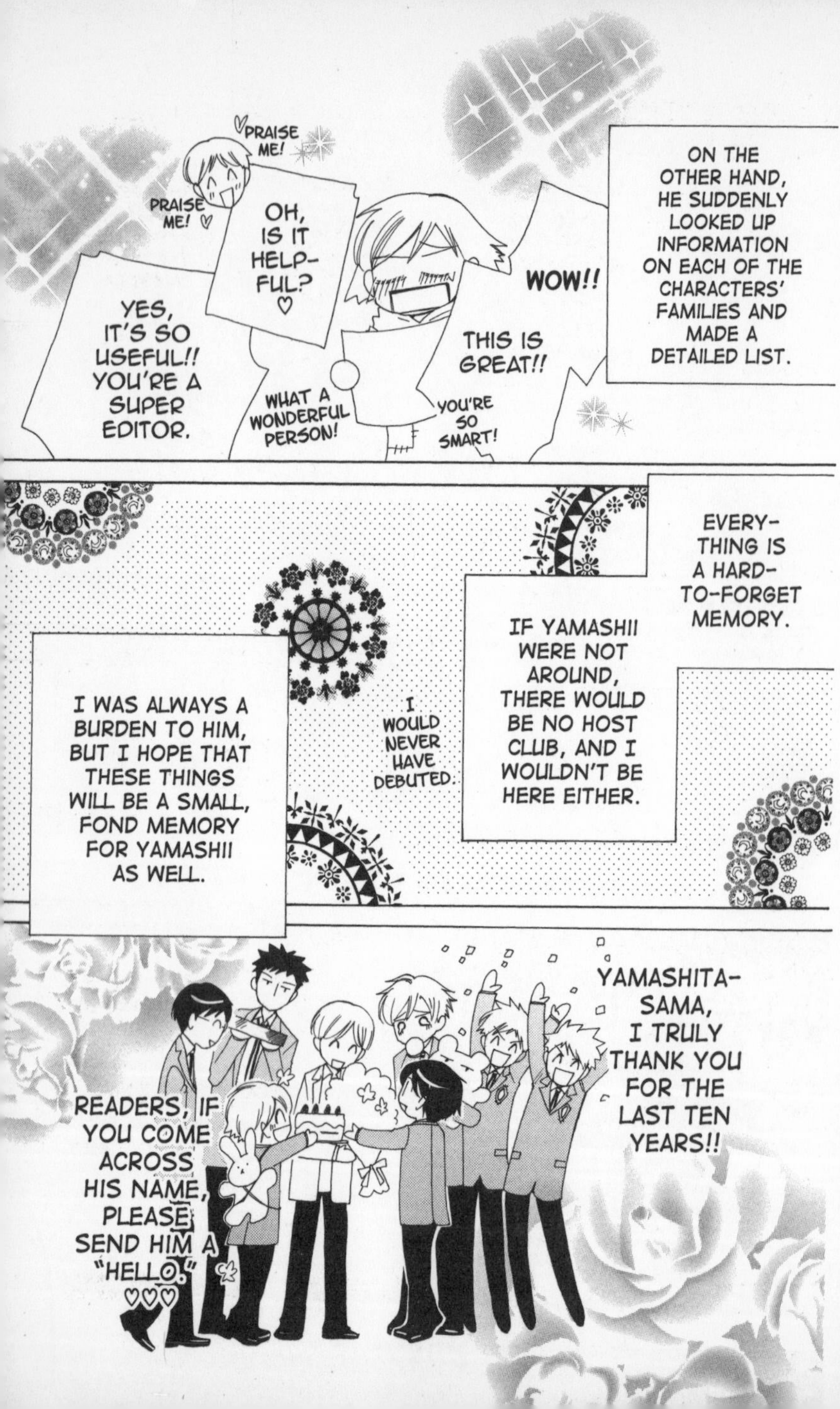
ON THE OTHER HAND, HE SUDDENLY LOOKED UP INFORMATION ON EACH OF THE CHARACTERS' FAMILIES AND MADE A DETAILED LIST.
WOW!!
THIS IS GREAT!!
YOU'RE SO SMART!
WHAT A WONDERFUL PERSON!
OH, IS IT HELPFUL? ♡
♡PRAISE ME!
PRAISE ME! ♡
YES, IT'S SO USEFUL!! YOU'RE A SUPER EDITOR.
EVERYTHING IS A HARD-TO-FORGET MEMORY.
IF YAMASHII WERE NOT AROUND, THERE WOULD BE NO HOST CLUB, AND I WOULDN'T BE HERE EITHER.
I WOULD NEVER HAVE DEBUTED.
I WAS ALWAYS A BURDEN TO HIM, BUT I HOPE THAT THESE THINGS WILL BE A SMALL, FOND MEMORY FOR YAMASHII AS WELL.
YAMASHITA-SAMA, I TRULY THANK YOU FOR THE LAST TEN YEARS!!
READERS, IF YOU COME ACROSS HIS NAME, PLEASE SEND HIM A "HELLO." ♡♡♡

NO FLIRTATIOUS
DRAWING
THIS VOLUME.
SORRY.
INSTEAD, HERE'S
A SKETCH OF A
2008 NEW YEAR'S
CARD IMAGE
(A GIFT TO THE
READERS):
LITTLE TAMAKI.

✿ I'LL BE WAITING FOR ✿
YOUR LETTERS. PLEASE
LET ME KNOW WHAT
YOU THINK!

BISCO HATORI
C/O VIZ MEDIA
P.O. BOX 77010
SAN FRANCISCO,
CA 94107

Special Thanks!!

✿ TO YAMASHITA, EVERYBODY ON THE EDITING TEAM,
AND EVERYBODY INVOLVED IN PUBLISHING THIS BOOK.

✿ NATSUMI SATO

✿ STAFF: YUI NATSUKI, RIKU, AYA AOMURA, YUTORI HIZAKURA,
SUBARU AMASAWA, AND BISCO'S MOTHER.

AND TO YOU, THE READERS OF THIS BOOK!!

THANK YOU VERY MUCH!

Bisco Hatori
2008. Apr.

EGOISTIC CLUB/THE END

EDITOR'S NOTES

EPISODE 52

Page 10: Kaoru's reference to a fourth-dimensional backpack is a nod to the *Doraemon* series. Doraemon has a fourth-dimensional pocket from which he can pull out useful gadgets.

Page 17: *Doujinshi* is self-published manga, usually made by fans of a particular series. *Moe* is an affection for or attraction to certain types of anime, manga, or video game characters.

EPISODE 53

Page 66: A *kotatsu* is a low table with a heater underneath.

EPISODE 54

Page 83: In the original, Tamaki is wondering about providing *horigotatsu*, or floor seating with a space for legs underneath.

EPISODE 55

Page 132: This was a Japanese TV series popular in the late 80s featuring two police detectives.

Author Bio

Bisco Hatori made her manga debut with *Isshun kan no Romance* (A Moment of Romance) in *LaLa DX* magazine. The comedy *Ouran High School Host Club* is her breakout hit. When she's stuck thinking up characters' names, she gets inspired by loud, upbeat music (her radio is set to NACK5 FM). She enjoys reading all kinds of manga, but she's especially fond of the sci-fi drama *Please Save My Earth* and *Slam Dunk*, a basketball classic.